Ethics and Decision Making in Local Schools
in Local Schools
Inclusion, Policy, and Reform

edited by

James L. Paul, Ed.D.
Neal H. Berger, Ph.D.
Pamela G. Osnes, M.A.
Yolanda G. Martinez, Ph.D.
and
William C. Morse, Ph.D.
University of South Florida
Tampa

D1369698

·P A U L·H·
BROOKES
PUBLISHING C^{O.}

Baltimore • London • Toronto • Sydney

Paul H. Brookes Publishing Co.
Post Office Box 10624
Baltimore, Maryland 21285-0624

Typeset by Brushwood Graphics, Inc., Baltimore, Maryland.
Manufactured in the United States of America by
The Maple Press Company, York, Pennsylvania.

The case study in Chapter 1 and the teaching case studies presented in the appendix to Chapter 10 are authentic, but the names of individuals, schools, and school districts have been changed to protect their identities.

Library of Congress Cataloging-in-Publication Data

Ethics and decision making in local schools : inclusion, policy, and
  reform / edited by James L. Paul . . . [et al.].
      p.   cm.
  Includes bibliographical references and index.
  ISBN 1-55766-282-7
  1. School-based management—United States—Decision making—Moral
and ethical aspects.   I. Paul, James L.
LB2806.35.E85   1997
174′.93712—dc21   96-53207
                                                                         CIP

British Library Cataloguing in Publication data are available from the British
Library

Contents

Ethics and Decision Making
in Local Schools

This book is printed on recycled paper. ♲

About the Editors

James L. Paul, Ed.D., Professor and Chair, Department of Special Education, College of Education, University of South Florida, 4202 East Fowler Avenue, HMS 421, Tampa, Florida 33620-8350.

Prior to joining the faculty at USF, Dr. Paul was on the faculty in the School of Education at the University of North Carolina–Chapel Hill. He has written or edited many articles and more than 20 books in areas such as emotional disturbance, learning disabilities, families, teacher education, school restructuring, inclusion, and ethics. He was a visiting scholar at Stanford University while this book was in production.

Neal H. Berger, Ph.D., Deputy Director and Associate Professor, Institute for At-Risk Infants, Children and Youth, and Their Families, Institute for Instructional Research and Practice, Department of Special Education, College of Education, University of South Florida, 4202 East Fowler Avenue, HMS 401, Tampa, Florida 33620-8350.

Dr. Berger has served as Coordinator of the Collaborative Research Group on Policy and Ethics and has taught various courses, including a graduate class in special education ethics. In addition to his special education departmental duties, Dr. Berger serves as Deputy Director of two research and development institutes at USF: the Institute for At-Risk Infants, Children and Youth, and Their Families and the Institute for Instructional Research and Practice. He has been a classroom teacher in public and private schools and a district-level school administrator, and he has served as a senior analyst and staff director for the Florida House of Representatives Committee on Education.

Pamela G. Osnes, M.A., Administrative Coordinator of Advanced Graduate Programs, Department of Special Education, College of Education, University of South Florida, 4202 East Fowler Avenue, HMS 421, Tampa, Florida 33620-8350.

Ms. Osnes's early work as a special education teacher of children with autism and severe emotional disabilities motivated her interests in the area of inclusion of young children with emotional disturbance and behavior disorders. She has written more than 20 journal articles and book chapters on self-regulatory functions of young children with disabilities and their role in inclusion. Her research interests include the systemic inclusion of students with disabilities within school reform efforts and the ethical foundation of these efforts.

Yolanda G. Martinez, Ph.D., Postdoctoral Fellow, Department of Special Education, College of Education, University of South Florida, 4202 East Fowler Avenue, HMS 421, Tampa, Florida 33620-8350.

Dr. Martinez holds a doctorate in special education from and is a candidate for the doctorate in applied anthropology at the University of South Florida (USF). She works as Coordinator for the Inquiry-Based Teacher Education Program, a collaborative project between USF and Pasco County, Florida, schools. She has conducted research with the Mexican migrant farmworker population in Florida and is especially interested in issues related to educational attainment and parenting.

William C. Morse, Ph.D., Distinguished Research Scholar, Department of Special Education, College of Education, University of South Florida, 4202 East Fowler Avenue, HMS 421, Tampa, Florida 33620-8350.

Dr. Morse is Professor Emeritus at the University of Michigan, where he was Chair of the Combined Program in Psychology and Education. For many years, he directed a multidisciplinary graduate training program for the graduate school in a group therapy camp setting. The first national analysis of educational programs for children with emotional and behavioral disorders was conducted under his direction. He is coauthor of the fourth edition of *Conflict in the Classroom,* and he continues to make contributions to the field of education for children with emotional and behavioral disorders, from a humanistic perspective. He was the author of the crisis teacher program, which enabled the inclusion of students with emotional and behavioral problems in the general education classroom while providing help to their teacher and educational therapy for the students.

Contributors

M. Yvette Baber, M.A.
Doctoral Student
Department of Anthropology
University of South Florida
4202 East Fowler Avenue
Tampa, Florida 33620

Dore Beach, Ph.D.
Assistant Professor of Applied Ethics
Student Affairs–Counseling Center
University of South Florida
4202 East Fowler Avenue, SVC 2124
Tampa, Florida 33620

L. Adlai Boyd, Ph.D.
Academic Administrator (Faculty)
Florida Mental Health Institute
University of South Florida
13301 Bruce B. Downs Boulevard,
    MHC 6238
Tampa, Florida 33612

Ann Cranston-Gingras, Ph.D.
Associate Professor
Department of Special Education
University of South Florida
4202 East Fowler Avenue, HMS 421
Tampa, Florida 33620

Van O. Dempsey, Ph.D.
Assistant Professor of Social and
    Cultural Foundations
College of Human Resources and
    Education
West Virginia University
608-D Allen Hall
Post Office Box 6122
Morgantown, West Virginia
    26506-6122

Patricia R. Fagan, M.A.
Education Coordinator
The Ethics Center
University of South Florida
100 Fifth Avenue South
St. Petersburg, Florida 33701-5010

Darrell J. Fasching, Ph.D.
Chair and Professor
Department of Religious Studies
University of South Florida
4202 East Fowler Avenue, CPR 107
Tampa, Florida 33620

Peter A. French, Ph.D.
Cole Chair in Ethics
The Ethics Center
University of South Florida
100 Fifth Avenue South
St. Petersburg, Florida 33701-5010

Susan Greenbaum, Ph.D.
Associate Professor and Chair
Department of Anthropology
University of South Florida
4202 East Fowler Avenue, SOC 107
Tampa, Florida 33620

Brian M. McCadden, Ph.D.
Assistant Professor
Department of Educational
    Administration and Higher
    Education
College of Education
Southern Illinois University
    at Carbondale
Mailcode: 4606
Carbondale, Illinois 62901-4606

Shirley Raines, Ed.D.
Professor and Dean
College of Education
University of Kentucky
103 Dickey Hall
Lexington, Kentucky 40506-0017

Cheryl R. Rodriguez, Ph.D.
Assistant Professor
Department of Anthropology and
  Africana Studies
University of South Florida
4202 East Fowler Avenue, SOC 107
Tampa, Florida 33620-2668

Hilda Rosselli, Ph.D.
Assistant Professor
Department of Special Education
University of South Florida
4202 East Fowler Avenue, EDU 208B
Tampa, Florida 33620

Anthony G. Rud Jr., Ph.D.
Associate Dean
School of Education
Purdue University
1440 Liberal Arts and Education
  Building
West Lafayette, Indiana 47907-1440

Ella L. Taylor, M.A.
Instructor
Department of Women's Studies
University of South Florida
4202 East Fowler Avenue, HMS 421
Tampa, Florida 33620-8350

Daphne Thomas, Ph.D.
Associate Professor
Department of Special Education
University of South Florida
4202 East Fowler Avenue, HMS 421
Tampa, Florida 33620

Theron D. Thompson, M.S.
Doctoral Student
Department of Education
University of South Florida
4202 East Fowler Avenue,
  EDU 208B CLAR
Tampa, Florida 33620

Brenda L. Townsend, Ph.D.
Associate Professor
Department of Education
University of South Florida
4202 East Fowler Avenue
Tampa, Florida 33620

Preface

We have two aims for this book. The first is to assist local schools in acquiring basic information about ethics and in understanding theoretical constructs that underlie ethical deliberation and decision making. The second is to assist in the education and training of professional educators, special educators, principals, school psychologists, and others who are participating or will participate in school-based decision making. The work presented in this volume represents some preliminary findings and tentative understandings based on 3 years of collaborative research on ethical policy making in schools. We draw on the work of ethicists and scholars interested in school culture, research on site-based management, our work in the Collaborative Research Group on Policy and Ethics (CRGPE) at the University of South Florida, and our study of ethical policy making in a collegium involving stakeholders in school-based decision-making committees (SBDMCs).

The central focus of the text is the ethical dimension of the policy-related work of SBDMCs. Established to implement the site-based management philosophy embedded in the national reform of public schools, these committees exist in local schools in most states. Their membership varies but generally includes the principal, teachers, parents, community representatives, and others with vested interests in the quality of education in the local schools. Their policy responsibility also varies greatly, ranging from little or none to major responsibility for policy development, depending primarily on the leadership philosophy of the principal. Also, the training, technical assistance, and staff support for these committees range from minimal to considerable.

Ethical deliberation in SBDMCs is a positive force in developing schools as ethical learning communities. When policy-making authority is delegated to local schools and when the leaders in those schools share their responsibility with stakeholders, the policy outcomes reciprocally shape and are shaped by the local school culture. The policy process in a local school occurs in the context of a dynamic culture that includes the school's traditions and normative expectations; the faculty's beliefs about learning, teaching, schooling, and education; and the vision and values of the school's leaders. These values and understandings help define goals, guide allocation of resources, establish rules for relationships, and establish a system of accountability. It is in this context that SBDMCs are created to assist with policy development and accountability in local schools.

The deliberative process of policy-related work in SBDMCs is heavily influenced by the interpersonal dynamics of the committee. Individual members of the committee have their own personalities, needs, reasons for participating, values, agendas, and moral perspectives, all of which come together to create the committee's dynamics and work style. In addition to considering the school culture and the political forces that shape the policy process, it is essential to consider the social dynamics of the committee in order to understand the deliberative process and productivity of the SBDMC.

In order to facilitate the ethical policy-making process of SBDMCs, one must appreciate the cultural and moral complexity of their task and the competing self-interests that affect their decisions. The CRGPE focused on understanding SBDMCs and identifying an ethical perspective that would be sensitive to the complexity of their work.

The goals of the first of the CRGPE's two-phase collaborative research program in school-based policy making, which is described in this book, were to

1. Understand the policy and practice of site-based management
2. Examine the issues facing site-based management committees, with particular emphasis on educational services for students with disabilities, that is, local school interpretations of the inclusion policy
3. Examine the theoretical foundations for ethical policy making in schools
4. Consider the implications of local school culture for the work of SBDMCs
5. Explore the impact of group dynamics and the values and perspectives of individual committee members on the policy process and outcomes
6. Determine an appropriate process for teaching ethical policy making to school-based committees
7. Develop a curriculum model for school-based ethical policy making

Some of the principles or beliefs guiding our work were commitments from the beginning. Others have come into focus as we understood more about the work in which we were engaged, that is, developing a curriculum to support ethical policy making in local schools.

Five principles or beliefs guide the ongoing work of the CRGPE and are reflected in this volume. The first is the belief that our understandings of ethics and the process of school-based policy making must be highly contextualized. We believe assistance to SBDMCs must be guided by understandings of the local culture and experience of policy makers in the school.

Second is the belief that constructivist philosophy and critical theory can provide useful framing for inquiry into and formulations of understandings about complex phenomena, such as ethical policy making, which do not readily lend themselves to positivist inquiry alone. The CRGPE is composed of both constructivist and positivist researchers. Our own iterative process of developing and evaluating propositions about ethical policy making in schools has been informed by an ongoing process of collecting data about SBDMCs.

We have been guided by the perspectives of the 12 faculty and doctoral student members of the group (the group's size has varied from 8 to 14). These members participate in the weekly dialogue. Four members of the group are also members of SBDMCs. The CRGPE's constructions of the understandings shared here have been informed by 1) the literature on site-based management, school policy, restructuring, inclusion, and ethics; 2) a small conference of principals, chairs, and members of SBDMCs that we organized to validate our understandings of their work; and 3) a collegium that we structured specifically to generate data to inform the propositions with which we were working.

Our third belief is that the inclusion policy is interpreted locally and that interpretation has a major impact on the education and social experiences of children with disabilities and those at risk for school failure. Acknowledging the lack of definitive empirical support either to accept or reject full inclusion, we believe an operational definition of an inclusion policy in a local school is an ethical construction reflecting the values and interests of the authors of the policy. Inclusion, then, is a major ethical issue for SBDMCs.

Fourth, we have been guided by our belief that narrative ethics, especially the ethic of hospitality to the stranger, is a useful and meaningful way to frame ethical policy making in schools. Although we recognize the value of principle-based ethics in addressing some policy issues, we have focused more on storied, or narrative, ethics and virtue ethics.

Fifth is our belief that the case method is an appropriate approach to ethics instruction. We have found that an authentic case reveals the complexity of situations and allows individuals to identify with different points of view in resolving a policy problem. With a long history in ethics education, the case method also fits the narrative ethics perspective guiding our work.

These five beliefs are guiding the second phase of the collaborative research program in school-based policy making, which is focusing on the development and field testing of a curriculum for SBDMCs. Although the theoretical foundations for the curriculum and the ethical theory guiding our work are shared here, the curriculum now under development will be the focus of a future volume.

Acknowledgments

This book reflects the work of many people over a period of 4 years. As with most complex interdisciplinary projects, there is no way to adequately acknowledge the efforts of all who made contributions along the way. Although the editors assume responsibility for the final product, the thoughtful and creative imprints of all of our collaborators are gratefully acknowledged.

The contributions of the Collaborative Research Group on Policy and Ethics (CRGPE) are especially noted. The project began as the work of this group. The ethics project reported in this book came out of the collective imagination and values of this group. Meeting for 2 hours each week over a period of several years, the group focused its attention on one of the most challenging issues posed by the site-based provision of school reform—namely, how will the ethical issues raised by culturally diverse schools be resolved and reflected in school policies? Besides the CRGPE members who contributed chapters to this book, Meme Eno-Heineman, Rosalyn Malysiak, and Sally Wade provided valuable assistance during the development of the Ethics Collegium and this book.

In addition, we wish to acknowledge the contributions of the participants of a miniconference for school principals and school advisory council (SAC) chairpersons held in 1994 as well as those of the 1995 Ethics Collegium participants. (A complete description of the Collegium can be found in the Appendix at the end of the book.) These people—principals, parents, SAC chairpersons, and teachers—lent their valuable time to us and were willing to work with us in testing some basic ideas and helping us learn more about ethical decision making in schools. They brought a great deal of wisdom about the work of local SACs to our general concerns about ethics and school policy. Their knowledge about schools and their enthusiasm for the project contributed to its positive outcome. These people were Robert Avossa, Mary Bidwell, Mark Brunner, Bruce Burnam, Barbara Chestor, Karen Dearolf, Janet Dunleavy, Donnie Evans, Janice

Froelich, Sue Gillum, Tina Gordon, Pam Hart, Laura Hassler, Jacque Horkan, Florence Jensen, Odessa Johnson, Brenda Jordan, Gloria Kaalberg, Geraldine Kelly, Pegoty Lopez, Jim McAlister, Marti Meacher, Sharon Mizner, John Nicely, Frank Roder, Mary Pat Spencer, Nancy Sutton, Connie Tzovarras, Diane Wilson, and Jim Yerman.

Each of the chapter authors helped shape the general understandings that we reached. Darrell J. Fasching, Peter A. French, and Anthony G. Rud Jr. substantially influenced the ethical perspectives that guided our work. Kenneth Howe also provided useful consultation to the project. Susan Greenbaum, Van O. Dempsey, and Brian M. McCadden provided useful analyses of the nature and process of the ethical decision-making task based on their observations of the Collegium proceedings. These individuals guided our thinking about ethical analysis, the social and cultural contexts of schools, and the process of decision making. Where we have understood something especially well, it is likely the result of the contributors' input. Responsibility for the limitations or errors in our work is ours alone.

Marilyn Katzenmeyer was a principal architect of the design of the Collegium, which yielded much of the information shared here. Her knowledge of group processes and her sensitivity to the complexity of the kinds of questions we were seeking to answer helped us to achieve our major goals.

Several individuals made valuable contributions to the work of the CRGPE, the administration and evaluation of the Collegium, and the production of this book. Special recognition is extended to Marseena Bobo and Erin Sapp for their important contribution to the Collegium and this book. The commitments and work of Patricia R. Fagan and Zena Rudo are especially acknowledged. Theron D. Thompson and Tom Terrell provided additional support to the CRGPE to ensure that the Collegium was a success. The competence, generosity, and patience of Caroline Lee were felt throughout the process. We appreciate the contributions of all of these individuals. We are also grateful for partial funding for the Collegium provided through a special project funded by the State of Florida, Department of Education, Division of Public Schools, Bureau of Student Services and Exceptional Education, through federal assistance under the Individuals with Disabilities Education Act (IDEA) Part B. We thank Bettye Weir and Doris Nabi of the Florida State Department of Education for their support of this work.

Introduction
Ethics, Research, and
School-Based Decision Making

James L. Paul, Neal H. Berger, and Pamela G. Osnes

The policy challenges facing public schools are largely a product of the national school reform movement that has been under way since the mid-1980s. This reform draws its strength from the larger cultural, economic, political, moral, and epistemological changes that are redirecting, restructuring, or otherwise reforming all of the basic institutions in our society, including schools. School reformers have promoted changes in all aspects of education and schooling from the curriculum, methods of teaching, and the education of teachers to the philosophy of governance, management, and approaches to policy development. These changes are reflected in a plethora of current literature in which researchers and professionals in education and in the social sciences broadly are challenging traditional understandings of child development, learning, knowledge, organizations, and human relationships (Paul, Churton, Morse, et al., 1997; Paul, Churton, Rosselli, et al., 1997). As evidenced by this literature, the discourse on school reform has become increasingly complex and multiparadigmatic. An important part of this intellectually rich and diverse discourse is the increasing interest in ethics and the moral perspectives that guide and inform decisions about teaching and the policies that govern schools (Cook, Weintraub, & Morse, 1995; Howe, 1997; Howe & Miramontes, 1992). It is this interest that has guided our study of ethical policy making in local schools that is reported here.

In the first section of this introduction, we discuss the school reform movement, with particular attention paid to school-based policy making and the implications for children with disabilities and those at risk and to the relationship between ethics and policy. This is followed by sections on ethics and public policy and on research and public policy. Both of these sections focus on implications for ethical policy making in local schools. In the last sections of the chapter, we provide an overview of the book, including a discussion of the threads that integrate the chapters and the perspective—the bias of choice—within which the book and the ongoing work of the authors are framed.

SCHOOL REFORM AND THE WORK OF
SCHOOL-BASED ADVISORY COMMITTEES

Current policy issues in public schools are a product of a series of waves of educational reform that have been under way since 1983, when Terrell Bell, then Secretary of Education, established the National Commission on Excellence in Education, which released its report, *A Nation at Risk*. Even then, some of this book's contributors who were working with education committees of state legislatures recognized two things:

1. *Reform and the need for it is not new:* The reform of educational goals, policies, and structures has historically characterized the U.S. educational system itself as educational and political leaders have tried to adapt to and influence the changing realities in our society.
2. *Difficulties posed by state standards:* The rigorous state standards being recommended could create special difficulties for students with disabilities, those in traditional vocational or other tracks, and those at risk of dropping out. These students were already struggling with academic and other school-related difficulties, thus placing the most vulnerable students at even more risk.

There was a great deal of energy and activity as the national education policy, giving highest priority to excellence, rigor, immediacy, and state mandates, was being forged with an apparent consensus of business and political leaders. These leaders were pushing the public and the state legislatures to enact new education laws to address the mediocrity and failure believed to exist in the public education system, which, they argued, predisposed the nation to economic risk. During the mid- to late 1980s, little attention was given to the needs of students with disabilities in the public policy debates. Perhaps it was assumed that these students were safe because of the Education for All Handicapped Children Act of 1975 (PL 94-142) and the court decisions won in the 1970s. We did not anticipate waves of reform in the future that would propose holding *all* students to the same standards of excellence and rigor, or a philosophy guiding policy changes that would consider sacrificing the principle of equity that was arguably being established. Neither did we foresee a deep shift in the management of public schools that would locate responsibility for control, choice, and accountability for students in local schools.

Since 1983, there have been more than 270 task forces and commissions appointed that fueled the analyses of problems in public education and proposals for change. More than 700 state statutes have been enacted (Timar & Kirp, 1987). The philosophy and foci of reform have been fluid, changing with new emphases or targets, a situation that has been characterized as different waves of reform. The first wave focused primarily on components of the public education system such as the curriculum, goals, teachers' salary increases, more teaching time, higher standards for students, elimination of tracking, teacher education, technology, and the relationship between schools and business (Paul & Rosselli, 1995). Cuban (1989) described these as "first-order changes," that is, changes that improve efficiency but leave the organizational structure intact. The interests of children with disabilities were not part of the policy debate.

The second wave, which occurred during the latter part of the 1980s, focused more on the conditions of teaching and on teacher preparation programs. The Holmes Group published *Tomorrow's Teachers* (1986), and the Carnegie Forum on Education and the Economy published *A Nation Prepared: Teachers for the 21st Century* (1986). The slogan for this period was "teacher empowerment." Specific recommendations for change were made by the National Board for Professional Teaching Standards (Paul & Rosselli, 1995), including raising admission requirements for teacher preparation programs, increasing recruitment of minorities to teaching careers, eliminating undergraduate degrees in education, instituting 5-year degree programs leading to a master's degree in teaching, raising teacher salaries and expanding their career opportunities, connecting rewards or incentives to student performance, and freeing teachers to make decisions while holding them accountable for student progress. Again, the education of children with disabilities was not a part of this wave. Hocutt, Martin, and McKinney (1991) commented that the "silence about the needs of or outcomes for [children with disabilities] . . . [was] . . . deafening" (p. 24).

The third wave of reform reflected a deeper interest in equity issues and incorporated the needs of children at risk, which helped to bring special education interests into focus in the reform. This wave culminated in the president's education summit in 1989 and a set of national goals (Ysseldyke, Algozzine, & Thurlow, 1992). During this period, a deeply rooted, morally complex reform had already taken shape in special education. The focus of this reform was not on restructuring schools but on the inclusion policy. Where should students be educated (in general education classrooms or in pull-out programs)? What are the goals of that education (primarily academic and behavioral or primarily social)? How is effective instruction to be ensured? A major challenge in the 1990s has been to integrate the two reforms. That has been difficult because of differences among different constituencies for both general and special education reform.

The practicality, ethics, and research on inclusion continue to be debated by parent and professional groups at the national level. Slogans like "All children can learn" and "All means all" are useful rallying cries for a social movement, but, like "Teach children, not subjects," they are ambiguous as moral concepts and have little empirical content. This has not helped state bureaucracies that, in many instances, have attempted to base an administrative policy on a slogan and ended up with a "one size fits all" approach to special education. At a local level, our own studies, as described in Chapter 1, have revealed that school-based decision-making committees (SBDMCs) are functioning in a variety of ways, from addressing relatively trivial matters that do not appear to have a major impact on school policy to engaging in long-range planning. We have not found SBDMCs generally involved in restructuring schools or adopting a clear stance about inclusion from which to develop policy. Given the lack of consistency in the policy alternatives posed at a national level, as well as the lack of either a clear empirical knowledge base or a strong moral foundation, the variability in practices and the lack of consistency in positions is not surprising. Still, the local SBDMC faces a complex challenge in crafting policies that reflect the interests of all students.

Elmore and Associates (1990) noted that policy makers, teachers, administrators, and researchers must deal with conflicting points of view and prescriptions in the policy debate on restructuring schools. They suggested three different and conflicting lines of argument. The first is that schools can improve only if they can ensure that teaching and learning practices in schools are based on systematic and validated knowledge. The second is that schools must give teachers more control over their classrooms and more opportunity to use their skills and exercise their own professional judgment. The third is that schools must become more accountable to students and parents. They argued that school restructuring could lead to the "complete transformation of . . . schooling, [the] adaptive realignment of schools that accommodates new knowledge and new political forces, [or] insignificant changes and a co-optation of restructuring reforms" (Elmore &

Associates, 1990, p. xv). The outcome, they contended, will depend on "the degree to which political, community, and professional interests coalesce around a common agenda" (Elmore & Associates, 1990, p. xv).

Local schools work in a community context; they also work in the context of local, state, and federal laws, policies, and regulations. Accepting the responsibility that site-based management accords, the SBDMC must concern itself with a common agenda. In the absence of state and national consensus even about fundamental policy issues, local school leaders, including the SBDMC, must align political, community, and professional interests.

A major part of this challenge is to employ a policy-making process that is both ethically and empirically defensible, that is, sensitive to the needs and interests of each individual student and based on valid and reliable data. A stable and dependable framework for ethical policy making is needed to anchor the diversity of interests of all members of the school community, even in a rising tide of national policy initiatives and disputes.

ETHICS AND PUBLIC POLICY

It is difficult to separate ethics and policy. As Noddings (1995) pointed out, "Since the days of Socrates, philosophers have been concerned with the concept of justice and different views of justice give rise to different views on matters central to education such as equality and equity" (p. 160). Plato (1968) saw a congruence between ideal individual virtues (i.e., wisdom, justice) and the highest virtues of society. Aristotle (1985), as French indicates in Chapter 4, saw ethics in terms of virtue, character, happiness, and justice. Ethics and politics, for Aristotle, were closely related, essentially opposite sides of the same coin, the good man.

The integration of policy and ethics is a challenge in a liberal democracy. Curriculum and governance issues in local schools are good examples of the difficulties that arise in negotiating individual and collective interests. A fundamental premise of this book is that a thoughtful integration of ethics and policy within the context of school restructuring and site-based management will serve the interests of school policy makers who have responsibility for maximizing positive educational outcomes for all students.

The themes that have undergirded philosophical and ethical debate in the United States throughout the 20th century—democratization, empowerment, responsibility (i.e., accountability), choice, and excellence (i.e., academic learning)—are basic issues in terms of the work of restructuring and site-based management, especially with regard to decisions affecting marginalized students. Those responsible for local school policy, whether they are principals or SBDMCs, are called upon to make decisions about children and families that are value based and not always—or even often—based on data or on objective criteria as is often assumed. Objective data are often used more effectively in identifying a problem or in defining the parameters of a problem than in guiding the policy response. This is problematic when one considers the demographic diversity of public schools and the mind-set of local school leaders who reflect the values and interests of the majority culture. The challenge is to give voice in the policy process to the ethnic, ideological, religious, economic, gender, and ability diversity of students and families who are a part of the school community.

What types of ethical policy dilemmas might site-based decision groups be confronted with today? Howe and Miramontes (1992) suggested the broad range and complexity of ethical issues that must be addressed:

> Education is rife with ethical problems—problems concerning how to treat individual students, how to ensure equal opportunity for all, how to respect the views of parents, how to deal with colleagues, and how to do all these things while maintaining one's personal integrity and allegiance to the practice of education. (p. 1)

A variety of ethical themes and concepts can quietly (and not so quietly) underlie a range of policy issues with which SBDMCs may be confronted. These include, for example, rights versus privileges of students, parents, and teachers; legal rights versus moral rights; the skillfulness of considering all factors (e.g., laws, personal beliefs, feelings, conceptions of the good life, empirical facts) in making decisions; relationships between facts and values; evaluating the rightness of a policy in terms of consequences to society (e.g., the greatest good for the greatest number) versus justice or equal respect for all people; ethical reasoning versus scientific reasoning; the shared values of a community or the welfare of individuals versus abstract ethical principles; and the impartiality of an abstract and universal perspective versus reasoning that takes into account an individual's personal history and family and community obligations.

The relationship between ethics, which reflects the moral precepts of an individual or group, and public policy, which structures the differential allocation of public resources (Gallagher, 1997) affecting the interests and welfare of an individual or group, is the subject of ongoing research. In this book, the focus of analysis is on ethics and the policy process in local schools.

RESEARCH AND PUBLIC POLICY

The relationship between data and policy is both interesting and complex. Policies are based on values, not on data. We pass laws and develop policies that reflect our beliefs and preferences. Sponsored research is generally aimed at understanding the consequences of policies in place. To be sure, policy makers have access to available data, and, in fact, short-term studies are commissioned to assist them in making policy decisions. However, the data are almost always inadequate to provide unambiguous guidance to policy makers about their options. That does not dampen the spirits of those who argue forcefully for the policy options they believe to be best. Clark Kerr, President Emeritus of the University of California, commented, "Seldom in the course of policy making in the United States have so many firm convictions held by so many been based on so little convincing proof" (1991, p. 30).

The relationship between data and policy positions is dramatically illustrated by Berliner and Biddle (1995), who argued persuasively that the presumed crisis in education fueling the reform of public education is based on misinterpretations of data, ignored data, and no data. The image created by the reformers is that students are not learning, classrooms are chaotic and often violent, and bureaucracy is strangling attempts at constructive change. This crisis, forcefully introduced by the publication of *A Nation at Risk: The Imperatives of Educational Reform*, a report of the National Commission on Excellence in Education (1983), was, according to Berliner and Biddle (1995), manufactured—a fraud. They begin their book, *The Manufactured Crisis*, with the statement, "This book was written in outrage" (1995, p. xi). Schools are doing much better, they argued, than the data reported, the interpretations of data, or the slogans based on no data would suggest. The manufactured crisis was not an accident or the misguided effort of naïve individuals or groups. Rather, "it appeared within a specific historical context and was led by identifiable critics whose political goals could be furthered by scapegoating educators" (Berliner & Biddle, 1995, p. 4). In addition, the case for the crisis was supported by "an assortment of questionable techniques—including misleading methods for analyzing data, distorting reports of findings, and suppressing contradictory evidence" (Berliner & Biddle, 1995, p. 4). The end result of these efforts, the strategies for reform, Berliner and Biddle believed, could be damaging to schools.

One might wonder about the parallel policy reform movement in special education: inclusion. Certainly, the debate among professionals and researchers in special education and parents has been strident, and the rhetoric has been problematic. Slogans like "All children can learn" and "All means all" have been banners for the full-inclusionists. Traditional special education has been reinterpreted by this group, in the reform environment that has developed since the mid-1980s, to be harmful to children. Those who disagree with these advocates argue that the complex learning and behavior needs of children require a range of services. Those defending features of traditional special education services are cast as conservatives, unwilling to change and too focused on academics and behavior. Those advocating full inclusion are cast as self-serving and dangerous to the policy interests of many students with disabilities. The debate has been heated, with strong, articulate, and informed advocates on both sides. Their differences are philosophical: What is the nature and role of education for children with disabilities? But the debate, centering on values and individual or class interests, is political. The relationships among data, values, and policy in the inclusion debate are very complex.

It is important to point out that it was not until the late 1980s, 5 or 6 years after the publication of *A Nation at Risk* (National Commission on Excellence in Education, 1983), that the parallel reforms—restructuring public education and inclusion—began to come together. Students with disabilities, arguably 12%–15% of the school-age population, were not included in the public education reform debates until the late 1980s and early 1990s. The reforms still have not been entirely integrated (Paul, Rosselli, & Evans, 1995).

In the present context, focusing on ethical policy making in local schools, our attention is drawn to the complexity of policy arguments being hurled at the local SBDMC. The national debates among researchers, policy groups, and leading professionals occur in the literature and at national meetings. The truth about an issue is somewhere—perhaps—in the spin provided to it by writers and speakers. Even if one makes the absurd assumption that SBDMC members are able to attend all professional meetings, have the time and ability to read all professional and research literature, and have the technical policy and research skills to evaluate claims and positions, the answers to basic policy questions would not be found in facts. For example, where and how should a child with a serious emotional disorder be educated? Certainly, available data accurately analyzed and reported and appropriately interpreted (a suspicious concept in this discussion) would be very helpful. However, the task for the local SBDMC is still to decide what is valued in the school, how children are understood, what is believed about the nature of education, who has a right to it, how children with disabilities are to be served, and how accountability will be established. Information helps. The frame (i.e., perspective, paradigm, world view, belief system) for understanding policy questions and making decisions that affect the allocation of resources and the quality of experience for all children, teachers, and staff in a school is a more difficult challenge. It is fraught with ethical dilemmas that must be addressed. An important question is whether these issues are addressed openly and directly—that is, whether the committee makes decisions about the frame that will guide its work—or whether the questions will be addressed by default. The former is a precondition for a self-guided and deliberative committee; the latter is likely to result in inconsistencies and to be more susceptible to the current membership and the strength of personalities on the committee.

In the present volume, the assumption is made that the SBDMC needs and, given the means and opportunity, will elect to address issues of interest, including its own, directly. SBDMC members, in the main, would prefer to consider the integrity of their own deliberative process and work on their approach to addressing ethical dilemmas rather than allow decisions to be made without full attention to the interests of students and families that could be compromised.

OVERVIEW

The content of this book is based on three assumptions:

1. SBDMCs have overriding ethical responsibilities as policy agents in local schools.
2. Their work is facilitated by being informed about the different professional and political forces that create, sustain, and continue to affect them as members of SBDMCs.
3. Knowledge about ethics and ethical analysis is useful in helping them understand and make decisions about school-based policies.

The first two chapters provide a context for examining ethical policy making in local schools. The first chapter includes a discussion of the history of school reform and the major concepts currently guiding changes in schools, including site-based management, which locates policy responsibility within the local school.

Boyd and Martinez, in the first chapter, define and examine the history of school-based decision making (SBDM). They identify themes and best practices and the role of ethics in SBDM, especially in decisions affecting the education of children with disabilities and those at risk. Quoting the work of Murphy and Beck (1995), they point out that governance, parent participation, student performance, transfer of authority, and resources are critical variables in the effectiveness of school decentralization. Referring to the work of David (1991), they note five internal elements of successful SBDM: a well-balanced and representative committee structure, enabling leadership, council members concerned with maximal student achievement, council members open and willing to learn new skills, and council members willing to look at school issues from a holistic perspective. Four external elements include a long-term commitment from members and leaders, guidance in making curriculum-related decisions, district support, and access to information needed to make decisions.

These authors' discussion of SBDM is grounded in a review of the literature, a case study, and a national survey of the 50 chief state school officers that they conducted. They conclude that there is a great diversity of opinion about, and approaches to, SBDM. There are no good data on the effectiveness, and there appears to be little effort to determine the impact, of SBDM on marginalized students and their families. These authors express concern that a common understanding of the utilitarian ethic (i.e., focusing on the greatest good for the greatest number) would defeat the interests of these students. They point out that "even if SBDM councils were to espouse no other ethic than that embedded in the U.S. Constitution, as amended by the Bill of Rights and further interpreted by legislative action (e.g., the Individuals with Disabilities Education Act of 1990 [PL 101-476]), the rights of marginalized students would at least stay in the forefront of discussion." These authors describe eight themes relating to SBDM appearing in the literature and in their own research:

1. Administrative and council leaders must be prepared to provide democratic leadership and to avoid politicizing authority or interests.
2. Parents must be brought into the process.
3. Attention to the variables that impinge on all student performance, not just academic achievement, is necessary.
4. A valid, reliable, and current database is needed.
5. Availability of resources to support the implementation of decisions must be ensured.
6. Training and other forms of external support must be available to the council.
7. Consistency in leadership and membership is essential.
8. The implementation policies and regulations supporting SBDM must be clear and consistent.

The integrity of the decision-making process, including the development and implementation of ethical policies, is predicated in large part on representative committee membership, support, and responsible functioning, as suggested in these eight themes.

Townsend and Paul, in Chapter 2, discuss inclusion, the major special education policy issue in the 1990s and certainly a central policy concern for SBDM. They review the history of the policy in the last third of the 20th century, describing the changes in language and emphasis from mainstreaming in the 1970s, to the regular education initiative in the 1980s, to inclusion in the 1990s. Leading professional special educators disagree on the service delivery arrangement that best serves the interests of children with disabilities and their peers who do not have disabilities. Full-inclusionists believe that all instruction should occur in the general education classroom. The negative effects of demeaning social stigmata can be prevented, they contend, by offering all of a child's instruction in the general education classroom, where he or she can receive instructional services that are at least as effective as those offered in pull-out programs. Others, however, argue for the need to maintain a continuum of services to support children with different kinds of educational and behavioral disabilities. They point out several barriers to providing a quality education for all children with disabilities in the general education classroom, including the complexity and size of the classrooms as well as the training of the general classroom teacher. The problem is that both policy positions are supportable with efficacy data and moral arguments.

When the research is inconclusive, as it is in this instance, and the arguments about the best interests of the child are in conflict, policy makers have a serious challenge in knowing what to do. For this reason, the philosophy of service delivery in a local school and the policy decisions that follow from that philosophy require considerable attention from SBDMCs. Because the composition and therefore the mix of interests among members on these committees is highly variable, the process by which the committees make ethically defensible policy decisions is extraordinarily important. It is this dilemma that provides the focus of much of the work in this volume.

Following these two chapters, which provide the substantive professional, political, and legal contexts of ethical policy making in schools, a section on ethics, policy, and schools includes four chapters on ethical foundations for school-based policy work. In Chapter 3, Rud provides an introduction to ethical policy making applied to SBDMCs. He discusses the different interests and concerns brought to the table by teachers, parents, community members, and the principal. He also describes the Collegium, in which authors in the present volume were brought together to observe the work of two hypothetical SBDMCs from the perspective of an ethicist. He then discusses the implications of the Collegium's work and pursues his analysis of the ethical agency of SBDMCs, which he proposes should become communities of inquiry. In addition to providing a general context for the work of the Collegium, Rud introduces the discussions of philosophical, religious, and feminist-womanist ethics that follow in Chapters 4, 5, and 6.

In Chapter 4, French discusses moral principles, rules, and policies. He reviews two theories that have had the most impact on the ethics of rules and principles in the 20th century. The first is the ethical theory advanced by the German philosopher Immanuel Kant (1788/1977) in the 18th century, which focuses on the categorical imperative. The second ethical theory is utilitarianism, advanced in the late 18th and 19th centuries by the Englishmen John Stuart Mill (1863/1987) and his teacher Jeremy Bentham (1789). French then contrasts this view of ethics as rules and codes with the philosophy of Aristotle, who focused on the concepts of virtue, character, happiness, and justice. In applying these ethical theories to considerations of policies addressing the needs of children with disabilities and those at risk, French suggests borrowing from different camps. He emphasizes the side-constraint conception of the Kantian principle of respect, arguing that an end-state theory such as utilitarianism could work against the interests of these children in educational policy. He raises questions about applying a virtue ethic when virtue is understood from an Aristotelian perspective. However, he does advocate an Aristotelian view of "seeking the mean" as we wrestle with the difficult issues of access, fairness, and equity in special education. He also emphasizes the need to acknowledge the uniqueness of individual cases in a way that rules and principles do not necessarily allow.

In Chapter 5, Fasching develops an argument supporting narrative ethics. He agrees with French that rules and principles—abstractions characterized by Nagel (1986) as the view from nowhere—do not serve the interests of those who must make meaning of the complexity and traditions of local cultural circumstances. Fasching, recognizing the storied nature of our lives and the importance of understanding the roles we tell ourselves we are playing, supports a narrative ethic that is highly contextualized. Fasching proposes an ethic of hospitality to the stranger as an encompassing ethic that must be situated within the community. It is, he believes, a litmus test for the character of a community. The community can be understood by how it treats outsiders, that is, strangers. The usefulness of this ethic applied to special education seems clear. Children with disabilities historically have not been a part of the general community in schools. They have been served outside the normative culture, and a special vocabulary has been used to certify their difference and distance from the mainstream. This, indeed, is a core of the current debate about the placement (Kauffman, Lloyd, Hallahan, & Astuto, 1996) or inclusion of children with disabilities.

In Chapter 6, Rodriguez, Taylor, Rosselli, and Thomas examine different feminist and womanist constructions of care and the implications of those constructions for school culture and policy. Caring, they argue, is not only connected to gender awareness but also embedded in feminist and womanist ways of knowing. The authors examine the ethical implications of different gender construction reflected in school policies. They consider the implications of the predominance of women in the teaching ranks and the discontinuity of the reform agenda and the voices of women in the classroom. They also examine caring in different contexts in school, including the experience of teachers, curricula, administration, and school policies. They take no short cuts in generalities, but focus on specific manifestations of sexism and racism embedded in the normative cultures of schools. An ethic of care guiding school-based policy committees can call attention to the explicit othering in schools, such as inappropriate segregation of students with disabilities (e.g., not all pull-out programs are appropriate), as well as the more subtle forms of othering embedded in sexist and racist language, curricula, and school rituals.

Section II contains chapters addressing the sociological, anthropological, and group dynamics aspects of school-based ethical policy making. The authors use the Collegium as a common focus for their analyses. All of the authors were participant-observers in the Collegium and use this experience, along with the observational and interview data they collected, as a point of departure for their analyses from different frames of reference.

In Chapter 7, Dempsey and McCadden, writing on power and the construction of meaning in school policy, focus on schools as moral communities in their critique of the Collegium from a sociological perspective. They note the unanticipated consequence of both groups (Day 1 and Day 2) participating in the Collegium developing a sense of community. The afternoon sessions were more engaging and probing than the morning sessions because individuals got beyond their identified roles and connected with each other. Unlike other observers, Dempsey and McCadden felt that the input from the ethicists had relatively little impact on the groups' analyses of the cases. They argue that meaning and moralities are constructed out of personal narratives.

Part of the challenge of SBDM is the predominance of rational and technical models and language that focus on outcomes of decisions rather than on building shared histories that can provide an inclusive context for diverse constituencies. Dempsey and McCadden point out the value of conflict as evidence of different voices participating in the process of authentic change. Quoting Tronto, they suggest that morality is always contextual and historicized, even when it claims to be universal. This understanding is especially important when considering the participation of marginalized groups that are "brought in" as they are able to embrace the values of those in power.

In Chapter 8, Greenbaum, Martinez, and Baber discuss culture and school-based policy issues. They define *culture* and describe the demographic complexity of education in the United States at the end of the 20th century. They provide a critical review of current literature and policy issues related to ethical and democratic decision making in local schools. Their analysis focuses specifically on cultural diversity in the classroom and raises basic ethical questions about the goals and processes of education in the future for children from different cultural and ethnic backgrounds. When teachers and school leaders are ignorant about or insensitive to the cultural histories of children, those children who are ethnic and racial minorities are placed in a position of adapting to majority norms, which results, over time, in these children losing their own sense of cultural place. This is a process by which many children, often silently, become strangers. The deep personal cost of belonging for these children, of overcoming the outsider status, is not usually considered in the cost–benefit analysis of policies promulgated by and in the interest of the dominant culture. When all children must learn the same thing in the same way, the creative potential of the learning community, as well as the integrity of individuals, is compromised. As Greenbaum, Martinez, and Baber point out, the cultural diversity agenda must be addressed in local school policies and in the policy process. Representative and diverse membership on SBDMCs is essential. The moral vision guiding the policy analysis and development process in schools shapes the quality of education and schooling for all children.

In Chapter 9, Morse, Berger, and Osnes discuss the role of group dynamics in the policy-making process. They propose a framework for relating group dynamic concepts and school-based decision making that focuses on the following six concepts:

1. Power
2. Leadership
3. Membership functions
4. Communication

5. Decision making and conflict resolution
6. Group maturity

Each of these contributes to the success or failure of a group to function effectively. The nature and ethical implications of each of these concepts are discussed in the context of the work of SBDMCs. The authors of Chapter 9 build a case for examining the ethical implications for all aspects of a group's dynamic functioning.

The last section of this book contains chapters on the process of ethical policy making, with an emphasis on the case method. Again, the authors of these chapters draw on their own experience and the literature and focus on analysis of the process employed at the Collegium as a point of departure. In Chapter 10, Cranston-Gingras, Raines, Thompson, and Beach discuss the case method as an approach to teaching ethics and to ethical deliberation. They review the two cases used at the Collegium on each of the 2 days and describe a framework for ethical deliberation and analysis. In Chapter 11, Martinez and Thompson present an analysis of the Collegium culture and the process of ethical analysis. As participant observers using ethnographic methods of observing, interviewing, reviewing records, and analyzing transcripts, they sought to understand the deliberative process, which revolved around the ethical analysis of two cases presented during the first 2 days of the Collegium. Different ethical perspectives guided the analysis of the 2 days. The authors of Chapter 11 were able to discern several themes, including the impact of the Collegium on the world views of the participants and the development of a sense of community. Their conclusions included the need for SBDMCs to construct common frameworks to guide their work as a community within a school.

In Chapter 12, Berger, Paul, and Fagan integrate the more theoretical aspects of the work of the Collaborative Research Group on Policy and Ethics (CRGPE) with the design, development, evaluation, and utilization of a curriculum for ethical decision making by SBDMCs. They synthesize what has been learned in the CRGPE, delineate a model for describing and integrating curriculum variables, and present a preliminary set of curriculum design and construction guidelines for a curriculum in ethical policy making.

In Chapter 13, Paul draws together the major themes of the book into a discussion of ethical policy making in schools. He focuses his discussion on some of the understandings gained from the work of the CRGPE and from the Collegium. He discusses the importance of SBDMCs considering the ethical dimension of their policy task and the challenge of offering training in ethical policy making to assist them in this work. He suggests some guidelines for training that he and his colleagues in the CRGPE at the University of South Florida (USF) are using in the continuing development of a training program in ethical policy making for SBDMCs.

There are seven connecting strands that integrate the chapters in this book:

1. School reform, including the emphasis on restructuring in general education and inclusion in special education
2. SBDMCs, which were created by the school reform movement as a means of restructuring accountability and have varying degrees of policy-making responsibility in local schools
3. Ethics and the relationship of ethical reasoning to SBDM
4. The work of the CRGPE
5. The Collegium, which was planned and implemented by the CRGPE as an experimental program to learn more about ethical policy making and SBDMCs
6. The research perspective guiding the work of the CRGPE
7. The case method, the methodology used in the ethical deliberations at the Collegium

The reform of public schools, the first strand, provides the broad context for the work reported here. Although the responses of schools to the national reform agendas vary, the discourse about public education has changed in dramatic ways since the mid-1980s, and there is considerable evidence that the policies and practices in schools are changing as well. The first two chapters of this book discuss policy changes brought about by school reform, with particular attention to SBDM, and by inclusion. This background and contextual information provide a general framework for understanding the work of school-based advisory committees and the policy challenges they face. Each chapter in this book is written within the broad professional, legal, political, and moral context provided by the school reform movement.

SBDMCs, the second strand, are administrative mechanisms established to support site-based management, a major component of the school reform movement aimed at changing the traditional top-down management philosophy in public schools. The SBDMCs vary widely in the way they understand their responsibilities, the amount of responsibility and authority they are given, and the quality of support available to them. These committees are discussed in detail in Chapters 1 and 9, but their role as ethical policy agents is discussed in several chapters.

The third connecting strand is the focus on ethics. A central concern in CRGPE has been to understand the ethical dimension of policy making in schools affected by site-based management. The articulation of ethical analysis with policy making, though not a new endeavor, has proved to be challenging. The ethical perspectives presented in Chapters 3–6 are different by design. The diversity of ethical perspectives as a source for learning is valued, and no pretense is made in attempting to reconcile it; rather, the authors of the present volume seek to enrich the ethical discourse applied to policy issues and the policy-making process in local schools. Although no claim is made that one ethical position is better than another, the present authors do express a preference for virtue-based and narrative ethics over principle- or rule-based ethics. Furthermore, we acknowledge the appeal of an ethic of responsibility and respect, as described by French, as well as an ethic of hospitality to the stranger described by Fasching, and the feminist-womanist critique of ethical constructions presented by Rodriguez, Taylor, Rosselli, and Thomas, as being especially useful in developing a philosophy and method for ethical policy making in schools.

The continuity of focus in this book derives primarily from the fourth strand, the work of the CRGPE in the Department of Special Education at USF, which has met weekly since 1993. The 3 years of work in this collaborative research group leading up to the publication of this volume builds on 3 years of work in another collaborative research group in special education at USF, which continues to focus on restructuring and inclusion. The focus of the CRGPE has been an exploration of ethical policy making in local schools. The work described here has been informed by systematic dialogue with chairs and members of SBDMCs, some of whom are members of the CRGPE. In addition, the present authors have engaged in consultation with professional ethicists, reviews of the literature on policy and ethics, a workshop with SBDMC chairs and principals to validate and expand our own understanding, and a 3-day Collegium that brought together stakeholders in SBDMCs (i.e., teachers, principals, parents, community leaders) for the purpose of examining the relationships between ethics, SBDMC stakeholder interests, and decision making.

The Collegium, the fifth strand, was designed specifically to help us understand ethical policy making in a local school context. Professional ethicists were relied on to provide the substantive foundation for an understanding of ethics and ethical analysis. French and Fasching, ethicists representing different ethical theories, participated in the Collegium. Their perspectives are presented in Chapters 4 and 5. A third ethicist, Rud, participated as an observer of the process and a leader of the discussions during the third day of the Collegium. His framing of the discussion of philosophical and religious ethics at the Collegium and his views of school-based committees as inquiry groups are included in Chapter 3. Also included in the section on ethics, policy, and schools is a chapter on feminist-womanist ethics (Chapter 6) by Rodriguez, Taylor, Rosselli, and Thomas. This chapter was invited when there was recognition at the Collegium that, though a narrative ethical perspective was presented, feminist and womanist voices in ethical constructions were not. Different aspects of the Collegium and different perspective-based interpretations of the ethical policy-making work of the Collegium are discussed throughout the book.

Collegium observers included educational sociologists Dempsey and McCadden; anthropologists Greenbaum, Martinez, and Baber; and special educators interested in group process Morse, Berger, and Osnes. The interpretation of data gathered at the Collegium by these observers—observations, records, and interviews with participants—is presented in Chapters 7, 8, and 9, which are devoted to perspective-specific or frame-dependent analyses and conclusions.

The research perspective, the sixth strand, generally follows in the constructivist and hermeneutic traditions of collaborative or cooperative inquiry groups (see Reason, 1988a, 1988b). Fosnot (1996) defined *constructivism* as "a theory of knowledge and learning [which] describes both what 'knowing' is and how one 'comes to know'" (p. ix). With roots in psychology, philosophy, sociology, and anthropology, the theory of constructivism views knowledge as "temporary, developmental, nonobjective, internally constructed, and socially and culturally mediated" (Fosnot, 1996, p. ix).

Grondin (1995) pointed out the traditional debate between continental and analytical philosophers on what has been seen as the irreconcilability of contextuality and objective truth. Grondin challenged the presupposition of relativism, noting that hermeneutics attempts to understand what is said by examining its motivation or its context.

> It is only if one inquires into the underlying motivation of what is being said that one can hope to grasp its truth. . . . Contextuality and truth belong together in a way that does not entail any kind of relativism, because the truth that emerges out of a given situation and urgency remains one that can be shared by others, provided they are attentive to the unsaid side of the discourse. (p. ix)

The CRGPE's approach to inquiry is generally equivalent to the constructivist view of learning, which is a self-regulatory process of struggling with the conflict between existing personal models of the world and discrepant new insights, constructing new representations and models of reality as a human meaning-making venture with culturally developed tools and symbols, and further negotiating such meaning through cooperative social activity, discourse, and debate (Fosnot, 1996). This view of learning and of inquiry has guided the work of several collaborative research groups in special education at USF (see Kromery, Hines, Paul, & Rosselli, in press; Paul, Marfo, & Anderson, in press).

Guided by a constructivist epistemology, the CRGPE has focused its work on ethical policy making in schools. We began with questions about the nature of policy making in SBDMCs and developed beliefs about the nature and process of SBDM work through literature reviews and the use of ethnographic field methods, including interviews and observations. The examination of our own perceptions, based on literature reviews and our continuing experiences, is generally recursive, which results in a continuous modification of what we understand to be the case.

The assumption that our understanding of the policy process in SBDMCs would be socially constructed was accepted, and thus there was interest in more than an inventory of activities, membership, policy products, or other objective variables that could be described in portraits of SBDMCs. There was interest in the particular meanings and interpretations SBDMC members assign to their work. It was here that the culturally, socially, and morally complex contexts and processes of policy work in SBDMCs, in which the interests of children, families, teachers, administrators, and community members are negotiated, could be understood. That is, individual SBDMCs were seen as storied forums where ethical issues are addressed in the context of institutional and other narratives. These narratives had to be understood sufficiently well that SBDMCs could be assisted in making story-conscious, or frame-reflective, decisions in the moral interests of all community members.

Complicating our efforts to understand SBDMCs was the fact that our own CRGPE had created its own narrative. The CRGPE is composed of faculty and doctoral students with different roles and interests. Some of the members of the group are also members of SBDMCs, by design. Most members are Caucasian, all are middle-class, and all have the opportunity to sit and talk together for 2 hours each week. The group has a convener and attempts to keep a flat social structure. It is interested in ideas, literature, and data. Most members are special educators, as well as being advocates at heart. The group includes different philosophical and religious perspectives. There are constructivists and positivists in the group, and most are active researchers. The group's constructions of the work of SBDMCs, therefore, are frame dependent (see Chapter 12) and limited by the ethnic, racial, ideological, gender, and class composition of our group.

The other major aspect of the CRGPE's work involves its ongoing study of ethics. The CRGPE accepted a pluralistic, not necessarily relativistic, view of ethics. The group reads and reviews ethics literature together and invites ethicists to teach and consult with them. The members of the CRGPE are not professional ethicists but have dedicated a great deal of time to the study of ethics, especially ethics as they apply to public policy and the policy process. This philosophical research, seeking understanding of ethics, ethical analysis, and ethical reasoning, has led the CRGPE, again, to some tentative understanding, or tentative (perhaps even fragile) hypotheses about the nature of ethical policy making.

The seventh strand is the case method. Just as most authors in the book concern themselves with the work of the Collegium and ethics, so, too, most also address some aspect of the case method. Although the nature and rationale for the case methodology and the two cases taught and analyzed at the Collegium are presented by Cranston-Gingras, Raines, Thompson, and Beach in Chapter 10, the two cases and the general philosophy of case method, which focuses on authentic narrative accounts of events, are discussed in different chapters.

CONCLUDING PERSPECTIVE: THE INTENDED BIAS OF THE BOOK

All who are not connected as valued, caring, and cared-for members of the school community are strangers, kept at a distance by long-established boundaries based on social class values, race, ethnicity, and gender. A stranger is not simply an unfamiliar face, someone unknown to us waiting at the door, or a new person in the neighborhood. A stranger is also someone whose life we know little or nothing about; someone whom we recognize by sight and whose name we may know but are just as likely to identify with a stigmatizing label or a derogatory nickname; someone who, if demeaned and embarrassed, is not likely to cause others lasting mental pain or guilt; someone from whom one would never think he could learn; someone for whom one might never consider making a sacrifice or defending if it cost us time, social status, or personal comfort; and someone with whom one would never want to make oneself vulnerable.

The concept of the stranger can be understood in the social ecology of schooling where children are known or unknown to other children and to teachers, where teachers are known or unknown to other teachers and to parents of the children they teach, and where parents are known or unknown to their children's teachers and to other parents of children known to their children. The school is a complex moral ecology in which individuals (i.e., children, teachers, parents) have a place that is either recognized or unrecognized, valued or devalued, and affirmed or ignored. The stranger is the person bearing the feelings of having no place, of being unknown, of being devalued, or of being ignored.

People do not generally set out either to be strangers or to make strangers of others. The process of becoming a stranger or participating in making strangers of others is complex. It involves the values and myths of different cultures, and the stated attributions have to do with the competitive and social competence of individuals. Less obvious are the rules and policies that govern the normative practices in the setting and support, often invisible, patterns of social life, either connecting all members of the community in a respectful way or singling out select members in ways that hurt, demean, or otherwise disadvantage them.

We have focused a great deal of our attention on policy issues related to the unmet needs of students who, historically, have been identified as marginalized, at risk, or disabled or who are non–English-speaking, for example, and given labels that identify them as outsiders. From an ethical perspective, these children are often strangers in school communities that accord them no valued place or positive social status. In an educational system that has traditionally focused on differences in terms of the attributes of the individual, it may seem more acceptable to think of strangeness as being a product of individual attributes rather than the norms, including social rules, that define and create valued spaces for the familiar.

Policy is, as Gallagher (1997) suggested, a blunt instrument. It does not make fine distinctions; it leaves a great deal to chance; and it is often uncritical of the assumptions that drive it. SBDMCs have the responsibility for developing or providing advice about policies that serve the interests of all members of the diverse communities that inhabit schools. Policies guide the allocation of school resources. Will an effort be made to give each student and teacher what she or he needs? Will resources be divided equally, or will those who show the most potential be given the most resources? Policies also reflect and enforce a philosophy of delivering educational services to all children. Will each child be guaranteed an appropriate education, as the law provides, in a place and in a manner that is not demeaning? Policy makers communicate their values by the quality of the principles that guide their work. Will the language used be sensitive to gender, ethnic, and ability differences? Will the school rules foster creative and responsible work and play? Will the emphasis in school policy be on control or on nurture?

The present authors believe that balance, as an ethical matter, is more defensible than an either–or position. Following the Greek counsel of the Golden Mean, extremes are likely not to serve the best interest of students and others in a school community. We may find, however, that, in some instances, it is morally right to be extreme, as Kant (1788/1977) suggested, in doing what we understand to be our duty. In the present context, one's duty may be understood as one's obligations to the core ethic of the community. Care and hospitality are examples of core ethics that define a community and do not need balancing with competing ethics. Applying this argument to the policy-making work of SBDMCs, one may ask the question "What is the extent to which available resources should be extended in school-based policies to foster an inclusive community where strangers are welcome?" The purpose of this book is to help SBDMCs in their deliberation about issues such as these and to assist in the education and training of professionals who participate in school-based policy making.

REFERENCES

Aristotle. (1985). *Nicomachean ethics* (T. Irwin, ed. & trans.). Indianapolis, IN: Hackett.

Bentham, J. (1789). *The principles of morals and legislation.* New York: Hafner Press.

Berliner, D.C., & Biddle, B.J. (1995). *The manufactured crisis: Myths, fraud, and the attack on America's public schools.* Reading, MA: Addison-Wesley.

Carnegie Forum on Education and the Economy. (1986). *A nation prepared: Teachers for the 21st century.* Washington, DC: Author. (ERIC Document Reproduction Service No. ED 12 322)

Cook, L., Weintraub, F., & Morse, W. (1995). Ethical dilemmas in the restructuring of special education. In J. Paul, H. Rosselli, & D. Evans (Eds.), *Integrating school restructuring and special education reform* (pp. 119–139). Austin, TX: Harcourt Brace.

Cuban, L. (1989). The district superintendent and the restructuring of schools: A realistic appraisal. In T.J. Sergiovanni & J. Moore (Eds.), *Schooling for tomorrow* (pp. 251–272). Needham Heights, MA: Allyn & Bacon.

David, J. (1990). Restructuring in progress: Lessons from pioneering districts. In R. Elmore & Associates (Eds.), *Restructuring schools: The next generation of educational reform* (pp. 209–250). San Francisco: Jossey-Bass.

Education for All Handicapped Children Act of 1975, PL 94-142, 20 U.S.C. §§ 1400 *et seq.*

Elmore, R., & Associates. (Eds.). (1990). *Restructuring schools: The next generation of educational reform.* San Francisco: Jossey-Bass.

Fosnot, C. (Ed.). (1996). *Constructivism: Theory, perspectives, and practice.* New York: Teachers College Press.

Gallagher, J. (1997). The role of policy in special education reform. In J. Paul, M. Churton, W. Morse, A. Duchnowski, B. Epanchin, P. Osnes, & L. Smith (Eds.), *Special education practice: Applying the knowledge, affirming the values, and creating the future* (pp. 26–42). Pacific Grove, CA: Brooks/Cole.

Grondin, J. (1995). *Sources of hermeneutics*. Albany: State University of New York Press.

Hocutt, A., Martin, E., & McKinney, J. (1991). Historical and legal context of mainstreaming. In J.W. Lloyd, N.N. Singh, & A.C. Repp (Eds.), *The regular education initiative: Alternative perspectives on concepts, issues, and models* (pp. 17–28). Sycamore, IL: Sycamore Publishing Co.

Holmes Group. (1986). *Tomorrow's teachers*. East Lansing, MI: Author.

Howe, K. (1997). Liberalism, ethics, and special education. In J. Paul, M. Churton, H. Rosselli, W. Morse, K. Marfo, C. Lavely, & D. Thomas (Eds.), *Foundations of special education: Some of the basic knowledge informing research and practice in special education* (pp. 215–228). Pacific Grove, CA: Brooks/Cole.

Howe, K., & Miramontes, O. (1992). *The ethics of special education*. New York: Teachers College Press.

Individuals with Disabilities Education Act (IDEA) of 1990, PL 101-476, 20 U.S.C. §§ 1400 *et seq.*

Kant, I. (1977). *Critique of practical reason* (L.W. Beck, ed. & trans.). Indianapolis, IN: Bobbs-Merrill. (Original work published 1788)

Kauffman, J., Lloyd, J., Hallahan, D., & Astuto, T. (1996). *Issues in educational placement*. Mahwah, NJ: Lawrence Erlbaum Associates.

Kerr, C. (1991, February 27). Is education really all that guilty? *Education Week*, 30.

Kromery, J., Hines, C., Paul, J., & Rosselli, H. (in press). Creating and using a knowledge base for restructuring teacher education in special education: Technical and philosophical issues. *Teacher Education in Special Education*.

Mill, J.S. (1987). *Utilitarianism*. Buffalo, NY: Prometheus Books. (Original work published 1863)

Murphy, J., & Beck, L.G. (1995). *School-based management as school reform: Taking stock*. Thousand Oaks, CA: Corwin Press.

Nagel, T. (1986). *The view from nowhere*. New York: Oxford University Press.

National Commission on Excellence in Education. (1983). *A nation at risk: The imperative of educational reform*. A report to the nation and the Secretary of Education, U.S. Department of Education. Washington, DC: U.S. Government Printing Office.

Noddings, N. (1995). *Philosophy of education*. Boulder, CO: Westview Press.

Paul, J., Churton, M., Morse, W., Duchnowski, A., Epanchin, B., Osnes, P., & Smith, L. (Eds.). (1997). *Special education practice: Applying the knowledge, affirming the values, and creating the future*. Pacific Grove, CA: Brooks/Cole.

Paul, J., Churton, M., Rosselli, H., Morse, W., Marfo, K., Lavely, C., & Thomas, D. (Eds.). (1997). *Foundations of special education: Some of the basic knowledge informing research and practice in special education*. Pacific Grove, CA: Brooks/Cole.

Paul, J., Marfo, K., & Anderson, J. (in press). Developing an ethos for change in a department of special education: Focus on collaboration and an ethic of care. *Teacher Education in Special Education*.

Paul, J., & Rosselli, H. (1995). Integrating the parallel reforms in general and special education. In J. Paul, H. Rosselli, & D. Evans (Eds.), *Integrating school restructuring and special education reform* (pp. 188–214). Austin, TX: Harcourt Brace.

Paul, J., Rosselli, H., & Evans, D. (Eds.). (1995). *Integrating school restructuring and special education reform*. Austin, TX: Harcourt Brace.

Plato. (1968). *The republic* (A. Bloom, ed. & trans.) (2nd ed.). New York: Basic Books.

Reason, P. (1988a). Experience, action, and metaphor as dimensions of post-positivist inquiry. In R. Woodman & W. Pasmore (Eds.), *Research in organizational change and development* (pp. 195–234). Greenwich, CT: JAI Press.

Reason, P. (Ed.). (1988b). *Human inquiry in action: Developments in new paradigm research*. London: Sage.

Timar, T., & Kirp, D. (1987). Education reform and institutional competence. *Harvard Educational Review, 57,* 308–330.

Ysseldyke, J., Algozzine, B., & Thurlow, M. (1992). *Critical issues in special education* (2nd ed.). Boston: Houghton Mifflin.

I

HISTORICAL, PROFESSIONAL, AND LEGAL CONTEXTS

The current school reform movement, which is challenging the traditional practices of public schools, has been under way since the 1980s. One of the changes with profound implications for school policy is the shift to a philosophy of site-based management. This shift, which locates more policy-making authority and responsibility in local schools than in state education agencies, occurs at a time when the social ecology of today's schools is complex and the interests of individuals and groups are difficult to discern. Students attending today's schools represent increasingly diverse social, cultural, political, and religious perspectives, a situation that is forcing more attention to the values embedded in school policies.

These values and the broad interests of diverse student groups must be addressed by school-based decision-making committees. These committees face many complex policy dilemmas, including the philosophy of service delivery for students with disabilities and others at risk. The policy on inclusion, for example, is informed by limited data, but it is also guided by the committee's belief about what is fair, equitable, and educationally appropriate. Developing a responsible ethical decision on inclusion requires a deliberative process in which the interests of all children in the school are adequately considered. In the absence of a set of rules or a formula, the committee must make informed ethical choices. Little information or training is available to assist these committees in the analysis and resolution of ethical dilemmas in policy. The purpose of this book is to provide some basic information and perspectives for developing a curriculum to assist school-based committees with this aspect of their work.

This first section of the book includes two chapters that provide a context for the study of ethical policy making in schools. In the first chapter, Boyd and Martinez discuss the history and current status of school-based decision making. They base their analysis on a review of the literature, a case study, and a national survey of chief state school officers. Concluding with 10 themes relating to school-based decision making, the authors emphasize the importance of valid and reliable data, as well as democratic values, in the policy-making process.

In the second chapter, Townsend and Paul describe inclusion policy, which is the special education part of the school reform movement. One of the critical issues facing those who must make policies at the school level is the philosophy that guides service delivery for children with disabilities. Data are available, but they are inconclusive in their support for full inclusion. More important, there is no consensus; strong opinions exist on both sides of the argument. Lacking adequate data, policy makers must rely on their beliefs and values regarding the rights and interests of all children.

1

School-Based Decision Making

L. Adlai Boyd and Yolanda G. Martinez

This chapter focuses on school-based decision making (SBDM) in the United States and abroad. Basically a democratic movement arising from the felt need to turn away from authoritarian or dictatorial schools and school systems that evolved as a result of urbanization and industrialization, SBDM, in its various forms, has flourished parallel to currently popular movements to downsize, deregulate, and decentralize almost all government.

As will become evident, SBDM has not yet succeeded, though there are islands of excellence here and there. Factors ranging from voluntary shared decision making with representatives of all school constituencies to legislatively mandated (and bureaucratized) local and state systems provide valuable information regarding not only the purposes and direction but also the perceived results of SBDM so far.

Finally, and more important for the purposes of this book, there is little evidence that the ethics and values that influence and sometimes underlie SBDM have positively affected marginalized students and students with disabilities. The risk, of course, is quite the opposite, for, as pragmatists, utilitarians, and other budget-minded law and rule makers move responsibility for educational decisions toward the local level, there appears to be a much better chance that the specialized nature of special (i.e., powerfully individualized) education will be forced to abate as well. This chapter seeks to highlight these forces, along with general findings, caveats, and conclusions.

SCHOOL-BASED DECISION MAKING IN
THE UNITED STATES: A HISTORICAL OVERVIEW

Definition of *School-Based Decision Making*

The concepts and practices associated with SBDM, sometimes referred to as site- or building-based decision making as well, appear to range rather widely in the schools of the United States and other nations. Marsh (1992) perceived that SBDM is inclusive of "decentralization of power, knowledge, information and rewards within school organizations" (p. 6), whereas Etheridge, Valesky, Horgan, Nunnery, and Smith (1992) described it as a formal process that includes the participation of school personnel, children, parents, and the community in decision making. Candoli (1991) presented the meaning and purpose of SBDM as a way for all aspects of the educational system to achieve a balance between accountability and freedom, which, of course, virtually necessitates some manner or method of decentralization as well. Tellingly, Wohlstetter and Mohrman (1993) referred to school-based management as an "organizational approach" to the school reform movement.

Despite the seeming diversity of descriptions, definitions, and applications of SBDM, across its various forms and acronyms, there appears to be equally wide agreement that it surely represents a shift in the locus of decision making in schools, as well as significant changes in the processes of those who have traditionally made those decisions (Garms, Guthrie, & Pierce, 1978; Murphy & Beck, 1995; Weiss, 1993).

Although there is also an equally diverse range of operational definitions, descriptions, membership mandates, and purviews involved in SBDM in different schools, districts, and states, SBDM just as certainly shares some central elements that are pervasive in all areas of implementation. Among such central elements are school-level autonomy and participatory decision making, usually involving a large or at least a representative number of stakeholders (Crosby, 1991; David, 1989; Garms et al., 1978; Lindquist & Mauriel, 1989; Mojkowski & Fleming, 1988; Wohlstetter & Mohrman, 1993).

For the purposes of this chapter, *school-based decision making* may best be defined as the sharing of the authority to make specific school-related decisions, based on the information necessary and sufficient to make them most efficiently and effectively, as well as the distribution of such authority to those in or closely associated with that school, usually on site, and who are most willing and likely to know how to evaluate relevant data; what to do about the meaning of those data; when, where, who, and how to do it; and who will evaluate the results of this process and make confirming or reforming decisions, as needed, over the long and consistent run.

Assumptions Underlying SBDM

One of the most evident assumptions for the implementation of SBDM is that those who work closest with students (e.g., teachers, parents, certain administrators) are better—perhaps best—informed about those students' academic and related needs. A related assumption is that specific remedial actions arising out of informed awareness of students' needs should result in improved student performance. It follows, then, that the empowerment of individuals at the school level should result in the improvement of the school as a community as well (Bryk, 1993; Mojkowski & Fleming, 1988; Murphy & Beck, 1995).

Although much of SBDM literature assumes that the central purpose of SBDM is improved student performance, the most challenging concepts also include specific decisions that are made to prevent student failure, as well as to remediate or compensate for competing conflicts and handicaps, however and wherever they may occur, on or off campus. This process may or may not involve formally established groups (e.g., school advisory councils, school improvement teams), but it almost always provides for a pooling of knowledge, information, and either advisory or final decision-making power among a group of experienced, interested, committed, and involved people, including school administrators, teachers, parents, students, and community representatives, who are either more or less permanently established or assembled on an ad hoc basis.

In short, it is assumed in this chapter that appropriate SBDM empowers those most likely to be most successful in specific types of decision making. This, of course, may vary with the types of decisions to be made, including disciplinary codes, curricular schedules and content, hiring and firing, budget priorities, attendance policies, parking decals, and special decisions that may require special waivers from district procedures or even from state or local statutes.

Finally, it is assumed in this chapter that virtually all site-based decisions inevitably and ultimately apply some specific value system or ethic in making each decision, even if that value system or ethic is unexpressed. The ethical base that undergirds, even nourishes, SBDM and its deliberative processes, then, should be recognized as a matter of crucial importance.

Historical Overview of SBDM

Moves to decentralize educational systems date at least to the turn of the 20th century. To be able to understand this movement, it must first be understood why centralized school systems came into being. Among some of the forces that contributed to centralization were the industrial revolution, with its emphasis on efficiency; stern, rigid, top-down management; assembly-line production; and inexpensive labor (including child labor). As more people left rural areas for the growing industrial opportunities of urban centers, education gradually shifted from home and community centers to larger regional schools. As laws were passed to protect children from inappropriate labor, more children were forced into these schools. Centralization of authority, both in principals locally and in local school boards and superintendents regionally, mirrored big business and a growing economy (Murphy & Beck, 1995).

John Dewey (1903), a student of William James, the father of American pragmatism, was among the first proponents of decentralized school power. Dewey argued that placing power in superintendents promoted autocracy rather than true democracy by moving power to those more knowledgeable about the particulars of its application and use. Dewey's ideas were favored and featured by several movements that promoted decentralization, including the teacher council movement (1909–1929), the democratic administration movement (1950–1975), and the community control movement (1950–1975). According to Murphy and Beck (1995), three types of decentralization have resulted from these movements: professional, administrative, and community. The first two of these seem clear enough. The purpose of the community movement, however, is to allow those community members who have episodically or traditionally been excluded from the decision-making process to have input in making policies, especially policies affecting them or their families.

Forces Behind SBDM Initiatives
The failing health of schools and education is cited as a force behind SBDM. According to Murphy and Beck (1995), today's school reformers generally resort to several logical measures to support their views for reformation. Among these measures of the success or failure of schools and school systems are the academic achievement of students, the level of functional literacy, the potential for employment of high school graduates, the development and application of higher-order thinking skills, and community involvement and citizenship. Underlying the push for reformation is the conviction that schools should promote political enfranchisement and empowerment, moving away from personalization by autocrats and toward more broadly democratic, less hierarchical management systems.

The changing socioeconomic and cultural environment has also contributed to the desire to reform schools through SBDM. There is abroad in the land the perception that the United States is losing ground as a powerful player in the world's economy and market-places. A major reason for this continuing attrition is widely said to be the failure of U.S. public schools. In addition, Murphy and Beck (1995) cited the political, organizational, and economic dynamics of a postindustrial society as pressures requiring adaptive changes, including SBDM, in our educational system.

Finally, the need to reinvent education has also played an important role in SBDM in the United States. According to Murphy and Beck (1995), the myriad problems whose roots lay at the schoolhouse door require paradigm shifts in the way in which we educate our young people. This effort would require a restructuring, even a reinventing, of a school governance system that would employ decentralized, nonbureaucratic administrative processes. Such a system would require alternative models of instruction that did not center around the traditional model of sorting students into broad categories based on their presumed or even tested abilities.

SBDM IN THE UNITED STATES

New York City was among the first cities to implement community-controlled schools in the mid-1960s. Several models were used, followed somewhat later by even more radical departures from centralization. P. Kries (personal communication, April 1996), a consultant to a state educational agency who is concerned with business and citizen partnerships with schools, saw several large, failing traditional junior high schools in East Harlem, New York City District 4, divided into several smaller, academy-like, theme-based junior high schools, with several operating in the same building. These schools used no administrators, apart from a single lead teacher who actually taught as well as handled minimally necessary administrative functions. The students who composed the earlier, larger junior high schools, as well as their parents and others in the community, chose themes (e.g., music, math, sports) that would characterize and identify each new school in addition to the "three Rs." Attendance, grades, decorum, interest, achievement, and pride shot up significantly, and dropouts, fights, failures, and other problems dwindled dramatically.

The high schools that the graduates of these decentralized, site base–managed junior high schools were slated to attend were not District 4 schools. Thus, they were unprepared to receive the education-seeking, academically stimulated, and unfettered students from East

Harlem who arrived at their doors being very accustomed to decentralized processes. Alas, the experiment was halted and the larger junior high schools reappeared, but not before the concept and the idea people received a coveted MacArthur Award for near-genius-level innovation. Other SBDM initiatives soon arose in cities such as Detroit and Washington, D.C.

Murphy and Beck (1995) pointed out five important areas that appear to interact with the effectiveness of school decentralization, such as in the New York City experiences:

1. *Governance:* Research has pointed to the lack of administrative expertise in some SBDM schools (e.g., in New York City) as one of the reasons why such schools can become too political, serving only the interests of a few sponsoring organizations.
2. *Parent participation:* Although parent participation was the cornerstone of the decentralization movement, studies of the initial years of the New York City initiative indicated that parents only minimally participated in school decision making.
3. *Student performance:* Although there were no careful studies validating the relationship between decentralization and improvement in student achievement, some studies found that student achievement increased most of all among minority groups.
4. *Transfer of authority:* Community control was limited, and, to a certain extent, decentralized schools continued to be controlled by districts and the schools themselves.
5. *Resources:* As decentralization efforts were beginning to be implemented, federal funds dried up, frustrating the schools' success.

Apart from New York City, according to David (1996), one third of all school districts in the United States had some form of site-based management in place from 1986 to 1990. Kentucky, for example, requires every school to have a site-based council, composed of three teachers, two parents, and one principal, that is given considerable fiscal and policy authority. In Maryland and Texas, SBDM teams do not have mandated, specific compositions, and power is not transferred from the districts. Chicago has local school councils made up of six parents, two community representatives, two teachers, and one principal, with each council enjoying considerable authority. Although Cincinnati has decentralized its system, no additional authority is given to school principals (David, 1996).

Successful SBDM Schools

David (1996) listed internal and external elements for successful school-based management in the schools she studied.

Internal Elements of Successful SBDM

1. A well-balanced, thoroughly reasoned committee structure, implying a representative committee composition with participants well informed about the decisions to be made
2. Enabling leadership, or the presence of strong leaders who are willing to delegate their authority
3. Council members who are concerned with issues related to maximal student achievement
4. Council members who are open and willing to learn new skills
5. Council members who are willing to look at school issues and decisions from a holistic perspective

External Elements of Successful SBDM

1. Long-term commitment from members and leaders
2. Guidance in making curriculum-related decisions
3. District provision of assistance and opportunities for schools to achieve change (e.g., waivers from district policies)
4. Easy access to all information necessary for informed decision making

In its November 1995 publication, *Goals 2000: Educate America Act State Profiles,* the Council of Chief State School Officers reported on progress made in 48 states toward applying the philosophy, funds, and purposes of Goals 2000: Educate America Act of 1994 (PL 103-227). This federal educational reform act provides substantial funds for each participating state (only a few are currently stalled or otherwise not participating) to develop a state plan that will improve student achievement through systemic changes, reforms, and deregulation by utilizing state planning panels composed of representatives of all major educational stakeholder groups, to integrate each state's educational technology with the objectives of Goals 2000 and to provide subgrant funds for local education agencies (LEAs) to initiate their own reforms as well. Although it has not yet tracked the specific use of SBDM in each of the state plans currently approved or being considered, there is specific recognition in virtually every participating state's plan that restructuring along the lines of additional community control of school and school system management not only is desirable but also is one of the ways in which Goals 2000 may best be accomplished. (See Figure 1 for the results of a survey of state education secretaries regarding the use and status of SBDM at all levels.)

The following questions may be answered, Yes, No, or ? (i.e., unsure).

1. Is there a written history or similar description of site-based public school management in your state? (If so, please send us a copy, as soon as possible.)
    Results: Yes = 54%, No = 43%, ? = 3%. Comments included the following:
    a. State's Goals 2000 planning usually included SBDM as an appropriate method of reform and restructuring
    b. Some states had already planned SBDM method of reform before Goals 2000 was enacted
    c. Some states answered "No" but sent obvious written histories anyway
    d. Several states noted that SBDM was merely optional for the state, but, in some, many districts were utilizing it
    e. See legislatively mandated Annual Report of the Task Force on Site-Based Management

2. Has any form or outgrowth of Goals 2000 (or any other statewide effort at student and school improvement through local site-based management means) been articulated through state or local laws in your state? (If so, please send us copies.)
    Results: Yes = 72%, No = 21%, ? = 7%. Comments included the following:
    a. Emphasis on alignment and accountability
    b. Several states wanted it understood that their Goals 2000 programs had little or nothing to do with Goals 2000, even though they were spending Goals 2000 federal funds to plan and implement their Goals 2000 program
    c. Many states reported that they were utilizing prior existing panels and other extant groups representative of school system stakeholders as the Goals 2000 required planning panels
    d. A few states answering "No" explained that their legislation permits or establishes charter schools (which, by definition, utilize SBDM)
    e. Several states reported that, though there was not legislation passed pursuant to this question, related state board regulations and policies were put in place by administrative fiat
    f. See Task Force Report
    g. Legislation has been passed in [*name of state*] that strongly advocates [only] a form of SBDM but requires each of the state's school districts to attend a workshop on partnerships [a form of SBDM]; each district decides for itself whether to foster, to allow, or not to allow SBDM
        (*Note:* Question 2 caused some confusion among a few respondents because Goals 2000 and SBDM are treated as two completely separate endeavors not officially related in some states, even though Goals 2000 clearly advocates for some form of SBDM.)

3. Have there been developed in your state any methods of tracking progress made toward Goals 2000 (by any other name) at the state, district, and school levels? (If so, please send us descriptions, analyses, and current data.)
    Results: Yes = 61%, No = 25%, ? = 14%. Comments included the following:

(continued)

Figure 1. Minisurvey of state education chiefs regarding site-based decision making and the Goals 2000: Educate America Act of 1994 requirements. (*n* = 29 [58% return].)

Figure 1. *(continued)*

---

    a. Several states cited state, district, or local school report cards, describing strengths and weaknesses, sometimes with recommendations regarding remediation

    b. Two states reported that tracking was an outgrowth of their student assessment systems

    c. See Task Force Report

    d. Goals 2000 plans are tracked, but not SBDM per se, except informally

4. Have there been developed in your state any methods of tracking and measuring the impact on marginalized students (e.g., special education, dropout prevention, teen pregnancy, substance abuse programs) of any site-based management methods implemented in your public schools? (If so, please send us descriptions and analyses.)

    Results: Yes = 3%; No = 90%; ? = 7%. Comments included the following:

    a. Only as a function of not including special education student scores on those tests used by the state or district to determine school effectiveness

    b. One state is conducting a study of this issue, but is not now tracking it

    c. One state has included such data in its interim report on school reform

    d. One state approaches the issue only in its state accreditation procedures (not explained)

    e. See Task Force Report

    f. [*Name of state*] is struggling with the issue of whether to count [marginalized] students' scores in their adherence to statewide requirements for school performance, based on each school's average scores: Some do, some do not

5. Does your state use any particular training literature for districts or local schools to use in preparing those responsible for implementing site-based management? (If so, please cite or send us copies.)

    Results: Yes = 54%; No = 39%; ? = 7%. Comments include the following:

    a. Some states have state-produced materials (including videos) and workshops, and others leave it to LEAs

    b. Some states allow professional organizations to train

    c. Some states only promote and provide assistance to LEAs, if requested

    d. This state created materials for a mandatory [SBDM] workshop and is still offering them when requested

6. It would greatly aid our work if you would place, in the space below, your candid impressions of the success or failure of site-based management efforts in your state, along with your best understanding of why. Your comments will be held in complete confidentiality.

    Results (Note: Because anonymity was promised to respondents to encourage forthright opinions, most states are not identified.)

    a. "Success seems to be related to: leadership style of principals; empowerment of the community; experience of superintendents; and history of support for building-based efforts. SBDM is tougher when there are trust issues, a lack of training and fear of loss of control."

    b. "Success is largely dependent on the principal's openness to SBDM, and her or his willingness to gather and empower stakeholders and to buck prevailing winds. The state's report card, per school, is a prod in this direction."

(continued)

Figure 1. *(continued)*

---

   c.   "SBDM is very successful in schools where there is trust and good communication and less successful otherwise. It is only a tool, and its success is very dependent upon those who use the tool! To be more successful:
- Legislatively require training for SBDM council members
- Legislatively mandate released time and compensation for teachers in SBDM process
- Legislatively allow compensation for participating parents (cf. paid jury duty)
- Did not see SIPs, SBDM, and Goals 2000 as part of the same movement"

   d.   "[Success] is limited by what local boards are willing to give up. They claim to support, but still want control of, most budget and all personnel decisions. Successful SBDM schools are due to effective leadership from the principal (which may have occurred, anyway, without outside prodding). Teachers' associations sometimes hamper school teams' efforts by insisting on extra compensation for anything beyond standard teaching hours. Some schools cannot afford this extra cost."

   e.   "Mixed review in [*name of state*], to date: though a specific component of the state's [legislatively mandated planning law], it is not openly endorsed by local superintendents or school boards. This difficulty is compounded by principals who use SBDM as another tool to manipulate staff and community while denying them true decision making authority. Parents and teachers frequently cite time as an important factor in making SBDM work—a commodity not readily available for SBDM. Finally, SBDM councils rarely cite student outcomes when outlining their goals. (If student achievement isn't the goal, why do it?)"

   f.   "In reviewing the efforts of school districts and schools to develop site-based management techniques, it is determined that it must be supported by the entire learning community, and it requires a great deal of ongoing, systematic, multilevel professional development."

   g.   "It takes several years for members [of school improvement teams] to comprehend fully the power they have. . . . Some tackled projects that could be termed 'beautification' more than education. . . . [A special governor-appointed] panel . . . is awarding [incentive grants] to enable [school improvement teams] to become more involved in school improvement efforts that affect student performances. . . . We believe . . . [incentive grants are] the incentive to begin working together as a community of stakeholders that leads to better understanding of their potential. We have come a long way, but true reform does not happen overnight. We know we are succeeding and are continuing to offer grants and technical assistance, if requested."

   h.   One northeastern state commissioned and completed a preliminary exploration of the extent and nature of site-based management practices in [*name of state's*] public schools. In addition to examining the breadth of shared decision-making practice, the study explored the purpose, form, level and nature of participation, and perceived impact of such practices. The following are some of the most striking findings from the study:
- Nearly all [*name of state*] public school districts report using shared decision-making practices in some form. However, definitions vary by district and school, regarding the intent, role, and effect of such practices. Similarly, the actual practices vary as well.

(continued)

Figure 1. *(continued)*

- Committees that currently exist in [*name of state's*] schools are more likely to serve in an advisory rather than a decision-making capacity.
- Curriculum and instruction, student discipline, and school climate are the most commonly addressed issues.
- Issues such as personnel matters, budgetary decisions etc., are rarely deliberated in these forums [*sic*].
- Most [*name of state*] educators view shared decisions as a means to facilitate school improvement.
- Teachers differ from building and district administrators in their opinions about the effectiveness of site-based management practices related to changes in curriculum and instruction.
- For site-based management to be effective, there is a need for all educators to set aside old conceptions of leadership and decision making and learn new ones.
- [*Name of state*] administrators, principals, and teachers view this as a complex process requiring time and external support. It requires attention to the skills of intervention and decision making, the roles and responsibilities of all parties to the process, as well as the provision of time and professional development support, to enable these processes."

i. North Carolina has been promoting and tracking legislatively permitted and encouraged site-based management for several years through an active Task Force at the state level. This report, entitled *Task Force on Site-Based Management: Annual Report to the State Board of Education* (Public Schools of North Carolina, 1995), is replete with the progress (and lack of it) this state has experienced, along with the opinions of a large number of principals, parents, and teachers as to the state of site-based management in their schools. It is the opinion of the authors of this chapter that this report does an excellent job of revealing and successfully representing the strengths, weaknesses, roadblocks, and needs of any state, district, or local school contemplating or implementing SBDM. The Task Force Report may be obtained through Dr. Emmett M. Floyd, Director, Task Force on Site-Based Management, Public Schools of North Carolina, 301 Wilmington Street, Raleigh, North Carolina 27601-2825, (919) 328-6208.

j. Although widely used throughout [*name of large western state*], SBDM is entirely voluntary, district-by-district. There is no effort to control this movement or to standardize practices.

k. [*Name of state*] has hundreds of districts, all of them locally controlled. Although [SBDM] is advocated, both legislatively and by the [state education association], and is a part of many local Goals 2000 plans, it remains optional, with some very vocal detractors.

SBDM IN SELECTED FOREIGN COUNTRIES

Israel

Since the creation of the state of Israel by the United Nations in 1948, the main goal of Israel's educational system has been to provide quality and equitable education to all of its minor subjects. To accomplish this, the educational system was initially centralized under the Ministry of Education. According to Vollansky and Bar-Elli (1996), this system soon experienced several severe problems, among which was its inability to tailor educational programs to meet the needs of specific populations. Specifically, purposeful positive discrimination plans for allocating additional funds to the schools in poor neighborhoods to even the playing field and improve educational outcomes there went awry. Somehow many of these funds found their way into the schools in the better neighborhoods instead, leaving the poorer schools disadvantaged even further by inadequate funding.

The educational system in Israel functions differently from that in the United States in that elementary schools and junior high schools are strictly administered by the Ministry of Education, which controls virtually every aspect of these schools from funding to curricula. High schools, however, are controlled by LEAs and local businesses in synergistic collaboration, although they too must follow a national curriculum guideline.

As is true in the United States, Israeli educators began to question the effectiveness of this system, suggesting that a decentralized administration would allow schools to design individualized school-based programs to meet the needs of the specific populations being educated at each school. Since the mid-1980s, Israel has begun to move toward just such decentralization.

In April 1995, the Ministry of Education launched a trial experiment in school-based management. Among the goals of the experiment were the adaptation of the national curriculum to the manifest needs of the students, the development of a school-monitoring system rather than national testing, and delegation of autonomy for principals. By October 1995, schools had experienced considerably increased control over their resources and staff. Although it is difficult to predict the long-term results of this experiment, it is clear that the movement toward school reform by way of SBDM in order to meet the needs of individual students is active internationally.

Other Countries
In an evaluative study of selected schools in the United States, Canada, and Australia, Odden and Wohlstetter (1995) found that schools that appeared to be implementing successful SBDM shared the following characteristics:

1. Articulation of a vision of restructuring, especially of curricula and instruction
2. Restructuring, not only of governance but also of other components of education as well
3. Empowerment of school personnel over a variety of issues, including budget, personnel, and curriculum decisions

4. Use of shared authority to effect changes in the teaching and learning processes
5. Effective decentralization of professional development and training and the provision of appropriate information and reward systems to effectuate improved teaching performance
6. Principals who exercised strong leadership while sharing authority and accountability

Odden and Wohlstetter (1995) also presented their conclusions regarding at least six major components of SBDM that they believed were necessary, if not sufficient, for success:

1. Shared accountability through some form of site-based councils in which are vested adequate power and authority to make far-reaching decisions concerning programs and resources
2. An emphasis on professional development through which schools create studied, professional communities that foster and expand the avenues for the professional growth and advancement of all staff
3. Broad dissemination of information to constituents and stakeholders to enhance the best decision making possible
4. Capable, dependable leadership (usually the principal) that incorporates delegation while sharing authority
5. A well-defined vision of the mission and the values and goals that relate to its accomplishment, especially regarding student performance and school and community development
6. Recognition and rewarding of accomplishment by individuals for progress made toward the vision and goals of the school's programs

SBDM: A CASE DESCRIPTION

The following is a brief description of a real-world school advisory council (SAC) of a 1,600-student high school in a suburban area of Tampa Bay, Florida. The focus of this brief account is how the pseudonymous Victory High School (VHS) approached, practiced, and evaluated SBDM over a span of 4 years.

Case Study: Victory High School

VHS is a fully accredited, multifaceted school that is well appreciated by its community, in which it has been a major force for more than 50 years. Although its buildings are relatively old, its spirit, curriculum, accomplishments (academic and otherwise), and challenges are quite modern and pronounced. It of-

---

fers all ranges of academic pursuits, from special education, dropout prevention, and teen parent classes to adult night school, vocational tracks, regular tracks, and all levels of honors courses. Its performance on such statewide measures as percentage of students to graduate, percentage of students to go on to college, grade point average, scores on the Scholastic Aptitude Test (SAT) and American College Test (ACT), and on Florida's required tests of the "three Rs" plus social studies, are at least at or better than the state and district averages. VHS's minority population fluctuates between 6% and 10%, and the families represented by its 1,600 students in 9th–12th grades fall slightly above the median income for its county and a bit more above the median income level for the state of Florida. It competes very well in all intermural sports and all other intermural events, including academic teams, forensics, drama, band, and chorus.

VHS has had for many years a SAC that is composed of anyone who wishes to be a part of that organization. In 1991, the Florida legislature passed Blueprint 2000 (similar to then–President Bush's Goals 2000 plan). This legislation mandated the creation of appropriately representative SACs (i.e., inclusive of all stakeholder groups: students, faculty and administration, parents, and community) in every public school. SACs are charged with the responsibility of creating and implementing school improvement plans (SIPs) based on state-, district-, and school-generated data concerning the school's performance across the six major goals of Blueprint 2000 (most of which are oriented toward student achievement and performance and related areas such as a safe environment for teaching).

During the ensuing 4 years (1992–1996), VHS and its SAC accomplished the following tasks successfully:

1. Compiling and evaluating trend data on virtually every measurable aspect of VHS, including student demographics; proportionate breakouts of all categories of students; graduations; dropouts; SAT and ACT scores; other mandated and selected norm-referenced test scores (e.g., reading, writing, math); teacher salaries, turnover, certification, and length of service; teacher : pupil ratios; class sizes; attendance; suspensions and expulsions (by number and category of offenses); mentoring; and other student and parent volunteer services

2. Writing four annual SIPs with objective, measurable timeline goals in all six of the Blueprint 2000 goal areas, calcu-

lated to further improve the school's obvious successes, while decreasing its few areas of weakness and failures (e.g., its 9th–12th grade dropout rate hovers close to 50%, which approximates the state's average)

3. Using a 6-month process to create a comprehensive vision statement facilitated by a special subcommittee that met more than 12 times, focus groups for all stakeholder groups, at least 10 written versions, tentative agreement, presentation and explanation to all stakeholder groups, and final adoption as the document that expresses the values, purposes, expectations, responsibilities, and privileges of the school for all stakeholder groups

4. Creating a broadly representative committee (mostly faculty, but inclusive of SAC, parents, students, and others) to study alternative daily academic schedules; go in small groups to visit schools already using alternative schedules; prepare a written proposal to the faculty; persuade the faculty to pass the proposal (for a 4 × 4 alternative schedule) with a 72% affirmative vote; devise appropriate committees to reform, restructure, challenge, and otherwise improve every aspect of the school's academic and extracurricular programs while preparing for implementation of the new schedule (for Fall 1997); and devise and prepare training for all faculty, including special requests for those who may not feel comfortable in using, or know quite how to use, four 90- to 100-minute class periods per day, instead of the usual six 50-minute classes, or for those who may not know how to plan and present an entire course within one semester, instead of over the course of two semesters

5. Incorporating an accountability system for planning, implementing, staffing, resourcing, evaluating, and changing SIP and other goals and their objectives as needed across all categories of SBDM

6. Planning for the implementation of an outreach program to VHS feeder middle and elementary schools to prepare their students to be fully assimilated when they enter VHS

7. Reducing the number of official, elected SAC members to 14 (i.e., 4 each of faculty and staff, parents, and students, and 2 community members), rather than continuing to allow anyone who attends its monthly meetings at least twice during an academic year to be a bona fide member, while continuing to invite the participation of all as often as they would like

It should be mentioned that the SAC chairperson was always a parent and that the principal, though empowered to shoulder much of the responsibility for all decision making, purposefully shared that responsibility as widely as was practical and prudent. The SAC agenda always began with stakeholder concerns, allowing literally any subject to be broached until consensus or closure was reached.

Regarding the value system and ethic that undergirds SAC deliberation, decisions, and advice, suffice it to say that it is not the seductive and prevalent utilitarian ethic of the greatest good for the greatest number that so often typifies monolithic systems of all sorts. Rather, the VHS SAC ethic is one determined to do everything possible to avoid taking from one group to bolster another, regardless of the relative size, proportion, or makeup of those groups, based on the accepted value that every student, teacher, administrator, and parent is entitled to expect and receive the very best the school has to offer, individually as well as collectively.

When it becomes obvious that a larger group is about to overshadow a smaller group, the VHS SAC deliberates how to continue to guarantee the rights of all the individuals involved and not to give in to the false democracy of service primarily to the majority. The employment of this ethic could serve other SACs well. In an effort to gather specific information about the degree, type, proliferation, and effectiveness of SBDM in this nation's school systems, the authors conducted a brief, six-item survey and mailed them to all 50 chief state school officers (see Figure 1).

The survey shown in Figure 1 was intended to evoke candid answers about SBDM and related activity from those who should have known how and how well each state was doing in this area. In addition, it was hoped that subjective as well as objective data would be adduced for evaluation. The results (see Figure 1) are a mixed bag, as expected, but help in understanding what is intended, as well as what is and is not happening in the United States with regard to SBDM.

CONCLUSIONS

It is clear from the literature cited in this chapter, the survey (see Figure 1), and the experiences of the authors that there is a great diversity of opinions about and approaches to SBDM in the United States.

Not everybody talking about SBDM is doing it, evidently, and not everybody doing it is talking about it through careful evaluation of results. Just as clear, there appears to be little effort being placed in determining how SBDM may affect marginalized groups of students and their families. It is precisely at this point, however, that it is imperative that SBDM be practiced from a specifically chosen and articulated ethical framework other than the greatest good for the greatest number, which tends to overlook the rights of the individual, especially the marginalized individual. Even if SBDM councils were to espouse no other ethic than that embedded in the U.S. Constitution, as amended by the Bill of Rights and further interpreted by legislative action (e.g., PL 94-142 and amendments, the Education for All Handicapped Children Act, now known as the Individuals with Disabilities Education Act [IDEA]), the rights of marginalized students would at least stay in the forefront of discussion.

However, based on available information, there appear to be several important themes associated with the successful practice of SBDM:

1. Administrative and council leaders must be well prepared, not only to delegate authority but also to orient those with less experience toward larger issues and truly democratic action. The trick here is to avoid the politicizing of authority or of interests.

2. Parental participation must be sought and increased to the maximum in the decision-making process, especially including those parents who belong to sectors of the community not previously vocal in the educational process.

3. Although student achievement is an appropriate goal for general determination of the success of SBDM, it is not necessarily the only marker for achieving such success. Determining those forces, negative and positive, that either help or hinder student performance, no matter where or when it occurs, is also the business of a truly community-oriented school or school system. Categorizing students only according to their problems, challenges, or expected outcomes may well be denying and defeating of the full measure of opportunity inherently promised in a public education system. SBDM councils must be aware of the propensity of even the best teachers to want to direct their best efforts toward those students who they perceive will most likely utilize what they learn while expecting and requiring far too little of others not perceived to be so potentially successful. Successful SBDM councils recognize the presence or absence of this underlying value system and take appropriate measures to inculcate and apply it.

4. Data complete and valid enough to enable SBDM councils to understand not only the apex of problems, opportunities, and challenges but also their probable causes and their potential solutions must always inform SBDM. This requires prodigious evaluation of current data and data-tracking systems, not only for comprehensiveness but also for reliability and validity, lest SBDM councils make wonderful decisions based on faulty information.

5. Diligent assurance that resources are adequate to guarantee that decisions made by SBDM teams or councils have a chance to be implemented fully and evaluated objectively must be obtained and maintained. Otherwise, the process itself becomes a futile exercise.

6. External support and training, extra incentives, demonstrations, and professional training must be proffered avidly to SBDM groups.

7. Consistency of membership and leadership appears to be crucial to ongoing and successful SBDM.

8. There must be appropriate and consistent commitment, determination, legislation, rules, policies, funds, and regulations that mandate SBDM at all levels of school systems. Otherwise, total failure is risked because the results may well resemble a top-down system of lip service, accompanied by the same power structures that existed prior to the current push for SBDM.

9. Goals 2000 legislation clearly advocates but does not mandate SBDM. Some states have accepted the underlying philosophy of local and building control of decisions, including budget authority; others clearly have not done so and have no plans to do so. There is some fear that if and when Goals 2000 federal dollars dry up, so will efforts toward establishing SBDM. Other SBDM advocates were well into SBDM before Goals 2000 and plan to continue SBDM efforts until results are clear, one way or the other.

10. Some states' Goals 2000 plans include new and specific roles for colleges and universities involved in teacher training, as well as surveying LEAs for their professional development needs. If SBDM could be addressed at both ends of this spectrum, as it appears it should, then perhaps SBDM will survive Goals 2000, regardless of each state's results.

In concluding this chapter on SBDM, perhaps the reader can be stimulated to continue the discussion within the purview of his or her own school or school system circumstances. Accordingly, the authors present a short list of questions partially distilled from David (1996) and partially from their own studies. Readers are invited to read, discuss, and answer them for themselves and to share them with others, including the authors of this chapter, if they so wish.

1. What policies and supports will ensure that site-based management will not exacerbate resource differences among schools (or among classrooms and classes)?

2. How can SBDM create a sense of community in schools that draw from large geographic areas?

3. Where and how effective are the opportunities for principals, central or district office staff, parents, and even participating students to learn new roles and ways to assist SBDM councils and teams?

4. How should teachers' jobs be redefined, compensated, and otherwise focused on collaborative SBDM, in addition to their teaching responsibilities?

5. How can SBDM be structured to balance school autonomy and flexibility with certain centralized operations that require consistency, cooperation, immediate decisions, coordination, and legal constraints (e.g., government regulations, transportation, college entrance requirements)?

6. What is the best public education analog to private sector work teams, and where do parents and community members fit in?

7. Should schools have mandates that require them to involve parents and the community in decisions?

8. What is the best way to underscore an ethic of inclusion and equity for all groups and individuals, despite the seeming cost to the majority? Should each SBDM council or team include one or more people whose constant responsibility is to remind the group of its obligations to minorities and marginalized groups and individuals?

9. What are the groups and individuals that either attend or support your school or school system whose rights, privileges, and responsibilities an SBDM council might tend to overlook?

10. To what idea, value, thought, or purpose should every member of an SBDM team or council be most committed? Why?

11. To what extent are Goals 2000 and SBDM related? Could or should Goals 2000 be better utilized to enhance SBDM efforts in your state?

These questions call attention to issues the authors have found to be some of the most challenging in SBDM. Most of the questions need to be raised periodically in the spirit of examining a group's (e.g., SACs) values and perspectives that tend to settle out of sight as the culture and modus operandi (i.e., routines and rituals) become established (see Chapter 9). These questions can be useful in opening deeper discussions of ethical issues (see Chapter 3) and coming to decide the prevailing ethic by which the group intends to be guided (see Chapters 4 and 5).

Before proceeding to a specific discussion of ethics and ethical analysis, we turn our attention to a discussion of inclusion, one fundamental policy that must be addressed by SACs and other SBDMs. Townsend and Paul, in Chapter 2, consider the social, pedagogical and moral complexity of the inclusion policy, which, within some broad legal parameters, must be addressed one school at a time.

REFERENCES
Bryk, S.G. (1993). The Chicago experiment: The potential and reality of reform. *Equity and Choice, 9*(3), 22–32.
Candoli, I. (1991). *School system administration: A strategic plan for site-based management.* Lancaster, PA: Technomic.
Council of Chief State School Officers. (1995). *Goals 2000: Educate America Act state profiles.* Washington, DC: State Leadership Center.
Crosby, S. (1991). *Teachers' opinions of school-based management.* (ERIC Document Reproduction Service No. ED 343 241 EA 023 785)
David, J.L. (1989). Synthesis of research on school-based management. *Educational Leadership, 46*(8), 45–53.
David, J.L. (1996). The who, what, and why of site-based management. *Educational Leadership, 53*(4), 4–9.
Dewey, J. (1903). Democracy in education. *Elementary School Teacher, 4*(4), 193–204.
Education for All Handicapped Children Act of 1975, PL 94-142, 20 U.S.C. §§ 1400 *et seq.*
Etheridge, C.P., Valesky, T.C., Horgan, D.D., Nunnery, J., & Smith, D. (1992). *School based decision making: An investigation into effective and ineffective decision making processes and the impact on school climate variables.* Paper presented at the annual meeting of the American Educational Research Association, San Francisco.
Garms, W.I., Guthrie, J.W., & Pierce, L.C. (1978). *School finance: The economics and politics of public education.* Englewood Cliffs, NJ: Prentice Hall.
Goals 2000: Educate America Act of 1994, PL 103-227, 20 U.S.C. §§ 5801 *et seq.*
Individuals with Disabilities Education Act (IDEA) of 1990, PL 101-476, 20 U.S.C. §§ 1400 *et seq.*
Lindquist, K.M., & Mauriel, J.J. (1989). School-based management: Doomed to failure? *Education and Urban Society, 21,* 403–416.
Marsh, D.O. (1992). *Change in schools.* (ERIC Document Reproduction Service No. ED 353 673)
Mojkowski, C., & Fleming, D. (1988). *School-site management: Concepts and approaches.* Andover, MA: Regional Laboratory for the Educational Improvement of the Northeast and Islands.
Murphy, J., & Beck, L.G. (1995). *School-based management as school reform: Taking stock.* Thousand Oaks, CA: Corwin Press.

Odden, E.R., & Wohlstetter, P. (1995). Making school-based management work. *Educational Leadership, 52*(5), 32–36.
Public Schools of North Carolina. (1995). *Task Force on Site-Based Management: Annual report to the state board of education.* Raleigh, NC: Author.
Vollansky, A., & Bar-Elli, D. (1996). Moving toward equitable school-based management. *Educational Leadership, 53,* 60–62.
Weiss, C.H. (1993). *Interests and ideologies in educational reform: Changing the venue of decision making in the high school.* Cambridge, MA: National Center for Educational Leadership.
Wohlstetter, P., & Mohrman, S.A. (1993). *School-based management: Strategies for success.* New Brunswick, NJ: CPRE Finance Briefs.

SUGGESTED READINGS

Association for Supervision and Curriculum Development. (1986). *School reform policy: A call for reason.* Alexandria, VA: Author.
Caldwell, B. (1990). School-based decision-making and management: International developments. In J. Chapman (Ed.), *School-based decision-making and management* (pp. 3–26). London: Falmer Press.
Carnegie Forum on Education and the Economy. (1986). *A nation prepared: Teachers for the 21st century.* Washington, DC: Author.
Chapman, J., & Boyd, W.L. (1988). Decentralization, devolution, and the school principal: Australian lessons on statewide educational reform. *Educational Administration Quarterly, 22,* 28–58.
Clune, W.H., & White, P.A. (1988). *School-based management: Institutional variation, implementation, and issues for further research.* New Brunswick, NJ: Rutgers University, Eagleton Institute of Politics, Center for Policy Research in Education.
Hallinger, P., & Hausman, C. (1993). Comprehensive school restructuring: Impact on the role of the principal. In J. Murphy & P. Hallinger (Eds.), *Restructuring schools: Learning from ongoing efforts.* New York: Teachers College Press.
Hill, P.T., & Bonan, J. (1991). *Decentralization and accountability in public education.* Santa Monica, CA: Rand Corp.
National Commission on Excellence in Education. (1983). *A nation at risk: The imperative of educational reform.* Washington, DC: U.S. Government Printing Office.
O'Brien, T.P., & Reed, R.R. (1994). *Implications of site-based management for the preparation of public school teachers and administrators in North Carolina.* Unpublished manuscript, North Carolina State University, College of Education and Psychology, Raleigh.
Simmons, Boyle, & Associates. (1994). *Site-based management.* (1994 opinion research project conducted for the task force on site-based management, North Carolina Department of Public Instruction). Chapel Hill, NC: Author.
Simmons, Boyle, & Associates. (1995). *Site-based management.* (1995 assessment conducted for the task force on site-based management, North Carolina Department of Public Instruction). Chapel Hill, NC: Author.
Wagstaff, L.H., & Reyes, P. (1993). *School site-based management.* (Report presented to the Educational Economic Policy Center). Austin: University of Texas, College of Education.

2

School Reform and the Inclusion of Children with Disabilities

Brenda L. Townsend and James L. Paul

Schools across the nation are implementing educational reform initiatives with hopes of improving practice in general education (Cuban, 1990), special education (Kauffman, Kameenui, Birman, & Danielson, 1990), or both (Paul & Evans, 1995). Special and general education reforms have tended to be parallel movements (McLaughlin & Warren, 1992) with little collaboration between the two.

Having few mutually planned goals and vested interests gives rise to competing forces; accomplishing the goals in one arena may actually compete with the goals in the other. An example is general education's increased emphasis on accountability and raising students' standardized test scores. Given the often-cited pessimistic reports of the lagging performance of U.S. children (e.g., Carnegie Forum on Education and the Economy, 1986; Goodlad, 1984; National Commission on Excellence in Education, 1983) and the thrust to prepare the 21st-century work force, aiming to increase student performance is both laudable and understandable. Yet achieving higher academic goals may in effect be in conflict with special education initiatives to include children with disabilities in general education settings.

The fear that including children with disabilities in the mainstream would lead to lower school aggregated test scores could dissuade meaningful inclusion of children with disabilities in mainstream settings. Other administrative concerns and constraints that have little to do with student characteristics affect the extent to which children with disabilities are included in general education settings (Evans, Townsend, Duchnowski, & Hocutt, in press).

Regardless of whether school reform is occurring separately in general education and special education or jointly, children with disabilities must figure prominently in decisions about reforming school practice. The timing is right. General education reform is currently in its third phase (see the Introduction). Outcomes for children with disabilities were not discussed in the early proposals to reform schools (Lavely & McCarthy, 1995). In the 1990s, unlike the mainstreaming and regular education initiative eras of the 1970s and 1980s, children with disabilities are acknowledged in general education reform (i.e., restructuring), and their needs are specifically addressed in the Goals 2000: Educate America Act of 1994 (PL 103-227) (Hocutt & McKinney, 1995).

Policy-making committees established within local schools are provided varying amounts of responsibility for guiding or facilitating restructuring activities. These school-based decision-making committees (SBDMCs), with membership typically including teachers, principals, parents, students, and community representatives, face complex ethical challenges. In particular, they must consider the extent to which children with disabilities and their families are provided valued social space within the school. Addressing this issue, the authors of this book discuss the metaphor of "hospitality to the stranger" as an ethic of care that ought to permeate local school cultures.

Special education reform movements have their own histories that include heated debates about how the interests of children with disabilities can best be served. In order for SBDMCs to do their work, it is helpful for them to have some awareness of these debates and the historical, ethical, legal, and political contexts in which they have occurred. An understanding of these contexts can help SBDMCs frame the critical questions about educational outcomes for children with disabilities.

HISTORY OF SPECIAL EDUCATION

The history of education parallels the history of mental health in the United States relative to policies that structure the social proximity of people with disabilities to mainstream society. In the history of mental health, institutions were built to protect individuals with mental disabilities who had previously been in jails and almshouses or chained in cellars. The mental health movement, started early in the 20th century, sought to improve the institutions that had been built in the middle of the 19th century and to develop community services. It was not until the 1960s, however, that community mental health centers received congressional endorsement with the passage of the Community Mental Health Centers Act (PL 88-164). The deinstitutionalization policy was developed during the Nixon administration to reduce institutional dependency and to support the development of community-based care.

The education of children with disabilities did not receive significant public policy support until the 1960s. Before that time, many schools, in response to lobbying efforts of parents, were offering special class programs for children with mental retardation. Children with obvious physical disabilities and some with central nervous system disorders were provided limited educational services in certain schools. It was not until the mid-1960s, however, that federal legislation provided support to prepare teachers for all children with disabilities. Still not all children were served in public schools, in part because public school policy is mostly a state and local government matter.

In the 1970s, parents of children with disabilities and special interest or advocacy groups were successful in litigation on behalf of children and adults with disabilities. The focus was on the right to treatment, the right to an appropriate education, and the right to due process. (See Turnbull, 1986, for an excellent discussion of special education law.) In 1975, with the passage of the Education for All Handicapped Children Act (PL 94-142), Congress established the right of all children to a free and appropriate education in the least restrictive environment (LRE). This law included several basic provisions that changed the political dynamics of the relationships among schools, parents, and students with disabilities. Parents were given the right to participate in decisions about their child's education. Children were given the right to a culture-fair assessment. Each child identified as having a disability was given the right to an individualized education program (IEP). Although it was not normative for children with disabilities to be served in the general education classroom, all children were given the right to due process and safeguards to protect them from being removed from general education programs without appropriate educational reasons and without the parents' support for the decision. These and other provisions changed the social contract between schools and children with disabilities and their parents. (The focus on families was to come later. See Paul & Simeonsson, 1993; Turnbull & Turnbull, 1997.)

The federal law did not change the culture of schools with respect to the social status and the generally devalued place of children with disabilities. The attitudes and feelings about children who learned differently or more slowly or about children who looked different were not suddenly transformed. The labels continued to serve their cultural function of structuring relationships between those who were considered socially deviant and those who were not. Historically, there had been labels of damnation, such as "emotionally disturbed," and labels of forgiveness, such as "mentally retarded" (Noblit, Schlechty, & Paul, 1991). Labels of forgiveness communicated victimization, a condition over which the individual had no control. Labels of damnation, however, held the person more responsible for his or her disability and expected the individual to change to fit culturally normative standards of behavior and the unmodified general education curriculum. The curriculum could be adjusted for the forgiven but not for the damned. The labels therefore helped maintain a moral and sociopolitical system of thinking about children and their education.

This general social dynamic continues to exist. The ideology of this system, held together by mental health specialists, special educators, and technobureaucratic patterns of assessing, labeling, and placing children, was not transformed by the law. Social attitudes, school cultures, and professional guilds had been knitted together in a strong web of caregiving and special education that would resist change. Part of the strength of the web, as well as the strength of resistance to change, was in the deep cultural roots of the system itself. Labeling and placing students was, among other things, a political activity with clear racial implications. Many have argued that the system has worked against children who are poor and members of minority groups.

Another challenge for the law was the problem of defining the legislatively mandated *least restrictive environment*. This concept was generally interpreted to mean something similar to what had previously been called *mainstreaming*. Again, the restrictiveness of the environment had to do with the social proximity of children with disabilities to their age peers. It was this proximity, among other things, that the policy sought to address. A cascade of services, a concept closely akin to the concept of a continuum of care in the mental health system, was advocated for special education. Some of the policy debate centered on the general education classroom as the standard for "least restrictiveness." For example, is the general education classroom the LRE for a child who cannot learn from a general education curriculum or cannot socially adapt to a general education environment?

As discussed later in this chapter, terms for this debate changed somewhat in the 1980s with the Reagan administration's political advocacy for the regular education initiative (REI). Again, the concept included provision for pull-out services where necessary, but the emphasis was on general education classroom placement. (Interestingly, the REI was not an initiative of "regular" educators but rather some of the special education leadership during the early to mid-1980s.) The inclusion movement of the late 1980s and 1990s placed the emphasis even more on general education classroom placement, with full-inclusionists rejecting all pull-out services.

The story of special education policy development, though socially, culturally, and politically complex, is relatively clear. During the last half of the 20th century, changes in culture, demographics, values, political ideology, power alignments, technologies, and the philosophy of education have dramatically altered the nature and culture of schooling. The cultural and moral issues embedded in the social contract between children and their families and schools are profoundly different from the substance of that contract before midcentury. The understanding of children with disabilities is different. Behavioral issues in schools are different. Concerns about out-of-seat behavior and running in the halls have been replaced by concerns about drugs and violence, including children killing children. The understanding of behavior disorders in an urban multicultural school with unresolved or unaddressed ethnic differences, gang violence, and police patrols is different from a segregated, white middle-class school with teachers who are known to and by the parents. The question now is, What policies will work at the local school level to serve the educational needs of all students?

The SBDMC is an organizational strategy in school reform being used to locate more policy authority in the local school, a shift from the traditional top-down, often autocratic, and even patriarchal approach of the past. The SBDMC is a relatively new organizational strategy reflecting confidence in the idea that the problems in a school can be addressed best by those who are in the school and those whose interests are directly affected by the school—teachers, principals, students, parents, and other members of the community.

The SBDMC faces difficult philosophical challenges in deciding the kind of school it wants and the kinds of policies that will lead the school toward that vision. In the cultural context of the 1990s, unable to rely on the authority of professional wisdom because it is inconsistent or on research because it is not definitive, SBDMCs must make responsible and ethically defensible choices in the form of policies or policy advisories about the allocation of resources to support the interests of all students. How can this occur? Attempting to be fair by simply dividing resources equally will work against the interest of students who need more than others in order to have an appropriate education. Deciding what is in the best interest of most of the students may result in a cost for those students who are fewer in number but who may have more to lose.

MAINSTREAMING AND THE REGULAR
EDUCATION INITIATIVE: GETTING TO INCLUSION

The Education for All Handicapped Children Act of 1975 in principle guaranteed all children and youth with disabilities the right to a free and appropriate education in the least restrictive educational environment. Although few would disagree with the intent and spirit of the law, there has been a great deal of debate centering on definitions and implementation regulations (Gartner & Lispsky, 1987; Hocutt, Martin, & McKinney, 1990; Kauffman, 1993; Reynolds, Wang, & Walberg, 1987). The issue of what constitutes an appropriate education for children with disabilities was central in the special education debates during the 1960s and 1970s. In large part, criticism of special education services focused on segregated class placements, racially biased assessment and placement policies, and lack of instructional efficacy (Dunn, 1968; Skrtic, 1991). Moreover, there was evidence of negative psychological and social effects of labeling and special class placement for students (Stainback & Stainback, 1990).

In addition to these indictments of special education, court litigation also helped spawn the mainstreaming movement. Cases such as *Diana v. State Board of Education* (1970), *Larry P. v. Riles* (1972), and *Pennsylvania Association for Retarded Children (PARC) v. Commonwealth of Pennsylvania* (1971) led to policy mandates to mainstream children with disabilities (Hocutt et al., 1990). *PARC v. Pennsylvania* (1971) established the legal right of students with severe disabilities to receive public education. The *Diana* and *Larry P.* cases addressed the classification of ethnic minority students in programs for children with special needs.

The Mainstreaming Movement

The mainstreaming movement was a response to political, historical, and legal concerns expressed about educating children with disabilities. According to Turnbull (1986), LRE was a judicial preference for children being educated in a general education setting. The premise of LRE is that children with disabilities can and should be taught with their peers who do not have disabilities. It was believed, with some support from efficacy research (Reynolds et al., 1987), that children with disabilities benefit more from instructional services in a mainstream classroom (i.e., general education classroom) than in self-contained settings. The research is inconclusive, in part because of the differences among children with disabilities and the large variability among teachers and general education classrooms.

Considering the general education setting as the LRE for all students has sparked much debate. According to Vergason and Anderegg (1992), the general education setting is not least restrictive for all children. They suggested that Congress intended a continuum of placement options for children and youth with disabilities. As evidence, they pointed to the language used to note the conditions under which children can be removed from the general education class. Under the Education for All Handicapped Children Act of 1975, removal from general education classes is to occur "only when the nature or severity of the handicap is such that education in regular classes with the use of supplementary aids and services cannot be achieved satisfactorily" (20 U.S.C. § 1412[5][b]). Vergason and Anderegg (1992) viewed LRE as placing emphasis on the instructional environment as opposed to focusing more narrowly on the physical setting.

Although the definitions have varied widely, *mainstreaming* typically suggests educating learners with disabilities in settings with their peers who have no known disabilities (Pappanikou & Paul, 1977). Originally, the movement focused on children with mental retardation, presumably because of Dunn's (1968) early charge that special education practice was not justifiable for children with mild mental retardation. It was later expanded to include children with emotional and behavior disorders and learning disabilities.

The mainstreaming movement, in proposing to physically integrate children with disabilities in general education settings, was somewhat innocuous. Although it questioned special education practice, it did not involve radical school reform (Skrtic, 1991). Its focus was on physically and socially integrating children with disabilities into general education classes. Little was done, however, to ensure that the mainstream settings were improved instructional placements for children with disabilities. For example, general education teachers were not prepared to work with children with special needs. Educators' and parents' paradigms of disability were not addressed prior to mainstreaming. The attitudes individuals held about children with disabilities and their needs and abilities were not discussed. The relative lack of reliable data and the variability of perspectives among SBDMC members contribute to the difficulty of reaching consensus about school-based policies. It amplifies the need for commitment to a process of ethical deliberation.

Technical assistance in behavior management and IEPs was seldom available. In some instances, class sizes were not reduced to accommodate children with diverse needs and abilities. There were several social concerns with mainstreaming, including the lack of social skills development for children with disabilities and for their peers without disabilities, as well as the lack of preparation provided for teachers to meet the social and behavioral needs of children with behavior disorders (Braaten, Kauffman, Braaten, Polsgrove, & Nelson, 1988).

Regardless of intent, mainstreaming for physical or social integration alone does not ensure quality educational opportunities. In fact, it has been argued that mainstreamed settings for some children constitute an even more restrictive environment; thus, such settings could jeopardize the quality of life for some children. Consider the child with behavior disorders who has difficulty establishing and maintaining peer friendships. If that child were removed from a smaller special education setting and placed in a general education setting with a teacher who had no pre- or in-service prosocial skill instruction training, that setting could prove disastrous for that child.

Even amid numerous concerns about its implementation, mainstreaming has had considerable value for children with disabilities and for the field of special education. The mainstreaming movement has provided a new discourse about special education as well as a conceptual bridge from segregated services to services better connected and integrated with general education. Mainstreaming has helped establish the case for the rights of children with disabilities to be members of the school community. In fact, critical lessons have been learned that are now of value to SBDMCs. Those lessons are discussed later in this chapter.

The Regular Education Initiative

Following the mainstreaming movement, REI presented another attempt at school reform. Keogh (1988) pointed out the irony of calls for special education reform at a time when general education was under considerable pressure to change. Several national reports regarding the status of general education presented evidence of its need for reform (Hocutt et al., 1990). Those reports included *A Nation at Risk* (National Commission on Excellence in Education, 1983), *A Place Called School: Prospects for the Future* (Goodlad, 1984), and *A Nation Prepared: Teachers for the Twenty-First Century* (Carnegie Forum on Education and the Economy, 1986).

During that same period, Will (1986) and others (e.g., Gartner & Lipsky, 1987; Wang, Reynolds, & Walberg, 1988) noted that special and general education operated as separate systems in educating students. They contended that the separation of these two systems was costly and ineffective, promoted capricious identification and service delivery practices, and fostered pejorative labeling. Attesting to the difficulty of defining the REI, Kauffman (1990) stated that it is "a loosely connected set of propositions and proposals for reform of the relationship between special and general education" (p. 57). Most REI proposals sought to provide an integrated system within which special and general educators would share responsibility for all learners.

Most REI advocates question the efficacy of traditional special education policies and practices. They believe there is little that is special about special education and that children with disabilities would benefit more in the general education setting. In support of that contention, they frequently cite studies of special education efficacy that call into question the instructional models for integrating children with and without disabilities (Lloyd & Gambatese, 1990). Critics of the REI characterize those studies as seriously flawed and inconclusive. These critics point to other studies that either support special education effectiveness or fail to rule out its ineffectiveness. What is clear, however, is the need for methodologically sound research that identifies instructional practices that are beneficial to students with disabilities and mechanisms to ensure that empirically validated practices are implemented.

At the core of most REI proposals is the claim that the general education setting is the place where all learners, without labels, can be optimally educated (Kauffman, 1993). REI proposals vary (Fuchs & Fuchs, 1994), with some focusing on one of two groups of students with disabilities: high-incidence disabilities, including students with mild to moderate learning disabilities, behavior disorders, and mental retardation; or students with low-incidence disabilities, including those with severe disabilities.

REI is said to be a more radical proposal for reform than mainstreaming. Although mainstreaming advocates questioned the ethics and effectiveness of segregated special classes, general education practice went virtually unassailed (Skrtic, 1987). REI proponents charge that both special and general education practices are ineffective and damaging to students with disabilities and those at risk for school failure. In their arguments, REI advocates have used emotionally charged analogies and metaphors to portray special education. Special education has been compared to practices leading to the civil rights movement: slavery (Stainback & Stainback, 1985), segregation (Gartner & Lipsky, 1989), and apartheid (Lipsky & Gartner, 1987).

Although REI proponents challenged the integrity of special education, they failed to identify clear and specific strategies for simultaneously reforming special and general education to serve children with disabilities and those at risk in general education settings better. Moreover, only two instructional models were proposed as alternatives to the dual instructional systems. They were the Adaptive Learning Environmental Model (ALEM) (Wang, 1980) and Cooperative Learning (Slavin & Stevens, 1991). ALEM involves implementing IEPs for all students and cooperative learning as an instructional grouping strategy.

Several special education professional groups raised serious questions about the REI. The Council for Children with Behavior Disorders (CCBD) cautioned that the general education classroom may not be the LRE for children with behavior disorders. They noted that general educators do not have training in strategies for behavior and crisis management. Additionally, removing the label of behavior disorders from those youth will not change the way individuals perceive them. That is, their behaviors will continue to cause them to be isolated from their peers.

Other groups were cautious of the REI for children with learning disabilities. The Association for Children and Adults with Learning Disabilities (ACLD) (1986) maintained that the debate centers on the cascade of services. REI advocates have suggested proposals ranging from eliminating the top or the bottom of the continuum of placement options (i.e., residential schools or pull-out special education programs) to eliminating the entire continuum and replacing it with the general education classroom. Fuchs and Fuchs (1990) categorized the REI backers as abolitionists and their critics as conservationists. The conservationists (i.e., Anderegg & Vergason, 1988; Hallahan, Keller, McKinney, Lloyd, & Bryan, 1988; Schumaker & Deshler, 1988) cautioned REI proponents against elimination of the continuum of options and proceeding without the benefit of empirical support.

The crux of the often-heated debate regarding the REI revolves around several questions, including the following:

1. Should the cascade of services be replaced by the general education setting as the most appropriate and LRE for all students with disabilities?
2. What instructional models are beneficial to students with disabilities and those at risk for school failure?
3. What facilitates social interaction among children with disabilities and their peers without disabilities?
4. Can children with disabilities be successful when returned to general education settings—the very settings in which they were unsuccessful?
5. Can general and special educators work together to serve all students in general education settings?

For the most part, the discussions about the REI involved only special educators. Many recognized the need for discussions to be expanded to address the complex issues of educating all children. Also, discussions were needed to involve more disciplines than education alone (Skrtic, 1988).

Fundamentally, early special education reform aimed to provide access to education for children with disabilities. Building on early intervention, the goal was to improve outcomes for these same children over time (Cook, Weintraub, & Morse, 1995). In comparing special and general education reform, Cook et al. (1995) pointed out that both general and special education reforms emphasize student outcomes and call for reshaping the educational processes used to achieve those outcomes.

DEBATE SURROUNDING THE INCLUSION MOVEMENT

The most current special education reform movement is the inclusion of children with disabilities. Often called *inclusion,* it too represents different notions to different people (Fuchs & Fuchs, 1994). For some, it involves educating children with disabilities for part of the day in general education classes. However, *full inclusion* usually refers to students with disabilities receiving all educational services in general education classes, as reflected in the inclusive schools movement. *Inclusive schooling* is defined as "the inclusion of all students in the mainstream of regular education classes and school activities with their age peers from the same community" (Stainback & Stainback, 1990, p. 225).

According to Stainback and Stainback (1992), inclusive schools focus on the values of community and diversity. Individual differences are valued, as are the development of communities in which all students' needs are met. Furthermore, inclusive schools promote combining resources and providing comprehensive supports to facilitate student success in general education settings, as opposed to providing individualized services only when students have labels (Stainback & Stainback, 1992).

Although mainstreaming and the REI were originally advocated on behalf of children with mild and moderate disabilities, full inclusion is promoted most aggressively for children with severe disabilities. For example, members of The Association for Persons with Severe Handicaps have ardently supported the inclusion movement. Similar to the REI movement, inclusionists do not have the full support of others in the field of special education. Several professional organizations have raised serious questions about the full inclusion of all students, believing that some children with disabilities can be served most appropriately in pull-out programs. Most of them advocate maintaining the continuum of placement options for educating children with disabilities. In that regard, they argue that previously won rights will not be guaranteed, that the general education setting is not prepared to meet the unique needs of all children with disabilities. The general education classroom, they contend, restricts some children more than part-time and self-contained special classes (Viadero, 1992).

Although few deny that there is a need for special education reform, full-inclusion advocates desire to dismantle special education and all vestiges of it (Biklen, 1985; Stainback & Stainback, 1985). That is, service delivery system options would be eliminated to make the general education classroom the only option for students with and without special needs. As evidenced by the organizations that work on behalf of children and youth with special needs, much concern rests with the quality of services delivered in the general education setting. Issues of teachers ill prepared to work with students with special needs, guaranteeing student rights in the absence of labels, ignoring student and parent setting preferences, and social stigmata and embarrassment are continuing issues in the debate.

Relationships between general and special educators pose another dilemma for the inclusion movement. Professional relationships provide the foundation upon which the inclusion movement is built. Inclusion proponents believe that special and general education professionals can jointly meet the academic and social needs of children with diverse abilities and needs in one setting. Several collaboration and consultation models are employed to integrate children with disabilities with their peers with no known disabilities (e.g., Harris & Evans, 1995).

Often relationships among professionals, parents, families, agency personnel, and community personnel are tenuous and fragile. Collaboration and consultation models seek to facilitate and improve these relationships. Special education reform may not truly occur until ways have been found to share expertise and responsibility for the education of children with disabilities with all stakeholders.

INCLUSION: ETHICAL POLICY DILEMMAS AND IMPLICATIONS FOR SCHOOL-BASED DECISION-MAKING COMMITTEES

Educational policy decisions in local schools are guided by many factors, such as prevailing professional wisdom, available research, and the values of those empowered to make and interpret the decisions. As indicated in Chapter 1, there are many different approaches to implementing school-based management, a priority of school reform. The policy environment in schools in the 1990s is complex and varies even from school to school within districts. The manner in which the policy authority of a local school is exercised depends a great deal on the history, organizational culture, leadership style, and political ecology of the individual school and the district in which that school is located. The variability in local school environments makes the approach to interpreting and implementing the inclusion policy especially difficult.

Part of the challenge lies in the fact that there are no definitions of *inclusion* that are acceptable to all stakeholders. As noted earlier in this chapter, professionals do not agree among themselves about inclusion, and the research does not provide a definitive resolution to the inclusion policy debate. How, then, do SBDMCs address inclusion in each school? Lacking clear guidelines based on research and professional wisdom, how does a school advisory committee make thoughtful and responsible decisions about meeting the educational needs of all students?

In the absence of definitive data or general consensus among professionals regarding the most appropriate service delivery system for students with disabilities, the central issues are related to understanding the relative interests and needs of all students, including those with disabilities, and developing effective educational services that address those needs in the context of a caring and welcoming community. That is, given the values and the understanding of what constitutes educational needs in a local school, the SBDMC must develop or provide advice about policies that will best meet the needs of all students. A major challenge for the SBDMC is to make responsible decisions that are in the best interest of the school as a community, without compromising the interests of a particular student or group of students.

It is necessary to understand that the student's interest is socially constructed. In one school, the student's interest may be construed as the ability to perform on an achievement test. Test outcomes, then, will be the indicator of whether the student's educational interest, as indicated by what he or she has learned, has been served. In another school, the student's ability to work well with others, to make moral choices, and to have a positive image of her- or himself may be at least as important as measurable academic achievement. In this school, performance on achievement tests is still a priority; but it is interpreted in the context of other variables of equal importance.

The construction of educational interest occurs in the context of a school and is reflected in the decisions made by SBDMCs, principals, and teachers. In order to understand interest and how it is constructed, it is necessary to understand those who construct it and the context in which they work. The characteristics of SBDMCs as decision-making or advice-giving structures embedded in the policy process in schools are relevant in this regard.

As discussed in Chapter 9, the membership of SBDMCs, the values and control agendas of different members, the information available, and other characteristics of the group substantially influence the outcomes of the decision-making process. Also, the authority structure and culture of the school, discussed in Chapters 7 and 8, provide a context within which the committee interprets its role and conducts its business as a policy-making body.

Since policy decisions guide the allocation of resources and thereby affect the lives of people, the ethical dimension is always present. However, in the current environment of local schools, the ethical dimension—deciding what is the right thing to do and doing it for the right reasons—is especially prominent. This is dramatically evident in decisions relevant to inclusion. The absence of professional consensus and the lack of definitive data about inclusion highlights the ethical nature of policy decisions in the local school.

Although there are no formulas or objective prescriptions to guide SBDMCs in making ethical decisions, SBDMCs should proceed in a deliberative manner that treats the issue of interests, including conflicting interests, seriously (see also Chapters 3–6). We believe that SBDMCs should refrain from a simple application of ethical rules, principles, or theories. For example, an SBDMC could agree that there are several ethical principles that should be applied to test the wisdom of a decision. These might include principles such as doing no harm, ensuring fairness in the equitable distribution of resources, and making certain that the interest of the largest number of students is best served. Many such principles could be agreed upon. However, difficulty arises in attempting to define terms such as *harm, equity,* and *interest* (see Chapter 4). Also, these principles are not necessarily internally consistent. If, for example, resources are distributed equitably, and *equitably* is taken to mean an equal share for each student (i.e., the student who needs more teacher time, or the student who needs materials that cost more than they cost for most other students), then those students who need more may be harmed by receiving only an equal share. This, then, leads to the question of a hierarchy of principles. Are some principles more important than others? Although even this could be discussed and agreed upon, the arguments presented by French and Fasching in Chapters 4 and 5, respectively, suggest that principle-based or rule-driven policy is not likely to be satisfying.

An alternative is to focus more on the community and the kind of place community members want it to be (see especially Chapters 5, 6, and 13). The ethical stance that understands virtue and care to be constructed in context suggests that it is important and useful for SBDMC members to consider the kind of school they want their decisions to create. This may be more difficult. It requires more work among members of the group in crafting a vision of the good school (see discussion of the "Great Good Place" in Chapter 4); that is, it requires the kind of learning environment that they want for students.

The inclusion policy forces attention to the community narrative: What kind of place is this school? A central issue in this context is the nature and quality of the relationship between children with disabilities and their age peers. Both of the current inclusion-related policy arguments—continuum of care and full inclusion—suggest a relationship between children with disabilities and their age peers in school. The debate centers on where and how the child with disabilities will be educated (see Kauffman, Lloyd, Hallahan, & Astuto, 1995, for an excellent analysis of issues related to the placement of children with disabilities). The moral stance and policy position supporting and protecting the place of the child with disabilities in the general education classroom is uncertain. Indeed, it always has been.

Two questions must be addressed by an SBDMC in developing a policy position regarding inclusion. First, does a child with disabilities have a right to be educated with her or his age peers in a general education classroom? Second, can a child be educated appropriately in a general education classroom? If the child has a right to an appropriate education, and if that education cannot be provided in a general education classroom, then the question of a right to be educated in the general education classroom is moot, unless, of course, the right to be in the general education classroom is about more than being educated in the general education classroom. In that case, education as a right is replaced by a higher right: the right to be in the general education classroom with his or her age peers for the purpose of socialization, for example. This is the nature of the full-inclusion argument made by some people, as suggested in the first part of this chapter. The SBDMC must decide its own moral stance relative to the rights of children with disabilities and must draw its own conclusions regarding the weight of the evidence on the educational efficacy of full inclusion. Kauffman et al. (1995) commented,

> Placement decisions and policy options are informed by few reliable data that explain how placement is related to the desired outcomes of education or treatment. Many factors and people with very different perspectives influence both the making of individual placement decisions and the making of rules about placement decisions. (p. 379)

CONCLUSIONS

Whatever one's position on inclusion, it is the case that the education of children with disabilities in the mainstream classroom is not normative. The history of public education is clear on this point. There are children who fit the general education curriculum and those who do not. Those who do not typically either have failed within general education classrooms or have been certified as unable to profit from the general education curriculum and other educational arrangements made for them. School culture is constructed in ways that separate those who fit the normative culture from those who do not. It is in this sense, then, that the concept of the misfit is a cultural construction of the school.

School policies are cultural constructions that make the tacit understanding about interests in the school explicit. Many strongly held beliefs and values are not stated or codified in policy until they are violated or until someone raises a question about them. The SBDMC serves the instrumental function of articulating policy positions that accurately represent beliefs and priorities of the school. This is a complex process that involves reaching tacit as well as explicit understanding.

The process occurs in an SBDMC made up of individuals who have their own views. The values and control agendas of different SBDMC members, the information available, and other dynamics of the group, as well as the authority structure and culture of the school (see Chapters 7 and 8), provide a context within which the committee interprets its role and conducts its business (see generally Chapter 9). An SBDMC with a member who is a parent of a child with a learning disability is likely to have a very different conversation about inclusion than is an SBDMC with a member who has a child with moderate mental retardation. The dynamics are likely to be different, and, depending on several things, including the kinds of information available to the SBDMC, the outcomes are likely to be different. Another factor is the history of the school in serving students with disabilities and the state and school district policies already in place. The product, then, of SBDMC deliberations reflects the values, interests, and culture of the school and the membership of the committee.

Although no simple solutions are offered that would allow SBDMCs to address the complex ethical policy dilemma of inclusion, a perspective is offered within which the dilemma may be resolved in different ways within individual schools. This perspective, described by Fasching in Chapter 5, suggests that students who have been labeled misfits may be understood as strangers in the normative, valued places of a school. He suggests a narrative ethic with hospitality to the stranger as an overarching moral vision for the community. As an alternative to principle-based theories that provide tests for ethical choices, narrative ethics focuses on the school's story as a guide for the deliberative process of making decisions about particular events or individuals. It is in this context that the ramifications of, for example, disability, race, and gender in the school community are considered. Doing what is right and doing it for the right reasons become a matter of doing the only thing that makes the most sense in the "narrative" of the community.

The ethic of hospitality to the stranger must be articulated in the context of an SBDMC involved in making sense of the local school's story. The stranger—a student with a disability, for example—has a place in which he or she is welcomed. That place, whether valued and in the school's general education classroom or devalued and peripheral to the life of the school, depends on the ethic of the community. Decisions are made on the basis of the community's understanding of what it must do to reflect its values. An analysis of technical barriers to inclusion does not lead to the development of a philosophy of inclusion any more than a child's ability to read leads to decisions about the child's place at the dinner table with family. Welcoming is a deliberate moral and political act. It is an act that includes or, by its absence, excludes. Students with disabilities have not yet been fully welcomed into the general education classroom.

The Education for All Handicapped Children Act of 1975 established the terms for students with disabilities being present in schools. Amendments adopted since that time (including the Individuals with Disabilities Education Act of 1990 [PL 101-476]) have maintained those terms, or principles, established in 1975. The policy debates that have followed (e.g., LRE, REI, inclusion) accurately reflect the ambivalence of the educational community toward disability and difference. SBDMCs therefore carry a serious moral responsibility in the context of public education policy in the latter part of the 1990s in recasting the narrative of public education, one school at a time. The most serious challenge for special educators is to work with general educators in crafting policies that emphasize ethics of care and welcoming while maintaining a commitment to academic achievement.

There are no definitively best and most appropriate ways to educate all children with disabilities. There is a lack of consensus on the most effective strategies for educating an increasingly diverse student population. SBDMCs function within the context of political, cultural, historical, moral, and legal forces that shape their responses to needs within schools. Education reformers are not in agreement about a vision of the future or about policies most likely to lead to the improvement of schools for all children. Moreover, relationships among professionals, parents, families, and other members of the community can be difficult when there are differences in their moral visions of education.

Special education historically promotes individualization. As special education and general education reform movements advance, educators still must be guided by that principle. With increased student diversity, it is necessary for school-based policy makers to avoid a simplistic interpretation or application of ethical principles such as effecting the greatest good for the greatest number. Rather, school policy makers must be diligent in their efforts to address the educational interests of all children. As schools become more complex, the imaginative capacities of school policy makers must be developed in order that people may see, together, better educational opportunities for children affected by decisions.

Similarly, school policy makers must be critical of simplistic slogans that do not translate into meaningful policies. At present, SBDMCs, which have limited information and technical support for their work, are at risk of overinterpreting the implied ethic of full inclusion and overlooking the educational interests of all children affected by such a policy. For example, a student who has a behavior disorder and needs a teacher who can effectively teach him or her to explore life events and problem-solve to prevent and manage crises may need to be in a smaller, self-contained setting. However, another student with a behavior disorder that requires less intensive interventions may be successful in a general education setting with a teacher who is willing to maintain the student in the general education setting.

SBDMCs must consider many factors in developing policies that genuinely and sincerely welcome the stranger (i.e., children with disabilities) into the life of the school. SBDMCs must ensure that children with disabilities, as well as their peers who do not have disabilities, receive quality and meaningful instructional and social opportunities. Without deemphasizing academic outcomes, social outcomes must be given additional emphasis. Many students with and without disabilities in general education classes are subjected to scapegoating and other mean-spirited behavior. The instructional and social quality of the educational environment makes it inclusive and welcoming or exclusive and inhospitable. SBDMCs must be guided by a moral vision of an ethical school, such as that described in Chapter 13, in discerning and developing policies most conducive to authentic inclusion.

REFERENCES

Anderegg, M.L., & Vergason, G.A. (1988). An analysis of one of the corner-stones of the regular education initiative. *Focus on Exceptional Children, 20,* 1–7.

Association for Children and Adults with Learning Disabilities. (1986). Position statement on a regular education/special education initiative. *Academic Therapy, 22,* 99–103.

Biklen, D. (1985). *Achieving the complete school: Strategies for effective mainstreaming.* New York: Teachers College Press.

Braaten, S., Kauffman, J.M., Braaten, B., Polsgrove, L., & Nelson, C.M. (1988). The regular education initiative: Patent medicine for behavioral disorders. *Exceptional Children, 55,* 21–27.

Carnegie Forum on Education and the Economy. (1986). *A nation prepared: Teachers for the 21st century.* Washington, DC: Author. (ERIC Document Reproduction Service No. ED 12 322)

Community Mental Health Centers Act, PL 88-164, 42 U.S.C. §§ 2681 *et seq.*

Cook, L., Weintraub, F., & Morse, W. (1995). Ethical dilemmas in the restructuring of special education. In J.L. Paul, H. Rosselli, & D. Evans (Eds.), *Integrating school restructuring and special education reform* (pp. 119–139). Fort Worth, TX: Harcourt Brace.

Cuban, L. (1990). Reforming again, again, and again. *Educational Researcher, 19,* 3–13.

Diana v. State Board of Education, No. C-70 37 PFR (N.D. Cal., Jan. 7, 1970).

Dunn, L. (1968). Special education for the mildly retarded: Is much of it justifiable? *Exceptional Children, 35,* 5–22.

Education for All Handicapped Children Act of 1975, PL 94-142, 20 U.S.C. §§ 1400 *et seq.*

Evans, D., Townsend, B.L., Duchnowski, A., & Hocutt, A. (in press). Addressing the challenges of inclusion of children with disabilities. *Teacher Education and Special Education.*

Fuchs, D., & Fuchs, L. (1990). Framing the REI debate: Abolitionists versus conservationists. In J.W. Lloyd, A.C. Repp, & N.N. Singh (Eds.), *The regular education initiative: Alternative perspectives on concepts, issues, and models* (pp. 241–255). Sycamore, IL: Sycamore Publishing Co.

Fuchs, D., & Fuchs, L. (1994). Inclusive schools movement and the radicalization of special education reform. *Exceptional Children, 60,* 294–309.

Gartner, A., & Lipsky, D.K. (1987). Beyond special education: Toward a quality system for all students. *Harvard Educational Review, 57,* 367–395.

Gartner, A., & Lipsky, D.K. (1989). *The yoke of special education: How to break it.* Rochester, NY: National Center on Education and the Economy.

Goals 2000: Educate America Act of 1994, PL 103-227, 20 U.S.C. §§ 5801 *et seq.*

Goodlad, J.I. (1984). *A place called school: Prospects for the future.* New York: McGraw-Hill.

Hallahan, D.P., Keller, C.E., McKinney, J.C., Lloyd, J.W., & Bryan, T. (1988). Examining the research base of the regular education initiative: Efficacy studies and the Adaptive Learning Environments Model. *Journal of Learning Disabilities, 21,* 29–35.

Harris, D., & Evans, D. (1995). Restructuring for inclusion. In J.L. Paul, H. Rosselli, & D. Evans (Eds.), *Integrating school restructuring and special education reform* (pp. 322–334). Fort Worth, TX: Harcourt Brace.

Hocutt, A.M., Martin, E.W., & McKinney, J.D. (1990). Historical and legal context of mainstreaming. In J.W. Lloyd, A.C. Repp, & N.N. Singh (Eds.), *The regular education initiative: Alternative perspectives on concepts, issues, and models* (pp. 17–28). Sycamore, IL: Sycamore Publishing Co.

Hocutt, A., & McKinney, D. (1995). Moving beyond the regular education initiative: National reform in special education. In J.L. Paul, H. Rosselli, & D. Evans (Eds.), *Integrating school restructuring and special education reform* (pp. 43–62). Fort Worth, TX: Harcourt Brace.

Individuals with Disabilities Education Act (IDEA) of 1990, PL 101-476, 20 U.S.C. §§ 1400 *et seq.*

Kauffman, J.M. (1990). Restructuring in sociopolitical context: Reservations about the effects of current reform proposals on students with disabilities. In J.W. Lloyd, A.C. Repp, & N.N. Singh (Eds.), *The regular education initiative: Alternative perspectives on concepts, issues, and models* (pp. 57–66). Sycamore, IL: Sycamore Publishing Co.

Kauffman, J.M. (1993). How we might achieve the radical reform of special education. *Exceptional Children, 60,* 6–16.

Kauffman, M.J., Kameenui, E.J., Birman, B., & Danielson, J. (1990). Special education and the process of change: Victim or master of educational reform? *Exceptional Children, 57*(2), 109–115.

Kauffman, M.J., Lloyd, J.W., Hallahan, D.P., & Astuto, T.A. (Eds.). (1995). *Issues in educational placement: Students with emotional and behavioral disorders.* Hillsdale, NJ: Lawrence Erlbaum Associates.

Keogh, B.K. (1988). Improving services for problem learners: Rethinking and restructuring. *Journal of Learning Disabilities, 21*(1), 19–22.

Larry P. v. Riles, 343 F. Supp. 1306 (N.D. Cal. 1972).

Lavely, L., & McCarthy, J. (1995). Early intervention in the context of school reform and inclusion. In J.L. Paul, H. Rosselli, & D. Evans (Eds.), *Integrating school restructuring and special education reform* (pp. 79–104). Fort Worth, TX: Harcourt Brace.

Lipsky, D.K., & Gartner, A. (1987). Capable of achievement and worthy of respect: Education for handicapped students as if they were full-fledged human beings. *Exceptional Children, 54,* 69–74.

Lloyd, J.W., & Gambatese, C. (1990). Reforming the relationship between regular and special education. In J.W. Lloyd, A.C. Repp, & N.N. Singh (Eds.), *The regular education initiative: Alternative perspectives on concepts, issues, and models* (pp. 3–13). Sycamore, IL: Sycamore Publishing Co.

McLaughlin, M., & Warren, S. (1992, September). *Issues and options in restructuring schools and special education programs.* College Park, MD: University of Maryland, Center for Policy Options in Special Education. (ERIC Document Reproduction Service No. ED 350 774)

National Commission on Excellence in Education. (1983). *A nation at risk.* Washington, DC: U.S. Government Printing Office.

Noblit, G., Schlechty, P., & Paul, J.L. (1991). The social and political construction of emotional disturbance. In J.L. Paul & B.C. Epanchin (Eds.), *Emotional disturbance in children: Theories and methods for teachers* (2nd ed., pp. 218–242). Columbus, OH: Charles E. Merrill.

Pappanikou, A.J., & Paul, J.L. (1977). *Mainstreaming emotionally disturbed children.* Syracuse, NY: Syracuse University Press.

Paul, J.L., & Evans, D. (1995). The national context of reform in general and special education. In J.L. Paul, H. Rosselli, & D. Evans (Eds.), *Integrating school restructuring and special education reform* (pp. 1–9). Fort Worth, TX: Harcourt Brace.

Paul, J., & Simeonsson, R. (1993). *Children with special needs: Families, culture, and society.* Fort Worth, TX: Harcourt Brace.

Pennsylvania Association for Retarded Children (PARC) v. Commonwealth of Pennsylvania, 334 F. Supp. 1257 (E.D. Pa. 1971).

Reynolds, M.C., Wang, M.C., & Walberg, H.J. (1987). The necessary restructuring of special and regular education. *Exceptional Children, 53,* 391–398.

Schumaker, J., & Deshler, D. (1988). Implementing the regular education initiative in secondary schools: A different ball game. *Journal of Learning Disabilities, 21,* 36–42.

Skrtic, T.M. (1987, April). *An organizational analysis of special education reform.* Paper presented at the annual meeting of the American Educational Research Association, Washington, DC.

Skrtic, T.M. (1988). The crisis in special education knowledge. In E.L. Meyen & T.M. Skrtic (Eds.), *Exceptional children and youth: An introduction* (pp. 415–447). Denver, CO: Love Publishing Co.

Skrtic, T.M. (1991). *Behind special education: A critical analysis of professional culture and school organization.* Denver, CO: Love Publishing Co.

Slavin, R.E., & Stevens, R.J. (1991). Cooperative learning and mainstreaming. In J.W. Lloyd, A.C. Repp, & N.N. Singh (Eds.), *The regular education initiative: Alternative perspectives on concepts, issues, and models* (pp. 171–191). Sycamore, IL: Sycamore Publishing Co.

Stainback, S., & Stainback, W. (1985). *Integration of students with severe handicaps into regular schools.* Reston, VA: Council for Exceptional Children. (ERIC Document Reproduction Service No. ED 255 009)

Stainback, W., & Stainback, S. (1990). A rationale for integration and restructuring: A synopsis. In J.W. Lloyd, A.C. Repp, & N.N. Singh (Eds.), *The regular education initiative: Alternative perspectives on concepts, issues, and models* (pp. 226–239). Sycamore, IL: Sycamore Publishing Co.

Stainback, W., & Stainback S. (1992). Schools as inclusive communities. In W. Stainback & S. Stainback (Eds.), *Controversial issues confronting special education: Divergent perspectives* (pp. 29–43). Boston: Allyn & Bacon.

Turnbull, H.R. (1986). *Free appropriate public education: The law and children with disabilities.* Denver, CO: Love Publishing Co.

Turnbull, A., & Turnbull, R. (1997). *Families, professionals, and exceptionalities: A special partnership* (3rd ed.). Englewood Cliffs, NJ: Prentice Hall.

Vergason, G.A., & Anderegg, M.L. (1992). Preserving the least restrictive environment. In W. Stainback & S. Stainback (Eds.), *Controversial issues confronting special education: Divergent perspectives* (pp. 45–54). Boston: Allyn & Bacon.

Viadero, D. (1992, November 4). NASBE endorses full inclusion of disabled students. *Education Week, 12,* 1, 30.

Wang, M.C. (1980). Adaptive instruction: Building on diversity. *Theory into Practice, 19,* 122–128.

Wang, M.C., Reynolds, M.C., & Walberg, H.J. (1988). Integrating the children of the second system. *Phi Delta Kappan, 70,* 248–251.

Will, M.C. (1986). Educating children with learning problems: A shared responsibility. *Exceptional Children, 52,* 411–415.

II

ETHICAL FOUNDATIONS
FOR SCHOOL POLICY

Given the basic interest of the Collaborative Research Group on Policy and Ethics (CRGPE) in ethical policy making in schools, it is essential to consider foundational knowledge about ethics as a point of departure. The CRGPE, which developed the present volume, examined several different ethical perspectives as a way to ground the development of a curriculum for school-based decision-making committees. This section includes chapters describing the views that have had the most influence on the CRGPE's work.

In Chapter 3, Rud provides an introduction to ethical policy making applied to school-based policy. He includes a discussion of the Collegium, which was planned and implemented by the CRGPE to help answer some of the questions related to ethics, group processes, and methods of examining policy dilemmas. Rud focuses on the ethical agency of school-based committees and proposes that they become communities of inquiry.

French, in Chapter 4, discusses moral principles, rules, and policies. He contrasts Kantian and utilitarian ethics with the virtue ethics of Aristotle. Considering the merits of different ethical theories, French suggests borrowing from different points of view. He emphasizes the need to acknowledge the uniqueness of individual cases in a way that rules and principles do not necessarily allow.

Fasching, in Chapter 5, develops a defense of narrative ethics. He agrees with French that rules and principles do not necessarily serve the interests of those who must make meaning of the complexity and traditions of local cultural circumstances. He proposes an ethic of hospitality to the stranger as an ethic situated within a school community. This ethic has particular appeal when thinking about the interests of students with disabilities.

Rodriguez, Taylor, Rosselli, and Thomas, in Chapter 6, examine different feminist and womanist constructions of care and the implications of those constructions for school policy. In a layered analysis of school culture and policy, they describe the intersection of the themes of rationality, caregiving, and education in women's lives. They examine specific manifestations of sexism and racism in the normative cultures of schools, arguing that the lack of a connected, empathic, caring culture silences women in their early development and shunts them into roles and careers that disadvantage them. They argue that a feminist-womanist ethic of care can be a substantive remedy in the policy-making process.

Although they are in no sense mutually exclusive, these four chapters articulate ethical arguments from different perspectives. In this section, no attempt is made to synthesize or integrate views; rather, the appeal of different views that have affected, and continue to affect, the CRGPE's work is emphasized. Arguments found to be most helpful, as indicated throughout the book, are French's counsel about being mindful of different theories; Fasching's argument for a narrative ethic that focuses on hospitality to the stranger; the focus of Rodriguez, Taylor, Rosselli, and Thomas on specific issues of gender and race in an ethic of care; and Rud's suggestion that school-based decision-making committees should be moral communities of inquiry.

3

Perspectives on Ethical Deliberation in Schools

Anthony G. Rud Jr.

The formulation of school policy should be a cooperative process capitalizing on the intellectual resources of the whole school staff. This participation in the development of educational policy should not be thought of as a favor granted by the administration but rather as a right and obligation. . . . [I]t provides a democratic process through which growth in service is promoted and the school service itself profits from the application of heightened morale and of group thinking to school problems. It makes the school in reality a unit of democracy in its task of preparing citizens for our democratic society. (Educational Policies Commission, 1938, pp. 67–68, cited in Sirotnik, 1990, p. 313)

A democracy is more than a form of government; it is primarily a mode of associated living, of conjoint communicated experience. (Dewey, 1916/ 1989, p. 93)

These two quotations from the first half of the 20th century capture the goal of the work discussed in this volume. Through local school policy making, a democratic process and a heightened experience of communication and community are enacted. In the following chapters in Section II, we are concerned with how values govern such a process. We ask how the areas of philosophical and religious ethics can help us in local school policy making, particularly in regard to special education. In this chapter, I set an introductory context for discussing the ethical aspects of site-based decision making. I begin by examining how local school policy making has developed in the context of educational reforms of the 1990s.

The locus of educational decision making has shifted since the mid-1970s from a more centralized, bureaucratic, authoritarian model to a decentralized, democratic, inclusive mode of operation.

One way to see this shift is in the manner Murphy (1992) described the education of school administrators.

The study and teaching of school administration has evolved in the 20th century. Behavioral science in the earlier years of the 20th century sought to establish a knowledge base for educational administration beyond the anecdotal and collected wisdom of previous approaches. This social science era of educational administration shunted philosophy and values to the periphery (Murphy, 1992) and sought a positivistic knowledge base to support centralized bureaucratic control of schools.

However, such a foundation of knowledge was never found, and the knowledge determined by behavioral science was not particularly useful in solving school problems. A new generation of scholars declared that school problems were inherently more contingent and complicated than the positivist behaviorists claimed; metaphors such as managing messes (Murphy, 1992) or uncertainty (McPherson, Crowson, & Pitner, 1986) more closely described how school leadership came to be viewed. As Murphy pointed out, the metaphors being developed for this new design of schools—for example, from principal as manager to principal as facilitator and from teacher as worker to teacher as leader—nicely portray these fundamental revisions in our understanding of social relations and in our views of organizations and conceptions of management. Underlying this change has also been the change in the view of knowledge and of teaching, from knowledge as received information to that of constructed information and from teaching as delivery to that of facilitation.

This involvement of the school site's teachers, administrators, and community members in the governance of the school has opened up new roles for these players, sometimes placing them in uncomfortable territory. Such governance forces a collective discussion of the aims and purposes of education and of the means to best go about accomplishing these goals in our schools and communities.

Site-based teams, such as those in Florida discussed in this book, must consider broader, more varied perspectives than previous arrangements. Schools that had been managed by a central administration, with directives given to middle managers (i.e., principals), would not have to deal directly with voices in the community or within the school itself.

Teacher perspectives on governance are critical because teachers are in the front line of work with children and their parents. Teachers are aware of the kinds of problems and issues that administrators at the central office and even at the building level may not notice. Teachers know students firsthand; in cases of exceptionality, this is important because the teacher must develop individualized education programs for these students.

Teacher lore and anecdote are rife with how administrative decisions have been made without consultation of teachers. Yet administrators, and even collaborative leaders who work well with teachers, may have different ideas of the aims and goals of education. School administrators must balance the needs of students with the demands, often highly politicized, of the community. Teachers are often unaware of the conflicting demands placed upon administrators.

Beyond the concerns of the school, community members bring their own special issues to the table. Community members often lack firsthand knowledge of how schools operate; however, they have legitimate concerns about the quality and scope of education offered. Community members often get involved in funding discussions at schools. Clashes can occur when a community fails to muster the political will to support needed programs or reforms.

Thus, new players have been introduced to the scene of educational policy making; though these previously mute voices enrich the conversation, conflicts over aims, purposes, and practices naturally come more sharply into relief. Teaching and learning are pervaded with issues of power, justice, and the good. I draw upon work concerning ethics and teaching (Goodlad, Soder, & Sirotnik, 1990) in arguing that ethical deliberation is needed in such situations, a different model than that of hierarchy and top-down control.

The immediate context of this book is the work of school advisory committees (SACs) or school improvement teams (SITs) in Florida. Many of the authors in this volume convened at a collegium in Florida to discuss school-based policy making via SACs or SITs. These authors were brought together to give various perspectives on such decision making, particularly in regard to special education, for the purpose of assisting participants in school-based teams like SACs and SITs in understanding the nature of ethical deliberation and the importance of school context.

This work of the SACs and SITs presents an opportunity to construct what Dewey and others have called a *community of inquiry*. Although there are a number of different senses of community discussed in educational literature that are quite interesting (see Sergiovanni, 1993), I focus upon inquiry as a guiding principle for the type of community we hope to construct. Such a community is defined by the following:

1. *Norms of collegiality:* Collegiality is characterized by the relative absence of automatic deference to the role of a single leader

(McPherson & Rinnander, 1988). There is a great deal of interaction among members of a group, rather than action focused solely upon a leader. Emphasis is given to finding the best way to do necessary work and in encouraging the best ideas, no matter what the source.

2. *Multiple sources of knowledge:* Members of a community of inquiry bring diverse perspectives to the table. This is particularly true of site-based management teams, such as found in Florida and elsewhere. Teachers, administrators, and community and business leaders all have valuable knowledge about aspects of the schooling enterprise. It is therefore important that these bearers of multiple perspectives be open to other points of view and that there be effort made to accommodate a synthesis and interpretation of perspectives.

3. *Critical inquiry:* Participants in a community of inquiry must be able to subject their views to debate and dialogue. This must become, as Siegel (1988) pointed out, a way of life, a manner of looking at the world. My previous work with teachers in North Carolina involved encouraging them to become active inquirers through modeling behaviors stated in our "Taxonomy of Thinking Skills and Dispositions" (Rud, 1992). Eager dialogue and debate are tempered by a respect for another person's point of view and a willingness to hear from all quarters.

Throughout the book we are concerned with the relation between theory and practice, a difficult issue in many fields and disciplines. It is particularly important in this context because the theory under consideration (i.e., philosophical and religious ethics) has become prominent in the work of school governance committees only in the 1990s. In the work of the group in Florida described in this volume, the relation between theory and practice involves the reading and discussion of issues in philosophical and religious ethics and in the use of this knowledge in actual deliberation.

THE COLLEGIUM: A FORUM FOR INQUIRY, ETHICAL DELIBERATION, AND CASE ANALYSIS

I draw upon the events of a 3-day collegium that involved many of the authors of this volume to provide further evidence of how the dialectic of theory and practice gets played out in educational contexts. The University of South Florida (USF) Department of Special Education Collaborative Research Group on Policy and Ethics (CRGPE) hosted the Collegium in May 1995. Participants in the Collegium represented school-based and school district stakeholders with the potential to affect special education policies and students. These stakeholders included school principals, SAC or SIT chairpersons, parents of general education and special education students, teachers of general education and special education students, directors of Exceptional Student Education, and members of the business community. A panel of professionals representing philosophy, social anthropology, instructional design, psychology, and group dynamics were responsible for observing and reacting to the activities of the Collegium.

The agenda of the Collegium included 2 days devoted to discussion of the views of French (Chapter 4) and Fasching (Chapter 5), in addition to case studies dealing with equity and fairness (see "Future Leaders" and "Are All Children Treated the Same?" presented in Chapter 10). The final day of the symposium was a synthesis session that included preliminary planning for this volume and future work now continuing in the USF Department of Special Education.

The diverse community of stakeholders and professionals, who both observed and participated in the process, reached substantive understandings of the deliberative process, training, and ethical analysis that are shared throughout this volume. The understandings are more like lights along a critical path of inquiry than conclusions that mark a destination. Those lights are guiding ongoing work in the CRGPE at USF, with two goals in mind. The first is the development of a curriculum for training SACs in ethical deliberation. The second is the development of a national consortium of universities committed to research on ethical issues in special education and training in ethical analysis for special education teacher educators, administrators, and policy makers.

ETHICAL PERSPECTIVES

The core of the Collegium was extended discussion of several views of ethics. How ethics can inform educational policy is presented in the following chapters in Section II. The ethics of principle discussed by French are summarized and considered for their merit in such work. What Fasching calls an "ethics without choice" and the use of narrative emerge as powerful themes. Feminist-womanist ethics brings to the table the issue of the relation of gender, race and ethnicity, and power. This view is particularly germane to K–12 governance, which is still dominated by men and by the white majority.

French's chapter gives a summary of the main points of two principle-based ethical systems, namely, Kantian duty-based ethics and utilitarianism. French wants to dispel the view that ethics is like law. *Law* and *ethics* are not synonymous terms. French discusses Kant's categorical imperative as an example of how rule- and principle-based ethics works, in the context of a discussion of Nozick's view of a "side constraint" apropos of the categorical imperative, and contrasts it with utilitarian ethics as a goal-oriented conception of ethical rules where considerations of context come into view: "Laws and rules speak universally, [Aristotle] tells us, and therefore they quite often fail to fit the circumstances [in which] we find ourselves" (Chapter 4, p. 96). French ends his chapter with a brief discussion of how these views can be used to discuss issues of special education.

Fasching's chapter underscores the social dimension of ethics. He declares that ethics can never be a private matter, because it is about relations with others. He focuses upon narrative as a major force in shaping our lives. Story or narrative is the way in which humans give shape to their lives, and it is a very powerful way to convey ethical principles. He uses the biblical story of David and Nathan to illustrate "the ethical point of view," which he describes as coming to see one's own actions through the eyes of those who will be affected by these actions.

Declaring that how we treat the stranger is a test of ethics, Fasching uses this story to show how narrative has the power to move us to an ethical point of view and inspires ethical action. Such use of narrative in ethics is superior to philosophical analysis in this regard; Fasching echoes Kierkegaard and others in his view that philosophy leaves one as a disinterested bystander.

Narrative may lead one to ethical action, and that ethical action needs to be grounded in an ethical life. Fasching explores a social ecology whereby leading an ethical life involves balancing roles (i.e., moralities) of citizen, spouse, parent, job holder, and so on. The more roles one has, the richer one's social ecology, which one can use to draw upon in moments of ethical tension.

These insights have particular importance for the construction of school-based teams such as SACs and SITs. In the communities of inquiry that we are seeking to establish, a varied and rich ecology of voices is absolutely necessary for optimum results. Groups so constructed offer us an opportunity to see another point of view, especially to see ourselves through the eyes of the stranger, particularly through the eyes of special education students. Moving from story to empathy, we achieve an ethical mode of consciousness (see Denti & Katz, 1995).

With more emphasis than French, Fasching decries the ethics of principle and rule. Although French advocates a virtue-based ethic following the Aristotelian notion of the complexity of actual situations, Fasching argues that story shapes the way we appreciate and act upon actual situations. What narrative forms of ethics show us is that the disinterested, passionless observer who may spin philosophical ethical theories (Fasching) is not engaged in the situation. A philosophical point of view of weighing the evidence and making judgments is included; but, for these religious traditions, one must go beyond, identify with characters, and take a stand. Fasching notes a different sense of objectivity from that of the disinterested scientist. In the biblical narrative, David becomes detached from personal concerns and identifies with the person most drastically affected by his actions, thus gaining a kind of objectivity born of involvement and passion.

In Chapter 6, Rodriguez, Taylor, Rosselli, and Thomas present feminist-womanist ethical perspectives. Since the 1960s, feminists have treated an ethic of care as a major theme (Noddings, 1992; see also Jaggar, 1995). Feminists have brought to closer attention school practices that treat students abstractly and do not focus on the particular needs of that student. Feminists have focused primarily on gender, whereas womanists have called more attention to the experiences of African American women. Issues of power, control, and equity embedded in the language, formal structures, and informal alliances are addressed in these perspectives. Noblit (1993) showed how the ethic of care manifests itself in the classroom. His portrait of an African American female teacher shows the power of care and its complexity.

The ethics of principle, story, and power can become grounded in the deliberations of site-based decision-making teams. It is certainly fundamental that such groups consider the development of an ethical outlook toward the concerns that are brought to its attention. We have seen how French discusses two versions of an ethics of principle, finally coming down in favor of a Greek conception of virtue. Fasching speaks most powerfully to the view that the test of one's ethics is how one treats the stranger. In our schools, the stranger is often the student with disabilities or another type of student at risk. Feminists and womanists focus on care and community, with particular attention to issues of power as they relate to gender, race, and ethnicity.

This insight is particularly powerful as we consider the two case studies used in the discussion by Cranston-Gingras, Thompson, Beach, and Raines in Chapter 10. In each instance, questions of justice and fairness were raised in the treatment of the children. A reading informed by ethics, particularly feminist views, of the two cases would emphasize the power differential between the teacher and the principal in the teaching case "Are All Students Treated the Same?" whereas the students in the other teaching case, "Future Leaders," are marginalized because of their race.

SCHOOL-BASED COMMITTEES: GROUP
ROLES AND THE DELIBERATIVE PROCESS

For the three treatments of ethics—virtue, narrative, and care—among others, to become grounded in the deliberations of school-based groups, the composition of such groups is very important. I consider in some detail the roles possible in these groups (i.e., administrator, teacher, community member, university faculty, student). By examining the norms and practices of one's role and that of others, participants in these groups can explore how much a role determines behavior in an unreflective way and how the infusion of ethical deliberation can enlarge one's conception of a particular role. The groups advising on school policy must be composed carefully. There are a number of roles possible in such groups. Here I briefly list and characterize each role:

1. *Administrator:* An administrator generally has overall responsibility for a particular aspect of the school or system operation and must lead and manage a staff toward the end of efficient bottom-line operation. Administrators must answer to a number of constituents, and principals must obey central office mandates, state and federal guidelines, and so forth. Building-level administrators (i.e., principals) are also responsible for the budget and must spend their money in accordance with rules and regulations. What such a person can bring to a site-based team is an appreciation of the overall viewpoint and an insight into policies at the district, state, and national levels that affect the way decisions are made.

2. *Teacher:* The teacher is the person working in the school who is closest to the students. Whereas the administrator must be the generalist with the view of the entire school or school system and its relation to the community and beyond, the teacher is the particularist who has detailed knowledge of each student in a class. To be a good teacher, one must have care and concern for each student and try, as much as possible, to tailor instruction to each student's particular needs. The teacher would also be able to speak most directly about the special needs of students with disabilities and how those needs affect the classroom. The teacher can bring to the discussion an appreciation of how particular policies and actions affect individual students.

3. *Community members:* The community served by a school is an important part of the school's fabric. Community members provide support for a school in many varied ways, and almost always the school's values and principles reflect those of the community. Community members support the school via taxes and also employ graduates of the school system. Thus, they are particularly concerned that stu-

dents be educated well and at a reasonable cost. A community member could bring to the table these concerns and in addition force the conversation to consider economic and political forces upon the school that impinge upon curriculum and teaching.

4. *University and college faculty:* Universities and colleges do the preservice training of teachers and administrators, in addition to providing most of the continuing professional education. University and college faculty, particularly those who work as partners in professional development schools, have one foot in the university and another in the world of school practice. Yet, by their training, they are more attuned to theoretical issues than most practitioners. Thus, university and college faculty can add insight to the discussion in this manner while taking back to their work at the university the particular aspects of practice that can inform teaching. In the May 1995 seminar, a number of faculty from different disciplines contributed to the discussion, including social anthropologists, educational sociologists, and philosophers of education. Their different perspectives (see Chapters 7, 8, and 9) helped participants construct new understandings of ethics and the policy process in schools.

5. *Student:* The perspective of the student often lacks the depth that would come with experience. Still, a student, if able to overcome a sense of awe in the presence of adults, might be able to add a valuable perspective to the mix. Students are often not consulted on their own education; furthermore, it would be a valuable learning experience for students to have a say in their teaching and learning.

Such considerations come together in the pedagogy for ethics considered in this volume: case studies. Case studies are particularly effective in the formation of communities aimed at practice because they provide a rich context in which to judge action. Cases, like narrative, bring the richness and ambiguity of particular situations. Case studies, as a form of narrative, draw the reader into taking a stand and identifying with the players, whereas it is not possible to fully identify with abstract principles. Discussion of cases with this manner of identification abets the formation of a community of inquiry.

The vision that animated the work of Goodlad and associates (1990) in their considerations of the "moral dimensions of teaching" has important links to our work in Florida. Goodlad and his associates argued forcefully that teaching and schooling are fundamentally moral enterprises. There is an inherent moral relationship in the classroom: Simply put, "Teaching the young has moral dimensions, however, simply because education—a deliberate effort to develop values and sensibilities as well as skills—is a moral endeavor" (Goodlad et al., 1990, p. xii). Moral responsibility in teaching is intensified through the lack of parity between teacher and student (Sirotnik, 1990). Schools are part of a large moral web (Sirotnik, 1990) or what Fasching calls a *social ecology*.

Sirotnik (1990) called for schools to be centers of critical inquiry where norms are explicit, provisional, and open for debate. By extension, I argue that the governance of schools is a similar moral enterprise. We must enable those who work in schools, those who attend schools, and those whom schools affect (i.e., everyone) to make ethically informed choices about their lives and the lives of all others. Sirotnik called for inquiry with a commitment to knowledge, competence, caring, freedom, well-being, and social justice.

CONCLUSIONS

SACs need to become cohesive communities of inquiry to be able to be effective in ethical deliberation in school-based policy making. Composition of the group must be diverse. The group's culture must be developed carefully and intentionally in order to embed the kinds of values that honor and communicate caring for all members of the committee.

One of the great problems of our society was pointed out by Bellah, Madsen, Sullivan, Swidler, and Tipton in *Habits of the Heart* (1985). Echoing Tocqueville's assessment of American culture, these authors struck an immense chord by criticizing modern American society as lacking community and for being instead just a collection of atomized individuals. The work of this volume points to a means to enhance communication around shared values important to a robust and caring community. Through such acts as the hospitality toward the stranger noted by Fasching in Chapter 5 (see also Rud, 1995), it is possible to achieve an enlarged sense of the self, as one connected to others in meaningful ways. By doing so, we indicate what kind of society and what kind of ethics we want to have.

Strangers in schools are often students with disabilities and other students who are at risk. In considering the role that philosophical and religious ethics can play, this view of the stranger in schools has epistemological and ethical import. Ethics are needed when we realize the social context of education (Liston & Zeichner, 1991). Ethics are vital when we make schools places that open up to the community, where site-based decision making allows more voices to engage in the conflict-laden work of schools. What we can learn of new and different people enlarges our knowledge and helps us define the kind of society in which we want to live.

SACs, charged with developing or providing advice about policies in local schools, have extraordinary responsibilities and opportunities. Policies may be guided by data, but they are based upon values that policy makers consider important and worthy. The decisions that interpret those values in practical ways to structure the allocation of resources reflect an ethic or set of ethics. Deliberately and consciously or casually and unreflectively, an ethic or set of ethics guides the deliberative process one school at a time. It is the purpose of this volume and of the work on which this volume is based to help define ethical perspectives and their role in the deliberative process of SACs.

REFERENCES

Bellah, R.N., Madsen, R., Sullivan, W.M., Swidler, A., & Tipton, S.M. (1985). *Habits of the heart: Individualism and commitment in American life*. Berkeley: University of California Press.

Denti, L.G., & Katz, M.S. (1995, August/September). Escaping the cave to dream new dreams: A normative vision of learning disabilities. *Journal of Exceptional Children, 28*, 415–424.

Dewey, J. (1989). Democracy and education. In J. Boydston (Ed.), *The collected works of John Dewey* (Vol. 9). Carbondale: Southern Illinois University Press. (Original work published 1916)

Educational Policies Commission. (1938). *The structure and administration of education in American democracy*. Washington, DC: National Education Association and American Association of School Administrators.

Goodlad, J.I., Soder, R., & Sirotnik, K.A. (Eds.). (1990). *The moral dimensions of teaching*. San Francisco: Jossey-Bass.

Jaggar, A.M. (1995). Caring as a feminist practice of moral reason. In V. Held (Ed.), *Justice and care: Essential readings* (pp. 179–202). Boulder, CO: Westview Press.

Liston, D.P., & Zeichner, K.M. (1991). *Teacher education and the social conditions of schooling*. New York: Routledge.

McPherson, R.B., Crowson, R.L., & Pitner, N.J. (1986). *Managing uncertainty: Administrative theory and practice in education*. Columbus, OH: Charles E. Merrill.

McPherson, R.B., & Rinnander, J.A. (1988, Fall). Collegiality: Its meaning and purposes. *Independent School*, 41–45.

Murphy, J. (1992). *The landscape of leadership preparation: Reframing the education of school administrators*. Newbury Park, CA: Corwin Press.

Noblit, G.W. (1993, Spring). Power and caring. *American Educational Research Journal, 30*, 23–38.

Noddings, N. (1992). *The challenge to care in schools: An alternative approach to education*. New York: Teachers College Press.

Rud, A.G. (1992). Building a rationale for teacher renewal. In A.G. Rud & W.P. Oldendorf (Eds.), *A place for teacher renewal: Challenging the intellect, creating educational reform* (pp. 45–62). New York: Teachers College Press.

Rud, A.G. (1995). Learning in comfort: Developing an ethos of hospitality in education. In J.W. Garrison & A.G. Rud (Eds.), *The educational conversation: Closing the gap* (pp. 119–128). Albany: State University of New York Press.

Sergiovanni, T.J. (1993). *Building community in schools*. San Francisco: Jossey-Bass.

Siegel, H. (1988). *Educating reason: Rationality, critical thinking, and education*. New York: Routledge.

Sirotnik, K.A. (1990). Society, schooling, teaching, and preparing to teach. In J.I. Goodlad, R. Soder, & K.A. Sirotnik (Eds.), *The moral dimensions of teaching* (pp. 296–327). San Francisco: Jossey-Bass.

4

Moral Principles, Rules, and Policies

Peter A. French

Everyone seems to have an opinion about ethics, and, indeed, everyone seems to think he or she knows what ethics is. I've had the opportunity to talk to groups and organizations all over the country, and seldom does it fail that someone will announce that he or she is a moral person but has no ethics. Or I'll hear someone say, "We have ethics in our organization; we just don't have good morals." And so it goes. What I suppose people in these situations are trying to say is that they think of ethics and morals as different things. Perhaps ethics is what one should do and morals is what one actually does. Or perhaps ethics are theoretical and morality is practical. During a visit to a business corporation, I was told by a senior manager whose company actually has a code of ethical conduct that ethics is a set of rules or a code, but morals is what he and his fellow workers either did or did not have. He was worried that they were lacking in that regard.

I use the terms *ethics* and *morals* interchangeably. I am a moral philosopher, an ethical theorist. For me, ethics (or moral philosophy) has to do with the theoretical foundations of our responsibility ascription practices. Importantly, it reflects and is grounded in a conception of the good community or the just community, or, as I would prefer to call it, the community in which the conditions necessary for the flourishing of all members is achieved and maintained. Mythically, it is founded in our shared conception of the "Great Good Place" (Auden, 1948).

The concept of the Great Good Place serves to ground, in the sense of being an end or goal, moral justifications for social practices while also motivating social reforms. No one, from the moral point of view, can sensibly ask why anyone would want to realize the Great Good Place or bring about a society that is more, rather than less, like it. We can dispute about the description of that place but not its being a proper moral goal.

Gauthier (1991) wrote, "Morality faces a foundational crisis" (p. 15). He quoted MacIntyre, Williams, Mackie, and Harman as suggesting that "Moral language fits a world view that we have abandoned" (Gauthier, 1991, p. 16). But what world view? Gauthier thinks it is the idea that the world is purposively ordered, and he maintains that, unless we locate an acceptable alternative, we will no longer be able to understand the moral claims we make on each other and ourselves. For Gauthier, moral constraints on behavior can be justified only on deliberative rationality grounds. Simply, rationality requires that people keep their rational agreements, and so it requires that people "comply with the constraints of a contractarian morality" (Gauthier, 1991, p. 13).

I think Gauthier misidentified the world view on which ethics is founded. When questions about the reasons for or grounds of ethics are raised, the answers do not always come back in terms of the individual rational choice theory favored by Gauthier. Sometimes they are framed in terms of communal or cultural aspirations, traditions, and myths that are so embedded in the cultural identity of a society that they have long since become invulnerable to the challenge of individual rationality. They lie beyond justification because, with respect to the practices, they give justification its sense. They are, in Wittgenstein's (1969) terms, "something animal." He wrote, "What people accept as a justification is shewn by how they think and live" (Wittgenstein, 1953). The Great Good Place seems to be one of those embedded conceptions.

Many of the claims ethics makes on us are founded in the cultural vision of the perfect human society. Many of us wish that the world were radically different from what it is. Many at least occasionally dream about different worlds, better worlds, places in which serious conflicts between personal taste and moral responsibility never occur, pain and suffering are avoided, duty and desire are not opponents, the individual's private aesthetics and social ethics are one, and people invariably do the right thing: the Great Good Place.

In the Great Good Place, there are no normative moral laws or rules. Residents of the Great Good Place are by nature happy and moral. They act on inclinations that always produce the morally appropriate behavior. In the Great Good Place, as Auden (1948) described it, universal moral imperatives are unknown because they are unnecessary. Inhabitants, like unrestrained, happy children, do whatever they like; but what they like to do is always morally right. They do not act on moral principles; sentiment motivates behavior that accords with moral principles. If there were a Great Good Place, moral rules would tell how the people there behave, not how they ought to behave. But that is the Great Good Place. As much as its conception may influence our thinking about ethics and even motivate our expectations regarding proper behavior, we certainly do not live there. Our behavior does not invariably accord with what we ethically ought to do. Is an ethics of rules and principles, a code of conduct, necessary in this less than great good place where we actually live? (For a more complete discussion of the Great Good Place and its role in ethics, see Chapter 18 in French, 1992.)

A rules-and-principles conception has dominated the thinking and theorizing about ethics in Western philosophy since the late 18th century. The roots of such a conception of ethics, in which concepts of right and wrong and duty and obligation are emphasized, are to be found in the Judeo-Christian strand of our culture and not in the Greek and Roman strand. The Golden Rule of Christianity is nothing like Aristotle's Golden Mean. Taylor (1988) wrote,

> To speak of an action as wrong is to say that it is in some sense or other forbidden—for example, that it violates some rule, law, or moral principle. To say of one [action] that it is right is to say that it is not in any such sense forbidden, or in other words, that it is permitted by such rules, laws, or principles. And to say that a given action is obligatory is to say something different still; namely, that some rule, law, or principle requires that it be done. (p. 61)

To see how an ethics of rules and principles works, let us briefly examine two versions that have become the most influential theories on the subject in 20th-century ethical thought. The first is the work of the great German philosopher Immanuel Kant (1724–1804). The central feature of Kant's ethical theory is his conception of the unconditional moral command, or what he called the *categorical imperative*. He formulated the categorical imperative in three ways, though he claimed that all the formulations are ultimately equivalent and will never produce conflicting results. The first formulation is that a person should always act so that the maxim of his or her actions could be rationally willed as a universal law. Kant, in effect, was claiming that ethical principles, as action-guiding rules, must be universalizable without committing a logical contradiction, without offending rationality. A person morally must not lie, because if lying were to become a universal rule, then lying would have no sense. For lying to ever have any sense, people generally must tell the truth. Lying would have no point were lying to be the general rule. Also, the very statement of the principle of always lying would break itself, for it would not be the case that one should always lie. Kant's second formulation of the categorical imperative tells us that we are always to act in such a way that we treat humans as ends and never as means only. This formulation implies that humans have absolute worth, that they have dignity and integrity that must not be compromised. Using them for one's own purposes without their consent would do just that. The third formulation requires ethical people to act always as both subject and sovereign in a kingdom of ends. What that means is that ethical people are autonomous. They both make and follow their moral rules, and they recognize that others do so as well.

Kant's ethics are rule and duty focused. In fact, Kant rather went to extremes in his denial of the ethical value of any motivation other than duty. He did not think that actions that are motivated by our emotions or inclinations deserve moral credit. The consequences of what one does are not as ethically important as one's motives. Kant did capture some of our intuitions in this regard. Suppose, for example, that a man rushes out of his house and rescues a woman who is being viciously attacked. The rescuer wrestles the attacker to the ground and beats him until he is unconscious. The police finally arrive and take the attacker into custody. The media lionize the rescuer; but, after basking in the limelight, the rescuer admits that the reason he risked life and limb was not that he saw it as his duty to protect the woman, but that he really gets a kick out of beating up people. The outcome of his actions, of course, was highly desirable; but his reasons for acting were hardly morally admirable. We should, on Kant's theory, give him no moral credit for rescuing the woman. A person's intentions are crucial to moral value, not just the consequences of what that person does.

One way to formulate the basic tenet of Kant's conception of morality is that one should always treat people with respect, regard them as having intrinsic worth, and, therefore, never use them solely as means by which to achieve personal goals. It is difficult to think of a more basic precept of ethics; hence, it is one that should receive wide support, regardless of one's commitments to other ethical principles. But how is such a principle supposed to work in our daily lives?

Nozick (1981) characterized the Kantian principle requiring respect as a side-constraint on our actions. A *side-constraint* is a prohibition against doing certain types of things as one pursues one's personal goals. The idea is that you are not morally forbidden from, for example, amassing a great fortune, but you are prohibited from doing so by using other people as mere means to that end, for example, by stealing from them.

Would such a side-constraint forbid all cases in which I might use you in any way toward the achievement of my ends unless you chose to be so used? If that were the case, it would create an utterly unworkable precondition that would block most contractual dealings between us. Surely we are not using those with whom we contract (e.g., employees) as mere means just because those people have not approved, and maybe would not approve, of all of the things we intend to do through their agency. People get hired to do certain jobs and are paid on contracted wage scales or salaries. As long as they agree to the wage, understand what they are employed to do, and consent to doing that, they are not being used as mere means, even if they do not or would not approve of all of the ends to which those hiring them plan to put the results of their labor.

We can, however, tell the story in a different way that may alter the intuitions that it stimulates. Suppose that you would most definitely choose not to interact with me if I were to tell you the ends to which I intend to use your labor. I do not reveal them to you, though you, taking me to be a fine, upstanding fellow, never ask. You assume I am about some purpose that you would endorse or at least would not find objectionable. After our interaction is completed, you discover my purposes, and you find them offensive in the extreme. Have I used you in a way that violates the Kantian side-constraint? I paid you the agreed sum for your labor. Should the moral matter turn on your likes and dislikes, your tastes?

How much ought the fact that I had or should have had reason to think you would not approve of my plans count? Suppose you are a bricklayer; I, secretly a Nazi official. You have just built a sturdy building for me that, unbeknownst to you, I intend to use to warehouse Jews before gassing them. Suppose you are Jewish or have Jewish friends. Ignorant of my plans and the way in which your labor was to be instrumental in bringing them to fruition, most of us would agree, you were used as a means and not treated as an end. In a similar kind of case, suppose you are vehemently opposed to abortion, and I, a doctor, hire you, a carpenter, to remodel my clinic, never telling you that I intend to reopen it as an abortion facility. Suppose I have seen you on the evening news protesting outside of other abortion clinics. You are a member of Operation Rescue. I find the irony most amusing, my private joke. Were you used as a means and not as an end?

I confess that my intuitions in the abortion clinic case are less clear than they are in the death camp case. Perhaps that is because I have not resolved the moral status of abortion in my own mind. That is my failing and should not affect our understanding of the way to deal with the cases, for what is relevant is not that I am certain about how I feel about the Holocaust and vacillate on abortion but how you feel, your beliefs, your commitments, what you stand for, detest, and so forth. If your views govern in the first case, then they should in the second as well. We should conclude that you were used as a means in both cases.

So, do I have a moral obligation to explain my plans to you when I have reason to think that you would not interact with me if you were apprised of them? Would I be breaking the Kantian prohibition if I kept you in the dark? I am inclined to say that I would. It would seem, then, that the Kantian side-constraints entail that humans have certain rights vis á vis each other: in particular, the right not to be used in a way they would not have approved of were they fully informed of the goals of the person interacting with them. This sort of right is codified in informed consent laws regarding medical procedures and has especially come into play in cases where doctors doing research on alternative therapies are disinclined to apprise patients of the fact that they are being administered experimental drugs because that knowledge in and of itself may have an effect on the outcome. Courts and medical ethicists in hospitals have been in wide agreement that patients must be fully informed or their rights will be violated.

A side-constraint conception of moral principles and rules can be contrasted with a goal-oriented theory. In a goal-oriented theory, the idea is to produce a society in which violations of the principle or the rule are kept to a minimum. But that does not exclude occasionally violating the principle in order to keep violations of it to a minimum in the society at large.

A goal-oriented conception of principles is incorporated in utilitarian ethics. John Stuart Mill (1808–1873) and his teacher Jeremy Bentham (1748–1832) are the most influential of the utilitarians. Utilitarians, it is widely but, I think, wrongly believed, support, as the basic tenet of ethics, a principle that says that an act is right in the circumstances if its consequences produce the greatest good for the greatest number of people. Their primary concern, it is said, is to ensure that the good be maximized throughout the population. Doing so could occasionally lead to sanctioning the use of people as mere means to that end, for example, giving up an innocent person to terrorists to prevent the deaths of a number of people.

There are many ways to formulate the basic tenets of a utilitarian ethics. They all share the position that the consequences or outcomes of actions are their morally relevant features and that the reasons why actions are undertaken are not ethically important. The classical version of utilitarianism maintains that the way consequences are distinguished is in terms of the pleasure and pain to which the actions give rise. John Stuart Mill (1987) wrote, "Actions are right in proportion as they tend to promote happiness, wrong as they tend to produce the reverse of happiness. By 'happiness' is intended pleasure, and the absence of pain; by 'unhappiness' pain, and the privation of pleasure" (p. 10). To hold the classical utilitarian theory of ethics as developed by Mill's teacher Bentham, one must believe that pleasure, and so pain, can be quantified. Feldman (1986) explained this notion in a useful way:

> Let us suppose that every episode of pleasure can be given a score, or rating. We can pretend that there is a standard unit of pleasure, which we will call the "hedon." The pleasure resulting from eating a tasty meal might be rated as being worth 10 hedons. . . . Our second assumption is that episodes of pain can be evaluated in a similar fashion. We can call our standard unit of pain a "dolor.". . . The third assumption is the most difficult. We must assume that hedons and dolors are commensurate. This means, roughly, that you can add and subtract hedons and dolors. (p. 24)

Using Feldman's version of the utilitarian calculus, if my doing something to you—for example, hitting you in the face with a lemon custard pie—gives me 10 hedons of pleasure, but you experience 8 dolors of pain, then the action has a pleasure-to-pain value—what may be called its utility value—of two hedons. Another act I could perform in the same circumstances might be giving you a magazine I had just sat down to read. Suppose this action gives you three hedons of pleasure but gives me one dolor of pain. Its utility value is also two hedons. It would seem that, for a utilitarian, there is no way to decide which of these two things that I could do in the circumstances is the right thing for me to do. Both have the same utility consequences. Both increase the pleasure of those in the world by two hedons. Isn't there something wrong with such a result?

One way that classical utilitarianism has been formulated is to say that an act is right, the thing one ought to do, if and only if, in the circumstances, its consequences have a higher utility than any other act the person could have done. If, in those circumstances, the only two things I could have done were to hit you with the pie or give you the magazine, then it would seem that, in theory, there is just no way for me to do anything right. Neither has a higher utility than the other.

The proper formulation of the utilitarian's position, however, as Feldman (1986) clarified it, is, "An act is right if and only if there is no other act the agent [i.e., person] could have done instead that has a higher utility than it has" (p. 26). Following that formulation, we would have to conclude, not that I can do nothing right in the circumstances, but that if my options are restricted to just those two actions, either would be morally permissible in the circumstances. There would be nothing morally wrong with my doing either. This same sort of reasoning can be applied to cases in which I am confronted with two morally required actions and cannot possibly do both.

Imagine you are sitting by a swimming pool and a child falls in the pool near you. The child cannot swim, you can, and you can easily pull her out. If no one else is around, you have a moral duty to save the child. But suppose there are twins and they both fall in. Do you have a duty to save both? Philosophers like Feldman (1986) point out that there is an important difference between the cases. We can all agree that when one child is drowning, it is your moral duty to save her. Nothing would be morally better in that isolated situation. But if the twins are drowning and you physically cannot save both, your moral duty is to save one or the other of the twins. Failure to save either would be wrong, but the choice of one rather than the other is not a moral one. The moral duty is to make the choice of which one to save quickly enough to at least save that one. So we may say that when the two (or more) things one has an obligation to do in a certain situation are indistinguishably worthy and you cannot do them both, you must do one.[1]

It should be noted that Feldman's formulation of the classical utilitarian position differs from the way that theory is typically presented. As I mentioned above, we are often told that the utilitarians maintain that an action is morally right only if it produces the greatest good for the greatest number of people. The problem here is "the greatest number." The Feldman formulation simply calculates in terms of pleasure and pain values in particular circumstances. If 10 people are made ecstatically happy by an action and 1 million people are pained to only a very minimal degree, the action may pass moral muster. Broad distribution of pleasure is not necessary to maximize utility across a population.

In fact, the "greatest good for the greatest number" version of utilitarianism would require the maximization of two independent variables, the pleasure variable and the population variable. Trying to do that not only can produce extraordinary headaches, therefore skewing the calculus by increasing the dolors, but also can lead to utterly ambiguous results in which the highest pleasure to be realized does not have the widest distribution, a wider distribution of the pleasure having a lower utility, and vice versa.

An obvious objection to the purely hedonistic interpretation of the utilitarian calculus will surely occur to you. It did to Mill (1987).

---

[1]See Feldman (1986, p. 201) for a comparable account of these "Buridan's Ass"–type cases.

The theory seems to reduce all of what is valuable in life to undifferentiated amounts of pleasure. Are there no higher ends, noble pursuits, that outweigh the mere obtaining of moments of even intense pleasure? Shouldn't quality count as well as quantity? Think of the following situation.

A wealthy man decides to give away $1 million to someone. He narrows his choice to two possible recipients. One, a medical researcher, tells him that he will use the money to further his search for a cure for an extremely rare disease that afflicts only the dozen or so males per generation of a very small, remote tribe in the Amazon jungle, causing a loss of eye–hand coordination, making it impossible for them to successfully hunt an endangered species whose skins are used in ceremonial dances intended to ward off the disease. (No part of the animal is included in the tribal diet. They are vegetarians.) The other candidate wants to throw a drinking bash for 2,000 people. He will rent a large hall, hire a famous rock band, provide all the beer his guests can guzzle, and lay out all the food they can eat. What would be the right thing for the wealthy man to do?

Clearly, the party giver will produce the greater pleasure and will do so for a larger number of people. A double maximization! But could it possibly be morally right to give the money to him rather than to the researcher, albeit that there are serious moral ambiguities in the researcher's proposal? Isn't there something morally undesirable about encouraging feckless behavior? There must be more to ethics than merely increasing the amount of pleasure in the world. Shouldn't quality count as well as quantity? The researcher's pleasure in trying to find the cure and, indeed, his ecstasy should he do so are going to be factored in; but shouldn't the relative value of medical research over party giving be a part of the equation as well? Mill thought so.

Feldman (1986) commented,

> We must assume that for each episode of pleasure there is a number that represents its quality. Perhaps a "low" pleasure, such as one of the pleasures allegedly enjoyed by those who engage in lascivious behavior, would rate a 1 or a 2. A "higher" pleasure, such as the pleasure one receives from exercising his intellect, would be scored a 20 or a 25. An even "higher" pleasure, such as the pleasure we experience when we behave nobly, would rate a 50 or a 60. In each case, the numbers represent the quality of the pleasure being felt. (p. 33)

As Feldman (1986) pointed out, there are major problems with this way of factoring quality into the utilitarian calculus. Most important, how do we know how to assign the numbers? Is the pleasure of exercising one's intellect really 10 or 20 times higher in quality than the pleasure of sitting around on a beach with some friends on a starlit night with a campfire blazing, drinking one beer after another, singing lewd songs? It doesn't get any better than this!

Against this rules-and-principles conception of ethics that tends to lead us to think of ethics in terms of codes and laws and to always look for ethical solutions to difficult matters in terms of the right and the wrong, we have the wisdom of the ancient Greeks, especially Aristotle. Aristotle (1962) framed ethics in terms of the concepts of virtue, character, happiness, and justice. His understanding of all of these terms, especially "virtue," was, however, very different from the one that is typical in discussions of ethics today. Taylor (1988) commented,

> Most persons today . . . would find nothing terribly incongruous in saying of some man that, while he might be uneducated and poor, and unable to point to any significant personal achievement, he might nevertheless be a good man—a description that would have been totally incomprehensible to Aristotle. (p. 55)

What did Aristotle (1962) mean by "virtue"? The Greek word for virtue, *arete*, in the Homeric epics means excellence in what one does. There is the arete of a runner and even the arete of his feet. When it is applied to humans, it refers to personal excellence. What is personal excellence? It involves many things, such as health, wealth, and public position, and it certainly includes the attainment of self-confidence and a very high level of rational thought. When it is achieved in someone, the result is Aristotle's idea of happiness. Happiness for Aristotle meant functioning well, doing well at what one is best suited to do. Insofar as the function of a human being, all the ancient Greek thinkers believed, is to exercise reason, to live rationally: The achievement by a human of a lifestyle governed by reason will allow that person to function well. Such a person will be happy. The crucial point, however, for our concerns, is that Aristotle did not believe that a human being had good character if that person had to think out the situations that confronted him or her and apply formal rules and principles to his or her circumstances before deciding how to act in an appropriate manner. To Aristotle, a person of good character acts habitually in the appropriate ethical way.

For Aristotle (1962), we are not born ethical, with good character. We must develop character. And how is that done? In the way all habits are established: by practice until it becomes a part of one's way of life. Aristotle wrote: "Moral virtue . . . is formed by habit. . . . None of the moral virtues is implanted in us by nature, for nothing which exists by nature can be changed by habit. . . . We are by nature equipped with the ability to receive them, and habit brings this ability to completion and fulfillment" (p. 1102).

Who would have thought that we are basically good? Aristotle was particularly concerned with a view that Plato attributed to Socrates:

"No one does evil willingly!" Such an idea permeates much of our 20th-century thinking about wickedness. We have been impressed with the notion that people never really are evil: It is just circumstances or misunderstanding that leads them to do wicked deeds. People are not wicked; only their deeds are. Perhaps the idea that all of us are basically good is one of the motivations behind the popular idea that the ethical thing to do in a group situation can best be arrived at by consensus. After all, if people are basically good, shouldn't they come to agree on the right thing to be done? The idea that ethics is to be found in a bargaining process, that arriving at a consensus is a guarantee that a group has discovered what it ethically ought to do, is attractive for many reasons. But why should we think that the achievement of consensus reveals anything more than the extent to which people will compromise to settle an issue or a dispute? Why should we believe that, even if people are basically good, their underlying goodness will somehow dependably percolate up through layers of self-serving considerations? The politics of liberal democracy may settle a number of issues, but they can also result in compromises that obliterate ethical considerations. For example, a school-based decision-making committee that reaches a consensus about alternating classes for students with disabilities and classes for students without disabilities in portable classrooms might get a decision, but not one that has taken all pertinent ethical concerns into consideration.

For Aristotle, virtue is obtained by being virtuous, by making virtue your habit, so that you are inclined to be virtuous without having to think about it. The task of ethics education, for Aristotle, is to ingrain habits of good character, and, as most people who have read Aristotle's *Nicomachean Ethics* (1962) remember, the key to doing that is to learn to habitually seek out and adopt the mean in most things and act accordingly:

> Virtue or excellence is a characteristic involving choice, and it consists in observing the mean relative to us, a mean which is defined by a rational principle, such as a man of practical wisdom would use to determine it. It is the mean by reference to two vices: the one of excess and the other of deficiency. It is, moreover, a mean because some vices exceed and others fall short of what is required in emotion and action, whereas virtue finds and chooses the median. Hence, in respect of its essence and the definition of its essential nature, virtue is a mean, but in regard to goodness and excellence it is an extreme. (p. 1107)

Aristotle wrote that there are some actions and emotions that, under no circumstances, can be said to be good, even in moderation. He wrote:

> Not every action nor every emotion admits of a mean. There are some actions and emotions whose very names connote baseness, e.g., spite, shame-

lessness, envy; and among actions, adultery, theft, and murder. These and similar emotions and actions imply by their deficiency which is called bad; it is, therefore, impossible ever to do right in performing them: to perform them is always to do wrong. (p. 44)

Of course, there is no excess or deficiency when a person does things that are virtuous or just (understood to go beyond the legal sense of the latter term). One cannot be too virtuous or too just.

Where the more modern writers favor rules and principles in deciding issues of ethics, it might be fair to say that Aristotle endorsed a policy approach that gives us the latitude to consider specific issues and persons in particular cases but that does not let us go too far astray from moderation and good character. Aristotle praised being equitable over a strictly legal conception of being just (understood as getting that to which you are entitled). Laws and rules speak universally, he said, and therefore they quite often fail to fit the circumstances in which we find ourselves. To enforce the rule might leave us feeling uncomfortable because we recognize that such human factors as kindness, caring, and so forth are ignored. Although we followed the rule, the outcome just seemed wrong. People got hurt or were disadvantaged when they didn't deserve it. We need to recognize such situations and apply considerations of equity to achieve truly ethical outcomes. Equity serves as a rectification for rules and principles that offend our moral sense when they are straightforwardly applied in particular cases.

> Not all things are determined by law and rule. There are some things about which it is impossible to enact a law, so that a special decree is required. For where a thing is indefinite, the rule by which it is measured is also indefinite, as is, for example, the leaden rule used in Lesbian construction work. Just as this rule is not rigid but shifts with the contour of the stone, so a decree is adapted to a given situation. . . . A man is equitable who chooses and performs acts of this sort, who is no stickler for justice in a bad sense, but is satisfied with less than his share even though he has the law on his side. Such a characteristic is equity. (Aristotle, 1962, p. 142)

So how should we deal ethically with the cases involving special education? I'd suggest borrowing from the various theoretical camps. In the first place, the side-constraint conception of the Kantian principle of respect seems to me to be fundamental. If the way a case is resolved violates that constraint, then it cannot be ethical. I shy away from any end-state theory such as that of the utilitarians. With respect to our concerns, it is likely that the children in special education programs will be factored out of many utilitarian calculations of the greatest good for the greatest number. Aristotle's doctrine of virtue, at least in the way he defended it, however, will not sit well with us in this regard, because he did not think true virtue was achievable by most people. Taylor wrote,

> Contemporary people would have no difficulty in pointing to masses of the meek, ignorant, and dispossessed and saying, with sincerity, that each and every one might be just as good as the best of us and every bit as deserving. Indeed, modern moralists are quite capable of declaring that they want nothing for themselves which they do not also want for others, even for the least among them. This would have seemed to Aristotle and the Greeks, if not self-contradictory, then at least sick and perverse. (1988, p. 56)

Setting aside Aristotle's lack of inclusiveness, we have much to learn from his approach to ethics. We ought to seek the mean as we wrestle with the difficult issues of access, fairness, and equity in special education cases. Doing so should acknowledge the uniqueness of each of those cases in a way that the rules-and-principles approach does not. The side-constraints requiring respect should serve as an outer limit on any resolutions to the cases. However, the side-constraints are generally not going to be inconsistent with seeking the mean when it is modulated by considerations of equity as we try to realize a society that approaches the Great Good Place.

REFERENCES

Aristotle. (1962). *Nicomachean ethics* (M. Ostwald, ed. & trans.). Indianapolis, IN: Hackett.

Auden, W.H. (1948). The guilty vicarage. In *The dyer's hand and other essays*. New York: Random House.

Feldman, F. (1986). *Doing the best we can: An essay in informal deontic logic*. Boston: D. Reidel.

French, P. (1992). *Responsibility matters*. Lawrence: University Press of Kansas.

Gauthier, D. (1991). Why contractarianism? In P. Vallentyne (Ed.), *Contractarianism and rational choice*. New York: Cambridge University Press.

Mill, J.S. (1987). *Utilitarianism*. Buffalo, NY: Prometheus Books.

Nozick, R. (1981). *Philosophical explanations*. Cambridge, MA: Harvard University Press.

Taylor, R. (1988). Ancient wisdom and folly. In P.A. French, T.E. Uehling, & H.K. Wettstein (Eds.), *Midwest studies in philosophy, XIII*, 61.

Wittgenstein, L. (1953). *Philosophical investigations*. New York: Macmillan.

Wittgenstein, L. (1969). *On certainty*. Oxford, England: Blackwell.

5

Beyond Values

Story, Character, and Public Policy in American Schools

Darrell J. Fasching

My book, *The Ethical Challenge of Auschwitz and Hiroshima* (Fasching, 1993), is an effort to take a narrative ethics approach to thinking about religion, ethics, and public policy in a century of technobureau-cratically administered mass death symbolized by Auschwitz and Hiroshima. It is also an attempt to respond to a prevalent cultural and ethical relativism that seems to undermine our ability to think constructively about ethics and public policy. I have been concerned to draw ethical lessons from this project that can be applied to the everyday ethical and policy issues of our own technobureaucratic society. In this chapter, I attempt to apply some of these insights to the concerns of educational policy at the local school level.

Let me begin by suggesting that how we engage in ethical reflection depends primarily on what we think ethical reflection is all about. It is very common to imagine ethics as a kind of moral calculus for solving ethical dilemmas. All we need is the right formula, and all of our problems can be resolved. It would be nice if it were really that simple. In the real world, however, life is complex, ambiguous, and often tragic—it does not readily yield to such a calculus. Ethics is not about being right as much as it is about being responsible. We must intend to discover what is right, but we can be mistaken and still be responsible. However, we can do this only if we are prepared to recognize both our own fallibility and our common humanity.

For many people, *ethics* is also synonymous with obeying the rules. Unfortunately, the rules that we are asked to obey are not always ethical. Therefore, ethics must always begin by questioning the very rules we are asked to obey. Socrates was arrested and executed in ancient Athens for impiety toward the gods and corrupting the youth because he dared ask the question, "Is what people say is the good really the good?" He was thought to have corrupted the youth because he dared to teach them to question the rules, and he was thought to be impious toward the gods because the gods were thought to have invented the rules, which were consequently considered sacred and beyond all questioning.

Raising ethical questions is dangerous because it requires questioning the morality to which we are already committed. We never come to an ethical situation with a blank slate. Every social and institutional context (e.g., the family, the world of work, civic associations) in which we find ourselves has an implicit set of roles and expectations built into it. These expectations constitute the morality of that social context.

Now, if I had only one role to play in life, living an ethical life might be fairly simple. Unfortunately, life is complicated by the fact that I am really more than one person. In fact, in complex modern societies like ours, we are all multiple personalities. That is, we develop not only a work self but also a family self, a friend self, a civic self, and so forth. When I leave work and go home, I am required to become a different person. I have walked into a social context with a different set of expectations and therefore a different morality. Like my boss and peers at work, my spouse and children also expect things from me, but they expect different things. These expectations define for them what it means to be a good spouse and a good parent. (You know—taking out the garbage, taking the kids to a ballgame.) When I leave home and go out to meet a friend for coffee, I am required to become yet another person responsive to yet another morality—that of friendship. After all, my friends expect me to be there for them whenever they need me. When I attend a meeting of the parent–teacher association or some other civic association, I become still another person meeting yet another set of expectations about good citizenship. Thus, we are all multiple personalities juggling multiple moralities.

Part of the problem is that these multiple moralities are often in conflict with each other, although, as we shall see, rightly handled, this is also part of the solution. Every morality has a tendency to become absolute. My boss wants all of my time, talent, and energy; but so do my wife and my friend and the members of my civic group. Sometimes being a good employee conflicts with being a good spouse and parent or with being a good friend. Another part of the problem is that sometimes one's boss or spouse or friend expects one to do things that he or she has no right to expect. In such situations, being a good employee, spouse, or friend might paradoxically require us to be a bad person. Both of these problems require us to go beyond morality and think ethically. Ethics is the task of questioning our moralities. It is the task of asking, as Socrates did, "Is what people say is the good really the good?"

Answering this question in our day and age has become very difficult because there is a pervasive assumption in our culture that ethics is about values, and values are a subjective, personal, and private matter. We hear people saying things like "There are no absolutes" or "Everybody has a right to their own opinion." Thinking of ethics as a private matter in this way, however, makes ethics impossible, for ethics is inherently public: It is about our relationships with others. Because this is so, ethical reflection requires dialogue and deliberation with others. It is not something we can carry out in private.

So, why do people want to privatize ethics? I think we retreat into our own private morality out of a fear that if we do not, we will have somebody else's values or morality imposed on us. That is, we tend to become libertarians, arguing that everybody has a right to make his or her own rules, in order to head off those we consider authoritarian—those who want to make the rules for us and impose them on us. Of course, from an alternative perspective, many feel we need to impose some rules to prevent the chaos and anarchy that they fear would follow from everyone being a libertarian.

If these are our only options, then doing ethics becomes impossible. Deciding what is the good is reduced to a political struggle between those who value their autonomy above all and those who fear such autonomy as the beginning of anarchy and the collapse of social order. How can we ask the question of whether what people say is the good is really the good without bias in this situation? If we are to get beyond this stalemate between libertarianism and authoritarianism, then we need to restore our confidence that ethical judgments transcend such value conflicts.

STORYTELLING AND ETHICS

Ethics today tends to be dominated by "value language," with its concern for rules and principles. Modern philosophical forms of ethics have sought to achieve the ethical point of view by adhering to rational objectivity. The ethical point of view that every person must strive to achieve is interpreted as the point of view that any disinterested observer could supply. This observer is thought to be objective because he or she has no stake in the outcome of the ethical decision that has to be made in a given situation and therefore is not biased for or against any individual involved. This disinterested observer is imagined to proceed as an objective outsider who can apply rationally derived universal rules or norms to a specific case. These rules are thought, by those influenced by Kant, to be deontological—a matter of profound duty or obligation (i.e., some things are right or wrong no matter what the consequences of our actions) and by others in the utilitarian tradition, such as Mill, to be consequentialist in nature (i.e., right and wrong are determined by the good and bad consequences of our actions as measured by the sum total of pleasure or pain they produce).

However, although rules and principles can be useful summaries of some of our best ethical insights, they are no substitute for genuine ethical insight itself. In fact, apart from such insights, which are derived from achieving an ethical point of view, rules and principles can seem to be only arbitrary and capricious. When it comes to communicating what genuine ethical insight is, I find it much easier to tell a story than to explain it in the abstract. In fact, without the story, the abstract explanation will itself seem unconvincing.

As every parent, elementary school teacher, and preacher knows, communicating ethical values is more effectively done by telling a story than by learning abstract rules and moral principles. However, it is less widely recognized that stories shape our very ability to engage in ethical thinking. I doubt that we could know what is good and what is evil, as well as what is right and what is wrong, apart from some story or other.

Storytelling is superior to abstract modes of reasoning (i.e., rules and principles) as a way of arriving at ethical insights. Let me demonstrate this by telling you a story about a story. It illustrates the way in which narrative can enable us to achieve an ethical point of view. The story is a biblical one. It has been told and retold through countless generations. It is about David, the greatest king of Ancient Israel (c. 1000 B.C.E.):

> It happened toward evening when David . . . was strolling on the Palace roof, that he saw . . . a woman bathing; the woman was very beautiful. David made inquiries about this woman and was told . . . "That is Bathsheba, . . . the wife of Uriah the Hittite." Then David sent messengers. . . . She came to him and he slept with her. . . . The woman conceived and sent word to David, "I am with child." . . . [David then called Uriah home from the battle field and tried to persuade him to sleep with his wife, but he refused all such pleasure while his comrades were still on the field of battle.] Next morning David wrote a letter to Joab and sent it by Uriah. In the letter he wrote, "Station Uriah in the thick of the fight and then fall back behind him so that he may be struck down and die." . . . And Uriah the Hittite was

killed. . . . When Uriah's wife heard that her husband Uriah was dead, she mourned for her husband. When the period of mourning was over, David sent to have her brought to his house; she became his wife and bore him a son. But what David had done displeased God. . . . [So the God of Israel sent the Prophet, Nathan, to tell David a story.] He came to him and said: In the same town were two men, one rich, the other poor. The rich man had flocks and herds in great abundance. The poor man had nothing but a ewe lamb, one only, a small one he had bought. This he fed, and it grew up with him and his children, eating his bread, drinking from his cup, sleeping on his breast; it was like a daughter to him. When there came a traveler to stay, the rich man refused to take one of his own flock . . . to provide for the wayfarer. . . . Instead he took the poor man's lamb and prepared it for his guest. David's anger flared up against the man. "As the Lord God lives," he said to Nathan, "the man who did this deserves to die! He must make four-fold restitution for the lamb, for doing such a thing and showing no compassion." Then Nathan said to David, "You are the man." (2 Samuel 11:1–12:7, NJB)

The logic of this story carries us beyond the typical approach of modern philosophical forms of ethics that have sought to achieve the ethical point of view by adhering to rational objectivity. It is doubtful that such abstract modes of reflection are really able to function effectively in the actual complexities of our everyday life. One could imagine Kant, for example, advising David to always act so as to be able to universalize his action without contradiction. (That is, "Don't do it if you are not willing to let everyone else do it as well.") The problem with applying such an abstract formulation to a concrete situation is that the very abstractness of the formulation makes it easy for a person to find countless reasons why this general rule does not apply to his or her unique situation. Abstract moral reflection may in fact make it easy to practice self-deception, a feigning of disinterestedness by those who would like to think well of themselves despite their ethical failings.

A narrative ethic differs from a rationalistic ethic of principles and reasons by insisting that it is not enough to know the good in order to do it. We seldom feel ourselves compelled to act on the basis of a logical conclusion. In ethics, reason must follow, not precede, emotion—not just any emotion, of course, but emotions of empathy that lead one to identify with the one who will be affected by our actions.

In the story of David and Nathan, for instance, whereas the story does create a moment of disinterestedness, it does not allow David to remain in that state of mind. Because it is a story—either fictive or at least about someone else—it disarms David. It creates a sense of aesthetic distance that places David in the situation of the disinterested observer who sees immediately that an injustice has been done and needs to be redressed. But the story then quickly moves David emotionally from disinterestedness to empathy—a sense of identification with the victim that outrages him and compels him to act. Only then is David prepared to reason objectively about what is good and what is evil and unwittingly stand in judgment of himself. Nathan's abrupt turning of the story into an allegory for David's own situation forces David to confront his own actions. The story has managed to capture the complexities of his own particular situation and offers him no place to hide.

In coming face to face with his own wrongdoing, David is not the victim of authoritarian values and rules imposed by others. No one, not even God, has imposed an arbitrary set of values on David. At the same time, David is unable to excuse his own actions with the libertarian claim to make his own rules. He tried that and failed. He failed because the story seduced him into identifying with the victim of his actions, which enabled him to see the injustice of his actions and experience the anger of the victim. No one (not God, the religious community, or the state) tells David he has broken a rule or violated a principle. The ethical point of view induced in David by Nathan's story transcends both libertarianism and authoritarianism and leads David to condemn himself in spite of himself. David's self-condemnation comes about when he identifies with the victim. Then he realizes that what he has violated is not a rule or a principle, but another person like himself. He recognizes the humanity of the stranger and the claim that humanity makes on his conscience.

The story acts on David emotionally but not irrationally; on the contrary, it meets the rational requirements for justice as proposed by one of the leading ethicists today, the philosopher John Rawls. For David arrives at his ethical insight behind what Rawls (1971) called a "veil of ignorance," which leads David to unknowingly stand in judgment of himself. Rawls introduced into ethics a novel perspective that brings rationalistic ethics into closer proximity to narrative ethics. Rawls defined the ethical point of view, not as that of the disinterested observer, but rather as that point of view a person would be forced to assume if he or she were to imagine and plan a society without knowing what particular role he or she would be asked to play in that society. Behind this "veil of ignorance," one would have to imagine a society in which even the least would be treated fairly in order to ensure fairness for oneself. Rawls's theory forces the individual to identify, not with everyone equally (i.e., the position of the "disinterested observer"), but rather with the least in the social order—the alien, the stranger, and the outcast—because one can never be sure that one will not be placed in that position.

This story of the encounter between a king and a prophet, David and Nathan, is an example of the ethical power of narrative. For, as our story indicates, in the real world, it is narrative that has the power to create the required veil of ignorance. It is precisely the aesthetic distance of the narrative, its disarming quality as a story, that puts David behind this veil, seducing David into identifying with the one most vulnerable to injustice in this particular situation. Then, when the veil is lifted, as Nathan draws the analogy, David stands condemned by his own judgment.

Narrative as a form of ethical reflection proves itself to be considerably superior to purely theoretical reflection. First, narrative reflects the complexity, drama, and subtleties of life in its concrete particularities in a way that theoretical reflection cannot. Second, the story, at least in the hands of someone as skillful as Nathan, has the power to induce a disinterested perspective without removing David from the complex particulars of the situation. Third, the seductive power of the narrative brings about a transformation of David's emotions and awareness. He sees and experiences his own actions from a new perspective—that of the stranger affected by them.

The power of Nathan's story, however, cannot be understood in isolation. Nathan is able to tell this story and David is able to arrive at the judgment he does because they have been formed by a shared tradition of stories: stories of origin and destiny; of creation and exodus; of exile and return; of promise and fulfillment; and of prophetic demands for justice, mercy, and hospitality to the stranger. Indeed, in the biblical tradition, the command to welcome the stranger occurs more often than any other command (some 36 times) in the Torah. In fact, this narrative tradition insists that to welcome the stranger is to welcome God. This is important, for the test of an ethic is how we treat the stranger. We are all willing to treat those well with whom we identify—those like ourselves. The test of justice is whether we are willing to recognize the humanity of the stranger, treating equally well those who are different from ourselves. Not all stories are ethical. Ethnocentrism is the most common bias of every culture. An ethical story is one that runs counter to this bias, a story that encourages us to welcome and protect the stranger and the outcast.

Such stories have helped to shape our own story as a country. The United States was originally founded by immigrants largely shaped by such biblical stories—immigrants who fled from the political orders of Europe that would not tolerate diversity and had no place for the stranger. The United States has taken pride in being a nation made up of many nations, a people made up of many peoples. Our social and political life, including our schools and school advisory boards, reflect that diversity. We are a people who have invited the world to send us their tired, their poor, and their hungry. We are a nation founded on stories of hospitality to the stranger. That is a narrative theme that ought to guide us in shaping our public school policies. To have embraced stories of hospitality as the very core of our American identity presents us with an awesome challenge and an awesome responsibility.

STORIES, HUMAN DIGNITY, AND THE SOCIAL ECOLOGY OF OUR CONSCIENCE

Modern human beings have been tempted to think that they can do without stories—that stories belong to the childhood and adolescence of humanity, before the ages of reason and science. Having reached the enlightened adulthood of the modern situation, so the story goes, one must put aside these childish stories. Far from being storyless, however, the contemporary person's actions are still governed by narratives or at least fragments of narratives.

I have already argued that every social or institutional context in which we live has an implicit set of expectations built into it that constitute the morality of that social context. But there is more to be said here, for each such morality is deeply shaped by storytelling. For instance, when I go to work, I enter a social environment that already has a morality attached to it. When I show up for the first day on the job, how do I learn that morality? Perhaps there is a personnel lecture that explains company policies but does not really tell me about the actual operating morality of the company. I learn that over coffee breaks when my new peers sit me down and start telling me stories about the company and its various characters. Through these stories, I learn what to do and what not to do. I learn how to be a good employee. I learn the story of the company and come to understand my role in the story. In this way, I absorb the morality of the company—the patterns of expectation that structure my role. Our understanding of good and evil, or right and wrong, is determined in these situations by the kind of story we think we are in and the role we see ourselves playing in that story.

The moral complexity of our modern lives has to do precisely with the fact that every one of the social roles we embrace in constructing our social identities has a story or complex of stories attached to it, which we consciously or unconsciously absorb. Our spouses implicitly convey to us a story about what it means to be good marriage partners and parents. Our bosses implicitly convey to us a story about what it means to be good employees. Our friends obligate us to incorporate yet other stories into our consciousness. And so it goes. With every social role that we embrace, we add a new narrative or collection of narratives to our repertoire.

The challenge of the ethical life in our time has to do with the complexity of the narrative expectations that are placed on us in each of the institutional contexts of our lives. The problem is that the narratives that structure our role in each institutional context seem to demand all of our time, our talents, and our very being. The narratives that structure the workplace seem to make being a good worker the ultimate value. The narratives that structure our marriage and family life seem to make another set of obligations absolute and primary; likewise with our friends. Nobody wants just a piece of us; everybody wants our whole being.

Despite these conflicting claims, having multiple personalities rooted in multiple social and institutional contexts, each of which embraces a unique morality, can actually enhance rather than diminish our ability to be ethical if we know how to respond to this complexity appropriately. In fact, having multiple moral identities is only an ethical problem insofar as we allow one or another of these moralities to become absolute to the exclusion of all others. I find it helpful to think of the ethical life through an analogy with ecology (see Figure 1). Ecologists tell us that the more complex a natural environment is, the more stable and life sustaining it is. By contrast, the more species that are removed from an environment, the more it is destabilized, until it comes in danger of collapsing and is no longer life sustaining. By anal-

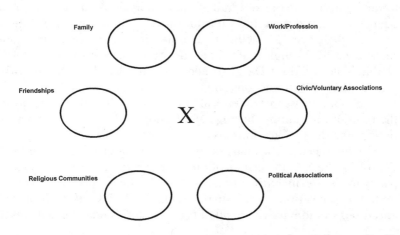

Figure 1. The social ecology of conscience. (X, the self in its capacity to choose.)

ogy, I would argue that the ethical life also depends on a complex ecology—a social one. The more complexity there is in our social life (i.e., the more roles we must play in various social and institutional contexts), the more sensitive and life sustaining our conscience will be. Conversely, the less complex and more simplified our social ecology becomes, the less sensitive our conscience will be.

Let me give you an example. Suppose I am a pharmaceutical executive and my company has been developing a new drug. We have spent a lot of money not only developing it but also testing it to be sure it is safe. Now suppose that the results are in and everything looks pretty good; but some of our test results are ambiguous, and, to be safe, we should really do some additional testing before putting it on the market. However, this drug has cost us a lot of money, and, if we do not get it on the market soon, it is really going to hurt our economic performance. We need to start recovering the cost of developing this drug.

Now, if my only identity is that of a corporate executive, I will be thinking only about the bottom line, and I will decide to put the product on the market now. However, if I am also married and a parent, and my spouse or one of my children might use this drug, or if I have a friend who might use it, suddenly my professional identity is called into question by my identity as a parent or friend; therefore, I will think twice about this decision and probably decide to run further tests before releasing it. The point is that every one of the social contexts in which I operate confronts me with genuine ethical obligations toward others. The tug and pull of these obligations sensitizes my conscience as I am drawn into their life stories and see my own actions through their eyes. My ability to assume more than one identity and see the world through more than one story functions much the way Nathan's story did for David: It allows me to identify with those who will be affected by my actions and to see my actions through their eyes. It enables me to assume an ethical point of view. It builds empathy on the basis of the genuine feelings of affection and obligation that I experience in the various contexts of my life.

In reference to the chart on the social ecology of conscience (see Figure 1), the X at the center of the chart represents the self in its capacity to choose, including its capacity to choose its social roles (represented by the various circles surrounding the X).[1] An ecologically balanced self would have ties to all of these circles. But as this self cuts its

---

[1]The presence of the X at the center suggests that there is such a thing as a "naked self"—that is, a self apart from its social roles. This is an optical illusion. The deciding self is really always in some social role or other; but, because it can move from one to another, it gives us the illusion of being in the center.

ties to all but one of these circles, this complex ecology is simplified and collapses and the self becomes a prisoner of a singular identity with no means of stepping outside itself to see its actions from another perspective. Injustice occurs when we are willing to sacrifice most of our obligations in the various circles of our life in order to excel in just one sphere. To do that, we will be forced to neglect and violate the dignity of the many people who need and depend on us in the various other spheres of our life. As we simplify the social ecology of our life, we cut the ties of empathy and obligation that enable us to identify with the joy and pain of others, and our conscience is desensitized. It ceases to be life sustaining.

In a world in which I have to juggle multiple identities, most institutions compete with each other for my absolute loyalty. Only a few—religious communities, universities, human rights organizations (if they are doing their job properly), for example—nurture narratives that ask us, not to give our ultimate loyalties to it as one more institution, but rather to weigh all our loyalties in light of a commitment to justice and human dignity. Their function, properly understood, is to ask us to put our whole life into perspective, weighing and balancing the obligations placed on us by the diverse narrative contexts of our lives. Justice occurs when we achieve an ecological balance between these diverse narrative contexts and the obligations toward the human dignity of others within each of them.

Neither individuals nor societies can be considered good if they sacrifice human dignity to either personal autonomy and ambition (i.e., libertarianism) or to established rules and principles (i.e., law and order) viewed as sacred and unquestionable (i.e., authoritarianism). Some laws are made to be broken, as both Socrates and Martin Luther King, Jr., knew, but only for the sake of protecting human dignity. Justice should be measured in terms of human dignity. No person, law, or society that violates human dignity can be considered good.

The only way I know to define *human dignity* is to say that it is indefinable. The violation of human dignity almost always begins by defining others (especially strangers) to show how they are not as human as we are (e.g., ethnocentrism, racism, sexism). The claim of human dignity is that we all share a common humanity despite our definable differences, that therefore what makes us human lies beyond all definition, and that every effort to define human dignity is a violation of it. We are equal, regardless of race, social class, gender, ethnicity, or religion. It is no accident that Jewish, Christian, and Buddhist ethics (to name three examples) emphasize the importance of welcoming the stranger and the outcast, for they all affirm that the human self cannot be defined and that therefore all selves are equal.

Key biblical stories affirm that human beings are all equal because we are all created in the image of a God without image. Hence, no one of us looks more like God than another. This is very different from creating God in our own image, so that God ends up looking more like "us" (e.g., white and male or whatever are the elite categories of a given culture) than like "them."

The Buddhist tradition came to a similar insight by another path, for although Buddhists do not believe in a god, they do affirm the spiritual truth that all selves are empty. Neither race, nor gender, nor any other characteristic defines our humanity. Therefore, no one is better than another because of some such characteristics. Our true self is "no self" or is "empty" of all self (i.e., indefinable) and therefore has no objective defining characteristics by which some selves can be thought to be more human than others.

The social sciences have led us to a similar insight by coming to the conclusion that no culture ever completely succeeds in socializing any of its members. (One does not have to be a social scientist to discover this, because every parent knows this through personal experience.) That is, no matter how hard our society tries to impose an identity on us, our humanity resists being completely defined by and confined to its social roles. It remains indefinable. Therein lies the mystery of our dignity as human beings.

STORIES, PROFESSIONAL
IDENTITY, AND ETHICAL RESPONSIBILITY

In our own time, the greatest ethical danger lies in our tendency to give primacy to professional identity, values, and goals. The narratives that seem to give meaning and direction to our lives are all too often exclusively scenarios of professional success. An instructive example of the danger this represents comes from the autobiography of Albert Speer, *Inside the Third Reich* (1970). Speer was a well-educated young man from a prosperous, liberal German family, a skilled architect who considered himself above politics. He was never a fervent Nazi. He married and had six children and was apparently a loving father.

Speer was drawn into the sphere of Hitler's influence by the promise of professional opportunity. Hitler wanted him to be Germany's architect—to rebuild the cities in magnificence once the war was over. In the meantime, he was made Minister of Armaments and threw himself into the technical details with zest and administrative skill.

As he relates how he came to play the role he did in Hitler's Germany, he suggests that he was seduced by his professional ambition. What Hitler offered him was the opportunity to fulfill his wildest professional ambitions. To put it in Speer's (1970) own words, "I felt myself to be Hitler's architect. Political events did not concern me" (p. 112). So, he ignored what was happening to the Jews. He did not want to know. Speer goes on to say that he seldom found time to reflect on himself, what he was doing, and what it all meant. He confessed, "I did not see any moral ground outside the system where I should have taken my stand" (1970, p. 375). What Speer lacked was a complex social ecology for his conscience and a story (e.g., hospitality to the stranger) that would have given him a vantage point from which to evaluate the narrative demands that governed his life in other contexts. In pursuit of his professional ambitions, he neglected his family and friends, and the only narrative he had to guide his life was a professional one. Consequently, his social ecology collapsed and, with it, so did his conscience.

All stories have moral implications. The morality implicit in many stories is ethnocentric, demonic, and destructive. Some stories, however, promote an ethical point of view. The only kind of story that can function as a mode of ethical reflection is one that encourages us to welcome the stranger and identify with the person who will be on the receiving end of our actions (as the prophet Nathan's story did for David).

The ultimate test of the ethical life is how we treat the stranger. To welcome the stranger is to recognize the dignity and humanity of precisely the one who does not share my story and is not like me. It is the antithesis of, for example, all ethnocentrism, religiocentrism, racism, and sexism. The goal of narrative ethics is to expand the horizon of compassion until the stranger has achieved the same status as our closest family and friends. Our ability to identify with the other is almost instinctive in the case of those who are like us and decreases in proportion as others are different, strange, and alien. Only those narratives that encourage us to welcome the stranger and that force us to question all things in our life, including our moral commitments themselves, in the name of human dignity, can function as ethical stories.

In the 20th century, one of the most vivid examples of demonic ethnocentrism was the Nazi myth of the pure Aryan race. As we ponder school-related public policy and the needs of special education students, we should not forget that the first to experience the gas chambers were those who were designated as "biologically inferior"— first people with disabilities and only after that the Jews, gypsies, and others. All were considered strangers, less than human, and not worthy of life. This is what makes us so nervous about contemporary "scientific" discussions of genetic differences in the learning capacities of different racial and ethnic groups, and rightfully so. The ethical danger of our time is that we may find ourselves without the narrative resources to resist the next such story to come along and seduce us with its own demonic and destructive logic.

ETHICS WITHOUT CHOICE

Although many would like ethics to be a kind of moral calculus for computing the answer to moral dilemmas, in the real world it has far more to do with story, conscience, and character formation. In 1988, Pierre Sauvage produced a documentary entitled *Weapons of the Spirit* on the community of French peasant villagers of Le Chambon sur Lignon that saved more than 5,000 Jewish lives during World War II and did so nonviolently (see also Hallie, 1979). He wanted to know how they went about making the decision to risk their lives for total strangers. He said that he had always envisioned such individuals as spending long, sleepless nights weighing the consequences of helping or not helping others and then, after weighing the pros and cons, finally making a decision to act (or not to act) with fear and trembling. What he discovered, however, was that, among these villagers, just the opposite was the case. They saw a stranger in danger, identified with the plight of that person, and acted spontaneously to help that person, virtually without thinking about it. Therefore, he argued, "I have come to realize people who agonize don't act, and people who act don't agonize" (McCarthy, 1990). When asked why they did what they did, the villagers said they felt they had no choice. In fact, in survey after survey of those who rescued Jews during the Holocaust, this is the typical answer. Paradoxically, not only the rescuers but also the perpetrators of the Holocaust frequently give this answer. The psychiatrist Robert Jay Lifton, in his book *The Nazi Doctors* (1986), asked physicians how they were able to reconcile their oath to be healers with their role as those who selected Jews and others for death in the gas chambers. They too responded by saying that they had no choice. Yet their actions were totally at odds with those of the rescuers.

What the doctors meant when they said they had no choice was that they feared for their lives if they did not follow orders. They also felt they were merely cogs in a larger bureaucratic machine in which others higher up made the real decisions, not themselves. If they refused to do the selecting, they felt, nothing would change: Somebody else—another cog in the machine—would do it. The system was totally bureaucratic and impersonal. Hence, they did not feel personally responsible for their actions. They were just following orders.

The villagers of Le Chambon and other rescuers, by contrast, meant something quite different when they said they had no choice. They meant that, given who they were, they could not imagine turning their back on a stranger in need, even if it meant risking their own lives. They were confessing the power of story, community, and character to shape their identity and school them in the virtues characteristic of compassionate human beings, especially the virtue of hospitality to the stranger. For these villagers were Huguenots, French Calvinists who had suffered a long history of discrimination and persecution by Catholics in France from the time of the Reformation. This history was part of their story, passed on from generation to generation.

Because of this story and their experience of being outsiders in their own society, they knew what it was like to be a stranger and to be persecuted. Thus, when these villagers encountered Jews running from the Nazis, they immediately identified with them and took them in because of their own story. This response was a matter of character and identity for these villagers. What these villagers meant when they said they had no choice was that they simply could not imagine turning these strangers away. In order not to respond to the need of the stranger, they would have had to abandon their very identity and they simply could not imagine doing that, even if it would lead to their own death.

What does all of this teach us about ethics? The lesson, I think, is that the ethical response is not a rationalistic process of weighing costs and benefits in order to solve dilemmas. For the French villagers of Le Chambon, there was no dilemma. They simply did what they had to do. Their response was rooted in their identity and character—the kind of people they were because of their own experiences and their own story. If we want to be ethical people, we shall have to learn to tap our capacity to identify with strangers. Without this capacity, we shall be without the strength of character needed for the ethical life, and we shall end up like the Nazi doctors, willing to follow even the most demonic orders on the excuse that we are merely cogs in the bureaucratic machine, without any personal responsibility—and, I would add, without conscience, character, or compassion.

This is a lesson we ought to take to heart in formulating and carrying out school policies that deal with special education students and their needs. Instead of saying, "What can we do? We are hampered by bureaucratic policies," administrators, teachers, and parents must be prepared to confront bureaucratic rules and regulations that ignore the needs of special education students or deliberately violate their dignity. Once we have identified with those whom our society treats as strangers, what choice do we have?

BEYOND VALUES: STORY, CHARACTER, AND PUBLIC POLICY IN AMERICAN SCHOOLS

If we are really engaged in ethics without choice, then what advice can be offered to school-based advisory groups about shaping school educational policies within their communities? If we think that ethics is about plugging in formulas based on our values and then calculating the right conclusion to the individual moral dilemmas that we face, this chapter will be of little use. If, however, we come to realize that ethics is about story, community, and character, then there are implications for those involved in shaping public policy. What is required for drawing them out, however, is a different way of thinking about ethics and the ethical life.

There is a lot of public discussion about moral decline in American life and about the failure of U.S. schools. U.S. citizens want their schools to educate their children to be responsible human beings. Typically, we hear this taking the form of a call to a return to traditional American family values. Too often, however, this turns out to be a code phrase for some idyllic picture of American life in the 1950s, before the moral decay of the 1960s and after set in. It dredges up images of the husband who supports his family while the wife stays at home to raise their 2.2 children, a world where sex either before or outside of marriage was a scandal, where homosexuals would never admit their identity in public, racial segregation was the norm, and women knew their place in the scheme of things.

The call to return to traditional family values is a nostalgic call to return to a time when life seemed simpler, when people knew who they were and seemed to agree on what was right and what was wrong—and, if they did not, they kept it to themselves. This is a call to a return to a less confusing time when there were no alternative lifestyles, at least none that were available for public display. The real dilemma of public policy to emerge since the 1950s and 1960s is not that people have departed from the norms of society (which has always been true) but that people now do so publicly and therefore destroy the illusion of such a normative public order. We are overwhelmed and bewildered by the diversity of our society. Public diversity of lifestyles undermines public norms and creates the impression (either real or imagined) of moral decay.

Consequently, we hear the call to return morality to American life, especially through the renewal of U.S. education. This has been taking the form of a call to return values to the curriculum. However, as soon as we hear such proposals, someone asks the inevitable question, "Whose values?" With this question, we are caught in the crossfire of the argument between libertarians, who insist everyone has a right to make their own rules, and authoritarians, who want to make the rules for everybody.

As I have already argued, this is a false choice that undermines our capacity to think ethically. Indeed, I would argue that the very appeal to values as the main subject of ethics undermines our ability to think ethically. The language of values is relatively new in the history of ethics. It first appeared in the 19th century with the emergence of the social sciences. Before then, ethicists talked about subjects like the good and the common good, honor and duty, obligation, character, and virtue. The new language of values was born out of the historical and comparative study of civilizations.

Until the 19th century, human beings everywhere assumed that they lived in a sacred and unchangeable natural order created by the gods or God and/or their sacred ancestors. Then, in the 19th century, the social sciences emerged. Critical historiography, ethnography, and cross-cultural studies gave birth to sociological and anthropological theory. As scholars examined and compared cultures across time and geographical space, it became apparent that though every culture saw itself as mirroring a sacred natural order, each culture imagined this natural order differently. Consequently, we became aware that human beings live, not directly in nature, but in culture and society, which mediates our relation to nature. For the first time, society, which, after all, is not an empirical object, became visible to the human imagination. It immediately became clear that human beings do not live directly in the order of nature but rather in language and culture—their second nature.

This comparative consciousness of the social sciences led theorists to look for a new language to express the diversity of human social worlds. For this purpose, a term that had primarily an economic meaning (as in "x is a good value," i.e., "a good buy"), *value*, gradually came to take on a new meaning expressing the collective preferences of each civilization and its individual members in contrast with every other civilization. That is, *value* became a term to express the new consciousness of cultural and ethical relativism. What cultures valued were often different. Why one valued *x* and another *y* seemed subjective and arbitrary because the reasons given within each culture had to do with the sacred natural order of things as perceived in a particular culture, which was now shown to be socially constructed and not natural at all. No reasons, it seemed, could be given for one preference over another that were not circular. Values were simply contingent and arbitrary objects of desire, which one person or culture preferred and another did not.

By the last decades of the 19th century, all of this seemed so obvious to the philosopher Nietzsche that he rewrote the history of ethics as a genealogy of morals or history of values in which he showed that values are arbitrary constructions that are not really about what is good at all but about the will to power. The language of values, he argued, in every age has been simply a mask behind which those with power and those without power express their conflicting tastes along with their approval of their own and their disapproval of all others. The future, Nietzsche argued, belonged to those who had the courage to transform the values of their culture in accordance with their own taste. He called this "transvaluing all values." Ethics was reduced to aesthetics—having the courage to set the standards of good taste, standards that would rise above common values of the herd (i.e., the common man) and allow one to be a creative and unique being. Such a person Nietzsche called an *Ubermensch* (literally, *overman*)—one who has the courage to rise above or over the common herd and its values.

From an empirical and comparative social science perspective, the language of values can have a certain functional usefulness. However, it should immediately be clear that once one accepts the language of values as the appropriate language of ethics, ethics becomes a subjective and arbitrary exercise. We end up with a kind of supermarket notion of value. Values are objects and commodities that come in all shapes and sizes, and we are free to wander through the supermarket of our culture, picking and choosing the ones we prefer—the ones we personally find most pleasing. The result is ethical emotivism: "X is good, and y is bad" means "I like x, and I dislike y." That is all there is to it. No reasons other than preference can be given why one should choose x rather than y.

The language of values destroys the possibility of ethical reflection because it treats ethics as if it is about objects toward which we have subjective preferences that are purely personal and fundamentally emotional and arbitrary. Such a view undermines ethics because it reduces ethical language to the language of radical individualism. Ethics becomes reduced to autonomy—the right of each individual subject to choose whatever objects he or she desires without regard for the choices other subjects make. If that is not pragmatically possible, then we modify our position slightly to allow that we all have a right to make these choices so long as our choices do not impinge on the rights of others to make their choices.

What is missing from this picture? Fundamentally, it is the fact that ethics is relational. It is about our relationship to other human beings. It is about the obligations we have toward the humanity of other human beings. It is about seeing our own actions from the point of view of the other to whom we are related, whether this is a relationship of choice or chance. Hence, ethics can never be a private affair. Because ethics is about human relationships, it is an inherently communal task. It can never just be about me choosing my values as if no one else mattered or were implicated by my choices and actions. I am obligated by my relationships to others to work out my understanding of what is right and good in dialogue with others. Ethics is about how we ought to relate to each other even though we may disagree with each other.

The language of values distorts the nature of ethics not only by privatizing and subjectivizing ethical reflection but also by technologizing it. When we think that ethics is about values and values are treated as objects that we subjectively choose, then our relationship to values becomes not only arbitrary but also technological. That is, we think of values as objects that we can change and transform according to our desires in the same way that we transform raw materials into finished products to satisfy our desires. Nietzsche's dubious accomplishment was to preside over the death of ethics by dismantling the language of ethics and replacing it with the language of transvaluation of all values.

A little reflection on our actual experience should tell us that there is something seriously wrong with this view. Nietzsche was reacting against the authoritarianism of the received cultural values of 19th-century urban culture—the bourgeois values of what he called the herd. Not willing to have the rules made for him, he responded equally but in the opposite direction of libertarianism—making up the rules for himself. But the ethical experience is no more constituted by libertarianism than it is by authoritarianism. As we have seen in the story of David and Nathan, ethical awareness is derived neither from the dictates of others (whether God or society) nor from one's own desires—as if we could arbitrarily decide what is good and right. On the contrary, ethical awareness is generated by the experience of obligation to another human that is constituted by our coming to see our actions from his or her point of view. David does not transvalue the meaning of justice—just the opposite. The insight he has into his own act of injustice judges and transforms him. The good is not transformed, but David's subjective will is. David is brought to crisis and transformed by his recognition of what is just, right, and good, despite his subjective desire that it be otherwise.

To use another example, if a friend turns to me in his hour of need and I am not there for him because I cannot be bothered, I have not transvalued friendship. I am simply a failure as a friend. I have demonstrated a significant ethical flaw in my character. To be someone's friend is to feel an obligation to assist him or her when he or she is in need. Thus, I do not transvalue friendship; rather, either friendship transforms me or I am a failure as a friend. There is nothing at all subjective and arbitrary about this; either I am a friend or I am not.

We are so seduced by the myth that ethics is about subjective values that I feel compelled to give one more example. If I am a scientist—say, a biologist—and wish to conduct experiments to test a hypothesis I have about the structure and behavior of viruses, I must make a profound ethical commitment to the virtues of honesty and integrity. I must be committed to following the questions wherever they lead me and to accepting the findings of my data, regardless of whether they are what I expected. If I choose not to embrace the ethical imperatives inherent in inquiry and fudge the data—out of a desire for fame and glory, for example—I may succeed for a while in acquiring fame. But if my data are not truthful, they will not lead to any genuine insights into the nature of viruses nor will they lead to any successful discoveries regarding how to combat them. Other scientists will not be able to build on my data to understand how the world works.

In doing science, then, it makes no sense to say that honesty and integrity are arbitrary values that are being imposed on me or to claim that I am free to choose or to transvalue my own values. Nature does not tolerate liars and cheats. Honesty and integrity are not values at all, but rather the virtues or skills inherent in the very process of scientific investigation. Either I incorporate these skills and commitments into my character and engage in real science, or I do not and therefore am not a scientist at all.

If one wants the good that comes from understanding how the world is constructed, one has to acknowledge the objectivity and validity of these virtues. Recognizing the obligations that come with the desire to pursue this good is to acquiesce to neither authoritarian values nor libertarian values, but rather to accept and embrace the ethical obligations of a scientist that are internal to the very structure of doing science. In accepting these obligations, the scientist does not transvalue science; rather, science transvalues the scientist who is transformed by the very activity of doing science.

To admit this is to understand the difference between the language of ethics and the language of values. The former has none of the privatistic, subjective, and technologizing qualities of the latter. Having articulated this difference, we should now be in a position to say why the question of whose values are to be implemented in the public schools undermines the goal we are seeking: that of raising the level of public morality in our society. For, instead of seeking to work together to clarify the obligations we have toward each other in our pluralistic society, we engage in a cultural war to see whose privatistic values will be imposed on whom—the very antithesis of an ethical point of view. Instead of seeing our own actions from the viewpoint of those we perceive as strangers, as different from us, we set out on a campaign to force others to see the world as we do. Instead of creating justice and peace, we end up creating conflict, prejudice, hatred, and violence. We end up becoming the kind of fanatical and authoritarian people we accuse others of being. Paradoxically, in our anxiousness to promote values, we end up destroying the very quality of community and character we are seeking to recover and protect. Instead of living by stories that encourage hospitality to the stranger, we settle for stories of hostility to the stranger, and society becomes the war of all against all.

School advisory boards are constructed to represent the communities they serve, including teachers, parents, and administrators, with sensitivity to race, gender, and ethnicity. They are models of society in miniature. If school advisory boards are to address the larger community's concern to reverse the moral decline in our society, they will have to begin by becoming ethical communities themselves—communities that model what it means to welcome the stranger and in which each individual sees his or her own point of view from the perspective of the others who will be affected by it. School advisory boards will have to be communities of character where people model what it means to work together, respecting our obligations to each other as human beings, despite our differences. They will have to model the core truth of the ethical life—that it is a public life, not a private life. Therefore, ethics is about thinking through our obligations to each other together in a community process of constructive and empathetic dialogue. Such advisory boards would come to see the ethical problems we face, not as isolated dilemmas to be solved, but as challenges to the integrity of the fabric of our life together—challenges that can only be met once we get beyond dividing ourselves into factions and engaging in power struggles to see who can win control to impose their values on others. In that scenario, no matter who wins, everybody loses, because the very thing that we all seek is destroyed—the ethical quality of our life together. We end up contributing to the moral decline we are seeking to reverse.

The question that must be answered by school advisory boards is not, Whose values?, but rather, how can we communicate by word and example the truth that our lives are all so interrelated that our own good can be achieved only if we seek to achieve what is good for others? The good is not private. I cannot achieve what is genuinely good and just for myself while ignoring the same for others. If one is diminished, all are diminished by the moral decline in our community and character. If one is uplifted, so are all.

How, then, ought we to prepare school advisory boards for the ethical dimension of their tasks? There is no quick fix for our problems. The development of community and character is a long-term, ongoing task that demands perseverance and a capacity for patience and even forgiveness on the part of every person involved. Nevertheless, the question was raised by the Collegium as to what form of training might help facilitate the ethical sensitivity of school advisory boards.

Answering that question will be a matter of trial and error. But I can think of one or two things I would suggest, based in part on my experience in the Collegium. I think that if school advisory boards are to be successful, they must have a long-term commitment to developing a sense of community among themselves. People have to be willing to share in each other's lives. That means occasionally gathering for social events as well as for business. It might also be facilitated by an annual 1- or 2-day retreat where both social and business concerns are part of the agenda. I also think short workshops to heighten the consciousness of these boards to the ethical dimension of their work might enhance their functioning successfully.

In our Collegium workshops, I noticed that when people understood that their task was to work on the ethical dimensions of school problems together (presented as case studies of actual problems) rather than each coming up with his or her private solutions, a kind of synergy occurred. People began sharing with each other and seeing the problem from each other's point of view. This process was enhanced by the fact that these school advisory boards reflect the diversity of the communities they serve and therefore offer each participant a rich selection of points of view. I also noticed that when role playing was introduced into the case study process, the likelihood of people achieving an ethical point of view increased because role playing required them to assume the identity of those who would likely be affected by their actions. In my own work, teaching ethics in the college classroom, I find that students evaluate role playing as the single most useful approach that they encounter in my courses. It has a powerful effect on them. They are forced to be involved and yet not from the viewpoint of what they think, but from that of how they imagine others feel and think.

School advisory boards will have to invent the kinds of communities they wish to create by living them. They will have to be communities of character. Public policy, especially (but not exclusively) at the local level, is shaped far more by community and character than it is by political movements and political elections. The latter only gets us more of the same; the former creates a whole new way of life in which we can all share. When that happens, we are on the way to the ethical renewal of society.

In this renewal, children with mental and physical disabilities and their parents have a special contribution to make. Teachers, administrators, and parents of children without disabilities are often uncomfortable when they have to deal with special students. It is not uncommon for special students to be isolated and set apart in our schools—in physical location, attitude, and access to resources. They are often truly strangers in our midst. I do not think that this is because "normal" people are inherently cruel and evil, but rather because whenever we encounter a human problem we cannot fix, we tend to isolate ourselves because we do not know what to say and do.

It is not uncommon, for example, for people who discover that they are terminally ill to suddenly find that many of their friends are too busy to see them. Misfortune makes strangers of us all. But it is in just such circumstances that we are offered one of the most important ethical lessons of friendship and community—that it is about being with one another and sharing one another's burdens even when there is nothing we can do. There is, of course, much we can do for special students. But there is also much that we cannot do. However, there is one thing we can all do—be there for one another. When we share our lives with others and allow them to share theirs with us, we discover that the bonds of friendship and community are the essence of our life in which our good and the good of others become one good.

There is no way to create a public policy that will reverse the moral decline of our society without bearing one another's burdens. In our school advisory boards and in all our communities, that is where the renewal must begin. The moral transformation of our society does not require more money. It does not require an elaborate public relations campaign or some new mass movement. It is not about putting things right and solving all our problems. Rather, it is about hospitality to the stranger—about making our burdens bearable by bearing one another's burdens even when we cannot solve all our problems. The good news is that the goal we seek is found not at the end of the process but in the process itself. For, when people are willing to bear one another's burdens, they are able to succeed even in the midst of failure, to succeed at being a truly human community.

REFERENCES

Fasching, D.J. (1993). *The ethical challenge of Auschwitz and Hiroshima*. Albany: State University of New York Press.
Hallie, P. (1979). *Lest innocent blood be shed*. New York: Harper.
Lifton, R.J. (1986). *The Nazi doctors*. New York: Basic Books.

McCarthy, B. (1990). *Bill Moyers interviews filmmaker Pierre Sauvage.* Los Angeles: Friends of Le Chambon, Inc.

New Jerusalem Bible. (1966). New York: Doubleday.

Rawls, J. (1971). *A theory of justice.* Cambridge, MA: Belknap Press of Harvard University.

Sauvage, P. (1988). *Weapons of the spirit* [Film]. Los Angeles: Pierre Sauvage Productions and Friends of Le Chambon Inc.

Speer, A. (1970). *Inside the Third Reich* (R. Winston & C. Winston, eds. & trans.). New York: Macmillan.

6

Gender, Schools, and Caring

Feminist and
Womanist Perspectives

Cheryl R. Rodriguez, Ella L. Taylor,
Hilda Rosselli, and Daphne Thomas

When we are guided by stories that encourage hospitality to strangers (as discussed in Chapter 5), we learn the importance of opening doors for people whose lives have been marginalized or whose capabilities have not been realized. In living our lives this way, we create an ethic of care. This ethic of care is defined by respect for and a sense of responsibility to all of humanity. Noddings (1988) defined *caring* as "a form of relational ethics. . . . One who is concerned with behaving ethically strives to preserve or convert a given relation into a caring relation" (p. 218). In terms of schooling and school-based policy making, the ethic of care means that educators must find ways to "validate and work with and for students and their families, whatever their culture, ethnicity, social class, or family configuration" (Henry, 1996, p. 124). Thus, caring, which stimulates a sense of connectedness and community building, is "a necessary underpinning of all educational and social work" (Henry, 1996, p. 124). Caring has significant implications for the education of all children, and, in this chapter, some ways are suggested in which feminist and womanist ideas can affect school-based policies, particularly for girls of various ethnic groups and social classes.

This chapter is also a collaboration involving diverse feminist perspectives on caring in schools and the school-based decision-making process. Although these voices represent the interweaving of ideas and theories that enhance and complement each other, there is also an acknowledgment of the distinctive diversity and autonomy of thought that is inherent in a nonhierarchical, interdisciplinary, multicultural endeavor such as this one. The interaction of different and diverse voices is as critical to the richness of scholarship as it is to the perpetuation of productive, creative, equitable communities and schools.

Unlike the preceding chapters on ethics, this chapter situates ethical analysis in the experiences of specific members of the human community—namely, women. The discussion centers on gender and on the history of the social and moral constructions of the relationships among gender, race and ethnicity, and class. Two authors of this chapter are African American and two are Caucasian. The reason for writing together was to reveal the complexity of the experiences of women and, without any pretense of integrating these divergent experiences, suggest substantive implications of a feminist-womanist analysis for school policies affecting girls. We also make explicit the power of voice in recognizing the need to affirm and support otherwise silent voices in the ethical deliberations likely to occur in school policy forums such as school-based decision-making committees (SBDMCs). The interlock of gender, race and ethnicity, and class has profound, though often subtle, implications for the philosophy of education, curriculum, approaches to teaching and learning, and culture in schools. The local construction of this interlock has implications with regard to which people are recruited to participate in the policy development process and for the quality and productivity of their deliberations.

The ever-evolving community of feminists is gradually beginning to understand that its internal differences are extremely valuable resources in working toward healthy changes in family, community, and education. It is coming to terms with the value of difference by discarding the fears and misconceptions of "otherness" and by allowing itself to learn about the historical, social, and cultural realities that characterize diversity.

This chapter attempts to move beyond gender awareness to a more complex feminist awareness within the context of schooling. The chapter's analysis is formulated with the knowledge that, even in the postmodern era, the term *feminism* is one that continues to be fraught with misunderstanding, mistrust, and even fear. Hogeland (1994) argued that it is not so much feminism that is feared as the politics of feminism that is threatening. In order to understand this argument, the distinction between gender consciousness and feminist consciousness must be clarified. Hogeland contended that women's gender consciousness (or self-awareness as women) is very high. One form of gender consciousness is women's heightened awareness of their special vulnerability to violence. Another is women's awareness of their cultural and social (as well as biological) differences from men. Through community action, education, and legislation, feminists have stimulated and fostered the public's awareness of women's vulnerability as well as women's differences from men and have "made it possible for women (including nonfeminists) to have an appreciation of things pertaining to women" (Hogeland, 1994, p. 18). Although gender consciousness is a necessary precursor to a feminist consciousness, these two concepts are not the same, for "feminism politicizes gender consciousness, inserts it into a systematic analysis of histories and structures of domination and privilege" (Hogeland, 1994, p. 18).

This chapter expands feminist theorizing by incorporating a womanist analysis that reflects the views and voices of feminists of color. In the 1990s, the term *womanist* has been found in both social science and literary domains. Although this term is not widely used, *womanist* is a distinctive descriptor related to the feminist consciousness, intellectual traditions, and humanistic activism of women of color, specifically African American women. As formally defined by Walker (1983), a womanist is a feminist of color who appreciates and prefers "women's culture, women's emotional flexibility . . . and women's strength" (p. 127). A womanist is also one who is "committed to survival and wholeness of entire people, male and female" (Walker, 1983, p. xi). Walker's definition also presents a womanist as one who has respect for and seeks human autonomy as opposed to separateness.

OVERVIEW

Within the domains of schooling and education, many feminist thinkers choose to remain comfortably gender conscious while ignoring the interlocking hierarchies of gender, race, and class oppression. There are historical foundations for this type of thinking. For example, the necessity of comprehensive educational opportunities for girls and women has long been addressed in the feminist literature. However, feminists have not always recognized or articulated the importance of education for people of color and other disenfranchised groups. Early feminists understood that gender, as one element in the universal human experience, should neither compromise the quality of one's education nor conflict with the basic principles of a self-proclaimed democracy. Thus, 18th-century feminists advanced the idea of women's formal education beyond the domestic sphere. Feminists also argued for the development of critical thinking skills that would facilitate women's self-determination. The development of the multiple capacities of women's minds was a recurring theme in the work of Wollstonecraft, a rationalist of the Enlightenment era, who believed that critical thinking could "liberate the individual from the mindless repetition of mere physical existence" (Donovan, 1987, p. 11). Writing in 1792, Wollstonecraft wondered,

> How many women thus waste life away the prey of discontent, who might have practiced as physicians, regulated a farm, managed a shop, and stood erect, supported by their own industry, instead of hanging their heads surcharged with the dew of sensibility? (1792/1975, p. 262)

More than 200 years later, Walker (1983) presented a similar discussion on the stifled intellectual and creative lives of African American women in America. In her classic essay *In Search of Our Mothers' Gardens* (1983), Walker posed painful questions about the forces that dictated compulsory ignorance for African American people and the enduring impact this intellectual darkness must have had on African American women in particular:

> How was the creativity of the black woman kept alive, year after year and century after century, when for most of the years black people have been in America, it was a punishable crime for a black person to read or write? (p. 234)

Walker, like generations of womanists before her, addressed the interlocking and systematic nature of domination and the ways in which such domination has been used to perpetuate compulsory ignorance. Historically, womanist thinkers have challenged narrow definitions of freedom and have used education as a tool of resistance and empowerment.

WOMANISM: A HUMANISTIC
PERSPECTIVE ON THE ETHIC OF CARE

In his poignant novel *A Lesson Before Dying*, Ernest J. Gaines (1993) wrote of the clarity and steadfastness that composes indigenous African American wisdom. Informed only by their life experiences with struggle and pain, two elderly women in rural Louisiana attempt to save the soul, the mind, and the dignity of their condemned nephew. As the young man, Jefferson, sits in a jail cell bitterly awaiting his execution for a crime he did not commit, the two women struggle with the idea that he has never learned to understand his own humanity. Despite their own lack of education, the women feel that their nephew must achieve some higher level of awareness about his rightful place in the universe, about his connection to his family and community, and about the unwelcome yet ever-present challenges confronting oppressed people. Powerless against a brutal and vindictive criminal justice system, the women call on an educated son of their community to bring some unnamed knowledge and light to the prisoner so that he will not die in the electric chair like a helpless animal. The women's undaunted faith in God, their belief in the power of the human spirit, and their quiet, unassuming moral strength help them to resist the unspeakable indignities that have been inflicted on their plantation community for generations. Certainly, these women have no public power or authority that anyone outside of the African American community is bound to recognize or respect. Yet their insistence that this young man achieve one small act of intellectual liberation— even as he faces an unjust death—is symbolic of many African American women's historic fight for enlightenment and survival for themselves and their children. This quiet, caring resistance has been the work of African American women. Walker argued, "This ability to hold on, even in very simple ways, is work black women have done for a very long time" (1983, p. 242).

Relationship Between *Womanist* and *Feminist*
Based on Walker's definition, the terms *womanist* and *feminist of color* are fairly synonymous with some similar political, social, and cultural implications. However, historically, African American women have mistrusted feminist ideas and have not used the label *feminist* as a descriptor of their liberatory work in African American communities. One of the recurring and painful problems with feminism and African American women is that feminist analyses and politics are generally associated with Caucasian women, who, along with Caucasian men, are the benefactors of systemic racism. Although the association of feminist analysis and politics with Caucasian women has a historical basis, it is erroneous and should be reconsidered by all feminists for at least two reasons. First, it is historically inaccurate to assume that Caucasian women were the initiators of liberatory ideas that supported women's full participation in society. Richardson (1987) argued that, as early as 1832, Maria Stewart mounted a platform to speak publicly on political issues. Stewart was the first American woman to lecture in public on the controversial issues of the day. She was an educator and a deeply religious, intellectually gifted abolitionist. Stewart was also particularly concerned with the state of African American women's lives in the United States, and, not insignificantly, Stewart herself was African American. Other African American women expressed a similar womanist consciousness through their work as abolitionists, organizers, activists, and educators. This womanist awareness became a part of the culture of survival among African American women.

A second reason to reconsider historic and contemporary notions about feminism is that there has never been one all-encompassing feminism. In fact, there are a multitude of theoretical perspectives on the definitions and goals of the various feminisms. Historically, these perspectives have included but are not limited to liberal feminism, cultural feminism, Marxist feminism, and radical feminism (Donovan, 1987).

Collins (1990) explored the dimensions of thought of African American feminist or womanist theorists and suggested that these women have created a specialized knowledge that clarifies a standpoint of and for African American women. Moreover, "Black feminist thought encompasses theoretical interpretations of Black women's reality by those who live it" (Collins, 1990, p. 22). These theoretical interpretations are extremely important because, as Henry (1995) argued, the realities of African American women and girls have often been misinterpreted, particularly in educational research. Emphasizing the value of womanist thought does not imply that all African American women embrace this political label; nor does it suggest that other groups of people cannot contribute to the advancement of womanist intellectualism and grass-roots activism (Collins, 1990). However, acknowledging and analyzing African American women's unique standpoint provides visibility for a previously invisible or misunderstood group of people. The definition of *womanist* also does not suggest that all African American women interpret the interlocking nature of various oppressions or respond to oppression and other social phenomena in a similar manner. The ways in which African American women experience their lives in relationship to the dominant culture varies greatly, depending on such factors as ethnicity, national affiliation, social class, geographic location, role models, and the quality of social and educational experiences.

Caring as Resistance

In attempting to articulate the unique experiences of African American women, womanist thinkers have advanced several core themes that compose an African American woman's standpoint. These core themes include a legacy of struggle against racism, sexism, and economic oppression; self-definition and the debunking of unidimensional characterizations of African American women; and activism in both domestic and public domains. Embedded within these core themes is the element of resistance. Resistance (see, e.g., that which was intimately described in Gaines [1993]) is a very important aspect of the ethic of care in womanist thought. In other words, for generations, African American women have illustrated their care and concern for the African American community by imploring their people to seek knowledge of themselves and the world.

Education, schooling, and intellectual pursuits have been the primary vehicles of resistance used by womanist thinkers. Womanist thinkers have always resisted oppression by refusing to blindly accept the barriers imposed by systemic racism. For example, Neverdon-Morton (1989) argued that, from 1895 until 1925,

> Southern women focused on many needs of Afro-Americans: the plight of working women, limited economic opportunities, inferior housing, severe health problems, the political strait jacket of Jim Crowism, care for the aged, and programs for the very young. But the key to solving all these problems, leaders of black women were convinced, was education of the masses of black citizens. (p. 6)

Womanist thinkers have also resisted racism by challenging the inconsistencies of racism. For example, in reflecting on her early explorations of Christian ethical thought, womanist thinker Katie Cannon expressed her most ardent intellectual, religious, and spiritual quest as one of attempting to "relate the Christian doctrines preached by the Black church to the suffering, oppression and exploitation of Black people in society" (1988, p. 1). Cannon's quest was a historical one. Decades before her birth in the 1950s, many people of African descent (both literate and illiterate) had attempted to reconcile Christian principles of universal fellowship and love with the reality of a brutal system of enslavement. Although the dismantling of the enslavement system challenged the economic, social, and cultural foundations of Southern life, it also precipitated new laws and policies that would perpetuate oppression. Such oppression guaranteed that the creative energies and intellectual endeavors of African American people in America would be stifled. This historical conflict in Christian ethical thought manifested itself most vividly in the wavering policies on literacy and education for African American people. Such policies would have a profound impact on the lives of African Americans throughout the 19th and 20th centuries. In fact, these policies have been far-reaching in their impact on African American youth. Fordham and Ogbu (1986), in their research on some African American students' lack of success in school, argued that there are at least three factors contributing to this problem:

1. African American children have been provided inferior schooling and have been treated differently in school.
2. A job ceiling has been imposed on African American people, thus allowing no reward for educational achievement.
3. African American students have developed coping strategies that often limit their striving for academic success. (p. 179)

Education has been a strong vehicle for the propagation of social mores and civic responsibility. However, controversy surrounding state and local education policies reflects the serious conflicts in American social, political, and religious thinking (Cornelius, 1991). A true ethic of care has not been apparent in teacher training, classroom interactions, and school decision-making processes. Resistance, both subtle and overt, by African American women has been an important force in identifying and changing discriminatory policies in education. A story told by Septima Poinsetta Clark, as cited in Lerner (1973), supports this point. Clark, who was born in 1898, was a teacher as well as a community activist in Charleston, South Carolina. In her autobiography, Clark tells the story of how African American teachers began teaching in the public schools in Charleston. In 1919, only Caucasian teachers were able to teach in the public schools. Employment for African American teachers was available only in the private schools. Clark became involved in the campaign to hire African American teachers in the public schools:

> I volunteered to seek signatures and started visiting the grassroots people. I worked Cannon Street, a very long street, from Rutledge all the way to King. Soon we brought in a tow sack with more than 10,000 signatures to the petition. I remember the number because of the fact that a white legislator known then as One-Eye Tillman had declared [that we] would never be able to get 10,000 signatures in all Charleston. The law passed. The next year, 1920, we had Negro teachers in the public schools of Charleston and the year following we had Negro principals. We had been victorious in this my first effort to establish for Negro citizens what I sincerely believed was no more than their God-given rights. (Lerner, 1973, p. 114)

As Clark's story shows, womanist resistance is "a part of the wider struggle for human dignity and empowerment" (Collins, 1990, p. 37). Such resistance speaks to humanism and caring. West (1993) viewed resistance as a vibrant tradition that has nurtured a collective and critical consciousness in African American communities. Collins connected resistance to humanism. Historically, resistance has been about survival. Ultimately, resistance, the foundation of womanist thinking, is about caring.

Unfortunately, far too many young African American girls are unaware of the work and struggles of their womanist foremothers. They are also unaware of the power of education as a means of resisting racial, sex, and class oppression. This lack of awareness persists in a patriarchal system in which African American students' school performance is gender differentiated at all levels of the academy, and African American females are often victimized by their race, sex, and class (Fordham, 1993). Furthermore, schools are not always welcoming places for African American girls. Fordham's research indicates that, for academically successful girls, "silence and invisibility are the strategies they feel compelled to use to gain entry into the dominating patriarchy" (1993, p. 23).

In the school decision-making process, the unique academic and social problems of African American girls can be addressed. Both school personnel and parents should be sensitive to the need for womanist role models in schools who can help African American girls envision themselves as successful people. They should also be aware of the need for safe, nurturing spaces for African American girls to express themselves verbally and in writing. Finally, there should be an awareness of the need for womanist leadership in schools. As Joseph (1995) argued, African American women historically have been central to educational change as teachers, survival technicians, administrators, and revolutionary thinkers. It is time to ask new questions in schools that will support the discovery of innovative answers for the problems of the whole of the human community.

GENDER AND THE ETHIC OF CARE: A FEMINIST ANALYSIS

Noddings (1992) suggested that the culture of schools rests upon the male experience as the standard. She asked, "If women had set the standard when schools were founded and curriculum designed, what might our students be studying today?" (Noddings, 1992, p. 67). Many in the past attempted to exclude women from an education by redirecting women's intellectual capacities toward housework and children. Rousseau may be one of the most explicit in his attempt to rationalize women's separate educational role. In *Emile,* Rousseau (1762/1979) painstakingly developed a bifurcated educational system in which proper development for boys rested on their free exploration of manipulated environments, but proper development for girls rested on their restricted movement and mental development. Rousseau noted, "For man this aim is the development of strength; for woman it is the development of attractiveness" (1762/1979, p. 365). He also stated, "It is for women to discover experimental morality . . . and for [men] to reduce it to a system. Woman has more wit, man more genius; woman observes, and man reasons" (Rousseau, 1762/1979, p. 387). Rousseau's views of education and gender were driven by his belief that morality rests on the relations of love between men and women. Men become what women desire; therefore, the solution to society's ills is to create women who will desire moral men. The issue for Rousseau then becomes how to create these women. His solution, unfortunately, is to create an image of women that real, living, breathing women must assume. In order to create such an image, women's education must be vastly different from men's. In a profound passage, Rousseau adroitly placed women's subjectivity outside their bodies. He noted,

> Observe a little girl spending the day around her doll, constantly changing its clothes, dressing and undressing it hundreds and hundreds of times, continuously seeking new combinations of ornaments—well or ill-matched, it makes no difference. Her fingers lack adroitness, her taste is not yet formed, but already the inclination reveals itself. In this eternal occupation time flows without her thinking of it; the hours pass, and she knows nothing of it. She even forgets meals. She is hungrier for adornment than for food. But, you will say, she adorns her doll and not her person. Doubtless. She sees her doll and does not see herself. She can do nothing for herself. She is entirely in her doll, and she puts all her coquetry into it. She will not always leave it there. She waits for the moment when she will be her own doll. (1762/1979, p. 367)

If *subjectivity* is defined as possessing self-reflective thought in conjunction with individual agency and *objectivity* is defined as not having those qualities, then we may argue that Rousseau placed women's subjectivity outside their bodies—in a doll. By meshing subjectivity and objectivity within one entity, Rousseau began to set the stage for women's unique educational role as wife or mistress and mother or educator. Women's role as wife or mistress is to continue to provide the allure of the virtuous woman for her husband to desire. Women's role as mother or educator is to provide a proper moral foundation for her children. In essence, Rousseau created women's role to be both keeper and conduit of morality.

Wollstonecraft's response to Rousseau, *The Vindication of the Rights of Women* (1792/1975), began to address the merging of women's statuses as subjects and objects. Using the Enlightenment idea that all humans possess rationality, Wollstonecraft argued that women, as humans, possess rationality and therefore are subjects in their own right—not objects:

> I will allow that bodily strength seems to give man a natural superiority over woman; and this is the only solid basis on which the superiority of the sex can be built. But I still insist, that not only the virtue, but the knowledge of the two sexes should be the same in nature, if not in degree, and that women, considered not only as moral, but rational creatures, ought to endeavor to acquire human virtues (or perfections) by the same means as men, instead of being educated like a fanciful kind of half being—one of Rousseau's wild chimeras. (Wollstonecraft, 1792/1975, p. 39)

As subjects, Wollstonecraft contended, women should be granted full and equal rights to educational opportunities.

Almost 200 years later, Betty Friedan (1983) proffered a similar argument in *The Feminine Mystique*. Friedan related the popular 1950s image of women as caregivers of home and children to the decline in women's college enrollment during the era. Specifically, recalling the anti-intellectual message designed for women of the 1950s, Friedan noted,

> If an education geared to the growth of the human mind weakens feminin-ity, will an education geared to femininity weaken the growth of the mind? What is femininity, if it can be destroyed by an education which makes the mind grow, or induced by not letting the mind grow? (1983, p. 172)

The themes of rationality, caregiving, and education have often intersected in women's lives. It is this intersection that has cultivated a philosophy of education that rests on the assumption that it is our web of interconnectedness as living beings that must be communicated to future generations.

Ruddick (1987) described this orientation as "maternal thinking." Maternal thinking can be equated with the capacity for attentive love or the empathic, selfless interest in another individual that, Ruddick posited, maternal practice develops. Although acknowledging that maternal practice should not be solely the purview of women, Rud-dick noted that "in most cultures, throughout most of history, the re-sponsibility and work of child care has been borne largely by women" (1987, p. 242). This primarily female practice has led to the internal-ization of maternal thinking by which women "mother." Mothering, according to Ruddick, is defined by the "demands to protect children, to nurture their growth, and train them to behave in ways acceptable to the social group" (1987, p. 241).

Chodorow, in *The Reproduction of Mothering* (1978), examined the effect that "mothering" has on the development of boys' and girls' core gender identity. She examined the development of the differenti-ation the child makes between self and other (i.e., the primary care-giver). Since women are predominantly the primary caregivers, differ-entiation has a profoundly different impact on boys from that on girls. A boy's gender identity must be developed away from his mother; therefore, separateness and difference become primary components of his differentiation. However, a girl's gender identity can develop in relation to her mother; thus, girls grow up with a sense of continuity and similarity to their mothers. A boy's gender identity emphasizes separateness and otherness, and a girl's gender identity emphasizes connections and relations.

In her landmark study of moral development, *In a Different Voice* (1982), Gilligan outlined the different impact males' orientation toward separateness and women's orientation toward connections has on moral decision making. Whereas men generally express a justice perspective concerned with equality and rights, women generally express a care perspective concerned with attachment and relationships. According to Gilligan,

> these perspectives denote different ways of organizing the basic elements of moral judgment: self, others, and the relationship between them. With the shift in perspective from justice to care, the organizing dimension of relationship changes from inequality/equality to attachment/detachment, reorganizing thoughts, feelings and language so that words connoting relationship like "dependence" or "responsibility" or even moral terms such as "fairness" and "care" take on different meanings. (1982, p. 22)

For Gilligan, women generally utilize an ethic of care, whereas men generally employ an ethic of justice. Noddings (1992) translated this ethic of care into a framework for schooling in which four components—modeling, dialogue, practice, and confirmation—guide students toward becoming independent moral beings. In modeling, one shows how to care for others through our own relations with others. Dialogue not only allows us to discuss the modeling relationships but also provides a mechanism through which we learn about one another to foster further relationship growth. Practice provides the experiences for incorporating caring into one's daily habits. According to Noddings, "if we want people to approach moral life prepared to care, we need to provide opportunities for them to gain skills in care giving and . . . to develop the characteristic attitudes" (1992, p. 24). Finally, confirmation is the act of affirming and encouraging the best in others. However, it is only through having developed a relationship with another that the continuity necessary for confirmation can occur: "In education, what we reveal to a student about himself [or herself] as an ethical and intellectual being has the power to nurture the ethical ideal or to destroy it" (Noddings, 1988, p. 227).

CARING ABOUT CHILDREN, FAMILIES, AND SCHOOLS

Families and schools are inextricably linked as a result of the tremendous influences of the home environments on schooling (Bronfenbrenner, 1979; Chavin, 1993). In conceptualizing family life, the quilt is a useful metaphor for care. That is, different components, separate but connected, form a whole picture. Children come to school wrapped in intricately woven quilts that outline the sociocultural contexts in which they live. The quilts provide information about children that extends far beyond the grades, standardized test scores, or labels assigned to them. Rather, the quilts include the ethnic and racial traditions and customs each family values and practices. Some quilts include religious and spiritual squares that illustrate the beliefs that guide families and link them to their present and past.

The quilt metaphor suggests multiple levels of analysis of relationships between parts and the whole: the status that the child is assigned as a female or male in the family, relationships among siblings, and the degree of personal power and control afforded each child within the family. Family structure, the economic and educational levels of the parents, and various aspects of rural and urban or suburban realities are other examples. The point is that each component or patch in the quilt has its own meaning and value. However, it is only in the larger and more complex context of the multicolored, multitextured quilt that each part can be fully appreciated.

Each family is different. These differences have a critical impact on the nature of the home–school partnership because they inform the level of family functioning, beliefs about child rearing (specifically behavior management), parent–child interactions, practices regarding homework, and home and school follow-through. Children also differ in the financial or other resources (e.g., time, space, leisure activities) that they have available (Hanson & Carta, 1996). To gain access to this valuable information, it is necessary for teachers to establish trusting, caring, mutually supportive relationships with key family members. Parents and other family members (including the child) can serve as key sociocultural informants. They can provide the information needed to transform our traditional conceptualizations of family life from images based on monolithic middle-class forms to a greater appreciation of the diversity of families present in schools. This should encompass the range of ethnic, social class, and gender constructions present across families. We learn of the realities of single-parent families. We address the issues of co-parenting and joint custody in merged families. We learn of the delicate balance of caring for an older grandparent and child with a disability in the same household. We learn of histories of family violence, both in the home and in the neighborhood. We learn of the isolation associated with suburban living when children are bused and regular public transportation is limited to the traditional workday. We learn of long-term unemployment and the impact of working for a company that offers no leave benefits and no provision for sick-child care. We learn to view families humanistically and connectedly rather than distantly.

Professionals in the field of education often enter into relationships with parents from hierarchical positions of authority (Harry, 1995). This is based on a number of factors, including the specialized clinical and instructional training professionals receive, the organizational structure of the schools and classroom environments, and the nature of the student–teacher relationship. These factors have contributed to the belief that professionals are more knowledgeable and objective than parents on matters related to the development and education of their children. Parents, it is often normatively assumed, should be willing to learn from professionals and return home to teach their children. In this patriarchal view, parents are expected to take and implement professional advice (often without questions) and defer most educational decision making to school personnel (Turnbull & Turnbull, 1990). When parents willingly participate in this hierarchical paradigm, they are considered to be cooperative and positive. When parents do not participate, they are often termed *noncompliant* or, worse, *uncaring*.

This hierarchical view of the relationship of parents to school ignores the adult status of parents. This view also fails to recognize the wealth of knowledge and information parents bring to the educational process by virtue of the intimate and historical relationship they have with their child. Parents have a long history of participation with schools in educational planning (Paul & Simeonsson, 1993; Turnbull & Turnbull, 1990). Their active involvement has been associated with many positive outcomes (Chavin, 1993). These outcomes include improved parent–child communication, improvement in the attitude of the student toward the school, increases in school attendance, and decreases in school dropout rates. However, much of the parental participation in schools has been limited to middle-income families from majority backgrounds.

Demographers Norton and Glick (1986) predicted that more than 86% of school-age children will spend some portion of their lives in nontraditional or non-nuclear family settings. The majority of these children grow up in families headed by women who are employed outside of the home in semiskilled service jobs. Often these women's work schedules are not compatible with the school day. In addition, they do not have the benefits packages that permit them to miss work and attend school meetings or other school activities. This means that child care is a critical link to the home–school partnership. Parents need more than baby sitters, who merely watch the children until their return.

Families experiencing major stressors in their lives sometimes seek alternative home environments for their children. In some cases, the child welfare agency or court system may make temporary placements in other environments with family structures that are dissimilar to the child's. These arrangements often create a range of kinship relationships that have major implications for home–school partnerships.

Multigenerational parenting occurs in many families (Beck & Beck, 1989; Pearson, Hunter, Ensminger, & Kellan, 1990). This also has a major impact on home–school partnerships in that the nature of the parent–child relationship changes as a result of the chronological age and life experiences of the parents. A universal nuclear view of families fails to recognize the variant adult–child and child–child relationships in families that can be supportive to educational goals.

We must begin to include the perspectives of these sometimes short-term and transitional parents in our plans for home–school partnerships. This will include expanding our definition of *parents* and considering the range of relationships present in the home environment of the children we serve (Harry, Torguson, Katkavich, & Guerrerno, 1993).

SCHOOL REFORM: CARING ABOUT TEACHERS

The influence of gender on ethics and policy in schools requires a multilayered analysis that not only examines feminist and womanist constructions of care but also explores the silenced voices of both women and teachers within the history of education. Being a woman and being a teacher are historically intertwined, and the implications can be traced back to the policies and traditions assigned to the profession when large numbers of women first assumed the job of teaching. This section explores the role of teachers in schools and the role of women as teachers, followed by an analysis of school reform from a gender perspective. Of equal importance, though not directly addressed in this section, are the influences of race, class, and gender that also affect the way teachers are viewed within the male-dominated power structures found in education.

From Whence Have We Come?

By the middle of the 20th century, teaching had already shifted from being a male-dominated profession to one that had nearly 75% female representation (Rury, 1989). Today's teaching force presents a stable demographic picture, a profession still dominated by women (71%), first-generation college graduates (80%), and working-class backgrounds (60%) (National Center for Education Statistics, 1994). Differences include a larger number of teachers who are married and have children, as well as a growing percentage who go beyond the baccalaureate level to attain master's degrees (47.5%). This demographic shift, known as *feminization*, has resulted in a plethora of policies and practices that define the lifestyles of teachers and affect an occupation that is defined, legislated, and confined by males, yet is populated primarily by females. Early rules governing the behavior of teachers were abundant and were often designed to bar teachers from marrying, thus creating the myth of teachers as lonely spinsters. Indeed, the profession of teaching has become sentimentalized as women's work (Darling-Hammond, 1990). Over the years, female teachers have systematically addressed many inequities, achieving tremendous strides toward equal pay for teachers of both genders, rights for married teachers, and maternity leave.

Teaching as an occupation continues to be affected by economic and social conditions, which, in turn, affect the quantity and quality of teacher supply. Ironically, even though many women have viewed education as an emancipatory factor and many women activists initially were teachers (Carter, 1992), the current status of teachers has not kept up with social and cultural expectations for professionalism. Teachers are still paid low beginning wages, are offered a flat wage and promotion structure, suffer from low societal estimation, work in relatively unattractive job settings, and are relegated to low levels of autonomy (Darling-Hammond, 1990).

Historically, women have been expected to serve as authority figures in the classroom while serving as subordinate figures in the school. Women teachers have also been expected to serve in the "mothering" role in school, whereas, in some cases, they are forbidden from being mothers outside of school (Quantz, 1992). These contradictory images have further contributed to the treatment of teachers as nonpersons with little control over their own activities. In addition, discussions regarding professionalization have relegated teaching to a semiprofessional status, seemingly ignoring the anomaly that this lowered status is found in an occupation predominated by women.

Connections between teaching and mothering have also influenced teachers in the elementary school model of the one-teacher–one-classroom system, which isolates the teacher from other adults and is characterized by caring, altruistic, repetitive labor (Acker, 1995–1996). This caring role, in Acker's view, is linked to a maternal image that is idealized, essentialized, and somewhat ethnoculturally ignorant. Yet some have suggested that teachers' caring behaviors may themselves be tied to survival strategies linked to women's subordinate position in society (Hare-Mustin & Marecek, 1990).

Teachers and School Reform
The concept of teachers' caring has curiously emerged as a perceived oppositional factor in the school reform picture. Teachers have sometimes been viewed as reluctant to embrace reform, particularly when it translates into valuable time away from students. Yet a number of other considerations must be examined that may influence school re-

form. To better understand the context for teachers' responses to reform initiatives, it is helpful to examine the critical perspective of teaching that views teachers as workers susceptible to deskilling resulting from increasing losses of control and greater fragmentation (Tabakin & Densmore, 1986). This has been witnessed in the increase of "teacherproof" materials, prescriptive teaching strategies, and models that replace the art of teaching with a mechanistic model (i.e., test, teach, retest). Accompanying these trends is what Apple (1983) described as "intensification," which seeks to extract more labor in the same amount of time. Teachers feel the weight of this phenomenon as they witness larger class sizes, increased responsibilities for reporting and documentation, and more emphasis on achieving measurable results in their classrooms.

The trends outlined above can easily be interpreted as another form of disempowerment in which outsiders have busied themselves with examining problems within an occupation predominated by women, without considering the views and voices of those doing the job of teaching (Glazer, 1991). As further evidence for this perspective, there was a noticeable dearth of women's voices, as well as teachers' voices, at the President's National Summit in 1990. As Conner and Sharp noted, "So often it seems that we speak of schools as though they are separate and distinct from the people who live and work there" (1992, p. 337). Once again, a message has been sent to teachers and women that "education and teaching are minor professions that benefit from instrumental control by a [male] power elite of state and federal bureaucrats, private foundations, professional associations, and research universities" (Glazer, 1991, p. 330).

Almost predictably, the first wave of reform movements was characterized by centralized controls and higher standards. "Prevailing assumptions of the day included: 1) poor student outcomes were attributable to poor quality teachers and teaching methods, and 2) mandated top down initiatives, particularly from the state, could improve teacher quality" (Evans & Panacek-Howell, 1995, p. 31). Consequently, this wave resulted in stiffer entrance requirements for getting into teacher preparation programs and competency assessments for licensure (Lewis, 1989). Described as first-order changes (Cuban, 1989), the reforms were designed to improve efficiency, but they left the organizational structure (and all of its inherent weaknesses) intact.

Considered more drastic in measure, the second wave of reform was at least viewed as more attentive to teacher voice and empowerment (McDonald, 1988), acknowledging the fact that "progress and change depend on what over two million teachers, working in relative isolation, know and are able to do in their classrooms" (Kennedy,

1991, p. 1). Yet many of the ensuing reform initiatives, such as merit pay, the National Board for Professional Teaching Standards, and alternative certification programs that focused on promoting professionalization again provided a vehicle by which outsiders could control the lives of teachers. In fact, the discussions on professionalism and teaching have been noticeably unconnected to gender (Tabakin & Densmore, 1986). In her seminal review of gender and teachers' work, Acker (1995–1996) criticized these reforms for assuming that a male orientation attended more to concerns for professional status. For many teachers, promotion may involve leaving the classroom and the children, which may be seen as a compromise to the profession (Al-Khalifa, 1989). Most likely, the concept of disposable careers that can be put on hold or abandoned in response to child-rearing needs has also contributed to what Acker noted is a significant absence of career structure in the teaching profession.

School reform movements have shifted toward school-based management and participatory decision making. Although viewed by many as a step toward teacher empowerment, this reform movement has not resulted in any one clear paradigm representing such empowerment (Webster, 1994); nor has it resulted in a noticeable increase in opportunities for women in management (Al-Khalifa, 1989). In fact, published reports and articles on educational reform have clearly ignored issues of equity in the profession, particularly at the administrative level (Sadker, Sadker, & Klein, 1991).

A Deafening Silence at the Reform Table
In order to examine the dearth of teachers' voices (i.e., women's voices) at the center of school reform, Webster (1994) suggested that factors related to empowerment must be examined. Although teachers are entrusted with the safety and development of children, there are still vestiges of teacher disempowerment. Teachers' lack of privileges becomes very clear to those who return to school settings in research or other professional nonteaching capacities. For example, privileges such as freedom to leave campus during the day, access to telephones, office support systems and personnel, and access to supplies and copying services are very often denied to teachers. In one specific example, teachers at a school received a memorandum announcing that the front office was receiving too many personal telephone calls for faculty and that they should not leave a work telephone number for doctors' offices to return calls.

Teachers still function in systems that necessitate working in isolation for the majority of the day. This creates a marked impediment to collaborative decision making. Unlike many other professions, there are limited opportunities for teachers to communicate with other adults. Their conversations primarily are with students and can be characterized as informational or directive. In a reform movement that still only rhetorically invites teachers' participation, the authentic involvement of teachers as site-based decision makers without appropriate time for acculturation may be an unrealistic vision. It would appear that collaborative decision making and participatory management may be highly correlated with women's styles of leadership (Conner & Sharp, 1992; Glazer, 1991); however, the success of these new reform approaches as a means of empowering women and teachers is still undetermined. Although 96% of the teacher respondents in a 1989 survey supported school-based decision making (Metropolitan Life Insurance Co., 1989), many teachers still felt that the reality was falling short of the goal. In his study of high schools, Webster (1994) found that although school advisory groups were often mentioned as a vehicle for school improvement, the majority of teachers and school administrators interviewed still believed that the principal has the final voice, which certainly limits the perceived level of invited participation. At one school, a 1-year analysis of the topics addressed by the school improvement team indicated that parking privileges, faculty dress code, and gum and hat rules for students were the most commonly discussed topics. Far from the most pressing issues of school reform, this finding may have symbolized the feeling of disempowerment experienced by the teachers.

Further complicating the matter is that women seeking to attain positions of leadership may camouflage their preferred styles of leadership in deference to more male-oriented approaches viewed as compatible with the bureaucratic and hierarchical structures associated with school and district administration. At the school examined, teachers who were innovative and who had ideas that could potentially be valuable were often ignored within the school structure if they did not also play certain roles. For example, they were expected to be ready at any given short notice to spotlight a particular feature of the school for guests or visitors. They were expected to carry additional responsibilities as school leaders on committees. Yet when elected to the school advisory council, most teachers chose to remain quiet and somewhat subservient to the wishes of the council. In addition, they were seldom genuinely asked for their opinions about the possible impact of a reform initiative on their working lives.

Applying an Ethic of Care to Schooling

Creating a caring environment has been said to be attainable with only subtle shifts in instructional strategy as well as needing substantial structural change within the education system. Noddings (1995) noted that caring can be conveyed in many ways, through the individual, through the curriculum, and through the institution. By examining relations of care and interconnectedness within these levels, we can more solidly describe what caring looks like within an individual school.

Noblit, Rogers, and McCadden (1995) emphasized that a caring connection between the student and the teacher can be developed through talk, appropriate physical contact, and recognition of cultural and classroom rituals. A teacher's attempts to recognize, understand, and respect her students build caring, trusting relationships within the classroom. These relationships create opportunities for academic and interpersonal learning to occur. According to Noblit et al., students recognized those opportunities in classrooms in which they felt the teacher was willing to help them with their work without demeaning them for needing assistance, allowed them to reveal their lives through dialogue, and supported and nurtured them when doing so.

In her discussions with middle-school students, Bosworth (1995) also found that caring teachers were described by students as those who helped students with their work and their personal problems, valued their individuality, showed them respect, and checked for understanding of assignments or directions. According to Bosworth, "it was through personal actions and attitudes that teachers demonstrated they cared, both in and out of the classroom. Broadly interpreted, these data say that a 'caring teacher' is an interpreter or guide to learning" (1995, p. 692).

Tharp and Gallimore (1989) described caring teachers as guides to learning as well. Utilizing instructional conversation, the teacher locates a common ground of understanding shared by both the teacher and the students. Through the use of questions, the teacher then assists the students in assembling the thoughts needed to comprehend the subject matter. The dialogue between teacher and students allows the students to move from "other regulation to self-regulation and thence to internalization and full development" (Tharp & Gallimore, 1989, p. 23). In their meta-analysis of what helps students learn, Wang, Haertel, and Walberg (1994) noted that the most strongly rated characteristic was classroom management in which the teacher maintained active participation by all students in metacognitive processes in which comprehension monitoring was done by the student.

Caring as conveyed through the individual involves a reciprocal relationship of respect, trust, understanding, and recognition between the teacher and the student. In a classroom environment, this relationship might be demonstrated by attending to student needs by modeling respect and consideration and through meaningful dialogue between teacher and student. On a curricular level, caring can be conveyed by developing themes of caring within the curriculum, either through interdisciplinary teams or individually by addressing these themes throughout the year (Noddings, 1995). Teams could weave one particular issue through all subjects. Issues such as sexism, crime, poverty, or racism could be addressed in every subject. According to Noddings (1995), it is critical to shape the curriculum so that teachers are "talking with students about problems that are central to their lives, and guiding them toward greater sensitivity and competence across all the domains of care" (p. 679). Noblit et al. (1995) stressed the importance of culture and school rituals in conveying to students that they are in a caring environment. They advocate the incorporation of stories and symbols that represent caring and connection in classrooms. Together, students and teachers can construct a meaningful curriculum with rituals that observe and celebrate relationships, moral responsibility, continuity, and constancy.

Noblit (1993) described one teacher-structured classroom in which each student was responsible for the collective good through a variety of daily tasks. Children understood the importance of the tasks and rotated responsibilities. Instruction was structured to take advantage of the collectivity of the classroom through both cooperative and competitive learning arrangements. The daily operation of the classroom rested on the reciprocal relationship of care between the teacher and the students.

It is on an institutional level that the most profound calls for restructuring occur. A caring institutional environment would be one in which the student–teacher ratio is low; students remain with the same teacher for more than 1 year (e.g., elementary school) or teachers teach more than one subject to the same group of students (e.g., middle or high school); modes of instruction and assessment allow for a caring, reciprocal relationship to develop between student and teacher; and the structure of school management is such that a caring, reciprocal relationship is allowed to develop between administrators and staff (Noblit, 1993; Noblit et al., 1995; Noddings, 1988, 1993; Tharp & Gallimore, 1989). Noddings argued,

> The odd notion that establishing national goals will make teachers work harder and more effectively, thereby making students work harder and more effectively, is part of a long, long tradition that assumes an autonomous agent can logically plot a course of action and, through personal competence, somehow carry it out, even if others are intimately involved. Such agents ... forget that the human objects of their project must also be autonomous. (1996, p. 196)

In essence, operating within an ethic of care requires relations of reciprocity. Such reciprocal relations necessitate an understanding of power and its movement among individuals. One type of reciprocal interaction is conversation. Conversation as method emphasizes an emergent conception of relationship wherein participants are jointly motivated to realize the good in the relationship. Each of the three functions provides a mechanism through which the development of relationships across power differentials can be achieved. The first function places an emphasis on the development of "we" relations such that all voices are included fairly. Thompson and Gitlin (1995) contrasted this to dialogue in which "each individual voice is honored . . . much in the way that votes are honored in a democracy" (p. 143). The second function involves a process in which participants experiment with shifts in the relationship to foster growth but use no preordained procedure to achieve that growth. According to Thompson and Gitlin, participants "feel their way, learning how to respond to one another *by* responding to one another" (p. 144). The third function, utilizing the emphasis on positive growth within the "we" relationship, begins to reevaluate expectations of appropriateness. Participants reevaluate accepted norms of appropriateness in connection to their relationship. Understanding that these norms may rest on preconceived ideas of personal and group power, participants begin to move toward the development of "new values and new perceptions of relevance or appropriateness" (Thompson & Gitlin, 1995, p. 144).

Conversation as method may allow those in institutional settings in which both differing and equal power relationships exist not only to understand the continuous flow of power but also to develop true reciprocal, caring relationships. Such an endeavor would also provide the modeling behavior that Noddings (1993) noted is pivotal for the development of an "ethic of care" in schools.

CONCLUSIONS

This chapter has sought to be a collaborative endeavor involving diverse feminist perspectives on caring in schools and the school-based decision-making process. We have attempted to move beyond gender awareness to an awareness of the interlocking factors that affect the female experience in schools. The factors are multiple and complex. However, feminist and womanist principles of leadership and decision making can contribute to the development of caring policies and practices.

REFERENCES

Acker, S. (1995–1996). Gender and teachers' work. *Review of Research in Education, 21*, 99–162.

Al-Khalifa, E. (1989). Management by halves: Women teachers and school management. In H. DeLyon & W. Migniuolo (Eds.), *Women teachers: Issues and experiences* (pp. 83–96). Philadelphia: Open University Press.

Apple, M. (1983). Work, gender, and teaching. *Teachers College Record, 84,* 612–628.

Beck, R.W., & Beck, S.H. (1989). The incidence of extended households among middle-aged black and white women. *Journal of Family Issues, 10,* 147–168.

Bosworth, K. (1995). Caring for others and being cared for. *Phi Delta Kappan, 76*(9), 686–693.

Bronfenbrenner, U. (1979). *The ecology of human development.* Cambridge, MA: Harvard University Press.

Cannon, K. (1988). *Black womanist ethics.* Atlanta, GA: Scholars Press.

Carter, P. (1992). Becoming the "New Women": The equal rights campaigns of New York City schoolteachers, 1900–1920. In R. Altenbaugh (Ed.), *The teacher's voice: A social history of teaching in twentieth-century America* (pp. 40–58). Bristol, PA: Falmer Press.

Chavin, N. (1993). *Families and schools in a pluralistic society.* Albany: State University of New York Press.

Chodorow, N. (1978). *The reproduction of mothering: Psychoanalysis and the sociology of gender.* Berkeley: University of California Press.

Collins, P.H. (1990). *Black feminist thought.* New York: Routledge.

Conner, N.L., & Sharp, W.L. (1992). Restructuring schools: Will there be a place for women? *Clearing House, 65*(6), 337–339.

Cornelius, J. (1991). *When I can read my title clear.* Columbia: University of South Carolina Press.

Cuban, L. (1989). The district superintendent and the restructuring of schools: A realistic appraisal. In T.J. Sergiovanni & J. Moore (Eds.), *Schooling for tomorrow: Directing reforms to issues that count* (pp. 251–272). Boston: Allyn & Bacon.

Darling-Hammond, L. (1990). Teachers and teaching: Signs of a changing profession. In W.R. Houston, M. Haberman, & J. Sikula (Eds.), *Handbook of research on teacher education* (pp. 267–290). New York: Macmillan.

Donovan, J. (1987). *Feminist theory.* New York: Ungar.

Evans, D., & Panacek-Howell, L. (1995). Restructuring education: National reform in regular education. In J.L. Paul, H. Rosselli, & D. Evans (Eds.), *Integrating school restructuring and special education reform* (pp. 30–42). Fort Worth, TX: Harcourt Brace College Publishers.

Fordham, S. (1993). "Those loud black girls": (Black) women, silence, and gender "passing" in the academy. *Anthropology and Education Quarterly, 24*(1), 3–32.

Fordham, S., & Ogbu, J. (1986). Black students' school success: Coping with the "burden of 'acting white.'" *Urban Review, 18*(3), 176–206.

Friedan, B. (1983). *The feminine mystique* (2nd ed.). New York: Dell.

Gaines, E.J. (1993). *A lesson before dying.* New York: Vintage Books.

Gilligan, C. (1982). *In a different voice: Psychological theory and women's development.* Cambridge, MA: Harvard University Press.

Glazer, J. (1991). Feminism and professionalism in teaching and educational administration. *Educational Administration Quarterly, 27,* 321–342.

Hanson, M., & Carta, J. (1996). Addressing the challenges of families with multiple risk. *Exceptional Children, 62,* 321–342.

Hare-Mustin, R., & Marecek, J. (1990). On making a difference. In R. Hare-Mustin & J. Marecek (Eds.), *Making a difference: Psychology and the construction of gender* (pp. 1–21). New Haven, CT: Yale University Press.

Harry, B. (1995). Communication versus compliance: African-American parents' involvement in special education. *Exceptional Children, 61,* 364–377.

Harry, B., Torguson, C., Katkavich, J., & Guerrerno, M. (1993). Crossing social class and cultural barriers in working with families: Implications for teacher training. *Teaching Exceptional Children, 26,* 48–52.

Henry, A. (1995). Growing up black, female, and working class: A teacher's narrative. *Anthropology and Education Quarterly, 26*(3), 279–305.

Henry, M. (1996). *Parent–school collaboration: Feminist organizational structures and school leadership.* Albany: State University of New York Press.

Hogeland, L.M. (1994). Fear of feminism. *Ms, 5*(3), 18–21.

Joseph, G.I. (1995). Black feminist pedagogy and schooling in capitalist white America. In B. Guy-Sheftall (Ed.), *Words of fire: An anthology of African American feminist thought* (pp. 462–471). New York: New Press.

Kennedy, M.M. (1991). *An agenda for research on teacher learning.* East Lansing, MI: National Center for Research on Teacher Learning.

Lerner, G. (1973). *Black women in white America.* New York: Vintage Books.

Lewis, A. (1989). *Restructuring America's schools.* Arlington, VA: American Association of School Administrators.

McDonald, J.P. (1988). The emergence of the teacher's voice: Implications for the new reform. *Teachers College Record, 89,* 471–486.

Metropolitan Life Insurance Co. (1989). *The Metropolitan Life survey of the American teacher, 1989: Preparing schools for change.* New York: Author.

National Center for Education Statistics. (1994). *Digest of education statistics: 1994.* Washington, DC: U.S. Government Printing Office.

Neverdon-Morton, C. (1989). *Afro-American women of the South and the advancement of the race 1895–1925.* Knoxville: University of Tennessee Press.

Noblit, G.W. (1993). Power and caring. *American Educational Research Journal, 30,* 23–38.

Noblit, G.W., Rogers, D.L., & McCadden, B.M. (1995). In the meantime: The possibilities of caring. *Phi Delta Kappan, 76,* 680–685.

Noddings, N. (1988). An ethic of caring and its implications for instructional arrangements. *American Journal of Education, 96*(2), 215–230.

Noddings, N. (1992). The gender issue. *Educational Leadership, 49*(4), 65–70.

Noddings, N. (1993). Excellence as a guide to educational conversation. *Teachers College Record, 94,* 730–743.

Noddings, N. (1995). Teaching themes of caring. *Phi Delta Kappan, 76,* 675–679.

Noddings, N. (1996). *Philosophy of education.* Boulder, CO: Westview Press.

Norton, A.J., & Glick, P.C. (1986). One parent families: A social and economic profile. *Family Relations, 35,* 9–17.

Paul, J., & Simeonsson, R. (1993). *Children with special needs: Family, culture, and society.* Fort Worth, TX: Harcourt Brace College Publishers.

Pearson, J.L., Hunter, A., Ensminger, M.E., & Kellan, S.G. (1990). Black grandmothers in multigenerational households: Diversity in family structure and parenting involvement in the Woodlawn community. *Child Development, 61,* 434–442.

Quantz, R. (1992). The complex visions of female teachers and the failure of unionization in the 1930s: An oral history. In R. Altenbaugh (Ed.), *The teacher's voice: A social history of teaching in twentieth century America* (pp. 139–156). London: Falmer Press.

Richardson, M. (1987). *Maria Stewart: America's first black woman political writer.* Bloomington: Indiana University Press.

Rousseau, J.J. (1979). *Emile, or on education* (A. Bloom, ed. & trans.). New York: Basic Books. (Original work published 1762)

Ruddick, S. (1987). Remarks on the sexual politics of reason. In E.F. Kittay & D.T. Meyers (Eds.), *Women and moral theory* (pp. 237–260). Totowa, NJ: Rowman & Littlefield.

Rury, J.L. (1989). Who became teachers?: The social characteristics of teachers in American history. In D. Warren (Ed.), *American teachers: Histories of a profession at work* (pp. 9–48). New York: Macmillan.

Sadker, M., Sadker, D., & Klein, S. (1991). The issue of gender in elementary and secondary education. In G. Grant (Ed.), *Review of research in education* (pp. 269–334). Washington, DC: American Educational Research Association.

Tabakin, G., & Densmore, K. (1986). Teacher professionalism and gender analysis. *Teachers College Record, 88*(2), 257–279.

Tharp, R.G., & Gallimore, R. (1989). Rousing schools to life. *American Educator, 13,* 20–25, 46–52.

Thompson, A., & Gitlin, A. (1995). Creating spaces for reconstructing knowledge in feminist pedagogy. *Educational Theory, 45,* 125–150.

Turnbull, A., & Turnbull, R. (1990). *Families, professionals, and exceptionality: A special partnership* (2nd ed.). Columbus, OH: Charles E. Merrill.

Walker, A. (1983). *In search of our mothers' gardens: Womanist prose.* New York: Harcourt Brace Jovanovich.

Wang, M.C., Haertel, G.D., & Walberg, H.J. (1994). What helps students learn? *Educational Leadership, 51*(4), 74–79.

Webster, W. (1994). Teacher empowerment in a time of great change. In D. Walling (Ed.), *Teachers as leaders: Perspectives on the professional development of teachers* (pp. 103–118). Bloomington, IN: Phi Delta Kappa Educational Foundation.

West, C. (1993). *Race matters.* Boston: Beacon Press.

Wollstonecraft, M. (1975). *A vindication of the rights of woman.* New York: Penguin. (Original work published 1792)

III

THE SOCIAL PSYCHOLOGY AND CULTURE OF SCHOOLS

Ethical Dilemmas

The three chapters in this section describe the social, cultural, political, and psychological ecology in which school-based decision-making committees function. They emphasize the subtle and not-so-subtle forces that affect the policy-making process. The authors of these chapters were observers at the Collegium, which brought together principals and members of school-based decision-making committees to help the Collaborative Research Group on Policy and Ethics (CRGPE) sharpen its insight into how to approach planning a curriculum in ethical policy making to assist these committees. The purpose of the observations was to help the CRGPE contextualize its understanding of the content and process of ethics instruction in local school culture.

In Chapter 7, Dempsey and McCadden, educational sociologists, address power issues and the construction of meaning in school policy. Focusing on schools as moral communities, they argue that an ethic of care and relationship should be the basis for ethical policy making in schools. They point out the value of conflict as evidence of different voices participating in the process of authentic change.

In Chapter 8, Greenbaum, Martinez, and Baber, anthropologists, discuss the culture of school-based policy issues. They focus their analysis on cultural diversity in the classroom and raise questions about the goals of education in the current environment. The cultural diversity agenda, they argue, must be addressed in school-based decision-making committees in order for the interests of all students to be respected.

Morse, Berger, and Osnes, in Chapter 9, examine the policy-making process from the perspective of group dynamics. They propose a framework for examining the role of group dynamics in the decision-making process that includes six concepts, and they examine the ethical implications of each concept.

7

Power and the Construction of Meaning in School Policy

Van O. Dempsey and Brian M. McCadden

One of the benefits of the school reform and restructuring movement in the 1990s has been the reconsideration of the nature and location of decision making about schooling. One of the main thrusts of this reconsideration has been to attempt to flatten educational decision making by moving more of the power to determine the course of educational policy to local contexts, with increasing emphasis on individual schools as the location for decision making.

This move is suspicious in its success on two counts. First, there is little evidence that the increased attention to local context as the basis for educational decision making has altered substantially the rational, top-down, bureaucratic model of decision making that was one of the targets of the 1980s critique of educational organizations. Most educational policy making still emanates from state legislatures and other offices of state government, and local decision making is left to devices created at the state level. Second, though there is some evidence that classroom teachers do participate in decision making in schools in ways that they did not before, there is little evidence that the nature of the decision-making process is considerably more democratic, participatory, flat (i.e., organizationally), or inclusive of stakeholders outside of traditional decision making by participants with professional status in schools and school districts. This is particularly problematic if it means that we have yet to seriously include the perspectives of a diverse set of community interests, including meaningful parent participation, as well as the needs, interests, and voices of students. In particular, we call attention to the interests and concerns of special populations who are all too often excluded from participation in deci-sion making outside of the specific area of special education and who provide the motivating concerns for this book.

This, at least in part, is due to the fact that far too much of the tra-ditional forms and context of educational decision making have gone unchallenged. Rational models still prevail—even in flatter, more par-ticipatory organizations—and many decisions are dominated by politi-cal agendas and fiscal concerns. Communities of decision makers in schools are still questionably exclusive, particularly in relation to par-ents, students, and other nonprofessional stakeholders. In addition, the moral nature of these communities and their decision making re-main incidental in far too many cases.

In this chapter, we offer a critique of traditional decision-making structures in education as well as the site-based strategies that are re-placing them in some locations. We also examine the nature of com-munity that those strategies presume. This includes a critique of those whom these forms privilege and empower, as well as those whom they disempower, marginalize, and silence. We also propose a different form of community for decision making, one that has a more inclusive nature and an extended sense of participation, perspective, and con-text. We argue in this proposal for a sense of school as a moral com-munity primarily nested in the relationships between those more tra-ditionally involved in decision making and those traditionally marginalized and excluded.

As part of these critiques, we include scenarios developed from the Collegium on Policy and Ethics of the Collaborative Research Group on Policy and Ethics. We reconstruct narratives from the par-ticipants' reactions to the teaching cases presented that reflect more traditional forms of school-based community out of which decision making might occur as well as alternative possibilities. We assert, through the cases, the limiting and marginalizing aspects of more tra-ditional forms of school decision making and examine how, if we look at schools as moral communities, more inclusive and relational con-texts for decision making might be created.

MAKING CASES OUT OF SCHOOL-BASED ADVISORY GROUPS

The Collegium organized by the Collaborative Research Group on Policy and Ethics and held in May 1995 was developed around two teaching cases (see Chapter 10 Appendix). One concerned differential treatment of general and special education students by school person-nel; the other concerned the defunding of a successful but maverick program for African American male students. These served as the medium through which all the participants—university faculty, school administrators, teachers, and parents—explored the ethical dimensions of site-based decision making.

The structure of the Collegium was to have members of various Tampa-area site-based groups come together to read and discuss the two cases, led by a university-based case facilitator. Two different groups of local citizens participated in the Collegium, with each being made up of three parents, three teachers, three administrators, and two school advisory committee chairs. One case was explored in a morning session, which was followed by a lecture-discussion of an ethical approach to decision making. (For a detailed discussion of the Collegium, see Chapter 11 and the Appendix.) Our (i.e., the present authors') initial objective, as educational sociologists, was to consider the cases and analyze to what extent the site-based teams employed the ethical frameworks in their decision making as well as what, if any, organizational issues arose from the discussions.

What we discovered in the course of listening to the interactions unfolding in front of us was the extent to which the participants employed neither of the ethical models as they were presented in their discussions and decision making. They exploited both rule-based and context-based morality throughout their discussions but articulated neither in the intellectual way they had been presented by the ethicists or in the technical language of the experts. Both were expressed in terms of the experiences of their everyday lives as parents, teachers, administrators, and school advisory team chairs.

The unanticipated consequence (see Giddens, 1979) of the Collegium for us was a deeper understanding of the real strength of such teams—the ability to construct a moral community out of the histories and contexts they brought with them to the setting. For example, the conversations of the different teams included, on the one hand, language such as relationship, communication, needs of differing people, empathy advocacy, sharing, and family; and, on the other hand, equality, authority, power, truth, and "doing right." That is, site-based teams, if they focus on the process of building shared histories rather than just on the outcome of making decisions, can provide a mechanism through which parents, teachers, and administrators can come to understand the constraints under which others work, the languages they use concerning education, and the logic that governs how each sees education.

People resorted to these multiple forms of ethics and morality while participating in meaning construction in the scenarios they were creating through the Collegium. Although intending no offense to the ethicists involved in the Collegium or to its organizers, we saw the ethical framework at best as only a small part of and possibly as irrelevant to this unintended outcome of shared meaning construction. As each day progressed, participants talked more and more past the models and the academicians and toward each other. The afternoon cases, which were explored after the ethics discussions, were, in our estimation, much more engaged and probing than the morning cases. This was a result of a move away from participants' self-identified roles within the teams and a move toward connecting with the other participants beyond the act of decision making. Because the participants had had icebreakers, the morning sessions, between-session breaks, and a lunch break in which to become familiar with each other, they were more willing in the afternoon to hear each other out, empathize, and collaborate. This attitude was further cultivated by discussing hypothetical decisions rather than real, immediate, and tension-filled decisions, which facilitated an openness that may not so easily occur in the latter situations.

During informal discussions of participants' home site-based teams, two general models emerged regarding team meeting styles and agendas. One type of team met in an ad hoc fashion when decisions needed to be made; the other type of team met on-site weekly, biweekly, or monthly, regardless of whether action items were on the agenda. Members of the latter type of team reported a stronger sense of cohesiveness, inclusion, voice, and satisfaction than the former type. This supports the idea that site-based advisory teams may function most effectively when they construct a shared identity that lies outside of the decision-making context for which they are organized. In this way, they can move past being simply site-based advisory teams in which no true power to generate decisions resides and become participatory site-based advisory teams (S. Goldman, personal communication, May 15, 1996) in which real decision-making power is shared by all members.

Following is a case of our own culled from our observations of the Collegium sessions that illustrates the participatory potential of site-based advisory teams. Neither case is a representation of one single event or of a single day; instead, they are pieces of the process of the 2 days that led to the formation of connections and community among participants. As with all such cases, the actions and sequencing of events are slightly fictionalized to create dramatic tension (Van Maanen, 1988).

SILENCED VOICES AWAKENING

In the morning session dealing with a special education case, the participants interacted in accord with their roles in the group as parent, teacher, or administrator. Principals in the cases, referred to as "he" by both males and females, talked about not being supported by higher administrative agents, the need for strategic planning, and the need to "serve all their children." Teachers, referred to abstractly as "she" by both males and females, talked about such things as the status of portable classrooms, or trailers, high student-to-teacher ratios, and the isolation of their jobs. Parents were oddly quiet, periodically referring to how much they cared about their children and not knowing what to do. As the facilitator probed participants' responses, attacks started forming on these roles; for example, teachers and parents attacked the principal for "trying to do it all himself," parents were attacked for "not coming to scheduled meetings," and teachers were attacked for being unable to teach special education students.

What was happening was not an exploration of decision-making processes but a letting off of steam—a venting of anger at the roles that each participant played in school and at the constraints that each role placed on the others. As we were to find out later, this letting off of steam was a necessary step in the formation of a cohesiveness, a sense of community among the participants. Members of the group were beginning to put forth the "dangerous memories" (Bellah, Madsen, Sullivan, Swidler, & Tipton, 1985, p. 153) that were reflected in the groups' discussions and began to draw voice and power through their articulation. Teachers argued among themselves about general versus special education needs, whereas parents voiced cautions about children without disabilities being neglected in favor of attention being focused on mainstreamed children with disabilities. The tide began to turn when a teacher questioned why the principal in the case was being "so autocratic" by not letting anyone else in on the decision-making process. This elicited an explanation from a principal in the group: "He might be new to the job. . . . [Because the principals] don't have a union, he might get canned if he opens his mouth too much or makes the wrong decision." The teacher paused, and the process of seeing the other as a person (see Noddings, 1984) was begun. That is, the participants began to break outside of a defense of their school roles and started to see the situation through the others' eyes, to empathize with others in their roles in the group. They also began to see past the particularity of any decision to be made and looked into the collective responsibility for the whole and for the relationships on which it was (or was being) built.

In the afternoon session, after an ethics discussion and a lunch in which informal conversation was emphasized, the role playing was continued. During the second case, the parents in the group, especially an African American woman, found their voices and began to assert themselves. The case revolved around a program designed to encourage African American male students to stay in school. Because the program was shut down in the case, the African American parent was moved to say, "Just goes to show how our men are an endangered species." The topic of racial marginalization was finally broached in a mixed-race Southern group. The Caucasian middle-class professionals in the group were visibly uncomfortable, as portrayed in their body language and more frequent silence, and they tried to steer the conversation back toward more comfortable issues of student rights, school politics, and support services.

The African American mother would not cede the floor. She talked of how difficult it is for an African American male to survive and how African American parents in her school care for their children but cannot always make it to parent–teacher conferences or to school events, owing to work or lack of transportation. "It might look like the parents don't care, but they do," she added. The Caucasian participants slowly began to listen to her and nod in understanding as she continued to talk of the constraints on African American parents— how they are perceived as "not having good parenting skills" and as "not wanting to participate in school." They began to understand that because membership in groups like site-based teams required either a vote-in or participation through volunteering, the onus was on the team to find ways to attract diverse representatives so that all school community voices would be heard. They came to realize, by listening to this woman's voice, that 9:30 A.M. meetings were not conducive to full participation. Gone was the overly technical, organizational language that was part of the early sessions of the Collegium. This language worked as a form of power and control in that it excluded those who did not possess it from the conversation. As the language shifted, so did power; and people who previously did not participate began participating.

Nothing monumental came of the discussion; no new policies were set, and no epiphanies occurred. But the Caucasian participants listened to an African American parent and actually seemed to try to hear what she had to say. They also began to see the power of the language they used and, by the end of the Collegium, were breaking away from that language. Conversely, the African American parent found the courage to speak within the accepting community that was beginning to develop, albeit slowly, among the participants. It is small steps such as these on which are built new forms of relation and connection. These relations and connections can change the nature of school-based decision making and ultimately policies about schools.

PARTICIPATORY DECISION MAKING

What this case demonstrates is the process by which site-based advisory groups can democratize schooling: They hold the potential to make decisions regarding how we organize our schools and how we formulate school policy. Through democratization, we can move from a traditional hierarchical model to a more egalitarian, participatory model. By spending time constructing a collective school culture with its own shared history, rituals, myths, and meaning (see McCadden, 1996; Noblit & Dempsey, 1996) rather than focusing only on objectified policy decisions, such a group can construct the framework for empathetic positioning and connection that necessarily moves them from antagonistic role players to supportive role sharers. It is our premise that such a move will take us closer to the ideal of site-based governance as a sharing of power and authority rather than as a shifting of accountability. It was not the ethics discussions per se that facilitated the fostering of community among the participants but the simple act of bringing them together and allowing them to talk with and listen to each other in a decision-making context. It is that ethic of care (Noddings, 1984) and relationship that can be the foundation for ethical policy making in schools.

One of the major problems with traditional forms of decision making about schools is that they have a long history of technical rationality (Tyack & Hansot, 1982) and do not typically attend to context and local meaning-making. This loyalty to the rational can result in bad decisions at best and marginalization, demoralization, and devaluing of people at worst. This "worst" comes in particular when we look at decisions in schools that seem as if someone has won, when in fact children have lost. Many times, as was discovered in the Collegium discussion, when students lose, adults do not necessarily lose; so, rational arguments about what happens to students fail to apply. The question, "How could they do this to students?" as one participant asked, is irrelevant because the decision-making process was not about students initially. Even when some in the group making a decision win, it is a losing proposition for all.

One of our concerns with the underlying assumptions of typical forms of site-based decision making is the adherence to the technical and the rational. When we act on rationally based assumptions, we "unacknowledge" concerns in order to have clarity (Collins, 1982). When we create clarity (or the appearance of clarity), we eliminate or suppress part of the context out of which people create meaning. Those whose (potential) contributions are eliminated or suppressed lose voice and power. Ambiguity, uncertainty, and the conflict they sometimes produce, though violating our rational assumptions, are many times evidence that multiple voices and perspectives are being heard and are also signs that we have a richer context out of which to make our meanings and, in a micropolitical sense, to construct decisions about schooling (Ball, 1987). Silencing this contextual noise to protect rationality and, in many cases, to protect a sense of ethics tied to traditional power relationships masks marginalization for those out of power as well as those in power (Tronto, 1993). This silencing robs us of resources out of which we might construct alternative stories and meanings. But, given our allegiance to the rational, we fail to celebrate these voices and include them. The problem that rationally based models of decision making present is that they lead some people— usually those on the margins of participation—to believe that what is important to them is not really important to the success of the broader world around them. What is left, given this problem, is a process in which these marginalized members cannot, or care not to, participate. Much of this contextual conflict and tension, ordinarily treated as a barrier to decision making and organizational success, not only is part of the process but also is likely the seed of authentic change (Fullan, 1993).

We have come to believe through our rationally based assumptions that in a decision-making process we always get conclusions. Conclusions are about clarity and finality; if we apply means, we are supposed to get ends. But we have no real claim to ends, conclusions, or even means. We go where we go in decision-making processes—no matter how rational we think they are—and we do not always get the conclusions we want, if we get conclusions at all. When we take ends or conclusions for granted and fail to get them, we see the process of decision making as having failed. We take resolution and consensus, like we do ends and conclusions, for granted. Sometimes they are not opportunities we can have. But they do not have to be taken as failures, and there are ways of interpreting them in which they need not be taken as such.

CREATING A MORAL COMMUNITY FOR SCHOOLS

As we have become more and more pawns of the organizational and distal agents of schooling, we have veered further away from the senses of community that at one time seemed to be more a part of schooling, particularly for historically marginalized groups (Delpit, 1995; Noblit & Dempsey, 1996; Walker, 1996). Although we cannot retreat into history and probably have no need or desire to, there are some aspects of community in and for schools that we want to have today. This path would take us more away from the rational, technical, and organizational or bureaucratic mind-sets of schools that have come to dominate decision making and more toward relationship building, community building, and collectiveness that would undergird an alternative frame. Some of the direction for this path comes from the Collegium, with the ethical position more grounded in context and relationship offering the idea of "inversion of values" (Fasching, 1995, pp. 10–11) that allows us or compels us to make choices or act in ways we otherwise would find unacceptable and to value that which would otherwise have limited or no value. Such inversions, as suggested at the Collegium, are most clearly recognizable in metaphors such as those used in war; but they also surface in the metaphors that reflect schools as bureaucracies, as political institutions, and as formal organizations. Such metaphorical contexts ironically provide us with a difficult double-entendre. Decisions in these contexts provide us with *sites* as locations as the word is typically used. They also provide us with *sights* as targets as they may come to be used in the more problematic atmosphere of political and organizational decisions regarding resources, as discussed in the Collegium. In such cases in which site equals target, the injustices that occur are taken for granted. Only who is "in sight" is left to question; in most cases, this becomes those on the margin with limited or no power.

MacIntyre (1981) suggested that our reclamation of the moral is to be found in our reinvestment in narratives and stories out of which our meanings and moralities are constructed. He argued that this connection has been lost through our concession to bureaucratic assumptions and organization and the distancing and discontinuity that comes with them. Our morality can be found once again, as presented previously, in the stories and narratives out of which we come to define who we are and that which is important to us in the sense of our virtues. Of the place of narrative in the moral constructions of our lives, MacIntyre stated,

> I am not only accountable, I am one who can always ask others for an account, who can put others to the question. I am a part of their story, as they are a part of mine. The narrative of any one life is part of an interlocking set of narratives. (1981, p. 218)

He later contended,

> For the story of my life is always embedded in the story of those communities from which I derive my identity. I am born with a past; and to try to cut myself off from that past, in the individualist mode, is to deform my present relationships. The possession of an historical identity and the possession of a social identity coincide. (1981, p. 221)

This discussion of the importance of life narratives in the broader sense brings meaning to the importance of narrative to the more immediate and local sense that arises in the kinds of concerns expressed in the Collegium. Participants bring stories, histories, and meanings to the context in which they will be asked to make decisions regarding the nature, qualities, and frameworks of local school policy. It is in these stories and narratives that any potential meanings, decisions, and possibilities for schooling will be constructed.

Tronto (1993) offered support in this reclamation of narrative as the basis for creating communities for school-based policy. Her thesis was based on the question of how we treat the "morally distant other" (Tronto, 1993, p. 13) who we think reflects our own beliefs. This morally distant other presents two problems that must be considered for negotiating moral boundaries in our lives. First, the very distance from the other creates a rationale for having no motivation to act out of concern. Second, if we do act, our assumptions that the distant other is like us could cause us to fail to attend to the fact that we cannot apply our morality to others in a different moral context.

These two concerns expressed by Tronto (1993) give us all the more reason to embrace the collective and shared meanings brought to a context such as that suggested by the Collegium. Connection and communication in a collective sense help us to become sensitive to and understand others distant from ourselves, and probably even those who are taken for granted to be close. We also begin to resolve problems presented by her first concern stated previously because, in the very acts of connecting and sharing collectively, we close the distance that creates the failure to understand in the first place. But this is not without its own set of concerns:

> I suggest that the questions interesting about moral life parallel the distribution of political power in our society. We are more interested in the moral views of those who are in positions of relatively more power than in the moral views of those who are relatively less powerful. Contemporary moral development theory reinforces the notion that those who occupy the centers of power are moral. As a result, the strategic dilemma of the outsiders . . . shapes the discussion of the moral views of the privileged and the less privileged. (Tronto, 1993, p. 61)

Tronto (1993) responded to her own concern in a way that holds promise for the kind of community we are advocating here. Morality, according to Tronto, arises out of the close and connected and is impossible in the distant and disconnected. "Morality is always contextual and historicized, even when it claims to be universal" (Tronto, 1993, p. 62). This collective sense and the connection that comes with it help us to begin to acknowledge the value of those who would have been positioned as distant and, therefore, devalued. Again she cautioned as a precursor to this acknowledging and valuing that an alternative but undesirable strategy is to "bring in" those on the margin by forcing them to embrace the values and the "clearly delineated path" (Tronto, 1993, p. 86) of the powerful, thus maintaining the status quo and the norms of those in power. Tronto also asserts that though they are on the margins of such contexts, those with a morally different voice do have a strategic location in arsenals of the outsiders and that this location gives them the ability to speak truth to power as they come to have a voice and to be heard. Such noise, tension, and voice have no place in the rational world discussed previously in this chapter; but they are, as we have suggested, essential to the community-defining moments that occur as distance is closed. As outsiders come to participate in redefining the inside, the powerful center is dismantled and renegotiated, and new meanings and values are collected and shared. The moral and the political become part of the same context, as Tronto would have it, and, within that context, new forms of participation and community are constructed. An ethic of care is critical to that construction, as Tronto argued: "Care is a way of framing political issues that makes their impact, and concern with human lives, direct and immediate. Within the care framework, political issues can make sense and connect to each other. Under these conditions, political involvement increases dramatically" (1993, p. 177).

Tronto, consistent with our thesis, saw the outsiders coming in and the possibility for a community as real. Also, consistent with our thesis, context takes primacy over abstract constructs, relationships begin to become valued over formal organizations and rational mindsets, and decisions about people cannot as easily be separated from the lives of people. Not only do we come to value the life narratives we have, but we also can share them and build communities with them.

CONCLUSIONS

What do we begin to value when we look at schools as moral communities? How does what we celebrate and value change the nature of how and what we decide for schools and for school communities? One possibility, playing off a suggestion by Sergiovanni (1994), is that the metaphors we use in the construction of meaning and narratives begin to change. Sergiovanni made his own call for schools as communities and stressed the importance of a "we" orientation over an "I" orientation. He also argued for a shift from a *Gesellschaft* (literally, *society*) orientation, marked by distance, formality, and order, to a *Gemeinschaft* (literally, *community*) orientation, characterized by relationship, interdependence, and mutual obligation. To apply his critique with a suggestion from the Collegium, site-based management is still management, and the managing of human beings may not be the image that captures what school advisory committees or any other school-based group should do. Terms such as *management* can be limiting and marginalizing without intention but nonetheless damaging in their consequences. *Site-based* implies a location of ownership, for another example. If one believes, as some parents and others in the nonprofessional community do, that schools belong to somebody else (e.g., the state, the district, the professionals), one is less likely to claim the power to alter or influence them. If schools are seen as communities, though, a different sense might be created. We take Sergiovanni's steps further—out into the community at large—whereas he concentrated more on the professional community within a school; but we applaud his emphasis on the sharing that comes with connection and relationship. We extend his emphasis on communities of kinship and place to include all the potential members of a school community, including those embraced in the Collegium context presented previously.

To get beyond the constraints and limits that have come to define participation in school-based decision making prevalent today, we offer a set of questions that provide the basis for the critique presented in this chapter and that might be useful to those who are examining their own assumptions about membership in school communities and participants in school decision making and policy making. Although these questions do not exhaust the possibilities for critique and reflection, we hope that they can highlight what might limit participation and silence valuable voices.

- What are the structures, beliefs, and meanings imposed on decision making by people in positions of perceived power?
- What is the source of the imposition, and who benefits?
- What is taken for granted in decision making?
- What is not being said in the decision-making group, and who is not speaking?
- How do people move into liminal space, helping them to become critics of their own cultural contexts out of which they make decisions (Bowers, 1984)?
- What do participants see as the boundary of the site in question?
- Who is considered to be in the site and who is not?
- What are the margins of the site—psychologically, relationally, geographically, politically, and sociologically?
- Whom, given these boundaries, are decisions made for?
- Is power diffused or centralized in decision making, and how?

- Does the shift in power change who participates in decision making (i.e., both the membership and the nature of their participation), or does it simply move to a new location within the same organization (i.e., holding membership and the nature of participation intact)?
- Are people previously on the margins gaining and using their voices and becoming valued members of the community?
- How does what we value change the nature of how and what we decide?
- What are the unanticipated consequences of decisions made?

These questions do not exhaust the possibilities for the construction of moral communities in schools, but they do expose the problems that come with power orientations and the marginalizing effects of traditional forms of decision making for and in schools.

REFERENCES

Ball, S.J. (1987). *The micropolitics of the school: Towards a theory of school organization.* New York: Methuen & Co.

Bellah, R.N., Madsen, R., Sullivan, W.M., Swidler, A., & Tipton, S.M. (1985). *Habits of the heart: Individualism and commitment in American life.* Berkeley: University of California Press.

Bowers, C.A. (1984). *The promise of theory: Education and the politics of cultural change.* New York: Longman.

Collins, R. (1982). *Sociological insight: An introduction to non-obvious sociology.* New York: Oxford University Press.

Delpit, L. (1995). *Other people's children: Cultural conflicts in the classroom.* New York: New Press.

Fasching, D.J. (1995, May). *Ethics without choice: Reflections on story, character and compassion.* Paper presented at the Collegium on Policy and Ethics, University of South Florida, Tampa.

Fullan, M. (1993). *Change forces: Probing the depths of educational reform.* Philadelphia: Falmer Press.

Giddens, A. (1979). *Central problems in social education theory: Action, structure, and contradiction in social analysis.* New York: Macmillan.

MacIntyre, A. (1981). *After virtue: A study in moral theory.* South Bend, IN: University of Notre Dame Press.

McCadden, B. (1996). Becoming a student: The moral significance of entry into kindergarten. *Educational Foundations, 10*(2), 23–36.

Noblit, G., & Dempsey, V. (1996). *The social construction of virtue: The moral life of schools.* Albany: State University of New York Press.

Noddings, N. (1984). *Caring: A feminine approach to ethics and moral education.* Berkeley: University of California Press.

Sergiovanni, T.J. (1994). Changing the metaphor changes the school. *Educational Administration Quarterly, 30*(2), 214–226.

Tronto, J. (1993). *Moral boundaries: A political argument for an ethic of care.* New York: Routledge.

Tyack, D., & Hansot, E. (1982). *Managers of virtue: Public school leadership in America 1820–1980.* New York: Basic Books.

Van Maanen, J. (1988). *Tales of the field: On writing ethnography.* Chicago: University of Chicago Press.

Walker, E.V.S. (1996). Interpersonal caring in the "good" segregated schooling of African-American children. In D. Eaker-Rich & J. Van Galen (Eds.), *Caring in an unjust world: Negotiating borders and barriers in schools* (pp. 129–146). Albany: State University of New York Press.

8

Culture and
School-Based Policy Issues

Susan Greenbaum,
Yolanda G. Martinez, and M. Yvette Baber

Cultural differences in the classroom pose a serious ethical dilemma for the development of policies that are both effective and humane. Should teachers enculturate all students into what is regarded as mainstream values and behaviors, so that they will have an equal chance to succeed in an increasingly competitive work force? Or should the values and beliefs of differing ethnic communities be respected in order to ensure that children from these communities are not alienated from their families or made to feel inferior? How much should teachers be required to understand about the histories and cultures of students of diverse backgrounds? How should such knowledge be incorporated into pedagogy, standards of behavior, and treatment of students?

This chapter is designed, not to answer these questions, but rather to illuminate the implications of them. Within the general theme of the Collegium on ethical decision making, the goals are to examine the broad concerns that are raised when the students in classrooms come from cultural and linguistic backgrounds that are different from those of administrators and most of the teachers. This chapter takes a critical look at current literature and policy issues related to ethical and democratic decision making in local schools. A key focus is the threat to minority interests in a zero-sum contest for shrinking resources.

Bilingual programs, enrichment programs, and special education programs compete with the basics. Another focus is on how issues of class, culture, and access to information affect parent involvement in schools. Specific issues include the unique problems of non–English-speaking parents; effects of busing on inner-city African American parents; and difficulties facing parents of children with disabilities. The concluding section discusses possibilities for strengthening school–community linkages and examines strategies in networks of parents, neighbors, grass-roots organizations, and business interests all building toward a social ecology of consciousness.

Culture is an elusive and confusing concept for most people that is often confounded with class or notions of race. Stated values that favor pluralism are set against a historical backdrop of intolerance and domination. The educational failures of ethnic minorities reinforce their disadvantaged position in the economy and society, which in turn may serve to reinforce general attitudes about their inherent inability to participate and contribute on equal terms. Schools have a critical responsibility to break this cycle and make it possible for democratic ideals of pluralism and fairness to be achieved. However, to realize that potential, it is necessary to understand more clearly the nature of cultural differences and the manner in which policies regarding diversity in the classroom both reflect and affect the larger society.

Culture is defined in two ways: first as the distinctive behavioral, linguistic, or other characteristics associated with ethnicity; and second as a set of unwritten rules, customs, and values that govern behavior within particular institutions or work settings. Cultural differences among students, between teachers and students, and between parents and school personnel represent a major source of misunderstanding and conflict affecting various aspects of schooling in the United States. Tensions result from communication failures, unconscious antipathies, and explicit conflicts spilling over from the larger society.

Prejudice and discrimination are included under the rubric of cultural concerns and extend to stereotypes and misconceptions about students with disabilities. The manner in which images of difference are framed—whether differences are racial, cultural, or behavioral—follows essentially the same pattern and reflects general values about acceptance and inclusion.

Those underlying values, the implicit assumptions of teachers, principals, and other actors who collectively form the culture of schools, are the object of the second usage of the term. As in any small group with a common purpose, it is possible to analyze the structure of roles and relationships, the flows of power and resources, customs, and the beliefs individuals share about the work they are doing. Decision making is powerfully shaped by such forces in ways that are often not easily apparent.

Both applications of the concept of *culture* are relevant to the ethical concerns raised in this volume. Culture is the incubator of ethical values; children bring theirs from home, as do teachers and administrators. More generally, the cultural systems of institutions both shape and reflect the underlying values of those who run them. For those who wield decision-making authority, belief in the rectitude of a particular position can justify overruling the beliefs of others. We are all enculturated to know what is right and wrong, but not all cultures emphasize the same mores. Universalistic notions of ethical behavior are confounded by culture or at least are impeded by its manifestations (Greenbaum, 1992). With regard to hospitality to strangers, cultural differences tag boundaries of exclusion; they identify the in and out groups. Pluralism in U.S. society and schools demands an examination of customs of exclusion. Such an inquiry requires consideration of cultural factors in the policies that guide the enterprise of education.

The two teaching cases presented in Chapter 10, "Are All Children Treated the Same?" (Case 1) and "Future Leaders" (Case 2), form the basis for an exploration of cultural issues emerging out of the Collegium. Case 1 provides a clear example of the power hierarchy in our schools that determines the parameters of "normality." Also illustrated is the policy battle being fought across the nation to provide children with special needs a learning environment that does not set them apart from the rest of the school population. Multilayered issues in this case reveal the complexities of decision making at the school level.

Case 2 exemplifies a range of issues affecting programs designed to aid minority students. Decision making in this case is also reflective of structural issues in administration and parent committees. Discussion of this case in the Collegium revealed some of the hidden problems in confronting the issue of race, as well as the complexities surrounding innovation in institutional cultures with unwritten rules about the conduct of outsiders.

A CULTURAL HISTORY OF
EDUCATIONAL POLICY IN THE UNITED STATES

Schools as we know them today developed during the 19th century with some basic guiding principles. According to Stout (1993), some of these principles were that schools were to serve all children equally; were to be supported by public tax dollars rather than by private means; were to teach citizenship in a value-rich, though secular, environment; and were to be as inexpensive as possible, governed by citizens in decentralized jurisdictions, and given very broad and significant responsibilities. Public education has been enshrined as the primary vehicle for developing an informed electorate and offering all citizens the opportunity to acquire necessary skills and achieve fully their human potential, regardless of the station into which they are born.

From the outset to the present, schools have confronted the need to provide public education for children from an ethnically and linguistically diverse population, forming a major ongoing policy challenge. Conceiving a solution first requires framing the problem, and, for much of our history, the problem has been viewed as correcting and conforming the deficient and nonstandard knowledge and beliefs of different groups. The educational system was also intended to play a major role in preparing an appropriate work force—skilled, compliant, and socialized into the dominant value system. Implementation overtly recognized and covertly reinforced the deep divisions between Caucasians and non-Caucasians in the economic scheme of labor and opportunity.

Unequal education of African Americans reflects the first and most obvious departure from the principles outlined by Stout (1993). For much of the 19th century, laws in southern states forbade the education of slaves, and free people of color were everywhere limited in their access to schools. The corrective activities of the Freedmen's Bureau in the aftermath of emancipation were short-lived and replaced by officially sanctioned segregation.

In many parts of the United States, especially in the rural South, primary schooling for African Americans was greatly curtailed, and high school was often not available (Franklin, 1994; Gill, 1991). These conditions prevailed well into the second half of the 20th century. It was not until the 1970s that many districts in the South yielded to the mandates of the *Brown v. Board of Education* (1954) decision. The massive court-ordered busing that was to remedy this intransigence has not been notably successful in erasing the disparities in educational attainment, and the social costs of this policy have been disproportionately borne by African American children and their families (Dempsey & Noblit, 1993). Many within the African American community view the trade-offs in loss of neighborhood schools and the burdensome distances between home and school not to have been worth the gains in improved learning facilities (Mwalimu, 1996). For a vast number of African American children, the facilities they attend in distressed and underfunded urban districts remain inferior to those in largely Caucasian suburbs located beyond district boundaries. According to Dempsey and Noblit (1996),

> School desegregation was a classic case of educational policy accompanied by ignorance. . . . We were ignorant of the taken-for-granted assumptions made by whites and the courts [that] African Americans would benefit from merely associating with the dominant culture. . . . We were equally ignorant of the culture of African Americans. In fact, school desegregation in many ways ignored the possibility that there could be desirable elements in African American culture. . . . [W]e seemed to ignore that there was an African American culture at all. (pp. 115–116)

For African Americans, the legacy of segregation, the inadequacy of efforts at desegregation, and the ongoing problems of inequality form the most daunting and urgent set of problems related to educational differences among groups in our society (Berry & Asamen, 1989).

The plight of Native American children represents another glaring contradiction in the mission of universal education for U.S. children. Native American education was initially intertwined with goals of military pacification and forced assimilation of tribes (Coleman, 1993). In the 1870s, with the end of warfare in the West, a policy of removing Native American children to distant boarding schools was conceived as an effective means of ensuring peace on the reservations while extirpating the tribal identities of subsequent generations. Quasi-penal institutions that invoked punitive treatment in the name of Judeo-Christian values, the boarding schools were highly ineffective in providing useful skills or knowledge, although the practice of holding children hostage in faraway places did contribute to the desired effect of eliminating armed resistance by their parents (Prucha, 1979). The goal of assimilation, however, was not attained in the vast majority of cases (Dumont & Wax, 1969). Most graduates returned home to their reservations ill equipped to compete in the non–Native American world, where even those who had marketable skills confronted discrimination.

The boarding school system remained in place until the 1930s and was not fully dismantled until the 1970s. The alternative of reservation schools fared little better; paternalistic systems that punished children for their traditional values still predominated (Redhorse, Shattuck, & Hoffman, 1981). In 1975, the Indian Self-Determination and Education Assistance Act (PL 93-638) established a new policy designed to promote tribal control of schools, although efforts to implement this act were slow to materialize and have suffered in the 1980s and 1990s from severe cuts in Native American allocations.

Federal policies affecting reservation schools, which are administered by the Bureau of Indian Affairs, have little relevance for the larger issues of educational policy in the United States. This is a marginal and somewhat exotic domain affecting even a minority of Native American children. As a result of relocation policies in the 1940s and 1950s, more than half of Native Americans now live off of reservations; their children attend public schools in the localities where they live. Districts with relatively large numbers of Native American children do receive some additional federal funding, and, in the 1970s, legislation was passed that encouraged special Native American programming and parent involvement in these schools. For the most part, however, Native American children in public schools represent a small minority population with special needs that go largely unmet, and one with unique cultural traditions that receive little attention, except around Thanksgiving.

Children of immigrants represent another special population whose needs and limitations have posed an ongoing policy challenge in U.S. schools. In the early part of the 20th century, the concentration of European immigrants in urban areas focused attention on the new residents, stimulating nativist ideologies and assimilationist practices (Banks, 1981; Mindel, Habenstein, & Wright, 1988; Steinberg, 1989). War against some of the mother countries of some of these immigrants aroused public suspicion and strengthened xenophobia against immigrants and their children. Public school policy reflected national pressures on the immigrants to assimilate as quickly as possible to reduce the distrust of immigrants caused by World Wars I and II. Schools promoted Americanization, demanding blind loyalty to the nation. Cultural pluralism was regarded as seditious and un-American. Schools embraced Anglo conformity goals, as did the rest of the dominant institutions, supporting the "melting pot" concept of U.S. society.

Although the melting of diverse ethnic cultures did not proceed nearly as smoothly as envisioned and the first generation continued to suffer from lack of educational and economic success, the second generation of European immigrants did find success in the post–World War II economy. Several factors converged in this outcome: the rise of labor unions, which secured a living wage for blue-collar workers; the GI Bill, which promoted higher education and home ownership; and the robustness of postwar economic conditions. Moreover, the fact that these groups were Caucasian should not be underestimated. Jim Crow segregation in education, housing, jobs, and unions helped reserve these benefits and heightened tensions between Caucasian ethnic groups and African Americans. Immigration policies in the first half of the 20th century also played a significant role. Demand for unskilled labor in the early years of the 20th century was the impetus for the vast influx of immigrants; but, by the end of World War I, the tide had turned, and severe restrictions against new immigration were imposed in the 1920s. This interruption enabled clear generational effects, in that new waves of immigrants were stanched, and the children of the early waves were thus more easily assimilated. Asian immigration was halted altogether, and the law specifically forbade non-Caucasians from entering the United States as prospective citizens (Takaki, 1994). These restrictions had varied success; large numbers of Mexicans were able to penetrate the long border in the Southwest and follow the railroad north into such cities as Denver, Kansas City, and Chicago (Barrera, 1979; Becerra, 1988). Puerto Ricans were exempted from the restrictions because of the unique status of Puerto Rico. Large numbers migrated from Puerto Rico to New York City during this period. The Cuban revolution in 1959 gave rise to a massive exodus of Cubans, mainly into Miami (Trueba & Delgado-Gaitan, 1988).

In the mid-1960s, immigration laws were liberalized, resulting in growing numbers of immigrants from Asia and Latin America. Children of new immigrants, who did not speak English and whose cultural traditions were in many cases very different from those of the host society, posed a distinct challenge to educational systems. Their arrival coincided with a policy environment very unlike that confronted by turn-of-the-century European immigrants. It was no longer considered appropriate to punish differences or to require children of immigrants to overcome language barriers without assistance. Following passage of the Bilingual Education Act of 1965 (PL 89-10), various approaches were implemented in an effort to speed the process of adjustment for non–English-speaking students. In addition, there was broader recognition of the need for teachers to understand cultural issues affecting the learning process of children from diverse backgrounds. During the 1970s and 1980s, there were serious efforts by policy makers to create a nurturing, multicultural environment in classrooms, based on the assumption that tolerance of cultural diversity and mutual understanding and respect would be beneficial to all groups.

In the 1990s, however, there has been a hardening reaction against immigrant students, reflected in efforts to dismantle bilingual education. Descendants of those who immigrated at the turn of the 20th century are often among the most vocal opponents of special programs for new immigrants, based in part on their own historical experiences (Portes & Rumbaut, 1990). Fiscal constraints and a conservative backlash against multiculturalism have created a harsh new policy environment in which children who do not speak English risk losing more than the programs that have helped them succeed in school. Their very access to public education, especially for those who are undocumented, is increasingly in jeopardy.

Migrant farmworkers, approximately 80% of whom are from Mexico, confront multiple challenges in obtaining an education for their children. Both parents and children have limited ability to speak English, and most are not cognizant of how the educational system works in the United States (Martinez, 1994). Most farmworkers assume a deferential position toward teachers and the decisions teachers make about their children's education. This pattern reflects cultural traditions in a region of the world where teachers are viewed as authority figures who are presumed to know what is best for students. In most Latin American countries, it is not customary for people, especially those who are poor and powerless, to question the authority of teachers. Parental participation in school activities is further complicated by the seasonal nature of their work. Migrant farmworkers are dependent on seasonal crops for their economic survival. This means that when crops are in season, farmworkers are out in the fields from daybreak to sundown, with very little time for anything else. It also means that they may have to move on to the next crop before the completion of the school year. Lack of sensitivity and understanding of these issues prompts many teachers to regard migrant parents as uninterested in their children's education. As a result, teachers themselves may take an uninterested stance toward migrant children.

Children with disabilities are another category with distinct needs and problems in the schools (Skrtic, 1991). In an effort to alleviate some of the problems faced by disadvantaged children in the schooling process, the federal government has enacted a series of policies to ensure equal access to education by diverse students. The school policy environment of the 1960s and 1970s reflects a marked awareness of the needs of children with disabilities, many of whom previously had been neglected. Some of the most important laws enacted during this period were those that protected the rights of minority children and children with disabilities.

The deficit model applied to children with disabilities has a long tradition, just as the cultural deprivation model that has been applied to culturally and linguistically diverse students. Although the Education for All Handicapped Children Act of 1975 (PL 94-142) provided for the education of all children with disabilities in the mainstream of U.S. schools, cases still remain of students who continue to be segregated and stereotyped. Case 1 (see Appendix in Chapter 10) illustrates the complexity of this problem. The sentiments of parents and professionals about pull-out programs for children with disabilities, which separate them from their peers without disabilities, are mixed, as indicated in the inclusion debate (see Chapter 2).

The inclusion policy in special education, though supported by many parents and special education professionals, also has the potential of creating resistance among general education teachers if it is not implemented with adequate support for teachers and the students with disabilities. The full impact of the inclusion policy will require thoughtful deliberation that takes into account the needs, values, and perspectives of all students and their families, as well as those of general and special education professionals. An ethic of hospitality must respect the interests of the familiar as well as the stranger in building a learning community. The complexity of this deliberative process is discussed in Chapter 5.

CULTURAL DIFFERENCES IN THE CLASSROOM

The foregoing extended sketch reflects the external forces affecting educational policy with regard to diversity in schools. Within classrooms, however, are found the practical problems and daily concerns that confront teachers attempting to do their jobs. Diversity in the classroom poses challenges on various levels, challenges that sometimes encourage teachers to resist policies that are welcoming.

With few exceptions, teachers reflect values that are both middle-class and mainstream. As individuals, their own experiences and beliefs are shaped by acculturation, a process so thorough and unconscious that it rarely provokes questioning or even awareness. A first step in understanding cultural differences is an inquiry into one's own cultural conditioning, a willingness to adopt a critical perspective on the values and attitudes that flow therefrom. For a profession whose explicit charge is to educate the young to be competent and responsible adults, it may be an unbridgeable contradiction to question basic tenets of what it means to be competent and responsible. But this is precisely what is needed. The second step is an examination of stereotypes and misconceptions about other groups that are also part of the enculturation process. The most debilitating aspect of interactions between teachers and children arises from negative preconceived ideas about limits on achievement. If children from different ethnic backgrounds or children with disabilities are relegated to a lower category of expectations, their performance is likely to match those expectations and preconceptions are brought full circle. The roots of this cycle of discouragement can be found in the literature on cultural differences in the classroom, which long stressed a deficit model. This model attempted to account simultaneously for the problems of non–English-speaking children and native ethnic groups who were poor. The assumptions were that these children enter the classroom with deficiencies arising from a culturally impoverished family background. This explanation drew from the work of Lewis (1966), who espoused a notion of the culture of poverty. According to this view, poor families reflect a lack of effective integration in major social institutions, inability to defer gratification or focus on long-range goals, mother-centered families, and a home environment that does not provide sufficient stimulation for normal development in language or social and cognitive skills. This theory drew heavy criticism from anthropologists (e.g., Leacock, 1971; Valentine, 1968), who argued that Lewis applied the concept of a culture of poverty inappropriately and overlooked the heterogeneity of language, ethnicity, and culture that exists among people with low incomes and that Lewis generally underestimated the resilience of poor children in the face of difficult external circumstances. Despite these objections, this model had considerable influence in shaping such policies as Head Start. The deficit model also provided a comfortably simplified perspective on why poor children did not do well in the classroom, as well as relief from institutional responsibility for those failures.

More recent analyses of minority educational problems have rejected the deficit model in favor of explanations that shift the focus of attention to structural forces in the labor market and larger society (i.e., the secondary cultural discontinuity approach) or that examine the nature of interactions between students and teachers as an example of bilateral cultural misunderstanding (i.e., the cultural differences approach). Proponents of the secondary cultural discontinuity model argue that schools reproduce the hierarchical social relations of the economy in the schools, thereby replicating the division of labor, channeling different groups into different economic slots, and reflecting the differential rewards typically available to poor and minority students. This is an ecological approach that focuses on the adaptation of different groups to the larger society. Ogbu (1982, 1992) argued that the main reason for the low school achievement of many minority students is that those students (and their parents and peers) are convinced that school success will not really help them to overcome either racism or the limited opportunities they correctly perceive in the labor market. Gibson (1987) observed that many minority students resist the forces of unwanted assimilation and the implicit devaluation of their own cultural traditions. In this conception of the problem, students are responding rationally to a series of genuine dilemmas that often result in opting out or in otherwise acting in opposition to the goals of schools and teachers. It is not that they lack the ability to perform; rather, they are unable to perceive the benefits or are unwilling to make the trade-offs required of them to succeed. This model also has critics, who point out that it does not account for those many instances in which minority students do succeed (Erickson, 1987); nor does it take into account the fact that African Americans and many other ethnic communities reflect a long tradition of valuing education and struggling mightily to gain access to it.

The cultural differences model stresses misunderstandings over malignancy; the notion of a deficit has been replaced by the value-neutral observation that cultures vary in ways that can have substantial effects. In this conception of the problem, differences in communication and learning styles of minority students present obstacles to effective interaction with nonminority teachers. Black English is an example of this type of problem. Although linguists have determined that Black English is a legitimate dialect, reflecting consistent and logical variations of standard English not unlike other regional dialects, many teachers have regarded the use of Black English as indicative of ignorance and stupidity. This attitude of teachers conditions inappropriate negative assessments of intelligence and can damage the self-esteem of children who would otherwise be capable of doing well in school.

Nonverbal differences among cultures are a less obvious source of difficulties in the classroom. Norms regarding eye contact during interaction vary considerably. In many Native American communities, for example, it is considered impolite and confrontational to look another person directly in the eyes while speaking, especially if the other person is a stranger or is older. When Native American children avert their eyes in response to a teacher's question, however, a non–Native American teacher may regard that behavior as indicating avoidance or hostility (Greenbaum & Greenbaum, 1983).

Differences in learning style that are part of a cultural pattern can also produce conflict and problems for minority children whose enculturation has taught them one way to learn but who are expected to perform differently in the classroom. Individualistic and competitive tasks are incompatible with the learning styles of many cultural systems in which individuals are embedded in extended families or tribal groups. Learning occurs through observation and participation in collective efforts rather than through individualized instruction and testing. Correction or punishment for incorrect behavior is intensely humiliating for students with cooperatively shaped learning styles. Even when successful, an individual required to perform in front of the group may be viewed as bragging and egotistical by peers from the same ethnic group, a social consequence most children prefer to avoid.

Cultural discrepancies between minority students and nonminority teachers represent a type of interference (Philips, 1983) in the learning process that is both needless and apart from the motives of either teachers or learners. Both may be intent on succeeding at the task of gaining skills and comprehension, but they cannot successfully communicate or effectively structure the process in order to make it work. Frustrations over the inability to make progress, however, may well engender or intensify hostilities in the relationship between students and teachers.

The preceding models represent efforts to understand the reasons for disparities in achievement by minority students. Although proponents of each tend to level criticisms against the other, both contribute some measure of understanding (i.e., cultural interference and the larger political economy may both be implicated in these outcomes), and neither answers all the questions that are raised. What is clear, however, is the need for educational policy and practice to incorporate these perspectives to a much greater extent, especially in the training of classroom teachers. Too many educators at all levels in the process continue to regard students who are from different cultural backgrounds from themselves as deficient.

DECISION MAKING: A CASE STUDY ANALYSIS

Decision making, according to Parker (1995), must satisfy three conditions:

1. There need to be two or more alternative courses of action, but only one must be taken.
2. The process by which the decision is made determines the best alternative.
3. The alternative chosen must accomplish a designated purpose.

In addition to the three conditions that must be met, Parker added that there are five components to decision making:

1. Data
2. A predicting system based on experiences, previous circumstances, and intuition
3. A value system
4. Decision criteria
5. Recommendations to be made

Decision making under simple circumstances can become a very complex phenomenon. The process is further complicated when the decisions to be made affect individuals who do not belong to the sociocultural group making the decision (e.g., ethnic, racial) or to groups that have been marginalized (e.g., poor, individuals with disabilities). Ethical decision making thus plays a very important role when the decision affects the lives of minority children and children with disabilities.

The rest of this section takes a closer look at one of the cases presented in the ethics collegium, "Are All Children Treated the Same?" from Parker's (1995) perspective. (For extended discussions of these cases, see Chapters 10 and 11.) Although the case study was not written to illustrate the areas addressed by Parker (1995), the information presented is examined to determine how Parker's conditions and components fit this particular case and what recommendations can be made from the outcomes.

Are All Children Treated the Same?

This case is a good example of the power hierarchy in schools that is used to determine who fits the parameters of "normality" and, as a result, who will receive an equal allocation of the resources. Although the case was not written to illustrate the decision-making process outlined previously, it serves as a good example. In Case 1, it is apparent that there is more than one alternative course of action dividing the special education students into smaller groups and moving the students to classrooms in the school building). In this case, although the final decision was delayed, the process by which the best alternative was chosen appears to be the most desirable. In other words, advocacy from the teachers and relatives of the students helped decision makers act, although not as fast as those involved would have preferred. Clearly, the alternative chosen (i.e., moving special education students to the school building) accomplished the designated purpose; that is, it provided students in special education classrooms an educational environment equal to that provided to students in general education. Furthermore, the ethical issue involved social equity.

There were overwhelming data indicating that the special education classroom was overcrowded beyond the limits established by the law. (The classroom had 20 students when the law allowed a maximum of 10–12 students.) Follow-up requests were made to the school administration to help solve the problem, and there was legal action from one of the student's grandmothers to bring about change. The predicting system indicated that the decision regarding this situation had been made on an established sociohistorical pattern of marginalization and segregation of students with special needs. The predicting system is also based on a value system.

Until the latter part of the 20th century, attitudes toward, and legislation for, individuals with disabilities rested on a view that these individuals were less worthy and less deserving. This led to placement of these students in isolated and run-down classrooms, often in basements or portable classrooms. An overarching assumption in Case 1 is that children with disabilities are a burden on society. The alternative ethic, reflected in federal legislation enacted since the late 1960s, is that all students have the right to receive equitable educational programs in environments free of stigma. The problem in this case was eventually addressed, but not without a great deal of advocacy. Unfortunately, though federal law protects the right of children with disabilities to a free and appropriate public education, deep differences continue to exist in the hospitality of school cultures. These differences are reflected in the ethical deliberations surrounding school policy making.

Future Leaders

The dilemma presented in "Future Leaders," Case 2, is one present in our educational system as a whole: allocation of shrinking resources. As in Case 1, there is more than one alternative course of action to be taken:

- Continue to fund the Future Leaders Club
- Eliminate funding altogether
- Provide partial funding, encouraging participants to find matching resources in the community
- Seek community alternatives for full funding of the program

As with many decisions, the choice to eliminate the club was an arbitrary decision made by individuals physically and, perhaps, philosophically removed from the circumstances of the children and families participating in the program. Moreover, the organizer of the club was an outsider in relation to the professional subculture of the school. His success may have been viewed as a threat that exposed the teachers' inability to achieve results with children regarded as deficient and difficult, and his lack of understanding of the implicit rules of protocol in winning support for an optional program may have handicapped the effort to retain the club.

Data indicated that involvement in the club resulted in improved grades and enhanced self-esteem. In addition, the parents showed greater enthusiasm for participating in school activities of their children. These outcomes should have been persuasive concerning the merit of the club; but, for unstated and largely inexplicable reasons, decision makers resisted this evidence. Again, the ability of an outsider to encourage participation among a segment of parents regarded as apathetic and problematic may have presented unwelcome evidence that the school had not been doing enough to encourage this behavior and thus that it was not the parents but the institution that had failed.

CONCLUSIONS

One of the major questions that concerns education scholars is to what extent are schools in charge of bringing about societal changes through education? This question might be rephrased as, "Have societal changes taken place that have not been reflected in the educational system?" As we approach the end of the 20th century, we see a growing political trend favoring cultural assimilation of ethnically and linguistically different students. Paralleling this trend is a major policy debate on the extent to which children with disabilities should be fully included in the educational mainstream. Minorities face the alternative of assimilation or marginalization (Schensul & Carroll, 1990); children with disabilities face marginalization. (The complexities of the inclusion policy debate are discussed in Chapter 2.)

Public pressure on the government to reduce services to undocumented immigrants and even to those with legal status is rapidly spreading across the nation. Biculturalism is no longer viewed as an asset but rather is seen as an impediment to full integration. Legislators concerned with education increasingly view biculturalism as a "handicap" preventing individuals from becoming fully Americanized and contributing to the fragmentation of U.S. society. This retrenchment and rejection of the approaches of multicultural and bilingual education, however, are not likely to produce better educational outcomes. Indeed, the problems that presently exist can be regarded as the direct legacy of policies that for more than a century have attempted to coerce children to give up their cultures and have punished those whose success is burdened by poverty and an inability to operate easily within the framework of monocultural classrooms. The divide that exists between rich and poor, Caucasians and non-Caucasians, natives and immigrants, can only be expected to widen. This may be true of those with and those without disabilities, as well.

Countering these trends are some of the provisions of Goals 2000: Educate America Act of 1994 (PL 103-227), particularly those that mandate more participatory structures that include parents and other important stakeholders. To the extent that these reforms lead to broader and more inclusive forms of policy making, diversity in the classroom can lead to more responsive and culturally appropriate pedagogy and curriculum. Parents of children who are culturally different or who have disabilities frequently have been unable to advocate effectively for the needs of their children and are too often regarded as incapable of participating effectively or as unwilling to do so. When teachers send home notes or written notices that go unheeded, they often assume that parents are apathetic without considering the possibility that the recipients may not be able to read. New approaches to parent involvement that do not rely on conventional forms of outreach or offensive beliefs that the poor do not care about their children are urgently needed if we are to realize the potential that the Goals 2000 plan holds for creating truly democratic and pluralistic approaches to schooling in our society.

There is an amalgam of clues to the diverse nature of the population. One need only drive down the streets of any large city to see the signs of diversity (e.g., ethnic restaurants, stores); one need only switch on the radio and turn the dial to find Spanish-speaking stations serving the Hispanic community and, in larger cities, other radio stations serving the needs of other language-minority communities. The same can be said for television. Assimilating this diversity of language, culture, ethnicity, and ability in a school requires thoughtful and caring leadership in the deliberative forums, such as school-based decision-making committees, where the policies governing the allocation of resources and establishing the social architecture of schooling are developed. An ethic of hospitality to strangers appears to have the potential of binding all students into a learning community.

REFERENCES

Banks, J.A. (1981). *Multiethnic education: Theory and practice.* Boston: Allyn & Bacon.

Barrera, M. (1979). *Race and class in the Southwest: A theory of racial inequality.* New York: Praeger.

Becerra, R.M. (1988). The Mexican American family. In C. Mindel, R. Habenstein, & R. Wright (Eds.), *Ethnic families in America: Patterns and variations* (pp. 141–159). New York: Elsevier.

Berry, G., & Asamen, J. (Eds.). (1989). *Black students: Psychosocial issues and academic achievement.* Beverly Hills, CA: Sage Publications.

Bilingual Education Act of 1965, PL 89-10, 20 U.S.C. §§ 7401 *et seq.*

Brown v. Board of Education, 347 U.S. 483 (1954).

Coleman, M.C. (1993). *American Indian children at school, 1850–1930.* Jackson: University Press of Mississippi.

Dempsey, V., & Noblit, G. (1993). The demise of caring in an African American community: One consequence of school desegregation. *Urban Review, 25,* 47–62.

Dempsey, V., & Noblit, G. (1996). Cultural ignorance and school desegregation: A community narrative. In J.S. Mwalimu (Ed.), *Beyond desegregation:*

The politics of quality in African American schooling (pp. 115–137). Thousand Oaks, CA: Corwin Press.

Dumont, R.V., Jr., & Wax, M.L. (1969). Cherokee school society and the intercultural classroom. *Human Organization, 28,* 217–226.

Education for All Handicapped Children Act of 1975, PL 94-142, 20 U.S.C. §§ 1400 *et seq.*

Erickson, F. (1987). Transformation and school success: The politics and culture of educational achievement. *Anthropology and Education Quarterly, 18,* 335–356.

Franklin, J.H. (1994). *From slavery to freedom* (7th ed.). New York: McGraw-Hill.

Gibson, M. (1987). The school performance of immigrant minorities: A comparative view. *Anthropology and Education Quarterly, 18,* 262–275.

Gill, W. (1991). *Issues in African American education.* Nashville, TN: One Horn Press.

Goals 2000: Educate America Act of 1994, PL 103-227, 20 U.S.C. §§ 5801 *et seq.*

Greenbaum, P., & Greenbaum, S. (1983). Cultural differences, nonverbal regulation, and classroom interaction: Sociolinguistic interference in American Indian education. *Peabody Journal of Education, 61,* 16–33.

Greenbaum, S. (1992). Multiculturalism and political correctness: The challenge of applied anthropology in curricular politics. *Human Organization, 51,* 408–412.

Indian Self-Determination and Education Assistance Act of 1975, PL 93-638, 25 U.S.C. §§ 450 *et seq.*

Leacock, E.B. (1971). *The culture of poverty: A critique.* New York: Simon & Schuster.

Lewis, O. (1966). *La vida: A Puerto Rican family in the culture of poverty: San Juan and New York.* New York: Random House.

Martinez, Y.G. (1994). *Narratives of survival: Life histories of Mexican-American youth from migrant and seasonal farmworker families who have graduated from the high school equivalency program.* Unpublished dissertation, University of South Florida, Tampa.

Mindel, C.H., Habenstein, R., & Wright, R., Jr. (Eds.). (1988). *Ethnic families in America: Patterns and variations* (3rd ed.). New York: Elsevier.

Mwalimu, J.S. (Ed.). (1996). *Beyond desegregation: The politics of quality in African American schooling.* Thousand Oaks, CA: Corwin Press.

Ogbu, J.U. (1982). Cultural discontinuities and schooling. *Anthropology and Education Quarterly, 13,* 290–307.

Ogbu, J.U. (1992). Understanding cultural diversity and learning. *Educational Researcher, 21,* 5–14.

Parker, L.M. (1995). Culture, class and race: Three variables of decision making in schools. In S.W. Rothstein (Ed.), *Class, culture and race in American schools* (pp. 225–239). Westport, CT: Greenwood Press.

Philips, S. (1983). *The invisible culture.* New York: Longmans.

Portes, A., & Rumbaut, R. (1990). *Immigrant America: A portrait.* Berkeley: University of California Press.

Prucha, F.P. (1979). *The churches and the Indian schools: 1888–1912.* Lincoln: University of Nebraska Press.

Redhorse, Shattuck, J.A., & Hoffman, F. (Eds.). (1981). *The American Indian family: Strengths and stresses.* Isleta, NM: American Indian School Research and Development Associates.

Schensul, J.J., & Carroll, T.G. (1990). Visions of America in the 1990s and beyond: Negotiating cultural diversity and educational change. *Education and Urban Society, 22,* 339–345.

Skrtic, T.M. (1991). *Behind special education: A critical analysis of professional culture and school organization.* Denver, CO: Love Publishing Co.

Steinberg, S. (1989). *The ethnic myth: Race, ethnicity, and class in America.* Boston: Beacon Press.

Stout, R.T. (1993). Enhancement of public education for excellence. *Education and Urban Society, 25,* 300–310.

Takaki, R. (Ed.). (1994). *From different shores: Perspectives on race and ethnicity in America* (2nd ed.). New York: Oxford University Press.

Trueba, H.T., & Delgado-Gaitan, C. (Eds.). (1988). *School and society: Learning content through culture.* New York: Praeger.

Valentine, C. (1968). *Culture and poverty: Critique and counter-proposals.* Chicago: University of Chicago Press.

9

Group Dynamics and
Ethical School-Based
Decision Making

William C. Morse,
Neal H. Berger, and Pamela G. Osnes

This chapter introduces and examines the critical relationships between school-based decision making (SBDM) (i.e., site-based management) and group dynamics, with an emphasis on the ethical aspects of decision making. Ethical decision making in groups means rendering a decision that goes beyond one's personal values and beliefs. Ethical decision making in site-based management groups permits such groups to be free from its members benefiting from individual preferences and decisions, to be more inclined to accommodate diversity, and to dream with their heads in the clouds and their feet on the ground about what it should be like. When ethical decision making is coupled with decentralized decision making by the full range of stakeholders who are closest to the action, powerful change can occur for school cultures and all students.

Following an overview of SBDM, this chapter focuses on the contextual aspects (i.e., the expectations and constraints) within which individual SBDM committees (SBDMCs) function. These contextual elements include implementing state goals, shifts in state priorities, relationships with school system authorities and other entities that affect the power base of the schools, individual stakeholders' agendas and vested interests, individual schools' flexibility for change through SBDM, community support, and group dynamics. Then, focusing on group dynamics, the bulk of the chapter proposes and explicates a framework for examining how effectively or ineffectively SBDM groups may function with respect to power, leadership, membership, communication, decision making, and group maturity.

Supporters of school restructuring believe that if schools are to resonate in harmony with parents and communities and with the strengths and needs of the students and their proximate educators (teachers and school-based administrators), then all of these parties must be involved in decision making or serve in an advisory role to the principal, who makes the decisions within the context of school board rules and applicable state and national laws and court decisions. Whether and how SBDM entities are willing and able to insert themselves into the continuum between purely advisory functions and actual decision-making and policy-making roles has a great deal to do with the nature and productivity of their groups' functioning, the manner in which ethical deliberation is likely to occur, and the advice or decisions made. Over time, it is conceivable that advisory site-based panels can become final decision-making and legitimate policy-making entities; however, this transformation may take time—something that some reformers do not seem to believe is available—as well as changes in laws governing the scope of their actions and the legitimacy of their decisions. Ultimately, if SBDMCs remain advisory (i.e., to the principal, to the district superintendent, to the school board) and their actual ability is only to influence those whom they advise, then the changes in power relationships that are necessary for real restructuring will be absent. However, improvement can still occur, and the quality and nature of their decisions (even as recommendations to higher authorities) may carry increasingly significant weight. SBDMCs and policy makers at all levels need to be cautious about empty empowerment, where recommendations are confused with the final and authoritative decision of policy and where deciding and real restructuring are camouflaged by halfhearted change.

Another major issue associated with SBDMCs, decision making, and ethical deliberation is to consider the potential good or harm that decision-making and policy-making actions can play in terms of improved educational outcomes for all children. Important decisions for the entire school may exclude or fail to appreciate and incorporate factors that may deeply and negatively affect marginalized populations such as minorities, students with disabilities, or those at risk of dropping out. Such decisions are particularly sensitive and acute because SBDMC participants may not have the collective judgment, expertise, or experience and training necessary to understand the unintended, potentially negative impact of decisions on marginalized populations.

Still another issue that affects ethical deliberations of SBDMCs deals with the restructured form of organizational culture typically associated with restructured organizations (Tönnies, 1957). What Raywid (1990) described as *Gemeinschaft* institutions are communities of people integrated with one another by virtue of their kinship, shared beliefs, commitments, and a wide range of interests over time (including the future). These school communities are concerned with full intellectual and character development of students. In such schools, tradition and knowledge would conceivably change, and marginalized populations, such as special education students, might be viewed in new ways within organizational structures. Such change efforts, argued Guerra, Jackson, Madsen, Ying Thompson, and Ward (1992), "cannot be meaningful unless efforts are centered upon a continuous moral dialog for it is beliefs and values which motivate professionals continuously, not new sets of rules, regulations, and expectations" (p. 28).

The process by which such groups work, the ethical nature of the decisions they make, and the impact of their decisions on students who receive exceptional student education services are of particular concern. When SBDM groups work within the guidelines of the same state mandate, *operational heterogeneity*, not *homogeneity*, appears to be the key term; no two school sites are identical. Thus, each group faces problems unique to its school. Even when SBDMCs are implemented under school district policy, a considerable range of operation and functioning is expected. Nevertheless, SBDMCs are working groups, and primary functions of group life, identified in theory and by research, may be employed to analyze how these groups can and do operate. We begin by attending to contextual aspects that delimit the playing field for a given site-based group.

CONTEXTUAL ASPECTS

First to be considered is the impact of the unique individual context in which a given SBDMC functions. Every group, be it an SBDMC, a classroom, an industrial committee, or an ad hoc group, functions within a given context that defines the purpose of its existence and describes its limits. The context includes a given set of expectations and restraints. Each SBDMC is a creature of its individual ecology and is in no sense an isolated island. In Florida, the SBDMC is called a school improvement team (SIT) or school advisory committee (SAC). It is a state-mandated group that is given the specific task to propose a plan to improve an individual school, thereby accomplishing school reform. If a school is only marginally performing up to state standards and there is inadequate progress in several years' time, the state board of education may step in and take action. Although the specifics of the action might be vague, the threat does constitute a prod to local schools, especially in the case of marginally performing schools. Producing school improvement to fulfill the seven goals of Florida's *Blueprint 2000* is the overriding SAC obligation.

Another contextual aspect is the changing nature of state priorities, which tend to change over time in response to political power shifts and associated priorities. Given the immensity of the task and the limited success of previous reform efforts, this top-down demand for a bottom-up effort represents a populist decentralization of power and responsibility. In the presence of past failures to induce lasting and meaningful school reform, there are great expectations for SBDM. The question is, Will this experiment in democratic decision making have enough bearing on the bureaucratic system of schools to effect significant change? Much depends on how SBDMCs function as groups.

The myriad parent concerns that may be expressed at any point in time within educational systems is to be managed by the representative parents who have been selected to be on their school's SBDMC. Parents of students with disabilities have independent legal power through acceptance or rejection of the individualized education program (IEP), which constitutes another specific power base; however, this involvement is typically governed under federal law, implementing state law, and conforming local school board policy. Can the schools be drastically altered without societal reforms (e.g., major shifts in federal and state policy) that are beyond the purview of the SBDMC?

There are many stakeholders and individual agendas when it comes to SBDMCs deciding the direction for school change. Each SBDMC member comes with an educational history, and most come with preconceived beliefs about how things should be done; these differences must be melded into a common group effort. Dreyfus, Keiny, and Kushnir (1989) described different stances members may take in savoring or resisting change, which is, after all, the basic business of SBDM. Involvement may favor or resist change in active or passive modes; it may be oriented by the task or serve an individual's need. How much risk capital do members have to invest in change?

Conservatives claim that the status quo is best; some follow a learned helplessness trail where the issue cannot ever be resolved, and still others are what can be termed *impatient-impulsive*. Those who are dissatisfied with the present condition and who want to solve the problem are labeled *authentically committed,* in contrast to the *floating indifferent,* who operate in the neutral zone until motivated by some external stimulation.

The unique personalities of the SBDMC membership and how they interact place considerable weight on the need to coalesce divergent views and values as the SBDMC does its work. What kind of power does the SBDMC command beyond the persuasiveness of its decisions? The control of the school rests with the local school board, working within the legal confines provided by the state. Unless the school board delegates or abrogates its authority, it retains the major policy-making authority within the limits of state law. The school principal is responsible for the administration of the local school. In the classroom, to varying degrees, the teacher has the power to create the actual educational experience for the student. In reality, teachers have wide jurisdiction over classroom activities, regardless of what an SBDMC might determine.

Vested interests reside in any given curriculum or instructional methodology. For example, there is a perennial struggle between equity and excellence for school resources. Particularly in special education, the courts have exercised power in acting on various interpretations of the law. Teachers, through organizations and ad hoc associations, influence schooling. Into this power maelstrom is thrust the SBDMC. Policy making is difficult enough in its own right, but getting actual school improvement is quite another matter. Perhaps the strongest limit on power comes from the ever-shrinking resources, a circumstance that leads to efforts to do the best that can be done, given the particular circumstances of each moment in which an action must occur. Many times, this becomes a choice between the less damaging of two inadequate possibilities. Lurking in the wings are issues regarding vouchers and charter schools and still more waves of state reform to add to the contextual wash in which SBDM occurs.

In addition to these general contextual aspects that bear on an SBDMC's group functions are elements that are unique to each school setting. Schools differ greatly in the "welcome index" for this enterprise. Some schools are relatively homogeneous, and others have a highly diverse student population. Many are subject to inner-city pressures or issues associated with rural or isolated situations. There are SBDMCs that believe that, as a consequence of the failure of past efforts, significant improvement is doubtful. This may seem especially true if the school's student population is composed predominantly of the lower socioeconomic classes. The membership of an SBDMC may see SBDM as a new chance to promote change and may embrace its potential to bring necessary change. Although there is criticism of education in general, parents in some locations can still be very positive that their child's school is already a good one. In this case, an SBDMC can be viewed as a threat. An additional threat is the perception that the school may already be doing too much for pupils who are at risk for school failure or who have special needs. The arena in which an SBDMC operates is the community of the school itself and the larger community of the area from which students come. Does the SBDMC really function as an integral component of these two communities?

Of course, seldom is there unanimity or consensus in the community about the present state of the school or what the school should and could be. Tinkering with schedules and planning change for a majority of students is one level of change, whereas a totally new concept of education for the 21st century, acknowledging the unique problems of students at the margin, is another. Suffice it to say that the climate within the school and within the community that surrounds the school will condition the SBDM operation. This is not to say that the SBDMC must rest on the climate that is there. A first task may be to assess the climate and, if appropriate, expand the community vision of what possibilities might exist. Taking all of these variations into consideration, it is clear that each SBDMC will develop and change its own styles of operation in response to its contextual conditions. There are many limitations, changes, and competing powers with which it must contend. Generalizations across SBDMCs concerning their motivations and the depth of their commitments are dubious at best.

SBDMCs are all working groups subject to common group processes as they struggle to fulfill their assignment of inducing a restructuring of the local educational experience. To that end, an analysis of group processes is presented here. A review of the literature on group functioning does not produce a consensus on terms: Overlap and ambiguity characterize the field, and little attention is given to the interaction of functions. To list group processes individually obscures the synergy at work in the group process. Given these limitations, six dynamic concepts have been selected to organize an examination of how SBDMCs work: power, leadership, membership functions, communication, decision making and conflict resolution, and group maturity. Table 1 provides a framework by defining each concept, describing ineffective and effective scale points on each dimension, and providing implications for SBDMCs. This framework can be used by an SBDMC to appraise its functioning. Each group dimension is discussed in some detail, with specific applications to the dynamics of SBDMCs being included.

POWER

In General
A critical aspect of group functioning is the power available to the group to accomplish its goals (Witte & Davis, 1996). An ineffective

Table 1. Group dynamics concepts and site-based decision making

Concept	Definition	Ineffective	Effective	SBDM implications
Power	*External* Ability to reach goals	*External* Reality or perception of low power to reach goals	*External* Clear delineation and exercise of adequate power	Authority to make final decision and policy versus authority to advise and recommend
	Internal Distribution of influence	*Internal* Concentration of influence to few members	*Internal* All members are empowered	Relationship between school community and external community Nature, quality, and support of decisions
Leadership	Ability to guide group and influence followers, keep group solving problems	Rigid, dictatorial or passive, floundering, Robert's Rules dominate	Facilitative, democratic, shared Keeps group focused Uses group expertise	Role that principal plays and power relationships among principal, group chair, and other internal and external leaders in the school community
Membership functions	Blending of various individuals into a working group	Low commitment, prominence of negative roles High turnover	High commitment	Elected versus appointed Composition: Professionals, community members, parents
		Significant roles missing	Feel safe to actively participate Presence of wide variety of roles	Representativeness to school community in general
		Low commonality Not supportive of group intentions of members	Common aspirations Support group intentions	

(continued)

189

Table 1. (continued)

Concept	Definition	Ineffective	Effective	SBDM implications
Communication	Interaction of members Dialogue	Tense, stilted, segmented, nonprogressive, tangential, uneven, and low participation Members feel threatened	Relaxed progression toward goals Broad participation Members feel it is safe to participate	Mature and formal Professional language versus a common language among all participants
Decision making and conflict resolution	Process of coming to decisions and resolving conflicts	Cannot agree on action Periods of disorganization, recycling, and off-task Disorderly action Issues unresolved or forced voting to end stalemates	Recognized process of decision making and conflict resolution Time spent to resolve differences High degree of consensus regarding decisions	Affective/normative versus rational choice Decisions versus recommendations
Group maturity	Groups go through stages in coming to a stable functioning level	Incoherent, unstable patterns Group members still feeling each other out Members do not yet feel safe Productivity stilted Low data usage	Members have achieved elements of community and have become a learning group High level of mutual acceptance and trust, with productive patterns of interaction Appropriate use of data	Maturity of SIT or SAC in terms of experience working together over time and a variety of issues How members are accepted and utilized

SBDMC has or perceives it has low power, whereas an effective SBDMC has a clear delineation of power to effect school change. The literature suggests two vectors of group power: One is influence on the world external to itself (i.e., the school community), and the other is the power distribution among the group members. As a facet of democratization of group process, a broad distribution of within-group power is advocated, including open agendas and the cultivation of group mores that are likely to encourage individuals to state their views. In within-group power, the ineffective group, power holding may be closely guarded, with a concentration of power in a few members or even, perhaps, in just the leader. In an effective group, all members feel empowered and have influence. Unevenness of member use of power may be a result of level of expertise assumed or reluctance to expose oneself to possible rejection.

Power to bring change to the local school springs from the mandate given the group by the state or by the local school board. The SBDMC typically has legal power to recommend decisions and to advise on policy, perhaps even to establish policy; but few SBDMCs have authority to punish, coerce, reward, or threaten. That power is typically retained by the state, the local school board, and the principal and is applied to the school.

There is also a possible power source in the recommendation and advocacy of policy that represents good judgment and displays sound reasoning. If recommended actions or decisions are logical, fair, and solve recognized problems, they have a better chance of being converted into sound practice and policy. This is the power of persuasion. SBDMCs have both theoretical power and real power, which they may choose to exercise. Given the broad SBDMC responsibilities discussed above, the delegated power is somewhat ambiguous. It may be seen as restricted to the pro forma concoction of the plan required by the state. At the other extreme, in the case of schools with severe and pressing problems, the SBDMC may demand reforms, even with the opposition of other power sources, such as the principal, professionals, the school board, the school superintendent, or traditional community forces.

To bring together a group of people and legally endow them with power to make decisions and create policy relative to school change is one thing. To convince and lead the membership to coalesce into a group to effectively wield that power is quite another thing. The actual power of an SBDMC is a reflection of how far the boundaries of delegated power are pushed, how willing the SBDMC is to take risks, and, often, how willing the principal is to let go of power.

Internal group power refers to who influences group dialogue when decisions are made. In a democratic group, the distribution of this power is broad, and members feel free to challenge the leader or other members. A single member can exert tremendous influence by exhibiting vigorous advocacy at given points in the group discourse. In contention over the exercise of power, effective groups develop mechanisms to curb predomination by leaders or outspoken members.

The SBDM experiment in site-level empowerment appears on the surface to be a democratic move consistent with the national restructuring movement to decentralize power. It serves as an end run on the educational bureaucracy. However, it is also an admission that central control has found no way to create the changes needed at the school level. This responsibility turnabout puts tremendous pressure on the local group, often with no discretionary budget or experience and training, to invest in accomplishing the heretofore impossible. Typically, SBDMCs do not have lump-sum budgetary allocation authority or authority for hiring principals and teachers, nor do they have the information or control over major components of the curriculum or policy-making authority. These are all critical definition points for site-based management and restructured change. The state level appears to escape responsibility, and typically it retains the right to intercede under only the most dire circumstances.

In effect, the development of group power depends on all six of the processes in the framework interacting at the effective level. If the tasks are well delineated, if the dialogue is thorough, if the information is timely and adequate, and if the decisions have broad support, the SBDMC will gather strength and exert influence. If policy recommendations and decisions are to become practice, the forum will have to be perceptive about the process of institutional change. It is not only how well the SBDMC exercises its power but also how circumspect the substance of the resulting recommendations and decisions are to deal with recognized problems with durable and effective change. The SBDMC must be cognizant of all power sources that bear on school practice—professional educators, the school board, the superintendent, the state department of education, the legislature, community stakeholders, and even the media may retain a balance of power in such matters as curricular change.

Power and Ethics

Granted, SBDMCs have acquired the power, or they can acquire the necessary power, to induce change. However, will their proposals be ethical, particularly with regard to the marginalized populations, such as those represented by students with disabilities? Have all who are to be affected and influenced by a policy decision been considered in the process? Have alternatives been examined before finalizing proposed policy? Is information adequate? Have the ethical issues been openly explored (Bottery, 1990)?

Particularly when it comes to students with disabilities and those at risk who need more investment to succeed, one needs to ask from whence will come the resources? How much more are these pupils entitled to, and on what basis is the provision of more resources justified for equity? These are parts of the ethical equation of being fair to all, although all outcomes will not necessarily be equal for all. The ethical basis for special education and other differential treatment programs centers primarily on equal opportunity policy.

LEADERSHIP

In General

Unless there is chaos, there will be a leadership function present in any group. This function may be conducted in a variety of ways, from a Quaker-like sharing of responsibility as the spirit moves, to a highly visible controller of group activity. Ineffective leadership may result in group passivity and floundering at one extreme and hostility to rigid, dictatorial leadership at the other. Effective leadership is facilitating, is democratic, and exploits the group's expertise to bring about sound decision making. Groups may develop more than one leader or heads of subgroups: In actuality, because of his or her role, the principal may be the de facto leader, regardless of any election. Presumably, the SBDM leader will be elected by the SBDMC's members, but there may be no hard-and-fast rules to ensure that this will occur.

How one sees oneself as a leader and how the group sees one as a leader may differ. Another complication occurs when some members want strong leadership to get things done, whereas other members resent the assumption of authority. An authoritarian leader may be tolerated if group achievement is high and the group's members are passive. An autocratic leader solves problems that are posed and uses members as sources of information. A consultative leader shares problems with certain individual members, and the outcome may not reflect the opinions of the broader membership. The democratic leader participates in the dialogue as a group member and encourages reaching a decision without unduly influencing it. In effect, the democratic leader carries out the will of the group.

At best, there is a two-way flow of information between the leader and the members. Various leaders have particular priorities, with some focusing on achievement and others being mindful of interpersonal group factors and relationships. Some leaders control the overt agenda, and both the leader and members may have covert intents. It is possible to use periodic feedback forms from the members to monitor membership reaction to the leadership, group processes, and achievement. The crucial ability of the SBDM leader is to guide the group in proposing feasible and desirable change that can be implemented and will be recognized as solving recognized problems. When focusing on SBDM issues, the leader is responsible for sensitizing the group to the relationship its work has to the forces external to itself.

Ethical Leadership
The leader is responsible to see that ethical implications of proposed recommendations and decisions enter the dialogue and are considered in a deliberate manner. She or he is responsible for ensuring that the members of the group have an opportunity to distinguish between their own personal ethics and values and those of the SBDMC itself. The leader in an effective group should also have his or her eye on helping to build the aforementioned *Gemeinschaft* community.

MEMBERSHIP FUNCTIONS

In General
In an ineffective group, the membership has low commitment and high turnover and is passive rather than active, and it does not fill roles necessary to enhance group accomplishment. In contrast, in an effective group, membership involvement is high, participation is active, adequate information is sought and used, and a wide variety of positive roles are enacted by the members. People behave differently in groups when compared with their behavior in isolation. Because the SBDMC is a voluntary group and members get involved in a variety of ways, the vigor of the SBDMC is subject to many unpredictable changes. What are the rewards for giving time to restructuring the school and participating in SBDMCs? Because a broad representation of stakeholders is to be included, there will be a variety of motivations with concomitant differences in how they approach the work, what they can contribute, and what they are moved to protect and promote. School personnel may have the highest stake because the results deal with their workplace, profession, and livelihood. Administrators are faced with sharing power and generating support for given changes in what has been their domain of control. Parents, especially those with children in school, have an immediate investment in what the proposed changes will bring. If they are parents of young children with special needs or who are at risk, they may be more alert to equity for the marginalized student. Business representatives are the ones who inherit the school product and have a vested interest in the ca-

pacities of the graduates. Although there typically are no younger students on elementary SBDMCs, adolescent members who are the consumers of the changed education system certainly have a stake. After all, time investment is an act of citizenship to help restructure our schools, which represent arguably the most significant institution in U.S. society.

To the degree that there is a sense of actual power to participate and do something to bring useful changes, it is an almost unique opportunity to counteract the general feeling of powerlessness that permeates U.S. society. But the work is difficult! Whether members volunteer or are selected because they can attend the meetings, whether they are elected, invited, or pressured to attend, each represents a constituency. However, when SBDM members are approved, they are presumed to be involved for the good of the whole—all of the school's endeavors and the welfare of all the students. What happens in schooling has an impact on the lives of every member, effects that can range from direct to remote. Because the membership is fluid, new members have to be oriented to the group and be nurtured to participate. Even the size of the group is an important variable—as numbers increase, participation decreases, and the depth of agreement may be reduced. Palazzolo (1981) pointed out that, with a group membership of 4, there are 25 possible relationships to maintain. If the group size is doubled to 8, the number of possible relationships increases to 3,025. Given this load, it becomes obvious why even seating arrangements that ensure eye contact are important.

Each member comes to the SBDMC with a given personality. Some members' roles are stable and predictable, and others' roles change with the group activity. Once part of a group, each member is subject to group influence and gives up a small or a large degree of individuality to become a participating group member. Some members play a variety of roles. There are reciprocal relationships between group members—as one member changes, the change influences all other members.

Roles emerge as the group develops a history and a culture. The work of the group is conditioned by the roles that are activated. Among the positive roles are contributor, information giver, seeker of information and opinions, evaluator, synthesizer, reality tester, harmonizer, and integrator. These roles may migrate from individual to individual over the course of time. There are negative roles: the egocentric dominator; distracter; generic opposer; data dismisser or manufacturer; and the bored, withdrawn, passive nonparticipator. Such roles detract from the quality of the group life. Role conflicts are common. Stohl and Schell (1991) described how such roles may create a dysfunctional group. From time to time, the leader can raise questions about the adequacy of group roles and can encourage the development of facilitating roles through consultation with the members. A "sick" group, dominated by negative role enactment, may need an outside consultant to challenge the operation.

The membership of SBDMCs represents different degrees of expertise regarding educational problems as well as different values that require attention. The relationship between expert and nonexpert members in SBDMC deliberations is a delicate one. Klein and Hoffman (1993) credited the true expert with perceiving a world different from the one other people perceive—seeing what is not there. They stated that the true expert sees a world that has levels of understanding from novice to proficient and with differing knowledge bases and fine perceptual discriminations. Experts are said to be better able to size up a situation and anticipate future events. One's self-perception of expertise may be at odds with the reality. Time served in an occupation may imply flawed expertise. In an SBDMC, in which members could be encouraged to participate on a level playing field, both the leader and the members must work to maintain the delicate balance between using group expertise and predomination by experts. There is also the quandary when the person has more understanding than the expert, yet the SBDMC may be dominated by the so-called expert. An SBDMC should cultivate a group culture that expects contributions to be sought from all members, without regard to status.

In an SBDMC, teachers are not in the role of teaching a class; the principal is not directing a school; and parents are not just demanding their special education rights. Members need to surrender their individual needs to working for the good of the whole school—something that is easier said than done. The following sections on communication and group growth address the quality of the dialogue as central in productive discourse.

Membership and Ethics

Again, the concern is for the infusion of ethical consideration for all children, particularly for the students with disabilities and at-risk pupils. If the ethical implications of policy proposals are not evident in the normal group process, efforts may be necessary to address them. One hopes that there will be a role taker for bringing ethical implications to the fore. If not, and if the leader does not inject ethical matters into the discussion, the role of the ethical sensitizer should be assigned. A member sensitive to ethical decision making should bring the SBDMC to see that a decision is a matter of ethical choice, even if the choice is only to minimize harm to a given population. There may be SBDMCs that become distracted by ethical issues; such committees would benefit from exploring ethical decision making in a formal manner to help them move ahead with their work. Ultimately, all members of SBDMCs are responsible for infusing ethical considerations into their deliberations and decisions. Unfortunately, we have found in our work with SBDMCs that there is little or no attention paid to the importance of ethics, the role of the ethical sensitizer, or the hows and whys of ethical deliberation.

COMMUNICATION
The communication in ineffective groups is characterized by tense, stilted, segmented, nonprogressive interaction. Few participate. Tangential talk and recycling of the same material occur. In an effective group, the interactions are relaxed. The dialogue progresses toward goal achievement. There is broad participation.

Although all factors of the group process interact, if there is one core around which other dimensions rotate, it is the nature and quality of the verbal and nonverbal communication patterns that are critical. Communication consists of dialogue, the give-and-take between people as they adjust to each other and work their way toward decisions. Dialogue includes both verbal exchanges and body language, which is sometimes more potent. Frowns, head nodding, eye contact, and vacant stares can speak more clearly than language utterances at times. A skilled group member can "listen to the silences." Usually, the longer a group of people interact, the smoother and more effective the dialogue becomes. In other words, effective communication should be a progressive process.

Cohesion is the glue that holds the members of a group together rather than simply keeping them as a collection of individuals. Cohesion results from the intensity of intermember bonds and the motivation to work together to achieve group goals (Palazzolo, 1981). In these groups, there is a sense of community to which all belong. Members care about the welfare of each other and enjoy each other's company. They feel the loss of absent members. It is interesting that research on group interaction warns that groups overvaluing cohesion can produce Orwellian "groupthink" in the desire to keep everyone content. There is a reluctance to rock the boat, and dialogue can become placating. Greene (1989) found that cohesion positively affects productivity, but only in groups in which group drive (i.e., members being energized by the group) was high. Actually, interactive dialogue is not an end in itself for SBDMCs. It should be a means to an end for effective decisions and policy making. Through dialogue, members deal with internal matters and bring information from external sources to the group's attention.

Membership Roles and Ethics

Most SBDMC members, in common with people everywhere, see themselves as acting ethically (i.e., as doing the right thing). Yet it is typical to ignore the many ethical nuances of a given policy proposal. Thus, it is critical that the dialogue include specific attention to the impact of a decision on all affected populations. This empathetic imperative may be viewed as a waste of the already limited time an SBDMC has to do its task, and it can be seen by some as an unnecessary diversion. The committee's priorities and values are revealed in their regard for this kind of discussion.

DECISION MAKING AND CONFLICT RESOLUTION

In General

The ineffective group cannot agree on actions. There are periods of disorganization, distraction from the task at hand, much recycling of discussions, and disorderly talk. To end disorderly activity and stalemates, the group often resorts to majority-rule votes. On the effective side, the group recognizes the process of decision making. Time is spent to resolve conflicts and to gain consensus for recommendations through voicing implicit ethical implications. Beatty (1989) underscored the importance of persisting until explicit or implicit consensus is reached.

Decision making, particularly in groups, is a very complex enterprise. The most predominant models and theory for decision making are the rational, or reasoned, choice models. Under these logical or empirical models, reasoned choices are systematically selected from among alternative courses of action, with information continually being integrated, and courses of action are taken. (See, e.g., Janis & Mann, 1977, for their descriptive variants of reasoned choice.) However, reasoned decision making has been criticized, and alternative theories and models have been proposed. These irrational socioeconomic models have a different view of human nature in which individuals are governed by normative commitments and affective involvement (Etzioni, 1992). In these models, information processing is often excluded, and decisions are made based on habit, regard for others, moral and ethical values, and emotion. The normative, or affective, model is also more inclined to see complex decision making being made by groups that operate within the context of larger social entities and organizations. Although the contrast between these models is interesting, it is beyond the scope of this chapter to conduct a full debate on the topic or to select a single theoretical model or hybrid for SBDM (see Zey, 1992, for a discussion of rational choice models and alternatives). Both models have their place in ethical decision making by SBDMCs. This is especially true, given the current laws that govern SBDMCs within an accountability and school improvement context, the developmental level of such entities, and the low prevalence of ethical deliberations of decisions.

It is crucial that SBDMCs deal with differences in member direction. These differences are frequently presented as competing values (e.g., freedom, justice, equality, excellence, choice) or as different interpretations of values. Making a decision is not an end in itself but rather is a step toward the goal of producing school change. Despite that, some experts hold that groups are inferior to individuals in decision making, and there are often circumlocutions. As groups struggle to make decisions, to take advantage of the wisdom of many participants, SBDMCs are being called on to guide or augment restructuring for U.S. schools.

Decision Making, Conflict Resolution, and Ethics

There are several prominent systems that groups can use to make viable decisions, especially decisions that incorporate ethical reasoning. Some advocate starting with a principled ethical base (e.g., the Golden Rule). This is to be followed by reasoning, clarification, and evaluation, leading to the decision. A second procedure for ethical decision making was offered by Paul, Gallagher, Kendrick, Thomas, and Young (1992) in their work dealing with ethical policy for implementing Part H of the Individuals with Disabilities Education Act (IDEA) of 1990 (PL 101-476). In this procedure (which adapts Kendrick's Ethical Method for resolving value differences that arise from conflicting values within groups), the group proceeds through a five-step process that involves problem description, proposing solution alternatives, identification of value conflicts, justification, and application. The cycle continues with monitored implementation, which is open to modification. Another decision-making process (Forsyth, 1990), called the rational series, starts with orientation (i.e., What is the problem?), followed by social discussion (i.e., collective induction) and then decision making and information processing, and ends with implementation. It is obvious in the case of SBDMCs that they recommend or make decisions or policy and monitor implementation, without doing the actual implementation.

Moscovici and Doise (1994) warned that superior decision-making performance of a group may be less than that of individuals. Groups tend to diminish cognitive faculties and accentuate emotional faculties. Member action in groups is directed at the more individualistic extremes. Collectivist life leads to uniformity in contrast to individuality.

Because certain SBDMC decisions may differentially affect given subgroups of children (e.g., children at risk), and because various SBDM members often advocate for particular subgroups, the presence of conflict in decision making is to be expected. Issues left unresolved or settled by majority vote, even after considerable dialogue, do not have the vitality of group decisions with consensus. Symptoms of uneasy decision making include the continuous recycling of ideas, periods of disorganization and tension reduction by humor in asides, or the introduction of irrelevant material. Usually, a healthy resolution requires backtracking to explore the ethical differences that undergird the conflict. There is often a dialectic between divergent and convergent thinking in groups. Poole and Roth (1989) argued in their research that there is no single path that groups use in arriving at decisions. Paths are dynamic, not static, and may be direct or recycled and interspersed with disorganized periods.

Causes of conflict in group decision making include real or supposed differences in goals, limited resources, a slowdown brought on by a gradual increase in awareness of the consequences of a decision, and an expectation that group loyalty should override differences. At times, a conflict may be a response to autocratic leadership or impassioned advocacy for a particular cause by a member. Gibson, Ivancevich, and Donnelly (1985) suggested that the following processes may apply to conflicts: rational problem solving, avoidance, soothing, compromise, and examining the ethics involved. Others have suggested far more complicated and less logical decision-making processes (Zey, 1992). Another strategy is to call in an expert on the debated issue as a way to expand the knowledge base concerning the matter in debate. Experts and lay members can share their knowledge.

The belief in the capacity of a group to resolve differences to a workable level is an item of democratic faith. Reasonable group members, through quality dialogue, will come to a resolution. However, there is ample evidence that this does not always occur in the case of societal conflict. Unresolved conflict encourages coalitions, polarization, and rigidity. One personal characteristic that sometimes enters into the consideration is the individual members' risk-taking index. Some want only safe bets (especially when authorities such as the state governments are watching), whereas others are happy to try things with a low probability of success.

Decision Making, Conflict Resolution, and Ethical Implications

Emerging values shape choices and attitudes. Basic value differences underlie much irresolvable conflict. A question to ask is, "How much complexity is entertained in the group process when different ethical propositions collide?" Although it may not be obvious during the discussion, one member may be operating from a principle-based ethic, such as the greatest good for the greatest number, whereas another argues from the desire for equity for the marginal as the right thing to do. Often the resolution of an SBDM conflict really satisfies no one's values, being merely what the SBDMC can live with for the time being. Palazzolo (1981) proposed a grid (see Figure 1) to understand different predominating values that motivate group members, contrasting those with concern for people with those concerned with results. Ethical behavior requires a respect for individuals in all aspects and the ability to prioritize goals from multiple viewpoints.

GROUP MATURITY

Over time, through dialogue and experience, a group develops patterns of interaction to accomplish its goals. In an ineffective group, the patterns tend to be unproductive. Members are unsure of each other and have developed patterns that show deep-seated differences that have never been resolved. Differences become obstacles rather

| | | Concern for Results | | |
		High	Moderate	Low
Concern for People	High	Surface harmony maintained		Valid problem solving Reservations and emotions worked through
	Moderate		Bargaining Compromise No winners	
	Low	Neutrality at all costs		Conflict suppressed by authority

Figure 1. Collective resolution grid. (Adapted from Palazzolo [1981].)

than sources of enrichment. The effective, mature group has become a learning group, with high mutual member acceptance of differences and the ability to use divergence to come to a more inclusive resolution.

SBDMCs, in common with most continuously operating groups, go through stages toward maturity. Forsyth (1990) listed five probable developmental stages for groups, along with a summary of major processes and group characteristics by stage:

1. *Orientation (forming):* Task exploration, identification of commonalties; discourse that is tentative, polite, and concerned with ambiguity; give-and-take of independent people
2. *Conflict (storming):* Resistance, disagreement, criticism of ideas, polarization, coalitions forming over procedures, and emotional responding
3. *Cohesion (norming):* Growth of unity, cohesiveness, establishment of roles, standards, relationships, "we" feeling, and agreement on procedures
4. *Performance:* Goal achievement, high task orientation and production, mutual cooperation, problem solving, and decision making
5. *Dissolution:* Completion of the task, reduction of dependency, and regret and withdrawal

Gibson et al. (1985) pointed out that groups learn just as individuals do. They proposed four stages in development:

1. Mutual acceptance as the members learn to trust each other
2. Communication and decision making with open exchange
3. Motivation and productivity with effort expended to accomplish goals as a cooperative unit
4. Control and organization where group affiliation is valued, members are regulated by group norms, and group goals supersede individual goals

The markers discussed in either Forsyth (1990) or Gibson et al. (1985) are useful in an SBDMC self-evaluation process.

The concept of a *learning group* expresses an ideal maturity state as described by the ongoing experimentation at the Massachusetts Institute of Technology (MIT). The rapid changes facing industry and social agencies as they adapt to new conditions requires continuous administrative group problem solving at a deeper level of interpersonal transaction than is traditional. Group maturity is achieved through dialogue, during which people gradually learn to suspend their defensive exchanges and probe into the underlying reasons why those exchanges exist. The result is a community group that is conscious of the processes by which assumptions and beliefs are formed. The goal is for members to have learned to think insightfully together. The result is shared meaning, which is of deeper significance than consensus. In effect, the secondary group incorporates aspects of a family primary group in function, especially deep intermember involvement. In this manner, the group becomes a learning organization with vision and values. The role of leader is that of facilitator, trying to solve problems through shared creative thinking and organizational learning. Although members may not always agree, they have a common goal. Such a learning group is not easily achieved, and SBDMCs have several limitations in such achievement: Their time together is so limited, membership is fluid, and the pressure to produce solutions short-cuts quality dialogue. Yet, to the extent possible, the SBDMC strives toward the maturity of becoming a learning group.

Over time, each SBDMC acquires an individual personality. Some exude warmth and cordiality while remaining task-oriented. Members care about and learn about each others' lives. A member comes to feel known, safe, and accepted. In other groups, the climate reflects interpersonal distance. There is little cordiality and little attention paid to the human element. Such groups remain arrested at the level of brief acquaintance, with weak and even negative connections and little intermember support. The climate is frequently a reflection of the leader's style. There are groups in which the whole style of group interaction changes with the presence or absence of a particular member. Groups may have think-alike alliances and sometimes spontaneously alienated pairs. A mature SBDMC takes considerable pains to welcome and incorporate new members.

The developing group culture supplies norms for member behavior, such as how much argumentative reaction to suggestions is proper. The norms may be a reflection of a strong leader's preferences. Input concerning the value loading of proposed actions may be approved or frowned upon. Some groups operate on a stable platform, whereas others are able to move from crisis to crisis.

The social structure of a group is the patterned regularity of member interactive relationships. The members are bound together in mutual respect and acceptance. Missing members are contacted. Cohesive groups often have vigorous and even contentious periods but come back together because of their social glue. In a mature group, active confrontation is no cause for alarm: The real danger is a group that cannot risk vigorous interaction. As has been mentioned, if members put comfort of each other ahead of sincere dialogue, the final product can suffer.

There are ways to promote group maturity through a group examining how it operates. Periodic feedback surveys can ascertain member satisfaction and reveal the state of development. Revisiting past decisions to see how well they hold up under reexamination provides a review of the quality of decision making. Group members can study group process and evaluate their own SBDMC. Sources of conflict can be examined, and conflict resolution methods can be explored. Incorporating ethical deliberation into the decision-making process should help the maturation process.

Group Maturity and Ethics
As the group work at MIT has pointed out, a mature group remains open to the examination of ethical matters. Members feel free to raise ethical issues and claim their individual stands. Members do not demand that all members value the same things. Power (1988) saw the mature group moving from moral judgments to a moral atmosphere. How can the SBDMC assist the school to become a moral or just community for all pupils, especially the marginal pupils? Where, and in what ways, can the SBDMC appraise possible injustice in policies? One way is a direct study of ethics as applied to the policies and practices in public schools. Certainly, given the individual differences between pupils, it is undesirable and inequitable to treat all students the same.

The choices that have to be made with inadequate resources are not easy. Alternatives have to be considered to make the most ethical policies possible. The role of group ethicist can be incorporated to ensure attention to ethical issues. One can use Bottery's (1990) instrument to assess the moral culture of the group. The study of ethical dilemma cases can sharpen awareness. Brainstorming groups, Delphi groups (i.e., members of relevant groups independently provide responses to a query), and focus groups on ethical issues are possibilities. Belief systems need to be overt. In planning for change, it is necessary to communicate in ways that respect individual differences while setting and prioritizing goals that originate from multiple viewpoints.

CONCLUSIONS
SBDM in U.S. schools is not only one of the hallmarks of school restructuring but also a complex group process, especially when one acknowledges the too frequently ignored and undervalued component of ethical deliberation. Nevertheless, such groups are subject to the same dynamic variables as many other groups: power, leadership, membership functions, communication, decision making and conflict resolution, and group maturity. Each of these concepts has been explored in depth in this chapter, with references to effective and inef-

fective site-based management and ethics. Implications of these variables on SBDMCs have been suggested. The authors strongly believe that the ethical deliberation in SBDMCs is essential to good policy in general and to well-thought-through policy for marginalized populations in particular. Indeed, the ultimate indicator of restructuring success may well be how achievement is obtained and how it can be achieved for all school populations, especially those at the margin. To ensure their meaningful role in our society, egalitarian and ethically informed recommendations, decisions, and policy need to be developed with the strong mark of each school's SBDMC. By coupling an understanding and utilization of the dynamic variables of groups with ethical deliberation, the quality of SBDMC policy decisions and the quality of lives for all members of our school communities can be enhanced.

REFERENCES

Beatty, M.J. (1989). Group members' decision rule orientations and consensus. *Human Communications Research, 16,* 279–296.

Bottery, M. (1990). *The morality of the school.* London: Cassell Educational Publishers.

Dreyfus, A., Keiny, S., & Kushnir, T. (1989). A search for self-renewal in school systems: Modes of participation. *Small Group Behavior, 20,* 333–343.

Etzioni, A. (1992). Normative-affective factors: Toward a new decision making model. In M. Zey (Ed.), *Decision making: Alternatives to rational choice models* (pp. 89–111). Beverly Hills, CA: Sage Publications.

Forsyth, D.R. (1990). *Group dynamics* (2nd ed.). Pacific Grove, CA: Brooks/Cole.

Gibson, J.L., Ivancevich, J.M., & Donnelly, J.H. (1985). *Organizations: Behavior, structure, process.* Plano, TX: Business Publications.

Greene, C.N. (1989). Cohesion and productivity in work groups. *Small Group Behavior, 20,* 70–86.

Guerra, P., Jackson, J., Madsen, C., Ying Thompson, H., & Ward, C. (1992). *Site-based management and special education: Theories, implications, and recommendations.* Paper presented to the University Council for Educational Administration. (ERIC Document No. EC 301 957)

Individuals with Disabilities Education Act (IDEA) of 1990, PL 101-476, 20 U.S.C. §§ 1400 *et seq.*

Janis, I.L., & Mann, L. (1977). *Decision making: A psychological analysis of conflict, choice, and commitment.* New York: Free Press.

Klein, G.A., & Hoffman, R.R. (1993). Seeing the invisible: Perceptual-cognitive aspects of expertise. In M. Rabinowitz (Ed.), *Cognitive science foundations of instruction* (pp. 203–226). Hillsdale, NJ: Lawrence Erlbaum Associates.

Moscovici, S., & Doise, W. (1994). *Conflict and consensus.* Beverly Hills, CA: Sage Publications.

Palazzolo, C.S. (1981). *Small groups.* New York: Van Nostrand.

Paul, J.L., Gallagher, J.J., Kendrick, S.B., Thomas, D.D., & Young, J.F. (1992). *Handbook for ethical policy making.* Chapel Hill: University of North Carolina, North Carolina Institute for Policy Studies.

Poole, M.S., & Roth, J. (1989). Decision development in small groups: IV. A typology of group decision paths. *Human Communication Research, 15,* 323–356.

Power, F.C. (1988). From moral judgment to moral atmosphere: The sociological turn in Kohlbergian research. *Counseling and Values, 32,* 172–178.

Raywid, M.A. (1990). Rethinking school governance. In R.F. Elmore (Ed.), *Restructuring schools.* San Francisco: Jossey-Bass.

Stohl, C., & Schell, S.E. (1991). A communication-based model of a small-group dysfunction. *Management Communication Quarterly, 5,* 90–110.

Tönnies, F. (1957). *Community and society* (C.P. Lumis, trans.). East Lansing: Michigan State University Press.

Witte, E.H., & Davis, J.H. (1996). *Understanding group behavior* (Vol. 1). Hillsdale, NJ: Lawrence Erlbaum Associates.

Zey, M. (1992). *Decision making: Alternatives to rational choice models.* Beverly Hills, CA: Sage Publications.

IV

ETHICAL DECISION MAKING IN LOCAL SCHOOLS

Developing a Curriculum for School-Based Policy Makers

Following the broad historical and policy context established in Section I, the ethical foundations presented in Section II, and the analysis of sociocultural and psychological forces affecting the policy process in Section III, the four chapters in Section IV focus on more specific methodological and substantive issues in developing a curriculum for ethical policy making in schools.

In Chapter 10, Cranston-Gingras, Raines, Thompson, and Beach discuss the rationale and uses of the teaching case method in ethics education. They present and discuss the two cases used at the Collegium: "Are All Children the Same?" and "Future Leaders." In their analysis, they find that a deliberative forum, such as a school-based decision-making committee, is especially well suited for the use of teaching cases. Martinez and Thompson, in Chapter 11, present an analysis of the culture and the process of ethical analysis employed at the Collegium. One of the principal conclusions of their analysis is that school-based committees need to construct common frameworks to guide their work as a community within a school.

In Chapter 12, Berger, Paul, and Fagan describe the approach employed by the Collaborative Research Group on Policy and Ethics to develop a curriculum for ethical policy making in schools. They summarize the group's current understanding and describe the model, an adaptation of Zais's eclectic model, being used to develop the curriculum. They discuss the curriculum content and an approach to evaluation as well as instructional design.

In Chapter 13, Paul returns to the discussion of the context of developing a curriculum for ethical policy making in schools. Focusing on some of the philosophical and practical challenges facing school leaders, he examines some of the overarching issues facing school-based decision-making committees and the changing social ecology of schools within which cultural interests are mediated, with or without an explicit ethical foundation. Integrating selected themes in the book, he examines the difficulties facing policy makers in discerning the interests of individuals and groups fairly, responsibly, and empathically. He also considers the challenge for philosophers to assist in clarifying what constitutes data, or evidence, in decisions, as well as the moral substance for ethical decisions.

10

Teaching Ethics Through the Case Method

Ann Cranston-Gingras, Shirley Raines,
Theron D. Thompson, and Dore Beach

> The key to fostering effective ethical deliberation is practice in reasoning
> and collaborating about ethically problematic situations, not mere mastery
> of a given set of principles and precepts. (Howe & Miramontes, 1992,
> p. xix)

Teaching case method, which has a long tradition in the fields of law
and business, involves the use of narrative accounts of actual situations
to foster deliberation about specific aspects of daily practice and to encourage the examination of complex issues from multiple perspectives. In this chapter, teaching cases are defined, teaching case method
is reviewed, two examples of teaching cases used at a small policy and
ethics collegium for members of school improvement teams (SITs) are
provided, and a framework for deliberation and analysis using the
case method to teach ethics is introduced.

TEACHING CASES DEFINED

Teaching cases are "a case of something, or an instance of a larger class
of experiences" (Shulman, 1986, p. 11). They usually are multidimensional, containing many plots and subplots that can be analyzed from
various perspectives. Most teaching cases are based on scenarios that
focus on problems. Some teaching cases include accounts of attempted
successful and unsuccessful resolutions, whereas others simply remain
unresolved, prompting discussion of possible solutions (Shulman,
1991). The teaching case method uses teaching cases as either a part
of or the central focus of a curriculum (Levin, 1995).

WHY USE THE TEACHING CASE METHOD?

The teaching case method employs the element of story in capturing reader interest and bridging theory with actual events. In contrast to case studies or vignettes, teaching cases are "sufficiently detailed, complex and substantive to foster multiple levels of discussion, analysis, and possible courses of action" (Merseth, 1991, p. 25). According to Bruner (1986), knowledge gained through the use of narratives is more personal and contextualized than paradigmatic knowledge, which is general and distant from the context of personal experience. Narrative allows for understanding about things with which one may not have had direct experience.

The real-life events represented in cases are not new in the study of ethics. Since the time of Aristotle, paradigmatic cases of complex ideas and situations have organized the study of ethics (Shulman, 1992). Four attributes of cases support their use in teaching ethics. Cases offer 1) a rich description of real events; 2) a situated scenario; 3) a relational, integrated environment; and 4) opportunity for discussion and social interaction (Richert, 1991).

1. *Description* Cases offer the opportunity for educators to record and relate practice. The case materials (e.g., journals, notes, plan books, annotated schedules, videotapes) may be transformed into teaching cases. The descriptive aspect of cases allows for addressing the complexities of school culture. Authors of teaching cases convey the intensity and understanding of events through the unique characteristics of people, physical environment, time, administrative involvement, and personal dilemmas.

2. *Situational* Cases are the representation of life in a specific context. Each case tells of particular actors, particular settings, particular plots, and particular perspectives. Cases offer an opportunity for learning because of their anchoring in narrative, time, and place (Shulman, 1992). Cases are stories, but they are stories written for a specific purpose and chosen for the purpose of teaching. They are chosen to connect theory with practice in the mind of the learner and offer a piece of experience that is vibrant and engaging. They are unique representations of the complex system of school culture.

3. *Relational* Cases demonstrate the interrelatedness of the multiple components of teaching practice. Activities do not occur in isolation. Teachers and schools operate in a causal environment where ideas, decisions, and actions interact with each other dynamically and multiply in response to numerous perspectives. This effect is admirably demonstrated by teaching cases.

4. *Social Interaction* The foundation of the case method is discussion and interaction within the pedagogy of cases. SITs are collabora-

tive, social groups assembled for the purpose of problem solving and decision making. The case method and teaching cases parallel the function of these school-based groups. The necessity of understanding and disclosure within the group is facilitated by the use of the case method, which welcomes and acknowledges the participation of people with varying perspectives and backgrounds. It opens a space in which diversity is celebrated and the risk of personal expression is minimized while providing an anchor for group interaction.

Teaching Cases Used at the Policy and Ethics Collegium
The teaching case method was used at the Collegium on Policy and Ethics organized by the Collaborative Research Group on Policy and Ethics (CRGPE) at the University of South Florida, in which the work of a hypothetical, school-based decision-making team was observed from multiple viewpoints. The background of the Collegium is discussed in detail in Chapters 3 and 11. A Collaborative Research Group on Teaching Cases (CRGTC) composed of special and elementary education faculty and advanced graduate students has been meeting weekly to develop, modify, and evaluate the application of teaching cases in the teacher education program. The CRGPE asked the CRGTC to identify two teaching cases that were cases of ethical issues. The following criteria were applied to the selection of cases for consideration:

- Did the cases present significant issues relevant to the concerns of SITs?
- Did the cases, in fact, present content that reflected ethical considerations?
- Were the cases well written, with enough description, characterization, and detail to engage the participants in the CRGPE and allow them to find meaning through group interaction?
- Was anonymity ensured?
- Was the case presentation risk-free for the characters and the authors?
- Could the cases be released for publication?

Two cases, "Are All Children Treated the Same?" and "Future Leaders," were selected and used at the CRGTC Collegium. The full text of these cases appears in the appendix at the end of this chapter. The authors of both cases have chosen to remain anonymous.

CASE ANALYSIS AND DISCUSSION
During the CRGTC Collegium, the teaching case approach allowed for reflection about real ethical issues. The authenticity of the teaching cases used was considered by participants and observers to be funda-

mental to this deliberation. Through the vehicle of teaching cases, participants were encouraged to think on two levels: to focus on the explicit content of the case as well as to examine their own reactions to the content in an effort to better understand their decision-making behavior.

Although teaching cases most often appear in written form, discussion of the cases is a critical component in case-based methodology. According to Hansen (1987), "Just as a piece of music exists only partially when it isn't being sung or played, a case comes fully to life only when it is being discussed" (p. 265). Proper facilitation during discussion of the teaching case is essential in arriving at conclusions based on deliberate decision making. By drawing out embedded issues in the case and deliberating them, participants are able to probe critically their responses to the circumstances of the case.

The Facilitator's Role
The facilitator's role in case analysis is much like that of the qualitative researcher. The facilitator proceeds with a set of open-ended questions to look for ideas that develop into emergent themes, perspectives, or understandings. Questions such as "What's going on here?" "What are the problems?" and "What else do we need to know?" require a response and have no particular correct answer. In fact, in case-based instruction, the focus is not on answers but on options and alternatives. The dilemma of the case is studied within a specific context and through the use of text and verbal reactions. The case method involves interpretation by the participants, facilitator, and observers.

To encourage participants to take different perspectives, the facilitator prompts, through questioning, a closer examination of what is actually said in the case, as well as what is not said. Questions such as "Why do you think the principal said . . . ?" or "What do you think the principal could have said?" prompt the participants to look at the principal's perspective in the case and to appreciate the tensions attendant to that role. Sometimes role playing is used to allow participants to defend one of the characters' positions, even if it is one with which they do not agree.

Since teaching cases have a contextualized scenario and a cast of characters, there is a specific basis for the examination of each case. The teaching cases presented in this chapter involve decisions of an ethical nature. Although an ethical viewpoint is not highlighted in much of the discussion, participants addressed issues that were connected to ethical perspectives. The case discussions that took place after formal presentations by ethicists included brief elements of labeled ethical discussion.

Questioning in Case-Based Instruction

The facilitating questioning used to analyze and discuss the cases provided opportunities for each individual to talk. The questions used during the 2 days of the CRGTC Collegium to analyze and discuss the teaching cases are presented in Table 1. Questions encouraged dynamic, fluid responses. They supported an atmosphere in which elaboration and open-mindedness were encouraged. Participants' utilization and acceptance of the opportunity to express themselves depended on their personal attributes, attitudes, and connection with the topic. The following statements provide a description of the overall questioning strategies used in discussing the two cases presented:

1. Questions ask for a factual response.
2. Questions ask for effective responses.
3. Questions ask the participants to interpret the case in light of their own experiences.
4. Questions ask participants to "read between the lines" and establish a rich context.
5. Questions ask participants for additional information that may not be included in the case.
6. Questions ask for judgmental or evaluative statements that reflect their life experiences.
7. Questions offer an opportunity for the expression of diverse perspectives.
8. Questions open undefined categories and invite participants to socially construct meaningful categories within the context of the case.

Responding to the Questions

Participants bring to bear their own individual backgrounds in case discussions and interpretations. How well participants apply the information constructed in the case discussion group to their roles in schools is an indicator of the effectiveness of the case-based teaching method. Responses offered during the case discussions were recorded on wall charts by the facilitator. The charts provided a concrete reference that illustrated the group's ethical reasoning process and progress. Viewing the charts as a data set produced categories and trends in the dialogue. Three strong themes emerged from the responses:

1. Evidence of a power structure and hegemony in school culture
2. Situated agendas
3. Options in consideration of a solution

Table 1. Sample questions in case-based instruction

	Case 1	Case 2
Day 1	What are the problems? What else do we want to know? Who are the main players? What do they think? What do school-based teams do? Will school-based teams address real or perceived needs? Offer alternatives? What are the by-products of school-based teams?	What are your initial reactions? What are the problems here? What else do we need to know? What could people have done to change the decision, before and after it was made? Any remaining issues? What are you sad about? What do you think should be done?
Day 2	Who are the major players? What are their views? What are the problems? What is the role of the school-based team? Who can help?	Who are the major players? What are their feelings? What are the problems? What is the role of the school-based team? What's going on here? Who are the good guys? Who are the bad guys? Who is the stranger? What would you have done?

With the examination of the generated text from the case discussion, a well-defined global theme emerged: power and the hegemonic power structure of schools. In support of this theme, textual descriptors from the data set are given in Table 2, in which the power structure of schools is evidenced by references to power structure in the discourse.

Each participant reacted to the cases in unique, role-oriented ways. Their responses, however, demonstrated the agendas within each perspective. In total, the responses showed the diverse, purposeful, and personal shading everyone brought to the case discussion. Agendas ranged from that of the concerned parent to that of the goal-oriented teacher to the organizational focus of administrators. Table 3 offers textual descriptors from the data set reflecting the diversity of the agendas.

Table 2. Textual descriptors: Evidence of power structure and hegemony in school culture

Silent	Powerless	Frustrated with the system	Separatist
Not a part	Double standard	Disheartened	Ashamed
Alienation	Frustrated	Left out and cut off	Prejudice
Abandoned	Failure	Impotent	Elitism
Caught	Hostility	Defensive	Power play
Discrimination	Students not valued	Isolation	Fearful

Table 3. Textual descriptors: Situated agenda

Single advocate	Courage	Needs assessment	Money
Best interests of children	Representative stakeholders	Parent's rights	District budget
Academics	Picket	Funding	Territoriality
Lack of support	Large group meeting	Involve the press	Values
Lack of sympathy	Due process	Valuing the children	Survival

The payoffs of case-based instruction are the mutually investigated and constructed options for addressing problems. The facilitator and group members provide multiple options for insight and action. In response to the multiplicity and acceptance of possible solutions, participants leave the discussion with a means of confronting problematic situations. This element of case-based instruction is one that was instrumental in the selection of the case-based method for dealing with ethical issues. Because ethics are constructed from relationships between people, they are most effectively discussed in a socially responsive setting. Table 4 offers textual descriptors from the data set reflecting the varied options presented in response to dilemmas posed by the cases.

Perhaps the most difficult task during ethical deliberation is recognizing and acknowledging the conflicting claims and obligations—the inherent dilemmas—within a particular situation. For example, in the "Future Leaders" case, the decision by the regional supervisor to eliminate funding for the Future Leaders club and to allow funding for continued parent involvement created a dilemma because both aspects of the program were important and were dependent on each other for success. This case is an excellent example of conflicting claims or obligations. At issue here are the following questions: What is the greater good? Which group of stakeholders (students or parents) could derive the most benefit? To which stakeholders is the regional director obligated? Was that obligation a consideration in his decision?

In the "Are All Children Treated the Same?" case, there are not only conflicting claims or duties at issue but also many other ethical considerations that must be addressed before an equitable and ethical

Table 4. Textual descriptors: Options in consideration of a solution

Good planning	Public relations	Needs assessment	Persuasion
Collaboration of goals	Honor children's voices	Involvement of shareholders	Evaluate
Teachers have confidence	Involve community in decisions	Broaden knowledge base	Ethics training

resolution can be reached. For example, What are the facts of the case? Who are the stakeholders? (There are many.) In what respect is the law relevant to the case? (That is, by law, the maximum number of students in a class of this nature is 10–12.) It appears that in the "Are All Children Treated the Same?" case, there was no ethical deliberation employed in any of the decisions regarding the children, because moral reasoning incorporates personal wisdom, understanding, and experience—it demands an understanding of human needs and requires that one adopt a broader, more flexible view of the situation than was exhibited by the individuals in this case. The ethical issue in this case was not whether all children were treated the same but whether the decisions were fair and just.

A FRAMEWORK FOR THE ETHICAL DELIBERATION OF CASES

Applying any one of a number of frameworks to the deliberative phase of case-based instruction allows for practice in analyzing situations in which there are ethical dilemmas or conflicting claims that may not be apparent on initial examination. This approach permits the study of the complexities and dimensions of cases at a deeper level, which may not be possible when only one aspect of a situation is addressed. Use of a framework specifically geared toward understanding moral reasoning encourages participants to sort out the contradictions, conflicting claims, values, and obligations that are relevant to the investigation of the situation.

The framework for the ethical analysis of the cases offered in this chapter is based on procedures for resolving moral problems that arose in particular real-life situations long ago. These procedures became known as *casuistry,* and those who employed these procedures professionally were called *casuists.* The *Oxford English Dictionary* defines *casuistry* as "that part of ethics which resolves cases of conscience, applying the general rules of religion and morality to particular instances in which circumstances alter cases or in which there may be a conflict of duties." The elements of this definition rest on the one important question: All things considered, what ought to be done? It is the nature of this question that helps us distinguish ethical deliberation from other forms of critical thinking that occurs in decision making. Moral reasoning takes into account but is not encompassed by such variables as legalities; the facts of the case; and the concerns, values, and beliefs of individuals who are affected by the outcome of the decision.

The framework is presented as a set of questions that are addressed systematically. Although not every question may be applicable in each case, this approach allows us to acknowledge the inherent values or obligations within the case, to explore and justify a range of options, and, finally, to examine in some detail the varying degrees to which particular options sustain or negate each of the relevant values or obligations of the case. The following is an example of a framework for ethical deliberation of teaching cases. In addition to the line of questioning discussed previously in this chapter, the additional questions below may be raised during the deliberative process to encourage examination of the case from an ethical perspective.

1. What are the facts of the case?
2. Who are the stakeholders?
3. In what respect are legal issues relevant to the case?
4. What underlying imperatives, values, principles, standards, or codes are invoked?
5. To what extent are there competing or conflicting claims or duties?
6. What social and intellectual traditions are invoked for support?
7. What factors in the case are given weight, and which are excluded?
8. In what respect do other cases (i.e., examples) or precedents fit the circumstances of this case?
9. To what extent are the circumstances of this case exceptional or atypical?
10. What are the alternative positions in this case?
11. What priorities do the options reveal (i.e., what underlying values and commitments determine priorities)?
12. What is or would be sacrificed for the sake of what is assumed to be the greater good in the various options?
13. Which position do you support?

Participants may then be asked to justify their position by applying the following questions:

1. What are the underlying ethics of the position you support?
2. With which stakeholders do you identify? Why?
3. What additional information could possibly change your position?
4. What action do you propose in support of your position?
5. What are the possible alternative courses of action available?
6. Are you comfortable with your position, all things considered?

CONCLUSIONS
In teaching ethics to school improvement and accountability teams, the teaching case method holds promise as a way of encouraging re-

flection about actual ethical issues that arise in school-based decision making. Teaching cases, usually written by or with teachers, constitute the core content of case-based instruction. The facilitating process of drawing out embedded issues in the cases and the resulting deliberations enable participants to critically examine the ethical implications of their actual and imagined responses to a variety of circumstances.

Merseth (1991) highlighted several reasons that case-based instruction is a useful teaching methodology. These same reasons, among others, underscore the value of this method for the continuing development of adult decision makers. According to Merseth, case-based instruction encourages reflective practice and deliberate action, provides practice in analysis and action in complex situations, involves participants in their own learning, and develops a community of learners.

The teaching case method provides opportunities for SITs and school accountability teams to practice analyzing the ethical dimensions of their decision making. The success of this method as a vehicle for teaching groups to critically examine the complex ethical realm of their work is dependent on the ability of curriculum designers to develop a collection of cases suited to the purpose, to refine procedures for presenting and discussing cases that encourage participants to focus on the ethical dimensions of issues, and to monitor and document the effectiveness of case-based instruction as a vehicle for teaching ethics.

REFERENCES

Bruner, J. (1986). *Actual minds, possible worlds.* Cambridge, MA: Harvard University Press.

Hansen, A. (1987). Reflections of a case writer: Writing teaching cases. In R. Christensen (Ed.), *Teaching and the case method* (pp. 264–275). Boston: Harvard Business School Press.

Howe, K.R., & Miramontes, O.B. (1992). *The ethics of special education.* New York: Teachers College Press.

Levin, B.B. (1995). Using the case method in teacher education: The role of discussion and experience in teachers' thinking about cases. *Teaching and Teacher Education, 11*(1), 63–79.

Merseth, K.K. (1991). *The case for cases in teacher education.* Washington, DC: AACTE Publications.

Richert, A.E. (1991). Case methods and teacher education: Using cases to teach teacher reflection. In B.R. Tabachrick & K.M. Zeichner (Eds.), *Issues and practices in inquiry-oriented teacher education* (pp. 130–150). New York: Falmer Press.

Shulman, L.S. (1986). Those who understand: Knowledge, growth, and teaching. *Educational Researcher, 15,* 4–14.

Shulman, L.S. (1991). Revealing the mysteries of teacher-written cases: Opening the black box. *Journal of Teacher Education, 41,* 250–262.

Shulman, L.S. (1992). Toward a pedagogy of cases. In J. Shulman (Ed.), *Case methods in teacher education* (pp. 1–32). New York: Teachers College Press.

Appendix

ARE ALL CHILDREN TREATED THE SAME?

In August, it was evident that the class for children identified as having developmental delays was overcrowded and needed to be split into two groups. The class continued to grow quickly and eventually reached 20 students. By law, the maximum number in a class of this nature is 10–12 students. The ideal number is closer to eight students. The teacher, who was my friend, mentor, and supervising teacher, prepared to make the classroom an appropriate environment for the kindergarten and first- and second-grade students. She contacted the site administration and departmental supervisors and followed the procedure for expressing concerns. She was continually disregarded. "We are doing the best that we can. You must be patient." So, instead of splitting the class, an extra teacher's aide was hired to work with the children. There were 20 children with developmental delays and 3 adults in a small classroom. Months passed, and no action was taken.

In December, the school's general kindergarten classes were large enough to get another unit allocation. Within 2 weeks, arrangements were made to hire a new teacher and to shuffle the school's physical arrangement to accommodate the new kindergarten class. Supplies were purchased. At the same time, a portable classroom was located to house the new class for students identified as having developmental delays, and interviews for a teacher began. Both of the new classes (i.e., general kindergarten and the special education class) opened on the same day, January 26. It had taken more than 5 months to get the special education class and just 2 weeks for the general kindergarten class.

At this point, a group of special education teachers and the school's guidance counselor had spoken at length about different approaches, solutions, and problems that the special education students were facing. The majority of concerns centered around the apparent double standard that existed at the school between general and special education students. We were continually omitted from schoolwide activities, assemblies, field trips, and the actual physical building. Of course, when we reminded others that students in our classes were left out, we

---

"Are All Children Treated the Same?" was written by a teacher not among the contributing authors of this book who wishes to remain anonymous.

were told that special education students were more than welcome to join. Through our discussions, we decided to take an active role in being advocates for our students by keeping them in the spotlight. We also decided to network with each other to promote awareness.

A grandparent whose grandchild was in the class for children with developmental delays was also advocating on behalf of the students in our school with special needs. She retained an attorney and contacted our site administrator, department head, district administrators, and the school board. She was stonewalled. Appointments were missed, telephone calls were not returned, and excuses were given for her concerns about overcrowding and location of the special education classes in portable units. The grandmother became discouraged with the district's lack of response and filed a complaint with the U.S. Office of Civil Rights.

On January 26, our site administrator received a call from the U.S. Office of Civil Rights. By noon, a decision was made to move three special education classes into the building and to move three first-grade classes into the portable units. This was very exciting because someone had fought the bureaucracy and made an impact. Children with disabilities would be in real classrooms and in the building. The three special education classes chosen to move were those with the nicest portables; meanwhile, my class remained in an old portable with no bathroom or running water. The carpet was splitting to show the plywood floor. The ceiling was water-stained and sagging. The cockroaches were a constant problem.

I went to my principal on January 29 to officially express my concerns and to allow him to explain the placement of students in a portable classroom while an unused computer lab occupied a classroom in the building. We had a productive conversation, although we did not agree on a solution. I was promised improved conditions within 2 years. I would be, if not in the building, in another portable with facilities to support the life skills components of my curriculum. His response to my concerns was, "I can't justify putting any more students with disabilities in the building." We agreed to bring up the issue at the end of the school year again. I left with my concerns on record.

Soon rumors were all over the school about my classroom being moved into the building. On February 1, I decided to go to the guidance counselor. The next day she asked the principal for clarification. "Eventually, but not right away," he said. Along with the rumors, I began to receive comments from the general education teachers. "Those students will always be a burden on society," one said. "They do not deserve to be in the building," said another. "How do you like being out in the leper colony?" I heard one teacher say to a teacher whose class had been assigned to a portable classroom. A teacher whom I had respected very much transferred from first to fifth grade to avoid being assigned to one of the portables. "I will not teach in a portable," she said. Needless to say, I realized two things: Do not believe rumors, and all students are not treated the same.

And now for the rest of the case.

In May, I was told that I would be in the computer lab in the fall. You can imagine my excitement. None of my students had ever been in a classroom in the building. It would be great for them. The next week I was told that I had been bumped from my position by a teacher with more seniority. I was very disappointed that I would not be there to share in the new experience with my students. I did, however, choose a position at a different school. My room is in the building, and I have a sink!

FUTURE LEADERS

Sinclair County school district encompasses a large metropolitan area in a growing region of the Midwest. Schools in Sinclair County are located in inner-city, suburban, and rural areas of the county. One of the regional supervisors of the school district decided to implement a program attempting to meet the needs of some African American male youth who were attending inner-city schools. These schools are identified as having at least 75% of the student population living in poverty conditions as defined by federal guidelines. Economic factors such as the percentage of students qualifying for free or reduced lunch and Aid to Families with Dependent Children are used to determine the school's ranking and eligibility for special programs. Designated federal funds are allocated to support the needs of these students in an effort to offset economic inequities.

A widely known educational consultant, Mr. Jones, who is himself African American, was contracted to search for a curriculum that would address the strength and potential of these children. Mr. Jones was chosen because of his reputation of extensive community involvement and leadership. He had been raised in a single-parent household of a housing project in a large city. Yet, through the encouragement of one teacher, Mr. Jones had attended major universities and earned several degrees. Mr. Jones had collaborated with this regional supervisor on numerous projects and had proved his ability to work with children, parents, and educators.

A commercially produced curriculum was purchased and modified to meet the needs of the children. Mr. Jones presented the package to all principals and lead teachers of the inner-city schools at a conference. They were instructed to share the idea with their respective staff and contact the county office if they desired to implement it. The regional supervisor would fund the project in only two of the schools. From the list of schools that responded, Mr. Jones chose Rogers and Clay Elementary Schools.

The lead teachers scheduled meetings with their fourth-grade teachers and asked them to identify areas of concern for the 15 male African American students having the most difficulty. The areas of concern were numerous referrals and suspensions, inappropriate behaviors and negative attitudes, low academic achievement, and lack of parental involvement. This program was to be evaluated on these criteria.

After contracting with the parents to meet monthly with him, Mr. Harris began the program with the boys, meeting them twice a week. The teachers were scheduled to meet with Mr. Jones once a month to discuss the children's progress and parental involvement.

"We need a name so we can be a club," said Joseph.

"Yeah, we gonna be the baddest club in this here school," Sam added.

"What do you mean when you say 'baddest club'?" asked Mr. Jones.

"Well my mom said you wanna help us be good in school, getting better grades and stuff like that. So we gonna be the cool guys getting good grades like the other kids. But see, we special 'cause we the only ones that get to do cool stuff with you," replied Sam.

After much discussion, the boys decided to name themselves The Successful Students Club/Future Leaders. Their sessions with Mr. Jones included reading texts about their African heritage, which led to geography discussions, which led to the boys interviewing their families about their ancestry and family travels. The children wrote about their families and shared this in group discussions. Each session involved journal writing and oral presentations.

Appropriate social skills were practiced, and the boys shared their most intimate triumphs and pains. During the time of these sessions, one student lost his father in a senseless neighborhood brawl; another lost a grandmother. The boys cried and hugged one of their fellow clubmates who was moving away. They were able to do this only after expressing their anger and disappointment about the circumstances of their lives to finally get to their feeling of loss.

Sharing their visions of their future enabled them to return to their classrooms with a sense of purpose. They visited a prominent African American judge and local African American–owned businesses. One principal remarked, "Mr. Jones, those boys of yours seem to be happy campers for a change!" Teachers commented on increased parental involvement and fewer behavior problems with the children.

Their parents attended their group meetings and openly discussed their individual problems with rearing their children. Some had to come to grips with some stark realities about their parenting skills. However, with the aid of the group, suggestions were generated and implemented that improved the parents' parenting skills.

"Mr. Jones, for the first time I feel that school is helping me and my boy. I don't mind having to wait longer to pick him up from school and being a little late to work, because my boy looks forward to coming to school now, and that teacher is sending home good notes for a change!" commented Mr. Greene.

The parents in both schools planned an end-of-the-year activity for the Future Leaders club. Rogers Elementary School's parents planned a banquet, and Clay Elementary School's had a picnic. Both events were attended by family members, staff, principals, and a representative from the regional supervisor's office. The highlight of the celebrations was the sharing of letters written to parents from their child and the parents sharing a letter to their child. Neither party knew of the other's intention. Needless to say, the emotion and appreciation was mutual and overwhelming. Mr. Jones was also presented gifts as a token of appreciation for his work with the boys. As one parent said, "We truly thank God for sending you to us. We have all learned a lot about ourselves, our children, and our school. We look forward to working with you next year."

The children and parents were looking forward to continuing the club the following year. As the school year was ending, the regional supervisor had to approve the budget for the upcoming year. Funds used for the Future Leaders program were no longer allocated. Discretionary funds were available, but his staff had already earmarked other projects to receive these funds. However, funding was available for continued parent initiatives and involvement. Therefore, he informed the schools that money was available only to fund further parent involvement at Clay and Rogers Elementary Schools. He also stated that the two schools would have to share these funds. However, funding for the Future Leaders club was not available.

Mr. Jones informed the participating principals that children, teachers, and parents were needed to have an effective program. He agreed to volunteer his services to continue the Future Leaders club and to work with the teachers. However, the principal at Rogers Elementary School decided that she wanted the SIT to make a decision about continuing any form of the program. SITs were established as part of a system of school improvement and accountability, implemented by the state. These teams include staff members, administrators, parents, and community members.

During the next meeting of the SIT at Rogers Elementary, one African American female administrator, five Caucasian female teachers, one African American teacher, and one African American parent decided that they did not want the program for parents or students. Their comments included

"I don't think Mr. Jones was the only reason the boys improved."
"Yeah, I worked hard on my social skills lesson in class. I think that had something to do with it."
"And parents really just need to continue to work with their kids. That's all they really need to do. We don't need the students involved in that club."

So, the Rogers SIT decided not to take advantage of the offer. When the Future Leaders club parents were informed of this decision, they called the regional supervisor's office and complained, saying, "This is the best thing that has happened to our children. We want this to continue."

The regional supervisor's office scheduled a special SIT meeting with the parent representatives and Mr. Jones present to express their concerns. All of the fourth-grade teachers attended with the regular members of the SIT. Mrs. Clark, the president of the Future Leaders club parent group, attended this meeting. She was accompanied by her oldest son, who was a teacher in the same school system. Mrs. Clark pleaded with the team to continue the program, sharing the parents' perception of improvement in the boys and supporting the connection the parents were feeling with the school.

"Don't you feel your children will continue to improve as long as you as parents continue to support them?" asked the principal.

"I don't know. But I do know that we as parents feel that we have been helped by this program and it gives us a chance to work with the school like we never have before," replied Mrs. Clark.

"My brother has really shown an interest in school since he started this program. I'm his older brother, and I've tried to work with him. But this program being housed in the same environment as his academics seems to say more to him than my involvement. He says that he likes coming to school now, whereas before he hated attending. How can you stop something like this that is giving these boys a sense of esteem?"

"I still think that our social skills activities have helped these boys, and we will continue that next year," answered one of the fourth-grade teachers.

The SIT meeting ended. The decision remained. As a result of this situation, some of the parents placed their children in other schools. Others continue to struggle with their children and the system to get their children through elementary school. Mr. Jones still gets numerous calls from parents and grandparents. He attempts to help them, yet the unity and focus has been lost, owing to the different schools the children now attend. Who really cares about the future of these African American Future Leaders?

11

Ethical Education
for Policy Makers
A Study of the Collegium

Yolanda G. Martinez and Theron D. Thompson

The cultures of school improvement teams (SITs) and school advisory committees (SACs) revolve around the process of decision making. Because this both defines and reflects the culture, the frame of responsibility and how it is interpreted plays a critical role in the success of decisions. Guided by this understanding, the Collaborative Research Group on Policy and Ethics (CRGPE) selected one concept for the Policy and Ethics Collegium to explore: ethics and decision making by SITs and SACs. The CRGPE recognized the pragmatic effect of these decisions on all members of the school community and decided to explore the level of ethical decision making and awareness within these groups. Was ethics considered a part of discussion and thought? Could ethical reasoning be identified in the decision-making process? What was going on with SITs and SACs in regard to thinking about ethics? How can the CRGPE help to develop an ethical base for decision making? What materials might be constructed from the exploration in this Collegium for use in training SITs and SACs? How can materials be tailored to meet the needs of SITs and SACs?

These questions were major concerns of the Collegium and framed the process of exploration that we undertook during the 3-day retreat (see Figure 1). This chapter describes the verbal interactions of participants and examines how these interactions, as a source of data, can aid in forming a base for building answers, understanding perspectives of SIT and SAC members, and framing their position within the decision-making process. In this study, the authors ob-

	Days 1 and 2
8:00 A.M.	**Introductions**
8:30 A.M.	**Case 1** Facilitator, Shirley Raines
10:30 A.M.	**Completion of evaluation of Case 1**
10:45 A.M.	**Ethicist's Presentation** Day 1: Moral principles, rules, and policies Peter French, Cole Chair in Ethics, University of South Florida Day 2: Ethics Without Choice: Reflections on Story, Character, and Compassion Darrell Fasching, Chair, Department of Religious Studies, University of South Florida
1:15 P.M.	**Case 2** Facilitator, Shirley Raines
3:15 P.M.	**Completion of evaluation of Case 2**
3:30 P.M.	**Ethicist reaction time** Perspectives on ethical decision making using teaching case methods
4:00 P.M.	**Group reflection and reaction time** Dialogue session with Collaborative Research Group members Facilitator, A.G. Rud
	Day 3
9:00 A.M.	**Synthesis session** Facilitator, A.G. Rud
1:00 P.M.	**Question and answer session** A.G. Rud with ethicists and panel members

Figure 1. Collegium schedule.

served and participated in the culture of the Collegium, were familiar with the language of the participants (i.e., educators and schools), and honored their perspectives. Their ideas and words are the basis for this chapter. Verbal interactions of the Collegium participants within the framework of teaching cases are reported and interpreted. In this chapter, we describe the setting, participants, and methodology used for gathering data. We also provide a discussion of the main themes that emerged during the 3-day Collegium. Finally, we discuss implications and recommendations for future work with SITs and SACs on the ethics of decision making.

SETTING

DaySpring Episcopal Conference Center, unconcerned with the blur of rush-hour traffic and only 3 miles from Interstate 75, was the perfect site for the type of work Collegium organizers had in mind. The secluded center rests on the banks of the Manatee River in Ellenton, Florida. The 90 acres of nature buffered the residents of DaySpring from the clamor and urgency of the outside world. The narrow, winding lane from the main road led the Collegium members to a place where live oaks and palms framed a setting amenable to reflection and introspection. DaySpring emanated a sense of seclusion, yet the conference facilities offered efficient, modern hospitality.

The reasons for selecting DaySpring as a meeting site centered on the site's attributes. First, it offered the benefit of being physically away from the business of schools and encouraged the community feeling of a retreat. There were no ringing telephones, job distractions, impromptu meetings, or emergencies. The center accommodated an uninterrupted focus.

Second, DaySpring supported the facilities needed for a 3-day Collegium. Overnight housing, dining facilities, and meeting rooms answered the physical needs of the Collegium organizers. The service rooms (meeting, dining, office, and lounge) were linked by a wooden deck, almost a verandah, with rocking chairs and a lake view. The complex of buildings seemed an integrated part of the landscape. Third, geography placed DaySpring close enough to the University of South Florida (USF) and schools to not be prohibitive, yet distant enough to give the feeling of being "away." In summary, DaySpring offered the environment Collegium organizers sought in which to introduce, situate, and focus a collection of people with no previous group history (for the schedule of events, see Figure 1).

Collegium Participants

Participants can be grouped into four categories: case discussion participants, CRGPE members, ethicists, and a panel of experts.

Case Discussion Participants People composing the case-discussion group were invited to participate for several reasons:

1. Each person represented the position of a stakeholder (mostly members) in a SIT or SAC decision-making process.
2. CRGPE members nominated people who would be outspoken and express their opinions in a newly formed group.
3. Ultimately, the final decision for attendance reflected the person's availability.

Roles of people attending included general and special education teachers, parent (of a child with a disability and a child without a disability), principal, SAC chair, SAC cochair, and elementary and secondary education director. The two racial groups represented in the Collegium were Caucasians and African Americans (for demographics of Collegium participants, see Table 1). In general, it can be said that each participant was purposely hand-picked for participation in the Collegium. Finally, permission was obtained from each of the participants to video- and audiotape the meetings for future analysis.

CRGPE Members CRGPE members attended the Collegium as observers and data gatherers. They were the designers of the 3-day Collegium, and their interests were vested in the long-term goal of de-

Table 1. Collegium participants

Day 1	
Case discussion participants[a]	
Teachers	3
Parents	3
School advisory committee chairs	2
Principals	1
Men	2
Women	7
Day 2	
Case discussion participants[a]	
Teachers	3
Parents	2
School advisory committee chairs	2
Principals	2
Exceptional student education directors	1
Men	3
Women	7
Day 3	
Case discussion participants	
Teachers	3
Parents	1
School advisory committee chairs	2
Principals	2
CRGPE members	12
Ethicists: Darrell Fasching, Peter French	
Panel experts: Van Dempsey, Susan Greenbaum, Brian McCadden, William Morse, Shirley Raines, A.G. Rud	

[a]CRGPE members, ethicists, and an expert panel were also in attendance as observers and were participants in the day's final session.

veloping curricular materials. Each member kept a set of field notes tailored to her or his particular research interests. All members had the opportunity, at the conclusion of the Collegium, to ask questions. Their observations served as a rich source of data collected through multiple perspectives and presented in this volume.

Ethicists Part of the Collegium design involved presentations by ethicists on each of the first 2 days. Their presentations were designed to take place between the discussion of Case 1 (Are All Children Treated the Same?) and Case 2 (Future Leaders) in order to assess the impact on discussion and meaning on the second case. Peter French, Cole Chair in Ethics at the St. Petersburg campus of USF, and Darrell Fasching, Chairperson of the Department of Religious Studies at USF, were the ethicists in attendance. Their ethical perspectives are presented in this volume.

French and Fasching fulfilled multiple roles. Aside from their presentations, each ethicist was also an observer, facilitator, and data gatherer. During the first 2 days of the Collegium, each ethicist observed, took field notes, presented, and facilitated a discussion at the end of the day. On the third day, both participated in a panel discussion involving a selected group of participants from the previous 2 days, including CRGPE members and panel experts.

Panel Experts In addition to the groups listed above, a panel of experts was also invited. The experts facilitated discussions, acted as observers, collected field notes, prepared reports, and contributed with their expertise in an area of study. They observed from the perspective of educational sociology, instructional design, anthropology, and psychology. Their theoretical contributions are also presented in this volume.

Methodology

Data Collection Data collection began the first day of the Collegium. It involved observation by the authors of this chapter, who took extensive field notes. The field notes were transcribed at the conclusion of the Collegium. The authors did not take part in the discussion of teaching cases, but they remained as nonintrusive observers.

Data Analysis The transcripts of field notes provided the basis for a review and interpretation of the case discussions. Transcripts from the 3 days were combined to form a bank of data. Even though the composition of the groups differed on each day, the setting, the cases, the outside role of discussion group participants, the observers, and the organization remained the same for the 2 days of the Collegium. On the third day, there was a change to a report-discussion format.

The authors disassembled the data in the transcripts and assigned them to various categories. The data gathered drove the category construction. Categorization was a strenuous 2-day process during which categories were changed, discarded, or combined to form the basis of this chapter's discussion section. The continual redesigning of this interpretive web aided in identifying commonalities emerging from the data. Figures 2, 3, and 4 represent those commonalities.

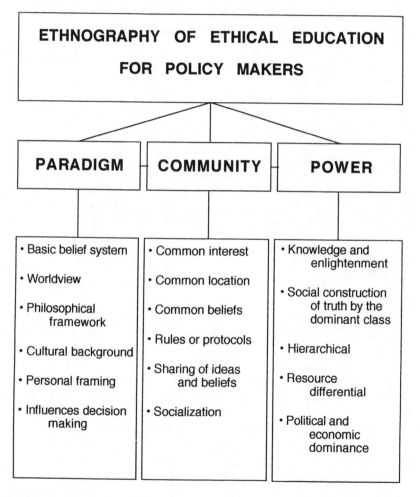

Figure 2.   Emergent themes and their attributes.

Figure 3. Paradigms identified from group discussions.

DISCUSSION

In the constructivist view, behavior and knowledge of people are formed by their lived experiences and encountered dilemmas. The experiential context determines how their stored information is used. How do cases activate the mental schema people possess and help them accommodate new information? Each person must cut and fit knowledge to make sense of it and fit it into what he or she already knows. Participants in the Collegium discussion group (see Table 1) made meaning by constructing three broad, influential categories: paradigm, community, and power. These categories appeared throughout the 3 days of discussion. The connections among these categories and the outside roles of the participants, as well as participants' personal agendas and experiences, can be identified. Nevertheless, case narratives are not enough. There must be discussion and application in a specific context—in this situation, ethical decision making in SITs and SACs. These connections are important and are reflected in the analysis of the data. Figure 2 lists the three emergent themes (i.e., paradigm, community, power) and the attributes of those themes considered by the authors in the analysis of the data. Once again, these themes were constructed by the authors upon analysis of the data.

Before beginning with the analysis, one more important issue is examined: talk space. The outside role of participants many times de-

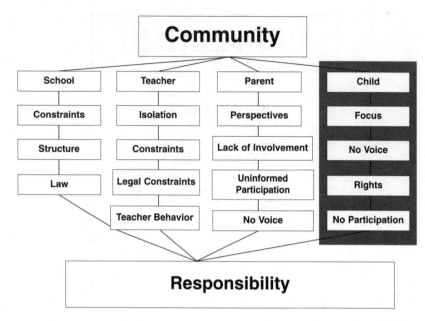

Figure 4. Community members as perceived by the Collegium.

termined who owned the talk space and for how long. Participants who were in outside roles that rewarded the ability to verbalize their thoughts and held administrative positions in the school spent the majority of their group time talking; that is, they were in charge of talk space. Parents were the least likely to volunteer information. Talk space was controlled to some extent by the facilitator, who shifted the focus from speaker to speaker and offered each person an opportunity to talk. Two elements of self-perception that influence the ability to control and persuade no matter what the context are "Who am I?" and "What is my role?" Making decisions, ethically or otherwise, is shaped by which group members control talk space. In the following sections, the three major themes that emerged during the 3 days of the conference are discussed: paradigm, community, and power.

PARADIGM
People construct basic belief systems in their lives for the purpose of dealing with real situations, dilemmas, and decisions. They use that world view as a means of personally and uniquely rooting themselves within a society or culture. The case discussion group exhibited basic belief systems that influenced their interpretations and perspectives concerning the cases. The life role of participants, life experiences,

personal agendas, and cultural backgrounds formed their world view. Each person reacted uniquely to the presentation of the cases.

The case discussion group did not specifically mention ethics as a consideration for decision making, even though the explicit purpose of the Collegium was for discussion of ethical issues. However, many of the topics they initiated could be considered ethical issues. Even with the addition of the ethics presentation at midday, discussions did not significantly increase in the afternoon group by specifically mentioning ethics. Four major paradigms within the group discussions were identified: skepticism, cynicism, resignation, and care (see Figure 3).

Skepticism

Many comments centered on the doubt of the maintenance of successful programs or the ability of SITs and SACs to provide the best programs possible for children. Teachers, especially, presented the skeptical paradigm with comments such as "successful programs are usually cut" and "I am not surprised that that happened," as in the teaching case "Future Leaders" (see Chapter 10). Parents also framed their responses skeptically: "Everyone has the answer except the parent."

Skepticism seemed to center on comments by parents and teachers. Perhaps these are the people who feel less empowered in the decision-making process. They felt that, even though the decisions were being made, they were not sure that they would be implemented. The case "Future Leaders" (see Chapter 10) specifically revealed feelings of skepticism from the teacher and parent perspectives. There was a question about whose voice would be heard and whose interests would be met. The case discussion group was skeptical that concern for the students was not foremost in each of the two cases. Whose interests were driving the actions in both cases? Does the discussion group have experiential knowledge that fosters this skepticism? Was it predetermined that the program in the "Future Leaders" teaching case would fail?

The case discussants seemed to be skeptical for many reasons: previous SIT and SAC experiences, role orientation, composition of the SITs and SACs, personal agendas in the school, and views of individuals within the school community. In many ways, the discussion is reflected in the statement, "Good does not always win." Who determines good, and what are the criteria for winning?

Cynicism

Devaluing the worth of events and decisions, or doubting the sincere motivations of players in the SIT and SAC context, constructed an interesting lens through which to view the two cases. How various members of the culture of the Collegium interpreted case events revealed experiences of the discussion group members.

"I've made up my mind. Don't confuse me with the facts."
"Do you want the truth?"
"What's wrong with the system?"
"We know how to do it. Why don't we do it?"
"Not all evil is delivered malevolence. No one is bad. It's the system."
"He's probably paying those kids."
"Write a letter to the editor and look for another job."
"This is so typical."

Similar to skepticism, cynicism was reflected to a large extent by parents and teachers. Their comments were of a critical nature and not only doubted the value of what was offered but also approached the cases and discussion with what we have termed a *postmodernist perspective*. Such a perspective examines decisions and decision making through a lens that postpones acceptance until those events have been reviewed in regard to appropriateness, motivation, stance, and reality.

Resignation

Another theme evident in the discussion is what we have called *resignation*. For those of us who are familiar with the bureaucratic and institutionalized functioning of schools, the idea of resignation by those who do not hold power positions in the hierarchy is not hard to accept. In most of the cases, as evident in the quotes gathered from the Collegium, resignation is practiced more often by teachers and parents, the two groups with the least amount of power:

"Teachers cover up and use their own money. Teachers take more than other people."
"Was it predetermined that it would fail? If not this, then what?"
"There are layers and layers; parents are treated like second-class citizens."

Some group discussion members seemed resigned to the fact that this would happen—almost to the point of not complaining or questioning.

Care

"Sometimes you have to not go to work and go and advocate for your child." Representatives from all outside roles put forth and operated within a paradigm of care. Each discussion group member displayed concern for children and their success. "Egos aside. Act on the best interest of students. What is best in this situation?" Interpretation of cases revolved around many points, but issues and interpretations of care guided numerous responses. The case "Are All Children Treated the Same?" (see Chapter 10) was telling in that discussion group members talked with genuine concern for special education students in the portable classroom. In the case "Future Leaders" (see Chapter 10), the care paradigm encompassed parents as well as children. Again and again, discussants repeated the phrase, "What is the best for all of us?"

However, those people deciding the best who are members of SITs and SACs represent the mainstream culture and define what is best for minorities and those from different backgrounds. Constant interrogation of motives and contexts needs to accompany the paradigm of care. What is best is in the direct control of the perspective and role of the provider. To situate the caregiver in the frame of the receiver requires reflection, knowledge, empathy, and analysis. Responses within the paradigm of care were grounded in personal and diverse perspectives.

COMMUNITY

Community refers to a group of people sharing a common location, interest, and belief system. Basic to the success of the community is the behavior of sharing (e.g., ideas, beliefs, resources) (see Figure 2). Communities also develop rules and protocols for operating in a productive and harmonious environment. Four types of communities (see Figure 4) are evident:

1. School community
2. Teacher community
3. Parent community
4. Community of children

Notice that we have the community of children in a shaded area to signify the absence of children from the Collegium (see Figure 4).

School Community

Most of the comments made by discussion group participants related to social, structural, and legal constraints that inhibited the functioning of the school. Societal constraints, for example, were thought to be present in social attitudes toward children (e.g., ethnic or racial minorities, children with disabilities). Structural concerns centered around problems related to school administration and lack of funding. An issue of noticeable concern was the principal's inability to take more responsibility in school problems and encourage communication between administration and teachers.

Teacher Community

Most of the comments made by participants regarding what we have termed the *teacher community* were related to the lack of collaboration between general and special education teachers. This is quite telling when most of the participants stress the need to work with the idea of putting children first. A recommendation provided by the participants was that special and general education teachers should exchange classrooms every once in a while to share experiences. There was also a shared concern about overcrowded classrooms, which may increase tension between teachers.

Parent Community
Despite comments on the general notion that parents "don't know anything," some participants agreed that parents are the children's best advocates. Administrators participating in the discussions, however, viewed parents as uninvolved. "Everyone else has the answer except the parent," they said. The frustration of the parents was evident. Parents also expressed that they were overwhelmed with the system and the lack of information and support. In other words, parents felt that they were not encouraged to become involved.

Community of Children
Interestingly enough, though the primary concern of the Collegium organizers was to find ethical perspectives on decision making that affected children, children were not invited to participate. Children are not regular members of SITs and SACs. Most of the comments—made by adults, of course—revolved around the idea that children are not made part of the decision-making process. Collegium participants saw children as devalued, which makes students frustrated, angry, and unable to share their feelings.

POWER
We define *power* as the ability of the mainstream culture to set the rules and interpret behaviors in the perspective of mainstream categories. Power is the chance to assign appropriateness and value to others in society and interpret their behavior from one's own viewpoint. It is the control of knowledge and the chance to use one's own frame of reference in evaluating others (see Figure 5).

Issues of power in the data emerged in relation to the outside roles of discussion group participants. Who felt power, who used it, who denied or remained unaware that they possessed it, and who defined it? Paradigms and community can be linked with perceptions of power in the classroom. The following quotes, taken from the conversation, illustrate power distribution in the school system:

"Yeah, I back my teachers."
"Teachers need validation."
"Focus on the parents. They can't advocate."

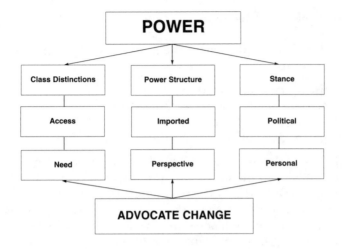

Figure 5. Relationships of power in SITs and SACs as perceived by Collegium participants.

"Even though it began wrong, the end result was successful and I would fight to keep it."
"Power and comfort. Resentment."
"Each individual is involved at a different level."
"The hidden teacher. There are different levels of the system and who we are serving."
"Where was all this information going? Where was the power?"
"They just need someone to blame."
"They blamed it all on the system. The ethical failure of professional jealousy."
"Don't assume everyone has the skills to participate."

Class Distinctions

The various representations of power within the Collegium discussion group help one to understand whose voices are heard in the decision-making process. Class distinction, as referred to in Figure 5, denotes that there are individuals in SITs and SACs (i.e., parents) who are powerless. This powerlessness may be the result, as stated earlier, of lack of support or lack of information.

Power Structure

The outcomes of SIT and SAC deliberations are effectively controlled by the structure of power, just as outcomes are controlled in the larger society. The comment "Don't assume everyone has the skills to participate" is descriptive of the position. Who is eligible for tenure on a SIT or SAC? Who has the skills to participate? The answers to these questions determine the outcomes, effectiveness, and intent of SITs and SACs.

Several elements document the power structure within the case discussion group:

1. The use of the pronoun *my*
2. The amount of talk space of each discussant
3. The seating arrangements
4. The perspectives offered by the discussants

First, the use of the pronoun *my* tagged people's position in the power structure. Who uses the word, and who does not? Phrases such as *my teachers, my parents,* and *my SAC* show the structure of power and where the speaker is placed and where the speaker places everyone else. Because *my,* by definition, is a possessive pronoun, it sets the hierarchy of the power structure and influences how events are interpreted.

Second, discussants with the perception of power owned far more talk space than those who did not perceive themselves as powerful in this setting. Dominance of talk space was an effective way to construct the structure of the group.

Third, and in combination with talk space, was the seating arrangement at each session during the first 2 days of the Collegium. With one exception, people who held roles of power outside the Collegium sat at the front of the room, and parents and teachers sat at the far sides or at the back of the group.

Fourth, the perspectives of the discussants were directly related to the degree of power they perceived that they possessed in the SIT and SAC environment. In the earlier "Paradigm" section, we noted that teachers and parents expressed viewpoints linked with skepticism, cynicism, and resignation far more frequently than did principals.

CONCLUSIONS

The power base that discussion group participants held was reflected in the paradigms they used to frame their discussion of the cases (see Figures 4 and 5). Skepticism and cynicism were most evident in discussion by parents and teachers. These discussions seemed to describe an element of powerlessness or, in the least, of being left out of the decision-making loop. Parents especially voiced a lack of control and devaluing of their knowledge and opinions relating to their children. Resignation was most disturbing of all because it portrayed the stance of unquestioning acceptance and hopelessness. Resignation and passivity by parents and teachers allow space and opportunity for carte blanche by SITs and SACs in school-based decision making. The paradigm of care fit most comfortably in the context of schooling. Nevertheless, people inside the education environment must examine their motives to ensure that decisions are based on an ethic of care. They need to view those decisions from the stance of other cultures, agendas, socioeconomic statuses, and beliefs. The major world view categories that emerged from the data in this section help to explain why and how people make decisions in the SIT and SAC context.

In summary, the Collegium gave the following two insights into major behaviors exhibited by Collegium participants: development of a basic world view and of a sense of community. The transcripts from the Collegium indicate a definite need to consider the perspectives of members of SITs and SACs in understanding the deliberative process. On what basis do they rationalize the ethical decisions? Have their perspectives been verbalized, examined, and applied in beneficial ways? It would be useful to assist the SAC in developing a framework, vision, and world view to guide their work.

Furthermore, just as discussants viewed material from the cases, members of SITs and SACs need to develop a sense of community. These committees should have a common goal and a common language. Although dynamic and short-lived, such committees should strive to construct a community within the school. They have the opportunity to engage in team building that empowers their work and, thus, benefits the school.

This review of the Ethics Collegium formulates far more questions than it could ever answer. Its prime objective was to cause an open space in our thinking that will allow the development of answers to those questions. Several specific questions emerged:

- How can the composition of SITs and SACs be representative of populations in the schools and not merely serve the function of dominant, traditional cultures or authority figures?
- What do the categories of paradigm, community, and power mean for the operation of SIT and SAC committees?
- How can the multiple perspectives of SIT and SAC members be combined or restructured to solve dilemmas in the school?
- What ethical dilemmas will arise because of the basic description of SITs and SACs?
- What are the chances of reaching ethical decisions with the roadblocks raised by unique, personal positions of each individual?
- Will the education of SIT and SAC committees help to moderate the effects of power and paradigm?

12

Developing a Curriculum for Ethical Policy Making in School-Based Decision-Making Committees

Neal H. Berger, James L. Paul, and Patricia R. Fagan

The purpose of this chapter is to help integrate the more theoretical aspects of our work and the design, development, evaluation, and utilization of a curriculum for ethical decision making by site-based decision-making committees (SBDMCs). Here we 1) present a synthesis of what we have learned and specify assumptions that we believe to be useful for developing a curriculum, 2) describe barriers to developing an ethical deliberation curriculum, 3) delineate a model for describing and integrating curriculum variables, and 4) provide a preliminary set of curriculum design and construction guidelines that we believe to be useful for guiding curriculum planners and writers. We are currently employing the model and the guidelines in developing a curriculum for ethical policy making in SBDMCs.

OVERVIEW

For the past 3 years, the Collaborative Research Group on Policy and Ethics (CRGPE) has pursued several different strategies in creating a foundation for developing a curriculum to assist SBDMCs in making or providing advice about ethical policies. One strategy has been a review of literature on policy, ethics, school reform, site-based management, site-based decision making (SBDM), and inclusion. Another strategy has been to seek the consultation of ethicists and individuals who are directly involved as members or leaders of SBDMCs. We integrated information gained from the literature and from consultants with our experience and knowledge in an iterative process of developing and refining understandings about ethics and the policy work of SBDMCs.

Besides the literature reviews and consultations, we established two forums to assist us in learning more about SBDMCs and ethical policy making. The first was a small conference of SBDMC chairs, other SBDMC members, principals, and community leaders. This 1-day conference was held approximately 1½ years into our work to validate or invalidate our understandings and to gain input relative to our long-range goal: development of a curriculum to assist SBDMCs in making ethical policy decisions. Since our CRGPE included four members who were either chairs or members of SBDMCs, we knew we had some grounding for our initial perceptions.

The conference helped us understand SBDMCs in several respects. First, it confirmed our belief that committee members, at least those involved in the CRGPE and those participating in the conference, have received no training in the ethical aspects of their work. Second, we found little or no representation of the needs and interests of students with disabilities. Third, we found a commitment to "doing the right thing," even if it involved bending or breaking some of the rules. Fourth, we found relatively little information about students and the school ecologies in which SBDMCs work. Fifth, we found a wide variability among and between groups regarding their perceptions of the amount of policy authority they could exercise. These findings were useful in assisting us with our planning.

The second forum, the Collegium, was a larger, 3-day gathering with a much more sophisticated format to help us obtain the kinds of data needed to help us clarify and extend the propositions with which we were working. The Collegium (for a description of the Collegium, see the Appendix at the end of the book) led us to what we believe are more definitive understandings of ethical policy making in SBDMCs, which are discussed throughout this book. Although these understandings continue to be modified by new information in the continuing work of the CRGPE, we believe we understand enough about ethics and the policy work of SBDMCs to have some confidence in the model for developing the curriculum in ethical policy making that is now the focus of our work. Before discussing the curriculum model, we briefly review understandings that have changed through the process we have followed over the past 3 years. These understandings form the basis for our work on the curriculum.

Our work began with our wish to understand and assist SBDMCs with their task of developing ethical policies or providing advice about ethical policies. We knew from the beginning that we would need a model to guide the development of a curriculum for ethical policy making. We believed we needed to become more focused on the moral perspectives informing policy making. Our historical commitment in special education to psychological theories and positivist research models has limited our sensitivity to and analysis of the existential and ethical dilemmas facing children with disabilities and their families as well as schools and service providers. Without rejecting or negating psychological knowledge or empirical research, we believed we needed to become better philosophers to address some of the policy challenges we now face. Our work in the CRGPE has reinforced this view as we have attempted to establish a philosophical foundation for developing the curriculum.

We believed a knowledge base about ethics was needed and would be helpful for SBDMCs in making ethical policy decisions. After 3 years and thousands of hours invested in understanding ethics and the policy challenges brought about by site-based management, our convictions have deepened about the relevance and, indeed, the urgency of developing a curriculum in ethical policy making for SBDMCs. Our perspectives about what this means and how it might work have changed dramatically. We have extended our belief in the importance of ethical policy making from students with disabilities to include other marginalized populations as well as the general school population.

At first, we were uncritically guided by a positivist model that led us to search for one or more principles, or criteria, that could be applied in an algorithm for decision making. We focused on developing a philosophical and technical framework for logical and normative ethical analysis. We also believed that our literature reviews and our consultations with ethicists would enable us to make a decision about a preferred ethical theory. It was not until we experienced the difficulties of applying ethical theories in our group and attempted to do the same with SBDMCs that we began to see the relevance and potential of narrative ethics. Our growing appreciation for the complexity of ethical theory and the policy environment of local schools directed our interests away from ethical principles and rules, although they can be useful in some contexts, and toward the ethics of story, or narrative ethics (see Chapter 5).

Our belief in a didactic approach to ethics also changed to a focus on the analysis of ethical dilemmas in policy from different perspectives. Rather than knowing only about ethical principles or knowing how to apply them, we came to appreciate knowing that some things are true and valued in one's experience and that those values need to be taken into account in ethical deliberations. To make ethical decisions, we came to believe that one must be able to identify with those involved with and affected by the problem (see Chapter 6). Furthermore, in teaching ethics, we believe one is more likely to change if he or she can identify personally with the issues involved (see Chapter 5). We came to view a narrative approach as the best match of the values and philosophy of our CRGPE with the ethical policy work of SBDMCs. Consistent with this view, we found the teaching case approach to be an appropriate medium for instruction (see Chapter 11).

Although our initial focus was on developing a technical framework for the analysis of ethical policy making, we have come to an understanding of SBDMCs as storied groups functioning within particular institutional narratives. We have found a narrative perspective to be more useful than a technical, principle-based perspective in thinking about the ethical policy work of SBDMCs. Although ethical principles, such as egalitarianism (i.e., equal treatment for all) or utilitarianism (i.e., the greatest good for the greatest number), are illuminating and helpful in considering specific policy questions, the deeper forces of individual and collective understandings of what the group is about (i.e., its story) and the roles each member tells her- or himself that she or he is playing help shape any group's ethic. The group develops a style and a character on which it draws for decisions: "This is who we are, what we are about, and how we do business here." For example, an SBDMC is more likely to be committed to a policy of including all children in the general education classroom to the maximum extent possible if it sees itself as part of a school that is welcoming, caring, and hospitable—that is, inclusive. Abstract principles, especially those that may be inconsistent with the group's ethic, are not as likely to change behavior. The group's ethic, which may or may not be openly stated or consciously acknowledged, can be brought into greater awareness and can be changed, but the process involves changing the culture and the community in which the ethic is held.

We started with the assumption that ethics education was an intervention that would have an impact on decision making, including decisions about inclusion. We came to appreciate even more fully the extent to which the ethical theory selected and the method of instruction validated or invalidated this assumption. We believed SBDMC members and local school leaders would be interested and willing to become involved in work on understanding how to support ethical policy making if they perceived it to be relevant and helpful. Our experience with the 1-day conference strengthened this belief, especially our experience with the Collegium. We believed we could gain cooperation if we could make an adequate case, but we were not certain we could interest SBDMC members in discussions of abstract principles that smacked of theory and what is perceived as "university-type" work rather than the practical work of SBDMCs. We found we could obtain cooperation as long as we were serious about real issues, such as the issues contained in teaching cases. The responses from those with whom we have worked to date have been generally enthusiastic. Some had thought about the value issues embedded in policy dilemmas they address; others had not. However, once they gained some experience with the analysis of a case and an ethical framework within which to analyze it, they saw the relevance and became motivated to learn more. Whether motivation and analysis of the case were aided more by the ethics instruction that preceded it, as occurred at the Collegium, or by the experience of community building, as occurred in the CRGPE, is not conclusive (see Chapter 7).

We knew we would find considerable variation among SBDMCs in membership, authority, and operational features, but we underestimated the variability and the differential impact of political and moral ecologies on SBDMC decisions. The ethical base for decision making in SBDMCs is extraordinarily complex when one considers the demographics of students and staff, the dynamics of groups, the external regulatory systems, the resources available, and the data available for decision making, which ranges from nonexistent to unreliable. The more we learned about the realities of SBDMCs, the more confirmation we felt for focusing on narrative ethics and case method.

The education of students with disabilities and others at risk for failure did not seem to be a specific priority for SBDMCs. Neither technical assistance and training for SBDMCs nor the participation of parents of students with disabilities in committees ensured even minimal information and advocacy for the interests of these students. We found this to be true, and we have not seen much evidence that this is changing. We do not believe the inclusion agenda is well understood or that there is enough information available to SBDMCs to ensure responsible ethical decisions about children with disabilities and those at risk. For this reason, if for no other, SBDMCs should look at the ethical dimensions of their decisions as these decisions affect the needs and interests of children at risk of school failure and those with disabilities.

We believed site-based management means that considerably more policy authority would be located at the local school level to effect a reform agenda and that SBDMCs would be organizational structures for mediating that authority to bring about significant change. SBDMC members vary widely in perceptions of their policy-making role, and, in fact, their policy-related role is generally unclear. For the most part, those with whom we have worked view themselves as strictly advisory, having no particular authority in the policy-making process. We have found SBDMCs to be engaged in different kinds of activities, including providing advice about relatively benign operational issues in schools and long-range planning. Although SBDMCs are, for the most part, performing some policy-related function, we found little by way of deep reform and serious restructuring initiatives. (For a discussion of policy reform that leads to real change in schools, see Corbett, 1990).

Beginning with very broad questions to guide our work, the CRGPE developed more specific questions that are guiding some of our research interests. Among those questions are the following:

- Assuming that the SBDMC passes through developmental stages within particular contexts, how does the maturity level of an SBDMC influence the ethical deliberation embedded in the decision-making process it uses?
- When compromise occurs, to what extent does ethical reasoning affect the outcomes?
- What ethical and other considerations govern consensus building in SBDMCs?

We have continued to believe that a thoughtful examination of philosophical problems would lead us to more valid accounts of the current policy challenges facing SBDMCs. However, we have come to appreciate even more the complexity and interdependence of the social, cultural, political, and psychological forces that contribute to the construction of ethical perspectives in local school policy decisions. For example, the cultural traditions of members, interpersonal group dynamics, and the political ecologies of SBDMCs are inseparable from the moral vision guiding policy deliberations and the ethical base for policy decisions. It is this thick and highly contextualized view of SBDMCs that now guides our development of an ethics curriculum to assist in their policy-related work.

In summary, the CRGPE has

- Developed an appreciation of the cultural, political, and moral complexity of SBDMCs and the ambiguity of their policy role
- Deepened our concern about the readiness of SBDMCs to support or provide focused advice about inclusion for all students

- Decided to employ narrative ethical theory as a primary framework for examining the moral dilemmas in school policies, especially the ethics of care, hospitality, and inclusion
- Decided to use the case method as a primary tool for teaching ethics

These decisions and perspectives, coupled with our understandings of the barriers to developing the curriculum (discussed in the next section), form the foundation for our work on a curriculum for ethical deliberation for SBDMCs.

BARRIERS TO DEVELOPING AN
ETHICAL DELIBERATION CURRICULUM

There is a growing concern about the erosion of moral and social values in the United States. Even high school students list this as a major problem facing teenagers. Students often state that they have cheated on homework and exams. They also report that they believe that their teachers are aware of the cheating but do nothing to stop it. These views of young people raise two interesting points. First, serious ethical dilemmas face students in today's schools. Second, students appear to place the responsibility for the lack of ethics outside themselves, preferring to see the problem as resting on the shoulders of their teachers rather than on their own but lamenting the current state of affairs. This second point has significant implications for the work of SBDMCs. The goal of building a moral learning community through SBDMCs in the public schools also addresses SBDMC members serving as role models for young people.

The main barrier is that adults as well as students see the locus of control in ethical issues as lying somewhere outside of themselves. Decrying the decline in moral and social values, too many people continue to do business as usual, whether cheating on homework, running a red light, or disregarding the effects of their actions on others. Creating a moral community within schools through the work of SBDMCs is a possibility, but only if people recognize their obligations and responsibilities to others in their community. The work in the Collegium demonstrated that SBDMC members are interested in improving the lives of students. Although it may appear presumptuous to assume that people who invested time in SBDMCs need to be taught ethical decision making, in our experience, the diversity of schools and the complexity of the policy process creates an environment in which good and well-intentioned people can use assistance.

The Greatest Good

In the CRGPE, we have devoted much discussion to trying to understand the underlying ethic that governs most schools. One member has remarked that, in the current political climate, he feared that the utilitarian ethic, loosely interpreted as striving for the greatest good for the greatest number, was taking over decision making. He was referring, of course, to policy being guided by the bottom line and marginalized students being left behind. The problem here is possibly not with the utilitarian ethic, but with the concept of the greatest good (see Chapter 4).

Stanley Hauerwas, in *Vision and Virtue* (1974), wrote about the principle of universalizability, a criterion of moral principles that everyone must acknowledge, regardless of status, particular biographical history, or commitments and beliefs held. Although Hauerwas acknowledged the criticism of this concept, he argued that the concept is a condition without which moral argument and judgment are not possible. The universal standard by which people judge themselves as members of a moral community, that is, the greatest good, is a central issue in moral philosophy. An example of such a standard, one that helps shape work on the curriculum, is that society is ultimately judged by the way the most vulnerable citizens of society are regarded and treated.

An *ethic of care* was defined by Fisher and Tronto (1990) as "a species activity that includes everything that we do to maintain, confine, and repair 'our world' so that we can live in it as well as possible. That would include our bodies, ourselves, and our environment, all of which we seek to interweave in a complex, life-sustaining web" (p. 40). As individuals, we are all metamorphically interwoven. That is just the point. Damage to those people who are most vulnerable damages the web, and all ultimately suffer. The ethic of care ideally should permeate the web. When Soltis (1990) wrote of taking the public perspective in educational research, he was referring to the need for those involved to recognize "the moral issues of our socially constructed and publicly shared lifeworld" (p. 251). Decisions made on the basis of half-truths have an eroding effect on the overall strength of our society. We believe an understanding of the interconnectedness of human lives will focus SBDMCs on the far-reaching implications of decisions made on behalf of others.

Who and Where?

A second barrier to developing a curriculum for SBDMCs is the nature and composition of the individual groups. This topic is discussed in detail in Chapter 9. Each SBDMC is composed of individuals with varying demands on their time and energy. In addition, each SBDMC has its own dynamic that influences the delivery of an ethics curriculum. Members vary in their level of commitment to explorations of ethical goals. Different people have different levels of ethical awareness and interest, and these differences must be accommodated in an ethics curriculum. How should these individual differences be addressed within groups? Is it possible that curriculum could be delivered along a continuum ranging from the whole SBDMC participating within an existing format to individuals or groups participating in workshops held away from the workplace?

Unfettered Individualism

A third barrier is the question of *whose ethics* are to be presented? This is perhaps the most controversial element to be faced. Much discussion has centered on this question—a question that deals with who we are at the most fundamental level. Educator and writer Theresa Richardson's (1989) discussion of the politics of individualism was very revealing in this regard. Richardson explored the evolution and impact of national character on public policy. The history of the United States and its national character are steeped in revolution and the idea of individual freedoms. Richardson wrote, "De Tocqueville, who criticized the oddities of democracy [in the 19th century], found the source of these discrepancies [between] democratic ideas and democratic practices in unfettered individualism" (pp. 173–174). In this discrepancy between the ideal of individualism and the implementation of social policy lies the origin of the debate over whose ethics are to be taught. Such a discussion, one would suspect, is largely a U.S. phenomenon. Is it possible that the revolutionary character of the U.S. national psyche, treasured by its citizens, has blinded Americans to the possibility of simply stating the case and allowing the audience to accept or reject it as they see fit?

A common theme that runs through most ethical perspectives helps to make the point (see also Chapters 4 and 5). Ethicist Peter French (1992) argued in favor of the existence of a universal morality. He stated that one can identify another agent's moral beliefs only if one agrees with those beliefs. According to French, just because large numbers of people in any culture hold a certain belief does not necessarily make it a moral belief. Only those beliefs that honor the rights of others are moral beliefs. Darrell Fasching (1995) called this philosophy "hospitality to the stranger." By any name, such an ethic focuses on the responsibility of the individual and, by extension, on the responsibility of the group to center the locus of ethical control within and to recognize the impact of individual and collective decisions on the others in the community. The next section uses the Zais (1976) model of the curriculum to help synthesize and expand the findings and barriers discussed previously.

A PROPOSED GRAPHIC MODEL FOR THE CURRICULUM

To summarize and integrate common understandings of a curriculum for ethical decision making within an SBDMC context, Zais's (1976) eclectic model has been adapted. The Zais model is patterned after the Tyler (1949) rationale. Despite numerous curriculum models, however, the Zais model appears easily adaptable for our purposes because it emphasizes the philosophical assumptions and other foundations that underlie the curriculum and focuses on understanding the bases and nature of the curriculum itself rather than on delineating a process for curriculum development. As Rogan and Luckowski (1990) pointed out, the Zais model "betrays its datedness" (p. 20) in that it was published when considerable reconceptualization was occurring in curriculum (see Figure 1).

Although the Zais (1976) model is not directed at curriculum construction, development, design, or implementation, its graphic presentation is used in this chapter to lay out the interrelationships among the variables critical for designing and developing an ethical

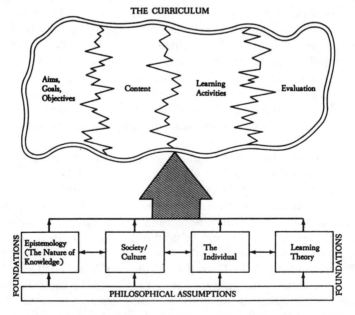

Figure 1. An eclectic model of the curriculum and its foundations. (From Zais, R.S. [Ed.]. [1976]. *Curriculum: Principles and foundations* [p. 97]. New York: Thomas Y. Crowell; reprinted by permission.)

deliberation curriculum for SBDMCs. The following description, summarizing Zais, should be helpful in understanding the model depicted in Figure 1. The curvy double line shows the curriculum and its four interrelated coherent components: 1) aims, goals, and objectives; 2) content; 3) learning activities; and 4) evaluation. The curriculum components (i.e., the curriculum design) are joined with irregular saw-toothed lines to emphasize the interrelatedness of the four components to one another, as in a jigsaw puzzle. Underlying the curriculum are the four coherent foundation blocks (i.e., epistemology, society and culture, the individual, learning theory) and philosophical assumptions. Although the double-ended arrows joining the foundation blocks suggest interrelatedness, such as in the curriculum, these components are not viewed as an integrated whole in the Zais model. Philosophical assumptions, which influence value judgments made about the foundational areas, undergird the four foundational areas. A large, dark arrow joins the four foundational blocks to the curriculum to indicate their influence on curriculum content and organization.

Starting at the bottom of the Zais (1976) model—the philosophical assumptions—and moving up and across the figure from left to right, this section summarizes a proposed SBDMC ethical deliberation curriculum and its foundations. Adaptations of the model may occur, and revisions will be necessary and desirable. For the purposes of this chapter and as a guide for future work, however, the Zais model satisfies the needs of this text, and references serve as a major source for delineating the curriculum and its foundations. Readers familiar with curriculum may feel that this section is somewhat basic and more explicit than necessary. However, this detail helps convey the depth and breadth of the perspectives that underlie current and future work in this area. At the end of this section, the Zais model has been adapted to display and summarize the beliefs and assumptions presented in the first three parts of this chapter. This summary includes the critical features that will guide the design and development of the curriculum during the next stage of our work.

Philosophical Assumptions
Philosophical assumptions influence the value judgments made about the foundational areas of the curriculum. Teachers teach what they believe to be good and are guided by what they believe people can become. When the authors of this chapter thought about what people may become, the targets were students, especially marginalized students, and adult members of SBDMCs, for whom the curriculum is being developed. In this case, adults (and occasionally middle and high school students) are the diverse members of the SBDMC (e.g., educational and other professionals, parents, community representa-

tives and leaders, secondary students, others). To construct the philosophical assumptions for this model, basic commitments and assumptions of the CRGPE's collective philosophy are identified. To do so, Zais's (1976) lead is followed by addressing three philosophical categories that have the greatest relevance for curriculum: ontology, epistemology, and axiology. It should be noted that the epistemological section here begins to move into the first foundational area of the Zais model, epistemology (i.e., the nature of knowledge), which is a philosophical category at the center of the educational enterprise.

Ontology addresses the question "What is real?" What is real seems obvious because it is embedded in our culture, which provides the assumptions and rules for constructing shared realities and beliefs at the most fundamental level. We believe that ideas such as justice, democracy, and love exist as symbols of human intelligence rather than as a physical entity such as a desk. We believe people can experience, communicate, and share ideas without having concrete physical representations of those ideas present because the idea is at least as important as a tangible thing. We believe that a symbolic idea such as justice is real and that it may be taught by placing the learner in direct contact with tangible cases and experiences that can be manipulated. We believe that one constructs a vision and shares that vision of reality with SBDMC colleagues. The reality for SBDMCs is the shared construction of meaning among group members that makes each group's vision highly idiosyncratic, experience based, and local as well as characterized by general principles of law and public policy. The real world is knowable by everybody; different groups construct their realities; and no authorities enjoy the special gift of knowing or declaring a universal reality.

Epistemological questions ask "What is knowledge? How do we know it?" A good illustration of an epistemological issue, in the context of this chapter, is an ongoing debate within the CRGPE whether SBDMC members must be consciously aware of the specific ethics that underlie their decisions. Is a decision authentic if the decision maker is not conscious of the ethic that underlies the decision? Or must the decision maker be aware of and able to communicate the ethic that guided the decision? (See Chapter 4 for a discussion of the relative importance of motivations versus outcomes.) Is the version of deciding without a conscious deliberation of ethical matters too ethereal or intuitive? Or can the truth of the decision best be reached by examining ethical matters overtly and scientifically, that is, empirically?

Epistemology and ontology are closely related. Indeed, postmodernists hold that these questions are inseparable. In this context, the point is that basic assumptions about what is real and how people come to know and understand what is true have a great deal to do with our understanding of decisions about what is of value. The construction of the good and the worthy is highly contextualized, in our view, and shaped by local culture. Local school policy issues are complex, and local circumstances need to be taken into account. Indeed, casuistry has long provided "a reasonable and effective set of practical procedures for resolving the moral problems that arise in particular real-life situations" (Jonsen & Toulmin, 1988, p. 10). This chapter is guided primarily by a constructivistic position based on two central principles: Knowledge is actively constructed by each cognizing individual, and cognition is experiential (i.e., it is not the discovery of independent reality).

A curriculum developed on an epistemology of constructed knowledge must have flexible content because all knowledge is viewed as changing. Consequently, it is critical for the curriculum to emphasize the process of generating and constructing knowledge rather than learning a specific knowledge base. It should be a curriculum of constructing the hows of solving ethical problems rather than a curriculum of what the solutions ought to be. Circumstances require that the content of the curriculum be prioritized because it would be unrealistic to include everything. Axiological considerations are helpful for establishing priorities.

Axiology poses value questions: What is good? What is preferable? What is desirable? The process of valuing entails identifying and weighing alternatives, sorting through choices, and making decisions. Axiological questions are ethical or aesthetic, with each having an impact on the curriculum. Ethical questions, discussed in Chapters 3, 4, 5, and 6, address the standards for moral behavior.

The curriculum we propose for SBDMCs cannot be value free. Commenting on criteria to justify a curriculum versus justifying the curriculum for a varied group of young students, Holmes (1991) observed, "It is one thing to develop a curriculum that can be justified on the basis of established criteria; it is another to deliver it to a varied group of young people" (p. 37). This ethics curriculum does not seek to be politically correct and value free. It must specify, unambiguously, underlying values that can be understood by those who teach them and those who learn them. The proposed ethics curriculum cannot be "de-ethicized" (Holmes, 1991). Indeed, it is essential that it be made explicit to those in authority whom we seek to persuade, so that they understand our underlying values and have the option to accept or to reject these values. Constructions of this curriculum are situated in the context of moral and political meaning (see Chapter 5).

Asking "What is good?" raises other questions. Should we develop a uniform curriculum for all SBDMC groups regardless of their interests, background, maturity, and school context? Should content focus on students with disabilities or on all students? Should a specific ethic be taught, or should SBDMCs be taught a variety of ethics? What is the authors' position on the value of inclusion? How explicit will this position be? The authors believe that a core ethical deliberation curriculum would be desirable for all SBDMCs in order to establish a common language to facilitate communication. However, these committees vary considerably in their composition, contexts, issues faced, experience, maturity, and other factors (see Chapter 9) dealing with group dynamics and describing SBDM (see Chapter 1).

Consequently, the core curriculum should be heavily augmented with content for ethical deliberation individualized to the SBDMC. Aesthetics deals with the question "What is beautiful?" In terms of the ethics curriculum, aesthetic issues to address are the manner in which our curriculum may be considered an art form; ways in which the delivery of the curriculum may interact with SBDMC members; and how it may affect how members see themselves, their tasks, and their interactions (see Beyer, 1991).

Society and Culture

A second foundational block underlying the curriculum deals with social and cultural factors. Chapters 6, 7, and 8 deal in depth with these factors as they affect constructions of ethical policy issues facing SBDMCs. This section summarizes and augments the major points made in those chapters, with an emphasis on curricular considerations.

Society is a group of individuals who perceive themselves to share common characteristics that enable them to belong. As a value-laden enterprise, culture provides members of a society with guidance for discerning what is good and what is bad as well as what one should and should not do (Zais, 1976). School policy makers acknowledge biases and, through the curriculum, seek to raise awareness of these biases against minorities, women, people with disabilities, and people who are poor, among others. The curriculum needs such awareness to be kept alive in order to avoid supporting and perpetuating such biases.

Zais (1976) and numerous other authors have discussed the curricular implications (e.g., DuBois, 1969) and the policy implications of values (e.g., Mitchell, Roysdon, Wirt, & Marshall, n.d.; Wirt, Mitchell, & Marshall, 1988). Traditional U.S. values, those adopted by the middle class, include compromise (a necessity for a democracy) and change (i.e., progress). The value of compromise reveals an appreciation that the values of neither compromise nor change represent truth. U.S. democratic ideological values center on the individual and the social institutions that support the value of the individual and the enhancement of the individual's life. From a social and cultural perspective, we embrace the concept that people can and should govern themselves because we have faith in the reason and freedom of thought of U.S. citizens. In fact, site-based management can be viewed as a strategy to democratize decision-making authority, as discussed in Chapters 1, 2, and 9.

Democracy goes beyond rule by the people. It includes a set of principles and a process for governing. Under this expanded meaning, democracy includes an impressive array of conceptions about humans—freedom, equality, equity, and justice, among others. Consequently, we see democracy as an ethic and a form of government. Thus conceived, democracy involves respect for individuality and support of conditions promoting individuals' growth, confidence in their intelligence and ability to inquire, and their rights and responsibilities to participate in the resolution of shared problems. A conscious effort must be made to ensure that the curriculum addresses the questions "How can an SBDMC member be disposed to act democratically? What will democratic participation feel like (e.g., invigorating, frustrating, aimless, conflict ridden, passionate, passive, perfunctory, rewarding)?" At the very core of democratic decision making is the conflict between competing interests that require valuing, judgment, and informed choice. It is important that the curriculum be flexible enough to accommodate these conflicting perspectives.

Democracy as it relates to the ethics curriculum is not a politically neutral goal, nor is it morally neutral regarding issues of social class, gender, race, ethnicity, or ability as reflected in policy decisions that affect diverse populations of students and their families. Competing fundamental social values underlie policies, and these values are tied closely to the ethical deliberation of policy matters. Kaufman (1956) was perhaps the earliest to address the classification of policies on the basis of support for competing public values. In working to develop a taxonomic framework for state education policy, Mitchell et al. (n.d.) gathered, defined, reviewed, and analyzed data from key policy actors on several fundamental social values that underlie public value preferences. Their work supports the idea of the competitive nature of social values. For example, when state-level policy makers responded to semantic differential type items ranking the importance of four public values (i.e., quality, efficiency, equity, choice), the equity theme prevalent since the late 1960s was replaced with the social value theme of quality. Suppose the study were to be repeated in the late 1990s?

Would the value of choice replace that of quality, given state legislative trends toward local control, for example, charter schools and site-based management?

When dealing with marginalized populations, we believe that the value of equity is most critical. Implied in equity are other values that underlie democratic principles, such as the worth of each individual and society's responsibility to acknowledge, enhance, and protect that worth in institutions such as schools. Hence, if state policy and corresponding local school board policy are not supportive of the core public value of equity, one might expect to see a decrease of this value as a factor in SBDMC decisions. In addition, Mitchell and colleagues (1988) pointed out, "Equity is complicated because it is a matter of redress rather than one of address" (p. 18). Hence, a policy action remedy is justified only after an inequity has been identified. Mitchell and colleagues (n.d.) and Wirt, Mitchell, and Marshall (1988) also summarized several problem levels and stages at which schools should address equity: inter- and intraschool provisions of equal opportunity for all children, gaps between social norms and the needs of citizens, and giving disadvantaged children educational resources to help them to achieve greater equity after completing school. We believe that ethical deliberation in SBDMCs also helps schools to move forward in addressing equity proactively by preventing or changing inequitable decisions, given the apparently conflicting presence of quality and choice values in state policy.

When equity is to be center stage as a social value, it is necessary to answer questions such as those proposed by Wirt et al. (1988). To which groups should attention be paid? How should their needs be addressed programmatically? How should programs be financed? What level of government should address the problem? Wirt et al. attempted to conceptualize the relationships among these four policy values as they relate to or conflict with each other conceptually. These relationships are important because they provide a window to the value conflicts that underlie policy making, conflict, and the ways in which such conflicts are resolved. Wirt et al. discussed the important oppositional relationship between quality and equity values. Their arguments have important implications. Essentially, they argued that quality "seeks uniform standards and services applied to all clients of schools," whereas equity "seeks special services or standards to meet the needs of particular clients" (Wirt et al., 1988, p. 280). Educational resources are not unlimited; thus, a conflict occurs because more funds are needed for special students and less funds and services are available to all other students. Consequently, equity is opposed by those who would not benefit and sought by those who support quality programs for special students. A loss of funds or services for the marginalized students is viewed by us as a reverse Robin Hood type of plan—take from those who need additional resources and give everyone an equal share.

Another dimension of social value conflict addressed by Wirt and colleagues (1988) is the opposition of choice and equity. Choice implies that one "may" choose, and equity implies that one "shall" choose. Wirt and colleagues called attention to the fact that the "historic unwillingness of a decentralized education system to redistribute resources to those with special schooling needs has generated the drive for equity-based state law" (p. 281). They also noted that various special schooling groups (e.g., poor, minority, handicapped, gifted children) had a similar local school district history of "inattention, discrimination, and underfunding" (Wirt et al., 1988, p. 281), and most had had to seek a redistribution of resources through the judicial system and the state legislature.

Another way to understand the equity–quality dilemma is to examine two types of equity: horizontal equity and vertical equity. Horizontal equity proposes to treat like students alike in terms of, for example, resources and services. For vertical equity, the proposal is to treat disalikes differently. Consequently, under *horizontal equity*, roughly the same resources would be distributed to all fourth graders, unless some important criterion such as being blind or having a severe mental disability distinguished a fourth grader from his peers. In this second case, under the concept of *vertical equity*, it would be inequitable to provide the identical resources to the fourth grader with special needs. In fact, such provision would not be equitable unless more resources were provided to compensate for their disadvantage or disparity relative to the rest of the population. One way of summarizing this equity issue is to say that it is inequitable or to say it is unfair to treat disalikes alike and likes disalike.

Another view of the quality-versus-equity debate is the question Gardner (1961) asked: Can we be equal and excellent, too? Gardner identified the apparent conflict for Americans who see positive virtues in egalitarianism and competitive performance: Both are advantageous. Americans simultaneously believe, in an Aristotelian manner, that all people are equal; but it is also clear that people are not equal in their innate gifts or potential for success. Hence, many Americans share a social philosophy supporting equality of opportunity. Egalitarianism, for Gardner, would protect the weak and define aspects of equity that cannot be ignored but would not attempt to "eliminate individual differences or their consequences" (p. 15). This leads us to a key foundation of this chapter, the individual.

The Individual

What assumptions and beliefs about the individual ought to affect the curriculum? With regard to the public school curriculum, this question is asked with the student in mind. Although the curriculum is to be developed by the adult members of SBDMCs, the assumptions about the individual as a student are critical to setting the ethical tone for site-based decision making. Three issues posed by Zais (1976) are addressed apart from the strict ontological issues associated with the question "What is a person?" These issues are as follows:

1. Are people of a constant or mutable nature?
2. Do people have free will?
3. Are people basically good or evil?

The comments below reflect the authors' thoughts on ontological issues raised by Zais.

The nature of the individual, whether constant or mutable, is of particular interest to those concerned with the educational needs of children with disabilities and those at risk of school failure. Individual variability within genetic constraints is recognized in educational and other environments. Given the failure of science to answer the question of whether human nature is fixed or mutable, the more optimistic conception of human nature, believing in the malleability and resilience of individuals, is favored here.

Does humankind have the capacity to choose and act freely, or do people react passively to external forces? We believe that the future depends on choices made in the present and on the consequences of those choices. Decisions about how the world must be are a powerful force in determining the curriculum. However, this freedom to choose which path to take carries with it the responsibility to use the best information available, whether it is empirical knowledge, self-knowledge, or affective knowledge. An important implication for the ethical school policy–making curriculum is the need to incorporate the skills of using decision-making processes and reflective and critical thinking. Such a curriculum should include skills necessary to envision and create the desirable society of the future. Implications of the assumption that people are basically good or evil are seldom considered in developing a curriculum. If it is assumed that the learner is basically good, then curriculum design assumes natural growth and types of activities that take advantage of an individual's willingness to learn and explore. However, if it is assumed that people are basically evil, a curriculum would not be designed to uncover good tendencies.

Rather, assuming wicked intentions, the curriculum would control behavior to a greater extent than content. If it is assumed that people are essentially ethically neutral, that is, people have the capacity for both good and evil, then responsibility for positive or negative outcomes is shared by the individual and the learning community. Adapting Zais's (1976) concept of the synoptic view of people for purposes of this discussion, such a learning community enables learners to become aware of their own perceptual limitations of the world, to understand the impact of culture on learning, to assess themselves relative to their environment in "self and social critical terms" (p. 239) and to develop an "openness to experience" (p. 239).

In writing about the types of educational institutions needed to produce healthy, productive adults, LePage (1987) expanded on a number of forgotten values that are especially worthwhile to consider in the development of an ethical policy-making curriculum: acceptance and trust, admiration, encouragement, wonder, play, creativity, celebration, choice, and consequences. These are values of nurturance consistent with the value of caring (see Chapter 5). These individual values must be incorporated into the tone and content of the ethics curriculum for SBDMCs.

Another issue associated with the individual was alluded to in Gardner's (1961) work. If the United States is to be a free and excellent society, we must "believe in the importance of the individual, and his fulfillment" (Gardner, 1961, p. 145). The individual must be cherished and protected, and his or her individuality must be encouraged. Gardner summarized this point for each free person as follows: "His goal must be not only individual fulfillment but the enrichment and strengthening of his society" (p. 145).

Learning Theory

The fourth foundational area of the curriculum deals with learning theory as it relates to generalized learning principles and adult learning components. Learning theory addresses questions such as "How do individuals learn? How can learning be facilitated?" Assumptions about adult learning influence the nature of our curriculum. For instance, if it is assumed that adults learn in highly sequenced steps ranging from easy to more complex, the curriculum will be organized accordingly. However, if we believe that learning occurs through insight and that aggregations of fragmented skills do not add up to usable learning, a less sequential curriculum designed to encourage discovery will be chosen. Unfortunately, there is no single theory of adult learning accepted by educators or psychologists (see, e.g., Langenbach, 1988). One basic principle seems to underlie the very definition of adult education: the choice to voluntarily participate (Langenbach, 1988).

Zais (1976) summarized Hilgard and Bower's (1976) principles of learning. These principles appear relevant to our work:

- The learner should be an active, rather than a passive, listener or viewer.
- Frequency of repetition is important in acquiring a skill such as typing.
- Repetition should take place under conditions in which correct responses are rewarded (reinforcement).
- Motivational conditions are important for learning.
- Conflicts and frustrations in learning situations must be recognized and provision must be made for their resolution or accommodation.
- Learning problems should be presented in a way that their structure . . . is clear to the learner.
- The organization of content is an important factor in learning and is an essential concern of the curriculum planner.
- Learning with understanding is more permanent and more transferable than rote learning.
- Goal setting by the learner is as important as motivation for learning.
- The learner's abilities are important, and provisions should be made for differential abilities.
- The learner should be understood in terms of influences that have shaped his development.
- The anxiety level of the individual learner is a factor affecting learning.
- The organization of motives within the individual is a factor that influences learning.
- The group atmosphere of learning (competition versus cooperation, authoritarianism versus democracy . . .) will affect satisfaction in learning as well as the products of learning. (Zais, 1976, pp. 291–293)

Joyce (1986) summarized five components in the training literature that are consistent with how teachers and other adults learn to incorporate a new approach into their active repertoire: 1) presentation of theory, 2) modeling or demonstration, 3) practice under simulated conditions, 4) structured feedback, and 5) coaching for application. These five interrelated training components can be generalized to apply to how adults learn and can be addressed by the curriculum we seek to develop. Joyce's components have been modified below to accommodate the adult learners on SBDMCs.

1. *Presentation of theory:* Although presentation of an ethical theory need not be the starting point for work with SBDMCs, the study of theory provides the rationale, conceptual basis, and common vocabulary needed to raise awareness and enhance conceptual control of the subject.
2. *Modeling or demonstration:* Modeling involves enactment of a skill or strategy that affects awareness and theory mastery by helping learners to better understand what has been modeled.

3. *Practice under simulated conditions:* Simulations involve trying out a new skill or strategy in situations where one might not have to manage an entire group. This practice allows fine-tuning and increases likelihood of transfer to other situations.
4. *Structured feedback:* Feedback involves a system for behavior observation (e.g., of self, observer, peer) and reflection on these observations. It may be combined with the practice component. Feedback will result in an awareness of one's behavior and knowledge of alternatives. Appropriate, regular, and consistent feedback should lead to change and change maintenance.
5. *Coaching for application:* For some people, direct coaching may be necessary to ensure learning and application of new skills and concepts. Feedback based on actual SBDMC meetings, for example, may be provided to individual members or to the group by those familiar with the ethical decision-making approach.

The social action model of adult education (Beal, Blount, Powers, & Johnson, 1966) appears to be consistent with the social change aspects of our model. This multipurpose, continuous evaluation model developed for use by the Cooperative Extension Service in the United States addresses the actors, the social system, and its elements and stages for social action. The model assumes a change agent role and works toward legitimization through leaders within the system. One factor to consider is that it is supportive of the system and may not be able to modify the status of formal and informal leaders (Langenbach, 1988).

The Curriculum
Curriculum may be understood as the various kinds of text suggested by Pinar, Reynolds, Slattery, and Taubman (1995): political text, racial text, gender text, phenomenological, postmodern, aesthetic, theological, and theoretical. These interrelated forms of curricular text are beneficial to acknowledge as we look into the more complex considerations of understanding curriculum. Several of these curriculum-as-text ideas are summarized below.

Curriculum, viewed as a political text by Pinar and colleagues (1995), takes into account political aspects of curriculum, the development and evaluation of which cannot occur in a politically neutral fashion. When viewed through the political lens, curriculum is best understood by attention to theories and concepts such as reproduction or correspondence theory (i.e., Marxist views of schools functioning as a part of society's economic superstructure, the hidden curriculum, social stratification, hegemony) and issues of race, gender, and class.

When curriculum is viewed as a racial text, according to Pinar and colleagues (1995), one takes into account the U.S. cultural identity and its relationship to exclusion and repression. Opposition to racism entails day-to-day commitment to freedom, justice, and diversity.

Viewing curriculum as gender text, one aims to understand curriculum in terms of the unequal ways people are viewed because of their gender or sexuality (Pinar et al., 1995). Among curriculum issues of importance within the context of gender are coeducation, the gender-centered curriculum, the importance or lack of importance of certain academic disciplines, the politics of feminist pedagogy, and gender and identity.

Curriculum as phenomenological text emphasizes the role of language as a lens through which one gains understanding of items in the curriculum that we take for granted (Pinar et al., 1995). Language and discourse may help bridge the gap between experience and meaning. From a phenomenological and deconstructivist perspective, curriculum is a series of never-ending stories told and retold by the narrator and listener, who exchange places as the story is passed on (e.g., narrator to listener, listener to narrator).

As presented in the Zais (1976) model, there are four components in a curriculum:

1. Aims, goals, and objectives
2. Content
3. Learner activities
4. Evaluation

Each of these components, the chapter authors' position, and implications for the SBDMC ethics curriculum are summarized below.

Aims, Goals, and Objectives Aims, goals, and objectives refer to end points toward which the curriculum is heading (i.e., its purpose). Once direction is identified, the question arises "How shall we get there?" These interrelated ends and means are influenced by philosophical assumptions and assumptions about knowledge, society and culture, the individual, and learning. It is critical that curricular aims, goals, and objectives be as congruent as possible and that they be consistent with the curricular foundations previously discussed and closely related to our views of learning theory and instructional strategies.

Zais's (1976) definitions of curricular aims, goals, and objectives and their relationship are summarized below. Collectively, these terms refer to curriculum purpose. Metaphorically, the three terms are like a target: "The closer they are the easier they are to hit" (Zais, 1976, p. 305). The broader the purpose, the more significant, abstract, and remote is curriculum purpose.

Philosophical Bases of Curricular Aims   The philosophical bases of curricular aims are statements that reflect values and describe expected life outcomes. They cannot be taken for granted (Gardner, 1961). As the distant target, they are not directly related to school outcomes, and the success of their achievement may not be determinable until some time in the future. Zais's (1976) examples of ethical character and civic responsibility as aims are consistent with curricular aims. Gardner's examples are also appropriate aims to share: peace with justice, freedom, the enablement of individuals to achieve their best, and equality before the law, including equal opportunity.

Curriculum goals are long-range and somewhat removed from immediate assessment. We will develop, implement, evaluate, revise, and disseminate a curriculum and related materials for educating SBDMCs to accomplish the following goals:

- Develop appreciation, understanding, and respect for the worth and dignity of the individual student.
- Develop an inclusive, hospitable, caring attitude toward students with disabilities and those at risk for school failure.
- Develop a sensitivity to and an understanding of barriers to and strategies for the inclusion of students with disabilities.
- Develop sound ethical and moral decision-making values, goals, and behaviors, and apply these in SBDMC settings.
- Develop a knowledge and appreciation of the importance of group decision-making processes and their implications for ethical decisions.
- Contribute toward the democratization of our schools through SBDMCs.
- Develop an ability to use information and ethical reasoning in SBDMC settings.
- Promote the development of ethical schools as moral learning communities.
- Develop an appreciation and understanding of the cultural, political, and moral contexts affecting the work of SBDMCs.
- Develop a willingness to take action to inform other SBDMCs and other decision makers about the critical and valuable role that ethics can play in SBDMCs in particular and education policy in general.

Curriculum objectives are the most proximate specific outcomes of instruction. Several important principles are set forth below to guide the development of these objectives. Eraut's (1991) work on defining educational objectives has been particularly helpful. Educational objectives should not be considered in isolation from companion objectives. Some objectives would be terminal and others would be enabling, in keeping with the importance of learning sequencing. It is necessary to separate objectives that are measurable from those that are aspirations. Objectives have a political status, and who specifies the objectives and whose authority may have a bearing on commitments to achieve them.

There are several systems for differentiating and classifying objectives (Bloom, 1956; Gagne & Briggs, 1974; Taba, 1962). Eraut (1991) cited Parker and Rubin (1966), who were critical of many of these systems, pointing out that they commonly treat knowledge as a commodity, with no place allowed for the learner's imagination and personal meaning. Learner objectives that encompass affective objectives and encourage learners to understand and apply their own value system should be valued for this curriculum. In terms of affective objectives, one strand deals with the areas of moral and social education. An issue here of particular value to our work is where on the continuum the target audience of our curriculum should be in terms of whether their value system and moral reasoning are typical of what their society or community considers right or wrong, as opposed to the moral and ethical understanding a philosopher would have of various situations. At the moral philosopher's end of the continuum, considerably more attention may need to be paid to the cognitive aspects of the affective objective. With social skills objectives, Raven (1977) suggested several personal skills objectives that may prove useful for our curriculum, such as the tendency to seek and use feedback and the willingness to accept frustration.

Curriculum Content

This section is divided into two parts. The first delineates some assumptions necessary to address major questions about curriculum content. The second part summarizes the core content for the curriculum. To achieve the curriculum's aims, goals, and objectives, a number of questions need to be addressed. Zais (1976) asked questions that provide some direction:

- *What is content?*
- *Does all content constitute knowledge?*
- *Which content . . . should be included in the curriculum?*
- *What criteria are the most valid ones to use in the selection process?*
- *Are there some things that everyone should know? Some things that only some students need to know?*
- *In what sequence should selected content be presented?*
- *What criteria should be used in determining sequence?* (pp. 322–323, italics in original)

Although it is beyond the scope of this chapter to respond in detail to these questions, some comments may help address these questions: Content should take into account the learner's prior knowledge and experiences to deepen the meaning and application of content. Content goes beyond knowledge presented from teacher to student. Knowledge, skills, and attitudes are content, and the learner makes judgments of content to be learned in a variety of ways besides direct instruction. The process of using and communicating content and creating knowledge itself is valuable for the learner. Content and the process by which it is learned are closely linked. It is desirable to develop a classification system for the content of the curriculum. This system should be heuristic for the learner and teacher.

It is important to determine the specific knowledge and skills necessary for the learner to acquire. Content related to ethics, group dynamics, policy analysis, collaboration, and other topics needs to be included. Decisions ought to be made about whether to teach the content in a manner consistent with the syntactic and structural organization of the subject matter disciplines or in some other manner that integrates the content of disciplines and ties the content to our immediate purposes.

The breadth and depth of curricular content are affected by the content all members of the SBDMC need to know about ethical policy making. They are also affected by the SBDMC's stage of development. To address the question of scope, the variables that influence the subject matter that members of an SBDMC learn and when they learn it must be taken into account. How and by whom these decisions should be made are important questions. In addition, portions of the content may be aimed at only some SBDMCs or SBDMC members. Such content will get in-depth treatment or, for some SBDMC members, no treatment at all.

Scope raises issues of the order in which the curriculum is to be learned. Scope is tied to the aforementioned beliefs about subject matter and psychological theories of learning. Zais (1976) suggested standards for selecting criteria: significance, utility, interest, and human development. Significance deals with agreed-upon acceptance or assumed worth; selection criterion is of particular interest to experts. Utility in our context deals with the application of the content to performing the SBDMC's ethics-related roles. (This selection criterion supports the status quo and may inhibit social change.) Interest as a criterion deals with the learner's selection of portions of content, but this choice may lead the learner to fail to take into account content that is critical to social aims and goals. The criterion of human development (i.e., individual and societal) within this context deals with a "democratic value orientation" (Zais, 1976, p. 346). Here the role of the school in society is to see that "knowledge and intelligence are brought to bear in the society's decision-making process" (Zais, 1976, p. 347). With a democratic orientation, content is selected because it has a value for addressing "moral values and ideals, social problems, human emotions, effective thinking processes, controversial issues, etc." (Zais, 1976, p. 347). Our work has led us to some preliminary decisions about the content of the ethics curriculum for SBDMCs.

Learner Activities

The activities of the learner acquiring content are at the core of the curriculum. How the learner experiences the learning activity is another important distinction. Content and learner activities coexist in a curriculum being implemented, and not all content is presented by the teacher (Zais, 1976).

The primary criterion for selecting a learning activity is its contribution toward curriculum purposes (i.e., aims, goals, objectives affected by foundational commitments). For instance, if SBDMCs are expected to develop ethical and democratic decision-making skills, they need to be placed in authentic situations where they are engaged in such decision making, and the learning setting itself needs to be democratic and ethical. It is possible and often desirable to aggregate a number of objectives into a single, active learning activity. For instance, group problem solving can be combined with group process skills and the social attitudes of compromise and community. Other criteria suggested for the selection of learning activities include regard for the learner's experience and existing abilities, the learner's culture and values, and the interests of the learner (see Zais, 1976).

One example of a learning activity is Rosen's moral negotiation method as summarized by Reagan (1984), which seeks the best and most rational actions within the constraints of the decision-making context. This method attempts to deal with moral or value conflicts by exploring the consequences of conflicting conditional statements (i.e., reasons) behind alternative courses of action. Conditional agreements are reached by focusing on whether the reasoning each position utilizes to support a judgment is warranted or true rather than on the conflicting moral judgments themselves.

Evaluation

The fourth curriculum component deals with evaluation. As with other components of the curriculum, evaluation design and method need to be viewed within the intent, assumptions, and foundations on which they have been based. Evaluation is viewed here within the context of use of the Zais (1976) model as dealing with both formative and summative evaluation. Formative evaluation assesses curriculum quality during the development process to improve the quality of curriculum products and the curriculum itself. The role of formative evaluation in this case is to describe the development and the implementation and to improve the quality of the enterprise. Evaluation is of particular value because of the evolutionary nature of curriculum. The role of the summative evaluation is to determine how well the curriculum performs (i.e., curriculum quality) based on some standards (e.g., benchmarks, goals, outcome measures, performance data). Before conducting a summative evaluation, which may occur at the end of the entire development process or at the end of development of a major phase of the curriculum, it is desirable to determine that implementation has stabilized and is being conducted in the same way it was written and intended, with the population intended, and with the materials and processes designed for it. Assessing the stability of the program, as described, is within the scope of what is often referred to as a process evaluation. Questions frequently asked in process evaluations were proposed by Berger and Dollard (1995) and by others. It is still necessary to develop a comprehensive evaluation design, but some features to consider are described below. Again, consistent with the Zais model, these features include comments on goal evaluation, curriculum coherence, and evaluation data collection methods.

First, goal evaluation will include an examination of the aims, goals, and objectives as set forth in this chapter. Besides the criteria previously discussed under aims, goals, and objectives, the curriculum is also evaluated. Also, adapting other evaluation matters set out by Zais (1976) is considered—for example, identifying which philosophical assumptions are desirable curricular outcomes and for what reasons; determining the impact of evolving SBDMC cultures and the impact that their value orientations have on curricular goals; specifying the curriculum's view of the educated person (i.e., learner) and the desired outcomes; and delineating the values being reaffirmed and modified, either through curriculum implementation or through other policy-making entities. To examine coherence of the curriculum using the Zais model, we will examine such issues as the consistency of the curriculum elements (e.g., relationships between goals and learning activities and between goals and content) and consistencies of curriculum components and foundational commitments (e.g., congruence between objectives and movement toward democratic schools and SBDMC decision making).

The collection of evaluation data can be viewed from the perspective of individual members or the full SBDMC using qualitative and quantitative measures such as direct observation, interviews, products, student outcomes, diaries, behavior analysis strategies, and even paper-and-pencil tests. In addition, we will gather rich data about the curriculum development process itself, including field testing, training, analysis of developed and used materials in terms of quality, appropriateness to curriculum, and follow-ups with SBDMCs and others.

Qualitative evaluation strategies are increasingly being used, especially in formative evaluations, and such strategies would appear particularly appropriate, given the proposed curriculum. Qualitative curriculum evaluation is referred to as educational criticism (see Willis, 1991). Educational criticism focuses on "expanding human understanding of specific educational situations and promoting moral action within these situations and social contexts" (Willis, 1991, p. 427). Qualitative curriculum evaluation's sources are hermeneutics, phenomenology, and critical theory. Meaning is derived from investigating personal and social contexts of specific situations, employing naturalistic methodology through a four-phase case study format entailing observation, description, interpretation, and appraisal.

Given that narrative ethics is a key philosophical concept underlying this ethics curriculum, it seems logical to assume that a narrative evaluation will be included as one among other approaches. The narrative approach to evaluation seems of particular value in the formative stages of the curriculum evaluation. Academics and practitioners implementing the curriculum could write compelling interpretive stories of implementation experiences. These narratives could also plausibly be used as part of the curriculum itself to show the real-life experiences of SBDMCs as they successfully or unsuccessfully tackle policy issues within an ethical context.

It is also important to address who conducts the evaluation. Too often, emphasis is placed on an external evaluator conducting the summative evaluation. An external evaluator at some point will help to ensure validity and avoid the inevitable blind spots in self-evaluation. Several evaluation methodologies seem useful to investigate. If the evaluation is to be useful, it must take into account the social and political ecology of the enterprise. Members of the CRGPE are not the only stakeholders in this curriculum. Lay and professional members of participating SBDMCs, various accountability commissions interested in site-based decision making, school boards, superintendents, legislatures, the public, and others are stakeholders. Taking into account multiple stakeholders, we will consider a participatory evaluation design, and it may include the narrative evaluation approach. In addition, we will involve practitioners in action research (see, e.g., Stringer, 1996), which makes sense, given the ongoing collaborative relationship the CRGPE has had with SBDMCs. Evaluation ought to be multifaceted channeling the CRGPE and stakeholders in a rich, ongoing flow of information for improving and documenting the enterprise and determining its actual impact.

Two evaluative phases for developing curriculum materials and processes are envisioned: prototype development and curriculum validation. These phases are summarized below. During the product development stage of the curriculum, prototypes are likely to be developed. Prototype evaluation permits the instructional design team to formatively examine the product's use and effectiveness in a real setting. Alkin (1991) reviewed the steps for prototype evaluation. In summary, these steps include 1) prototype review by subject experts for information on goals, objectives, content accuracy, and relevance; 2) field tests with small numbers of subjects to get detailed information from subjects in short time periods; 3) tryouts with actual student groups to clarify instructions, instructional methodology, and usefulness of examples (e.g., with data from observations, debriefings, work samples); and 4) assessing learner attitudes toward the curriculum products with questionnaires, direct observations, and interviews. At the conclusion of prototype evaluation, curriculum developers are prepared to make versions ready to consider in real-life settings.

Curriculum validation as an evaluative activity addresses knowing whether the program delivers on its intended outcomes. Such an activity raises underlying epistemological concerns. Depending on one's epistemological position, one would need to select a compatible validation procedure. Smith, Stanley, and Shores (1957) identified four procedures for curriculum developers to use in validating curriculum: judgment, experimentation, analysis, and consensus. Consistent with our stated epistemological position, judgment and consensus methods seem most appropriate. However, experimentation and curriculum analysis are also examined during the evaluation design process.

This concludes our use of the Zais (1976) model to outline the proposed curriculum. Figure 2 provides the reader with a summary of the CRGPE curriculum, taking into account the first three sections of this chapter. The next step is a practical one: to operationalize our curriculum and create actual instructional materials and a delivery system.

INSTRUCTIONAL DESIGN
CONSIDERATIONS FOR THE SBDMC CURRICULUM

This section sets forth preliminary instructional design considerations that should prove useful as we attempt to operationalize an ethical policy-making curriculum for SBDMCs. It is beyond the scope of this chapter to propose either a specific instructional design for the cur-

The Curriculum

Aims, Goals, Objectives	Curriculum Content	Learning Activities	Evaluation
• Curriculum may be viewed as different "texts" — political, racial, gender, phenomenological, postmodern, aesthetic, theological, and theoretical • *Aims* — Ethical character, civic responsibility, peace with justice, freedom, the enablement of individuals to achieve the best in him- or herself, and equality before the law (including equal opportunity) • *Goals* — Develop appreciation, understanding, and respect for the worth and dignity of the individual student — Develop an inclusive, hospitable, caring attitude toward students with disabilities and those at risk for school failure — Develop a sensitivity to and an understanding of barriers to and strategies for the inclusion of students with disabilities — Develop sound ethical and moral decision-making values, goals, and behaviors and apply these in SBDMC settings — Develop a knowledge and appreciation of the importance of group decision-making processes and their implications for ethical decisions — Contribute toward the democratization of our schools through SBDMCs — Develop an ability to use informative and ethical reasoning in SBDMC settings — Promote the development of ethical schools as moral learning communities — Develop an appreciation and understanding of the cultural, political, and moral contexts affecting the work of SBDMCs — Develop a willingness to take actions to inform other SBDMCs and other decision makers about the critical and valuable role that ethics can play in SBDMCs in particular and education policy in general • *Objectives* — See six principles for guiding the development of objectives	• Eight assumptions to address curriculum content	• Content and learner coexist in a curriculum, and not all content is presented by the teacher • Primary criterion for selection — contribution toward purposes of curriculum; other criteria — learner experience and existing abilities, learner's culture and values, and interests of learner • Teaching case method — the use of narrative accounts of actual situations to foster deliberation of specific aspects of practice and examination of complex issues from multiple perspectives • The SBDMC as a storied group	• Formative and summative • Features — goal evaluation, curriculum coherence, education criticism (qualitative curriculum evaluation), narrative evaluation, action research, prototype and curriculum validation

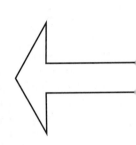

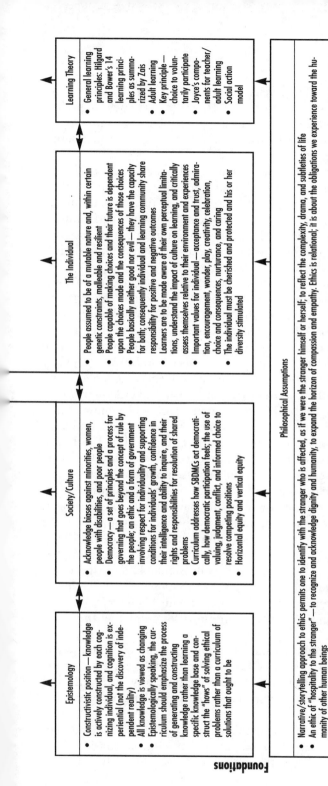

Learning Theory

- General learning principles: Hilgard and Bower's 14 learning principles as summarized by Zais
- Adult learning
- Key principle — choice to voluntarily participate
- Joyce's components for teacher/adult learning
- Social action model

The Individual

- People assumed to be of a mutable nature and, within certain genetic constraints, malleable and resilient
- People capable of making choices and their future is dependent upon the choices made and the consequences of those choices
- People basically neither good nor evil — they have the capacity for both; consequently individual and learning community share responsibility for positive and negative outcomes
- Learners are to be made aware of their own perceptual limitations, understand the impact of culture on learning, and critically assess themselves relative to their environment and experiences
- Important values for individual — acceptance and trust, admiration, encouragement, wonder, play, creativity, celebration, choice and consequences, nurturance, and caring
- The individual must be cherished and protected and his or her diversity stimulated

Society/Culture

- Acknowledge biases against minorities, women, people with disabilities, and poor people
- Democracy — a set of principles and a process for governing that goes beyond the concept of rule by the people; an ethic and a form of government involving respect for individuality and supporting conditions for individuals' growth, confidence in their intelligence and ability to inquire, and their rights and responsibilities for resolution of shared problems
- Curriculum addresses how SBDMCs act democratically, how democratic participation feels; the use of valuing, judgment, conflict, and informed choice to resolve competing positions
- Horizontal equity and vertical equity

Epistemology

- Constructivist position — knowledge is actively constructed by each cognizing individual, and cognition is experiential (not the discovery of independent reality)
- All knowledge is viewed as changing
- Epistemologically speaking, the curriculum should emphasize the process of generating and constructing knowledge rather than learning a specific knowledge base and construct the "hows" of solving ethical problems rather than a curriculum of solutions that ought to be

Philosophical Assumptions

- Narrative/storytelling approach to ethics permits one to identify with the stranger who is affected, as if we were the stranger himself or herself; to reflect the complexity, drama, and subtleties of life
- An ethic of "hospitality to the stranger" — to recognize and acknowledge dignity and humanity, to expand the horizon of compassion and empathy. Ethics is relational; it is about the obligations we experience toward the humanity of other human beings
- Schools as moral communities — a vision of a school as a learning community whose members are joined by a shared pursuit of common values and goals, where what is ethical advances the common good; and where individuals are bound to the good of the whole
- An ethic of care
- Ontologically — experiences and ideas can be communicated; the real world is knowable by everybody; different groups construct their own realities, and there are no authorities with the special gift of knowing or declaring a universal reality; the reality or vision for SBDMCs is highly idiosyncratic, experience based, local, characterized by principles of law and public policy and the shared constructions of meanings among the group's members
- Axiology — curriculum explicit to those we teach so that they can understand our position and have the opinion to accept or reject it
- Aesthetics — manner in which we deliver or facilitate learning will affect how SBDMC members see themselves, their interactions, and their tasks

Foundations

Figure 2. A curriculum for ethical policy development in school-based decision-making committees. (Adapted from Zais [1976].)

273

riculum or a total plan for developing an instructional design and curriculum planning and writing strategy. However, some helpful preliminary curriculum and instructional design elements are summarized so that these elements may be used in the forthcoming formal design process.

The curriculum design and instructional design are as consistent and coherent as possible with the four curricular foundations, their philosophical underpinnings, and our views of the curriculum. Although inconsistencies are likely in implementing the curriculum in real school settings, we must be vigilant in minimizing inconsistencies and taking them into account as we continue with curriculum design, implementation, and evaluation efforts.

To integrate subject matter democratically, we seek to acknowledge the needs, interests, and abilities of individual students and groups (i.e., SBDMC members and groups) in a manner intended to deal with genuine SBDMC problems. The balanced approach is centered on problems, decisions, and policies; it has a common core of learning for all students; and it focuses on social problems and group actions needed to alter the course of social problems (e.g., policy making that underplays the importance of an ethical deliberation process). It is necessary to explicitly identify the type of school community and society toward which one intends to work. The design will emphasize ethics, ideals, and cultural norms instead of empirical and technical considerations. A systematic action research model developed by Smith et al. (1957) seems appropriate because it assumes a close relationship between curriculum change and social change. This close relationship may be facilitated by involving parents, students, teachers, the school system's structure, and individual and group relations among members of the school and community (Smith et al., 1957), thereby bringing together human relations, school and community organization, and the authority of professional knowledge (Zais, 1976). To the knowledge of school-level professionals, we will add the knowledge of university faculty and graduate students. Although Smith and colleagues specified their steps for implementing four phases of action research, researchers such as Reason (1988, 1994) expanded our views about the value of and methods for collaborative action research. We see opportunities to blend collaborative action research (i.e., between the CRGPE and SBDMCs) with Smith and colleagues' curricular action research to develop a dynamic method of curriculum design.

The work of environmental educators (e.g., Stapp, 1978) and environmental ethicists (e.g., Leopold, 1949) has led us to consider a series of interrelated phases through which our curriculum can be framed and developed. We consider five interrelated phases through which an individual or group can progressively mature in ethical development in SBDMCs: activity, awareness, understanding, appreciation, and action. Operationalized to our task, during the activity stage, SBDMCs participate in activities that may involve ethical decisions; but little or no awareness of ethical content or its importance in this aspect of the work may become conscious. They are doing the work in good conscience, but they are not necessarily aware of overt or covert ethical considerations or dilemmas. Over time, they can become or can learn to be more consciously aware of some ethical dilemmas they face and their implications, but they may lack conceptual tools and learning experiences necessary to understand optimally and deal effectively with these issues. Next, with understanding enhanced by educational activities and experience, they develop increasingly more in-depth and conscious appreciation of ethical issues and how to deal with them more effectively. The more one understands, the deeper one's appreciation for recognizing the importance of viewing ethical deliberation as a critical part of the SBDMC role. This appreciation leads to political and social action with a foundation of experience in ethical deliberation as well as an awareness, understanding, and appreciation of the nature of ethical dilemmas embedded in SBDMC policy decisions.

During the later stages of development and implementation of the ethics curriculum, we will consider establishing a demonstration program at various SBDMC sites. Datta (1991) described several forms of demonstration programs. Some programs entail using training and dissemination sites of the curriculum as collaborative research sites for integrating research and practice, those that serve as levers for local participation in innovative change, and those dissemination sites that serve as variants to stimulate major shifts in programs. These demonstration forms may serve as a guide for establishing such a demonstration program. An instructional design consultant will work with the CRGPE and selected SBDMCs to develop a detailed design for the ethical policy-making curriculum.

CONCLUSIONS

This chapter should help the reader understand the historical context and the complex, interrelated factors that we believe need to be considered in developing a curriculum in ethical policy making for SBDMCs. We hope this chapter has provided the reader with a nexus between the conceptual aspects of our work and the more concrete task of developing, implementing, and evaluating the curriculum itself. We have described the philosophical and conceptual foundation for the work in which we are engaged—namely, writing, teaching, evaluating, revising, and disseminating a learning and teaching strategy to improve ethical decision making and policy at the school site— by 1) synthesizing our assumptions and what we learned in the CRGPE, 2) identifying major barriers to developing a curriculum for ethical decision making, 3) using the Zais (1976) model to systematically lay out our philosophical assumptions and foundations that influence the curriculum itself, and 4) providing preliminary design guidelines. A second big task will be to revise and broaden a research agenda that fits with our general interest in ethical policy making in school-based management settings.

REFERENCES

Alkin, M.C. (1991). Prototype evaluation. In A. Lewy (Ed.), *The international encyclopedia of curriculum* (pp. 435–436). Oxford, England: Pergamon Press.

Beal, G.M., Blount, R.C., Powers, R.C., & Johnson, W.J. (1966). *Social action and interaction in program planning*. Ames: Iowa State University Press.

Berger, N., & Dollard, N. (1995, May 1). *Evaluating child abuse prevention programs: What are the questions and how can we answer them*. Invited presentation, Ninth Annual Statewide Florida Child Abuse Prevention Association Conference, Tampa.

Beyer, L.E. (1991). Curriculum deliberation. In A. Lewy (Ed.), *The international encyclopedia of curriculum* (pp. 304–306). Oxford, England: Pergamon Press.

Bloom, B.S. (Ed.). (1956). *Taxonomy of educational objectives: The classification of educational goals: Vols. 1, 2. Cognitive domain*. New York: David McKay.

Corbett, H.D. (1990). *On the meaning of restructuring*. Philadelphia: Research for Better Schools.

Datta, L.-E. (1991). Demonstration programs. In A. Lewy (Ed.), *The international encyclopedia of curriculum* (pp. 375–376). Oxford, England: Pergamon Press.

DuBois, C. (1969). The dominant value profile of American culture. In W.F. O'Neill (Ed.), *Selected educational heresies* (pp. 10–13). Glenview, IL: Scott, Foresman.

Eraut, M.R. (1991). Defining educational objectives. In A. Lewy (Ed.), *The international encyclopedia of curriculum* (pp. 306–317). Oxford, England: Pergamon Press.

Fasching, D. (1995). *Ethics without choice*. Unpublished manuscript.

Fisher, B., & Tronto, J.C. (1990). Toward a feminist theory of caring. In E. Abel & M.K. Nelson (Eds.), *Circles of care: Work and identity in women's lives* (pp. 35–62). Albany: State University of New York Press.

French, P. (1992). *Responsibility matters*. Lawrence: University Press of Kansas.

Gagne, R.M., & Briggs, L.J. (1974). *Principles of instructional design*. New York: Holt, Rinehart & Winston.

Gardner, J.W. (1961). *Excellence: Can we be excellent and equal too?* New York: Harper & Brothers.

Hauerwas, S. (1974). *Vision and virtue: Essays in Christian ethical reflection*. Notre Dame, IN: Fides Publishers.

Hilgard, E.R., & Bower, G.H. (1976). *Theories of learning*. New York: Appleton-Century-Crofts.

Holmes, M. (1991). Curriculum as ethics. In A. Lewy (Ed.), *The international encyclopedia of curriculum* (pp. 37–40). Oxford, England: Pergamon Press.

Jonsen, A.R., & Toulmin, S. (1988). *The abuse of casuistry: A history of moral reasoning*. Berkeley: University of California Press.

Joyce, B.R. (1986). *Improving America's schools*. New York: Longmans.

Kaufman, H. (1956). Emerging conflicts in the doctrines of public administration. *American Political Science Review, 50,* 1057–1073.

Langenbach, M. (1988). *Curriculum models in adult education*. Malabar, FL: Robert E. Krieger Publishing Co.

Leopold, A. (1949). *A Sand County almanac*. New York: Oxford University Press.

LePage, A. (1987). *Transforming education*. Oakland, CA: Oakmore House Press.

Mitchell, D.E., Roysdon, G.W., Wirt, F.M., & Marshall, C. (n.d.). *The structure of state education policy*. Unpublished manuscript.

Parker, J.C., & Rubin, L.J. (1966). *Process as content: Curriculum design and the application of knowledge*. Chicago: Rand McNally.

Pinar, W.F., Reynolds, W.M., Slattery, P., & Taubman, P.M. (1995). *Understanding curriculum: An introduction to the study of historical and contemporary curriculum discourses*. New York: Peter Lang Publishing.

Raven, J. (1977). *Education, values and society: The objectives of education and the nature and development of competence*. London: H.K. Lewis.

Reagan, G.M. (1984). Applied ethics for educators: Philosophy of education as something else? *Proceedings of the 39th Annual Meeting of the Psychology of Education Society*. Normal: Psychology of Education Society, Illinois State University.

Reason, P. (Ed.). (1988). *Human inquiry in action: New paradigm research*. Beverly Hills, CA: Sage Publications.

Reason, P. (Ed.). (1994). *Participation in human inquiry*. Beverly Hills, CA: Sage Publications.

Richardson, T. (1989). *The century of the child: The mental hygiene movement and social policy in the United States and Canada*. Albany: State University of New York Press.

Rogan, J., & Luckowski, J. (1990). Curriculum texts: The portrayal of the field: I. *Journal of Curriculum Studies, 22,* 17–39.

Smith, B.O., Stanley, W.O., & Shores, J.H. (1957). *Fundamentals of curriculum development* (rev. ed.). New York: Harcourt, Brace and World.

Soltis, J.F. (1990). The ethics of qualitative research. In E.W. Eisner & A. Peshkin (Eds.), *Qualitative inquiry in education: The continuing debate*. New York: Teachers College Press.

Stapp, W.B. (1978). An instructional model for environmental education. *Prospects: Quarterly Review of Education, 22,* 495–507.

Stringer, E.T. (1996). *Action research: A handbook for practitioners*. Beverly Hills, CA: Sage Publications.

Taba, H. (1962). *Curriculum development: Theory and practice*. New York: Harcourt, Brace and World.

Tyler, R. (1949). *Basic principles of curriculum and instruction*. Chicago: University of Chicago Press.

Willis, G. (1991). Qualitative evaluation. In A. Lewy (Ed.), *The international encyclopedia of curriculum* (pp. 427–429). Oxford, England: Pergamon Press.

Wirt, F., Mitchell, D., & Marshall, C. (1988). Culture and education policy: Analyzing values in state policy systems. *Educational Evaluation and Policy Analysis, 10,* 271–278.

Zais, R.S. (Ed.). (1976). *Curriculum: Principles and foundations.* New York: Thomas Y. Crowell.

13

Ethics, Schools, and the Work of Local School-Based Decision-Making Committees

James L. Paul

Site-based management is one of the most challenging provisions of the current school reform movement. It is an attractive policy initiative from the perspective of developing democratic schools, but not all educators agree that all policy responsibility could or should be located at the local school level. It is more likely that both local and national interests can best be served with a sharing of responsibility. The local aspect of that responsibility is expanding, however, and the rhetoric associated with the implementation of those responsibilities is, in our experience, far in advance of the reality. Furthermore, there is not a well-developed training and technical assistance system to support local schools in this responsibility. The lack of support is especially evident in addressing the ethical dimension of the policy process. Discussion in this chapter centers on the opportunities and challenges facing school-based decision-making committees (SBDMCs) and the kinds of support they need.

The discussion is divided into three sections. The first section focuses on the development of ethical schools as an overarching purpose for SBDMCs. This discussion draws heavily on Starratt's (1994) work *Building an Ethical School: A Practical Response to the Moral Crisis in Schools*. In the second section, consideration is given to the understandings about ethical decision making in schools we have reached in our Collaborative Research Group on Policy and Ethics at the University of South Florida. Drawing on preceding chapters, the focus in this section is on an analysis and synthesis of some of the concepts we now consider to be especially relevant to the work of SBDMCs. A primary emphasis is on the need for SBDMCs to function as learning communities with an ethic of care and hospitality to the stranger guiding both the process and outcomes of the policy process. The third section includes a delineation of five general principles that we believe may be useful to SBDMCs. These principles are guiding the work of our research group at the present time. A brief conclusion follows these three sections.

DEVELOPING SCHOOLS AS ETHICAL LEARNING COMMUNITIES

There is a reciprocal relationship between SBDMCs and the organizational and political cultures in which they function. While developing or providing advice about school policies, they are influenced by state and local school board policies and regulations, values manifest in the school, patterns of operation, and attitudes of school personnel who are members of the committee. Indeed, the committee's agenda comes from issues that emerge in the school and the particular goals, needs, and strengths of the school it serves. The committee has the potential of having a culture-shaping impact on the school. In seeking to become an ethical learning community with decisions or advice centered in an ethic of care, the SBDMC can focus its work on developing and advocating policies aimed at building an ethical school. This focus leads the SBDMC into the most challenging and, potentially, the most rewarding aspect of its work.

The idea of schools as ethical learning communities is replete with basic questions and issues such as the role of schools with respect to affirming particular values. School leaders make ethical choices and school-based decision making bodies, such as SBDMCs, make policy-related decisions that belie a set of assumptions about what is believed to be good and appropriate. These are value issues and often matters of aesthetic taste, not universally agreed-on principles. Sizer (1984) pointed out the moral and political complexity of schools fulfilling their obligation to stand for certain values and to teach these values to students. Reasonable people, he observed, can disagree about basic concepts such as decency. For example, individuals can hold strong differences on issues such as whether demonstrations about social or political issues such as nuclear disarmament should occur during school time or how revealing cheerleader uniforms should be.

Part of the challenge has to do with the perceived role of schools in our society. The organizational, moral, and political roles of SBDMCs must be understood in the context of the perceived role of the schools in which they function. More than 50 years ago, Barzun

(1945), in *Teacher in America*, described the exaggerated hopes for schooling in America:

Sociologists and the general public continue to expect the public schools to generate a classless society, do away with racial prejudice, improve table manners, make happy marriages, reverse the national habit of smoking, prepare trained workers for the professions, and produce patriotic and religious citizens who are at the same time critical and independent thinkers. (p. 24)

Many of these expectations continue today, alongside more cynical and defeatist views of public education. Disagreement abounds about what schools ought to do, and radically different understandings exist as to what schools are, in fact, doing. Berliner and Biddle (1995), for example, argued that school reform is politically motivated and that schools are performing much better than school reformers claim.

Starratt's (1994) excellent work on building ethical schools is sufficiently clear and relevant to the issues SBDMCs are likely to confront in making ethical decisions; an extended discussion of his arguments is included here. Starratt described five obstacles to building an ethical school. The first is the fear that addressing ethical issues directly in our pluralistic society will become divisive. Teaching moral and ethical values, or attempting to promote an explicit ethical stand in school, could result in controversy and conflict among different ethical viewpoints. In response to this issue, Starratt argued that we can agree on certain basic values. He cited Lickona's (1989) contention that respect and responsibility are the essential values. Fox and DeMarco (1990), however, suggested three general moral principles: 1) do no harm, 2) do not be unfair, and 3) do not violate another's freedom. Starratt supported Green's (1985) view of the function of education in nurturing conscience, which Green conceived as unitary and personal. Green described five voices:

1. *The call of craft:* The sense of integrity in our work, including feelings of guilt or shame about work done poorly
2. *The call of membership:* Focusing on responsibility to the community that has primacy over the individual
3. *The call of sacrifice:* One's duty in going beyond self-interest (keeping promises or confidences, for example, when not to do so might serve your own ends)
4. *The call of memory:* Being rooted in the stories of our people and our place
5. *The call to imagination:* Feeling connected and in solidarity with those who have gone before, mourning their suffering and celebrating their humanity, and responsibility for future generations

The second obstacle, Starratt (1994) argued, derives from the assumption that objective knowledge is independent of subjective ethical preferences and religious beliefs. That is, ethics is understood to be based on values, not facts. An ethical view from this perspective reflects cultural traditions and religious beliefs and, therefore, should be addressed in the home and church, synagogue, or temple. Schools can teach obedience to laws and rules, so the argument goes, but there is no need to consider the ethical rationale supporting the laws. Even the legal profession, according to Starratt, does not concern itself with such ethical support. Starratt drew on the work of Jennings (1983) and Kuhn (1970) in challenging the view that objective knowledge is the only valued knowledge and questioning the traditional assumption about objectivity in science. Ethics is not, he argued, a purely subjective choice, neither is it necessarily relegated to religious beliefs.

Emphasizing its importance in public debate and consensus, Aristotle (1962) viewed ethics as practical knowledge gained from living in a community. Ethical understanding, from Aristotle's perspective, is gained from reflecting on life in the community and the ways practical problems are solved. As Starratt pointed out, "One learned how to be an ethical person by living in the community and learning the normal ways the community conducted its affairs and relationships" (1994, p. 10).

Following Aristotle's (1962) arguments, Starratt (1994) believed ethics is concerned with the public life of the community, not narrowly constrained "to subjective individual choice or to principles derived from religious dogma" (p. 10). Furthermore, he argued, it is the very diversity of our society that creates the necessity for schools to be places where children learn a common ethic that can bind them together.

The constitutionally mandated separation of church and state in the United States has led to numerous Supreme Court decisions and caused explicitly ethical content and moralizing to be removed from the curriculum. The question for teachers became how to teach an ethic that does not presuppose a religious foundation. In this context, Starratt (1994) suggested, the question "is not so much whether to have ethical schools; rather, … how do we do it within state and federal laws?" (p. 11). It is important to point out that, though the discussion of religion in schools can be problematic, current literature is beginning to reflect a deeper analysis of the role of religious thought in public schools. Nord's (1995) scholarly treatise *Religion and American Education: Rethinking a National Dilemma,* for example, suggests that public schools and universities must take religion seriously. Jacob Neusner, a scholar in religious studies, has described Nord's work as "a starting point for the debate that is coming" (Nord, 1995 [jacket copy]). In another publication, Thiemann (1996), Dean of the Harvard Divinity School, which has been traditionally associated with liberal thought, suggested that it may be timely to revisit the values of liberty, equality, and toleration that James Madison sought to inscribe in the First Amendment. Thiemann, in *Religion in Public Life: A Dilemma for Democracy* (1996), pointed out that the strict separation of church and state did not come into common constitutional usage until a 1947 Supreme Court opinion. He believes the view that religion has no legitimate place in public institutions needs to be reexamined, noting that

> the fragile bonds that hold the American Republic together are under considerable stress. The narrative that for more than two centuries provided a coherent framework for the aspirations of the American people now seems to many struggling citizens a story of exclusion and oppression rather than hope and opportunity. (p. 171)

Thiemann proposed a revision of political liberalism that would provide a more legitimate place for religious voices in public debate.

The important work of Nord, Thiemann, and other scholars in religious studies has profound implications for the work of SBDMCs. In taking their role in ethical decision making seriously, SBDMCs will be engaged in reflective work on the interests of all children in an increasingly diverse and complex society. The difficulties and challenges of serious debates in these committees will echo and, indeed, be a part of the public discourse that is becoming less accepting of unexamined assumptions. It will be necessary to develop an ethos in committee deliberations that makes liberty, equality, and tolerance explicit values. For SBDMCs, the virtues manifested in an ethic of hospitality to the stranger, a disciplined approach to policy, and an empathic regard for the interests of all children in the school must be grounded in a strong foundation of civility, respect, and care among the members. SBDMCs become learning communities, with the morally grounded policies they advocate being continually constructed from the struggles and growth of the committee itself.

The third obstacle Starratt (1994) described is more pragmatic: Schools do not have enough time to teach ethics. Viewed as already falling behind in teaching basic skills, ethics education would divert even more time away from the school's basic purpose. Starratt responded to this argument by suggesting that schools are already teaching ethics; the challenge is "to improve the quality of the ethical lessons students experience in the regular school day" (p. 11). He suggested that it is impossible to run an ethically neutral school: Adults and peers model appropriate behavior, a school's discipline policy defines unacceptable or negatively valued behaviors and their consequences, moral lessons are implied in the curriculum, and ethical lessons are learned on the playground and in extracurricular activities. It is, therefore, not a matter of needing more time as much as recognizing the ethical content of existing materials already in the curriculum and of promoting institutional consistency in reflecting agreed-upon values.

Although the SBDMC has a policy function rather than a teaching function, it exists in a milieu of tacit assumptions and priorities. The idea that the school does not have enough time to focus on ethics suggests something about the values and priorities in the school. The committee can have an influence on elevating ethics to a higher level of awareness by having the courage to get it on the table for discussion and by making discussion of the ethical rationale associated with school policy normative. The committee can aid in effecting explicitly agreed-upon values in the school and assist in addressing the issue of consistency in institutional response.

A fourth challenge is more subtle, more rarely articulated, and, Starratt (1994) argued, more difficult to overcome. That challenge is the growing indifference and belief that a common ethic is not needed. Behavioral standards have changed, and many behaviors that once were considered ethically objectionable are now acceptable, representing a decline in ethical standards and civility described by Starratt:

> Driven by a relentless pursuit of material accumulation, recreational thrills, and a self-centered desire for power and status, more and more adults have accepted a privatized ethic of social Darwinism, where the individual is pitted against everyone else in an aggressive pursuit of self-interest. (1994, p. 3)

Parents who have this view, Starratt contended, are likely not to hold their children to any ethical standard beyond competition and survival.

Ethical education is perceived as having no practical value in the school or in the home. Starratt's (1994) response to this objection is that the disintegration of public life is in some measure a product of parents abdicating their responsibility to teach their children the difference between acceptable and unacceptable behavior based on some concern for the common good. Since parent involvement is an essential component of building an ethical school, it is essential to confront apathy and indifference encountered in parents.

The SBDMC can play a pivotal role in this regard. As a representative body that includes parents and other community members, this committee can, in effect, engage in what Bellah, Madsen, Sullivan, Swidler, and Tipton (1985) called "doing public philosophy." The committee can create public discussions of value issues and moral dilemmas in a manner that affects the ways in which people think about and act on policy problems. An open discourse valuing responsibility, integrity, and hospitality, for example, can change the collective imagination about the place called school.

A fifth obstacle is the perception that teachers are not competent to teach ethics. Teachers reflect the diversity of ethical perspectives found in the larger society, and they are expected to teach students with different ethnic and economic backgrounds; yet they are given no special training or education in ethics. Starratt (1994) responded that teachers are already teaching ethics; the question is, "How well?" He suggested that attention needs to be given to in-service and pre-service ethics education for teachers.

Respecting the idea that the curriculum in the classroom ought to be cut from the same moral cloth as the policies governing the school's affairs, ethics education is also needed for administrators and school decision makers, including SBDMCs. That is, indeed, one of the basic arguments of this book.

Starratt (1994) argued that ethics education in schools is one aspect of reversing deterioration in the ethical life of society. He suggested proceeding by the following method:

1. Taking a look at some of the underlying frames of mind in schools and in the culture that create barriers to the ethical growth of children
2. Considering the values that ought to provide a foundation for ethical education
3. Examining perspectives currently guiding ethical education
4. Attempting to develop an overarching framework that incorporates features of different ethical theories

The same general approach can work in the analysis and development of policy.

Starratt (1994) described what he called the "moral problematics" in schools. These include individualism (as in, e.g., "You're on your own"), superficial forms of rationality (i.e., overreliance on memory rather than relying on problem solving or critical thinking), competition, a focus on achievement unrelated to the real world, and conformity to authority rather than independent thinking. He argued that patterns of school life work against the experience of belonging to a community or of having obligations to others. Schools fail to be concerned about deeper human purposes and values or general moral involvement with satisfying human relationships. Neither do they focus on social responsibility or participation in civic governance.

The values and virtues missing in schools, in Starratt's (1994) analysis, are part of what the school reform movement should be about. Although the authority given to SBDMCs varies considerably, school-based decision makers have the potential to profoundly affect the qualities of the school as a moral community and to model civic virtue in the management of schools.

Starratt (1994) used foundational qualities of an ethical person and a multidimensional framework for decision making as bases for planning an ethical school. He described three qualities of an ethical person:

1. Autonomy, that is, independent and able to act on intuition about what is right
2. Connectedness, that is, sensitive and responsive to others within a context or a community
3. Transcendence, which has to do with reaching for excellence, turning one's life over to something or someone else, and achieving something heroic

Starratt's (1994) framework for making ethical decisions incorporates an ethic of critique, an ethic of justice, and an ethic of care. He viewed this framework, not so much as a theory, but as a way of providing general coherence to the project of developing an ethical school. His focus, he said, is not so much to develop and test a theory as "to engage in the practice of ethics while engaging in the practice of education" (Starratt, 1994, p. 45).

We have taken a similar perspective in our work on ethics and school policy. We have not defined our work as developing and testing a theory so much as developing a framework to assist SBDMCs in engaging in the practice of ethics while making policy. Whereas Starratt's (1994) framework focuses on the ethic of justice and the social contract more than we have in this book, his perspective has a lot of appeal for those engaged in policy work. Therefore, the three ethics he proposed—critique, justice, and care—are briefly described below.

Ethic of Critique

The ethic of critique focuses on issues of power, privilege, interest, and influence in the political and social life of the school. It calls into question those practices that are legitimized by tradition, assumed rationality, and law:

> Whether one begins from the less radical perspective of the recent proponents of school reform such as Boyer (1983), Goodlad (1984), or Sizer (1984), or from the deeper critique of Apple (1982), Bates (1987), Freire (1970), or Giroux (1988), it has become increasingly evident that schools and school systems are structurally ineffective. (Starratt, 1994, p. 46)

Within this context, the school's bureaucracy is seen as a persistent problem that reproduces the status quo. From a critical perspective, a school can be reorganized in ways that reflect greater fairness to all students.

Starratt (1994) listed several structural issues involved in the management of education that are based on unjustifiable assumptions and may advantage some at the expense of others: homogeneous tracking, grading on a curve, absence of important topics from textbooks, calculating class rank, lack of appropriate due process, labeling criteria, and interrupting instruction by standard time allotments for class periods. These are examples of the kinds of issues that must be addressed within an ethical framework by school-based decision makers.

Ethic of Justice

The ethic of justice relates more directly to issues of governance. Unlike the ethic of critique, which calls governance and management practices into question, the ethic of justice is more useful in developing a response to the perceived abridgment of ethical values such as equality, the common good, democratic participation, and human and civil rights.

Ethic of Care

The ethic of care "requires fidelity to persons, a willingness to acknowledge their right to be who they are, an openness to encountering them in their authentic individuality, and a loyalty to relationship" (Starratt, 1994, p. 52). The ethic of care moves beyond formal contracts and specified obligations to a relationship. The integrity of relationships is held sacred, and the school as an organization is obligated to treat as sacred the good of individuals within it. Individuals are treated as ends, never as means only. An ethic of care challenges motives involving a wish to dominate, intimidate, or control. It resists stereotypes of race, ethnicity, age, and gender that thwart authentic and caring communication. The school culture, from the language used in formal memoranda to school songs, mottoes, rituals, reward systems, and other symbols, Starratt observed, is saturated with messages that communicate what it cares about. When students participate in a school culture that is welcoming and affirming, they learn to respect, support, and care for one another. "With some help from peers and teachers, they also learn how to forgive, to mend a bruised relationship, to accept criticism, to debate different points of view" (Starratt, 1994, p. 54).

REFLECTING ON WHAT WE HAVE LEARNED

A major focus of the restructuring of public education in the United States under way since the early to mid-1980s has been the location of more authority for making policy decisions in local schools. The implementation of the site-based management policy has met with varying levels of success in overcoming well-entrenched public school bureaucracies and traditions. Committees vary significantly in how they function and the extent to which they address major policy dilemmas such as the inclusion of children with disabilities in general education classrooms (see the Introduction and Chapter 1).

To the extent that the policy has been effectively implemented, school-based control has brought new challenges for local school policy leaders. As formal structures have been established in which teachers, principals, other professional staff, parents, and community representatives can participate in the policy process (i.e., SBDMCs), new questions are being raised regarding the values and moral visions guiding the decision-making process. Some of these questions emerge as a function of the increasing demographic complexity of schools. The policy deliberations in democratic schools are now more likely to be highly textured, with different cultural and moral perspectives on the developmental and educational interests of children.

The scope and moral implications of the present policy environment in schools is captured by Bottery:

> The ethicality of school management must be tested in terms of a number of values. These will be of a personal, social, and a political nature, for the treatment of the individual and the group within the school must have profound implications for the political processes of the country in which pupils will come to be adult participants, and ultimately for the planet on which they live. The questions which must be asked, then, move along a continuum from issues about individual development at one end to those concerning a world community of citizens at the other. (1992, p. 5)

The questions must be asked, but how will they be answered in a multicultural community, and by whom? In an economic environment with limited resources that must be allocated to meet almost unlimited needs, what criteria will be employed in making policy decisions? The importance of these kinds of policy questions is being amplified by the implementation of site-based management in public schools.

Although the specific authority of SBDMCs varies from school district to school district, most share at least five characteristics. First, each one functions in the social context of a school that has its own political and moral ecology. This means, among other things, that the quality of the relationships reflecting the cultural diversity among the students and between students and faculty, the leadership style of the principal, the school's history and traditions, the resources available, and the relationship of the school to the community will produce different kinds of policy opportunities and problems.

Second, each SBDMC is made up of individuals, each having his or her own needs, information, world view, values, agenda, and perception of her or his role in the committee. The diversity of perspectives, needs, and values and the intellectual and moral resources of each member contribute to the group's work style and its productivity.

Third, the SBDMC brings together professionals and nonprofessionals to share responsibility for making policy decisions or for providing policy advice. When functioning in a collegial manner, the SBDMC develops a culture that blurs the traditional lines that help structure the social contracts between experts and nonexperts. The duties and moral obligations are not always clear. The law and public policies tend to be clearer about the roles professionals or nonprofessionals should play than they are about the ethical criteria for responsible conduct in collaborative roles that involve sharing responsibility such as is expected of SBDMC members.

Fourth, each SBDMC has its own dynamic life as a group. The dynamics of these committees, like the dynamics of any group that works together over a period of time, are shaped by the personalities of the members and the quality of their relationships in resolving power and control issues. The decisions made in each committee are, in large part, a function of the group dynamics involved in the decision-making process.

Fifth, each SBDMC functions within a policy environment with a particular set of expectations. These expectations vary from school to school or, more specifically, from principal to principal; nonetheless, local guidelines help establish a work scope and a method of operation.

These characteristics of SBDMCs, among others, which are embedded in the social psychology and culture of schools, are discussed in Chapters 7, 8, and 9. Dempsey and McCadden, in Chapter 7, focus on power issues and the construction of meaning in school policy. In Chapter 8, Greenbaum and Martinez focus more specifically on the cultural context of the committees' work and the kinds of issues school cultures present to SBDMCs. Morse, Berger, and Osnes, in Chapter 9, describe the kinds of dynamics that affect group functioning and influence decisions. Although each committee is different, each one functions in a social, cultural, psychological, and policy context.

Although SBDMCs have broad policy-mandated authority and are located in some form in most schools across the United States, we have found in our work with schools in Florida, in our review of the literature, and in a national survey (see Chapter 1) that they have little guidance in how to go about their work; they especially have little help in deciding how to address serious policy dilemmas. They are typically provided little or no assistance in understanding school policy and even less in framing policy issues for discussion and resolving differences that may exist among group members. That is, with few exceptions, SBDMCs are not aided in analyzing policy problems or thinking about solutions. Without either conceptual or methodological assistance, it is not likely that these committees will play a serious decision-making role in the formulation of local school policies. Of particular interest in the context of this book is that there is no evidence that SBDMCs are given any assistance in understanding and addressing ethical issues in policy. When one considers, as we do, that policies need to be understood for their ethical implications as well as their factual basis, this general lack of preparation and technical support is a serious deficiency in the implementation of the site-based management aspect of school reform.

The nature of the ethical issues that must be addressed and the approaches to addressing those issues are directly affected by the five defining characteristics described previously. That is, the ethical perspectives of an SBDMC are determined by the views of individuals and the contexts within which they function. Whether consciously or not, each committee member faces two levels of analysis. The first level is an examination of one's own values and moral vision. The second involves understanding the values and moral vision of the group. The fit between individual perspectives and the emergent group perspective is very important. Discontinuities should be addressed and resolved in order for the group to function successfully. Depending on the styles of individuals in dealing with differences, the perceived seriousness of the issue, and the group culture, it is most likely that either the group will become dysfunctional or one or more members will leave if the discontinuities are not addressed.

Noting that professional ethics incorporate personal ethics in establishing ethical standards, Kalish and Perry (1992) observed,

> Compassion, fairness, integrity, moral courage—these are key elements of the ethical life to which we all aspire, professionally and personally. Lawyers, doctors, school executives, and others who lack these traits rightly are regarded as poor professionals as well as incomplete persons. (p. 24)

The ethical perspectives set out in Chapters 3, 4, 5, and 6 lead one to conclude that SBDMCs would do well to ground their work in these virtues (i.e., compassion, fairness, integrity, moral courage).

Authors throughout the book have argued that it is important for each SBDMC member to have some awareness of her or his own values and the social, cultural, and policy contexts in which the committee works. Several have also commented on the importance of individual members having some awareness of the dynamics that guide and influence the group's decision-making process. However, self-knowledge on the part of individuals or the committee as a whole is not sufficient to guide the work of the SBDMC as an ethical policy-making body. Some knowledge of ethics and of approaches to ethical reasoning is also required.

In turning for assistance, the SBDMCs do not find a well-developed literature on applied ethics in educational policy. Very little attention is given to ethics in the school reform literature. Although there is a vast literature on moral development and moral education or character education, educational practitioners are not well educated about ethics or trained in ethical method. Whereas the study of applied ethics has not been a high priority of philosophers of education, this is changing, as reflected in some excellent literature that has appeared since the mid-1980s, focusing, for example, on teaching (Strike & Soltis, 1992), educational management (Bottery, 1992), professionals in education (Strike & Ternasky, 1993), schools (Starratt, 1994), and special education (Howe & Miramontes, 1992). The study of applied ethics in education, indeed, takes analytic philosophers into new territory. Reagan (1984), in his presidential address to the Philosophy of Education Society, observed that if those in the "analytic camp" in philosophy get involved in applied ethics, "they will find that in addition to doing philosophy as they have generally seen that task, they will also be expected to 'do something else.' That 'something else' is essentially taking seriously the practical reasoning concerns of practicing educators facing ethical problems" (p. 15). The practical concerns now facing policy makers in local schools also must be taken seriously by philosophers of education.

Ethical methodology is complex and requires, as Neukrug, Lovell, and Parker (1996) pointed out, high-level thought coupled with deep reflection. Ethical perspectives differ greatly and, therefore, result in different approaches to ethical decision making. As a result of deliberative work and our studies of ethics and local school policy over the past 3 years at the University of South Florida, it is apparent to this book's editors that the ethical perspectives presented in Chapters 3, 4, 5, and 6 can be especially helpful to SBDMCs.

The general ethical perspective that emerged from our studies and from our deliberations as a research group that seemed best to fit our own values was a focus on care in the context of particular narratives. An individual's integrity and the integrity of the group in which she or he is a member relies on, among other things, the respect and quality of relationships in the group. Hospitality to the stranger, according to Fasching (see Chapter 5), is part of the narrative of an ethical community. Hospitality and care should form both the anchor for the collaborative ethos of an SBDMC and a moral compass for the policy-making process. Mayeroff (1971) said it well: "In the sense in which a [person] can ever be said to be at home in the world, [he or she] is at home not through dominating, or explaining, or appreciating, but through caring and being cared for" (p. 3). Children can be at home in a school in which they feel cared for and in which they are supported in caring for others. An ethic of care is the center of an inclusive culture in which acts of respect, kindness, hospitality, and compassion are normative.

The challenge, of course, is to create a school community centered in caring. The work of Noddings (1984, 1992) is especially helpful in understanding the nature and substance of this challenge. For SBDMCs, composed of individuals with different agendas and different perspectives on care and education, the challenge is to understand how to respect the differences while affirming a core ethic. This is a culture-building task that involves, from a narrative perspective, developing a common story centered in the group's shared values and understandings. It is a process aimed at each member contributing to and having a valued place in the group's story.

In order to develop a core ethic of care and hospitality to strangers, SBDMCs must have the discipline to carefully monitor and develop thoughtful policies that reflect caring for all students. Such discipline coupled with empathy—to follow the argument of Etzioni (1994) regarding the two capacities necessary for value-based decisions—for all students will substantially increase the likelihood that the committee will develop ethical policies. That is, policies will be developed and advocated that include students in all aspects of the school's life—female students, students who are minorities, students with disabilities, and those on the social margins and at risk for school failure.

A corollary to an ethic of care is the ethic of responsible action that requires that the committee view itself as part of the school's ethical learning community. To care responsibly means, among other things, that one has reliable and valid information. In making thoughtful and moral choices, the facts must be known and understood. Differences among decision makers that appear to be ethical in nature are sometimes differences in knowledge about or interpretation of the facts.

A great deal of imaginative work has been done in thinking through the concept of a learning community (Block, 1993; Senge, 1990). This concept has considerable appeal for SBDMCs, both for understanding themselves and for understanding the schools they seek to serve. A learning community understands itself to be responsible for the reality it constructs and the vision it chooses to follow. Each member shares responsibility for the welfare of the whole community. The community grows and matures as it learns, that is, as it continues to construct or re-create itself. This is an empowering and dynamic perspective that helps give definition to imaginative work in community.

The role of an SBDMC is partially determined by the principal in the school it serves. However, the reality with which it works, its view of policy, its understanding of the needs of students and staff in the school, and its concept of itself as a volitional community within the school are determined much more by its own constructions. The SBDMC can see itself as the victim of a controlling principal, a lack of expertise, or some other deficiency in its composition or assignment. Although not denying the influence these factors may have, the committee's reality, whether futile or filled with opportunity, is under its own control. The nature of the committee's work depends on the manner in which it is constructed, and the quality of that construction depends on the committee's deep investment in care, learning, and renewal.

This is the general perspective guiding the work of the Collaborative Research Group on Policy and Ethics at the University of South Florida. Our experience as a learning community has helped us imagine the potential of SBDMCs working with the mind-set of constructive learners. The locus of control is within the group, and each person has responsibility for the group's work. No special expertise is recognized, except when questions arise for which there is some knowledge or skill base. If a group member has that expertise, it is made available to the group; if not, the literature or individuals with the expertise outside the group are consulted.

This does not mean that the group is closed or works apart from other contexts. The group is, in fact, open, requiring only that individuals choosing to work with the group take their responsibility for participation seriously, that is, to be present and participate in meetings and to regard all members of the group as colleagues, no matter what title individuals may have. The group thus has a flat social structure with the leader serving more to convene and facilitate than to direct the group. An emerging literature on collaborative research groups (Paul, Marfo, & Anderson, in press; Reason, 1988) complements the growing literature on learning communities in providing a useful perspective for how SBDMCs can function. There is a great deal of potential for SBDMCs using the collaborative, learning community perspective.

TOWARD PRINCIPLES AND GUIDELINES FOR SBDMCs

Although we continue to hold most of our beliefs about ethical policy making in schools as tentative or working hypotheses, we do have some understandings that are guiding our work on a curriculum focused on ethical policy making in schools. As products of our work in progress, the five interrelated understandings, or principles, discussed below have grown out of several studies of SBDMCs, many reviews of the literature in several fields, and deliberations as a collaborative research group. They are grounded in the values and experiences of members of our collaborative research group, several of whom are active members of SBDMCs. These five general principles reflect our overarching focus on ethics, our bias in supporting a narrative approach to ethics, and our particular interest in a policy on inclusion for all children.

1. SBDMCs must have a long-term commitment to a sense of community among themselves. Several authors have made the argument throughout this book that we see ethics as being about community, story, and character. Ethics is relational, involving the inherently communal obligations we experience toward others. As Fasching suggests in Chapter 5, ethics is about relationships, even in the presence of differences of opinion such as may exist in SBDMCs. It is essential for committee members to consider and deliberate their obligations to each other in a constructive and sympathetic way. Each member of the committee, as French (see Chapter 4) suggests, must have integrity in the deliberative process.

2. SBDMCs should be self-conscious and deliberative about the kind of narrative they construct for defining themselves and their work over time. This involves more than establishing goals or establishing a work scope for the committee's work. It involves examining the values and moral vision that will guide the committee's work. It involves ethical reflection and the risk of questioning the group's morality and commitments. The committee's story can be one of an interested, committed, and caring agent of thoughtful change in a school, or it can be little more than a bureaucratic mechanism understood to be satisfying the policy requirement that an SBDMC be established. The committee's story is the soul of its work. It should develop rituals to define and remind itself of its story and the moral course it sets for itself. The committee should make certain that there are members with stories of their own—about diversity, poverty, disability, and single parenting, for example—who can help the group construct an inclusive and empathic story.

3. SBDMCs should be guided by an ethic of care and hospitality to the stranger. Ethics is storied; it is not a guide for disinterested observers. It embraces a profound existential principle that suggests our

own good can be realized only as we seek what is good for others (see Chapter 5). In order to truly seek the good of others, it is necessary to have empathy with the needs of others. This means, among other things, overcoming ethnocentrism and self-interest in the group as a hidden agenda. The imperative of welcoming a stranger is not a rule to be imposed but a matter of character, a defining value for a community. It is with this ethic in mind that SBDMCs can develop inclusive policies that are responsive to the diverse learning needs of children with disabilities. These children, as Rud indicates in Chapter 3, are strangers who are labeled, ostracized, and "othered" in the history of education. They have been viewed by many as sources of grief for parents and excessive burdens on the budgets of local schools.

We do not see a simple one-size-fits-all solution to the issue of where and how children with disabilities can best be served. Neither the research nor the moral arguments lead to a single solution to the ongoing national debate about inclusion. However, the SBDMC in each school has the opportunity to see these children differently, as resources of a diverse community, as individuals with gifts to be celebrated as well as special needs to be met. SBDMCs can be buffers in the policy process to resist simplistic solutions that marginalize and stigmatize children and tether our institutions to moral visions of the past.

4. SBDMCs must have valid and reliable information about the school. It is not likely that committee members will function effectively in making or providing advice about inclusive and caring policies unless they have an accurate understanding of realities in the school. Obtaining good data is not always easy. When provided some tables with numbers by "people in charge," there is a tendency to interpret them as if they were accurate and meaningful accounts of reality. The data, in fact, lead us to think in particular ways about the realities to which they refer. It is important, therefore, that committees decide the kinds of things they need to know, based on their own vision, and the kind of information they need to gather in order to know it.

Although objective data are helpful, committee members must know more. They need their own experience in the school. They need to see and smell the cafeteria when children are having lunch, walk in the hallways when classes are changing, attend faculty meetings, talk informally with teachers and the principal at appropriate times, and sit and observe teachers in their classrooms. How are the children arranged for instruction? What is the political geography of the school? That is, are some children separated from their age peers? If so, what is the rationale and how is it working for those who are separated? What are the rituals and routines, or regularities, in the school? What are the reasons given for these regularities? How do students feel about their experience in school? What is the quality of conversations among and between teachers and students?

SBDMC members will need to invest time in getting involved, learning the stories of children and their families, and understanding the interactions between poverty, ethnicity, and gender and our traditional approaches to identifying, labeling, and placing children with disabilities. SBDMC members will need to become generally familiar with different service delivery options and to know something about the empirically validated instructional practices all teachers should be able to employ. This information can be made available by the school district office or the state department of education if the committee asks for it. The committee needs this kind of information in order to develop an informed ethical stance about school policy issues. The committee needs to have valid and reliable knowledge and to know firsthand the realities in the school in order to effectively advocate a welcoming and caring community while avoiding the policy "potholes" of the past. Without this kind of knowledge, the committee is greatly disadvantaged in making any decisions relative to the development and nurture of an ethical learning community.

Obviously, committee members have their own time constraints, and the amount of time available for observing in school is limited. As a committee, however, it is possible to develop some strategies that result in each member having some experience in the school and the committee, as a whole, having a sample of the total school day. At a minimum, SBDMC members should have a clear, personal, rich, and well-illustrated picture of a typical day in the school.

5. SBDMCs must know their business. SBDMCs can be strategically disadvantaged in several ways. Their roles often are not clearly defined. Individual members have their own agendas. Resources to support the committee are usually meager, and little training is available. Yet the substantive issues they must address and the group process issues related to how they will work as a committee can be very complex. Given these realities, the committee must have some knowledge about and access to expertise in several areas, including group process, school policy, and ethics. Although there are other important areas in which assistance may be needed, SBDMCs must have access to information and assistance in these three areas in order to make or provide advice about ethical policies.

CONCLUSIONS

A thoughtful discussion of ethical policy making in schools is, from the outset, challenged to define policy and ethics and to indicate how schools are to be understood in framing the discussion. In this chapter and throughout the book, the focus is on how SBDMCs develop and mature as ethical decision-making bodies, whether central to or tangential to the policy process in local schools. We have viewed policy broadly as including all decisions regarding the allocation of limited human and financial resources to meet almost unlimited needs (Gallagher, 1981). Although a clear and important role for both principle-based and virtue-based ethics is evident, the authors of this book have leaned toward a narrative perspective because we believe it is especially helpful to SBDMCs in understanding and addressing the ethical challenges and opportunities they face in their decision-making role. The committee itself is a storied political and organizational medium in which some of the school's most crucial concerns affecting the educational and social welfare of all students may be addressed. As such, the committee must have substantial mooring in a sense of the shared values of its members and a moral foundation for its vision and its work in the school. It should have some commitment to building an ethical learning community in which all children have a valued place. In order to work effectively as part of the policy process in local schools, SBDMCs must have valid and reliable information, including their own personal experience in the school, and they must develop the necessary capacity and competence needed to implement their policy-related responsibilities.

REFERENCES

Apple, M. (1982). *Education and power.* Boston: Routledge & Kegan Paul.

Aristotle. (1962). *Nicomachean ethics, Book III* (M. Ostwald, ed. & trans.). Indianapolis, IN: Hackett.

Barzun, J. (1945). *Teacher in America.* Boston: Little, Brown.

Bates, R. (1987). Corporate culture, schooling and educational administration. *Educational Administration Quarterly, 23*(4), 19–115.

Bellah, R.N., Madsen, R., Sullivan, W.M., Swidler, A., & Tipton, S.M. (1985). *Habits of the heart: Individualism and commitment in American life.* Berkeley: University of California Press.

Berliner, D.C., & Biddle, B.J. (1995). *The manufactured crisis: Myths, fraud, and the attack on America's public schools.* Reading, MA: Addison-Wesley.

Block, P. (1993). *Stewardship: Choosing service over self-interest.* San Francisco: Berrett-Koehler.

Bottery, M. (1992). *The ethics of educational management: Personal, social, and political perspectives on school organization.* London: Cassell Educational Ltd.

Boyer, E. (1983). *High school: A report on secondary education in America.* New York: Harper & Row.

Etzioni, A. (1994). *Spirit of community: The reinvention of American society.* New York: Simon & Schuster.

Fox, R. & DeMarco, J. (1990). *Moral reasoning: A philosophical approach to applied ethics.* Fort Worth, TX: Holt, Rinehart & Winston.

Freire, P. (1970). *Pedagogy of the oppressed.* New York: Herder and Herder.

Gallagher, J. (1981). Models for policy analysis: Child and family policy. In R. Haskins & J. Gallagher (Eds.), *Models for analysis of social policy: An introduction* (pp. 37–77). Norwood, NJ: Ablex.

Giroux, H. (1988). *Schooling and the struggle for public life.* Minneapolis: University of Minnesota Press.

Goodlad, J. (1984). *A place called school.* New York: McGraw-Hill.

Green, T. (1985). The formation of conscience in an age of technology. *American Journal of Education, 93,* 1–38.

Howe, K., & Miramontes, O. (1992). *The ethics of special education.* New York: Teachers College Press.

Jennings, B. (1983). Interpretive social science and policy analysis. In D. Callahan & B. Jennings (Eds.), *Ethics, the social sciences, and policy analysis* (pp. 3–35). New York: Plenum Press.

Kalish, J., & Perry, D. (1992, February). Setting ethical standards. *Executive Educator, 24–26.*

Kuhn, T. (1970). *The structure of scientific revolutions* (2nd ed.). Chicago: University of Chicago Press.

Lickona, T. (1989). *Educating for character.* New York: Bantam Books.

Mayeroff, M. (1971). *On caring.* New York: Harper & Row.

Neukrug, E., Lovell, C., & Parker, R. (1996). Employing ethical codes and decision-making models: A developmental process. *Counseling and Values, 40,* 98–106.

Noddings, N. (1984). *Caring: A feminine approach to ethics and moral education.* Berkeley: University of California Press.

Noddings, N. (1992). *The challenge to care in schools: An alternative approach to education.* New York: Teachers College Press.

Nord, W. (1995). *Religion and American education: Rethinking a national dilemma.* Chapel Hill: University of North Carolina Press.

Paul, J., Marfo, K., & Anderson, J. (in press). Developing an ethos for change in a department of special education: Focus on collaboration and research. *Teacher Education and Special Education.*

Reagan, G. (1984). *Applied ethics for educators: Philosophy of education as something else?* Proceedings of the 39th annual meeting of the Philosophy of Education Society, Illinois State University, Normal.

Reason, P. (Ed.). (1988). *Human inquiry in action: Developments in new paradigm research.* Beverly Hills, CA: Sage Publications.

Senge, P. (1990). *The fifth discipline: The art and practice of the learning organization.* New York: Doubleday.

Sizer, T. (1984). *Horace's compromise: The dilemma of the American high school.* Boston: Houghton Mifflin.

Starratt, R. (1994). *Building an ethical school: A practical response to the moral crisis in schools.* London: Falmer Press.

Strike, K., & Soltis, J. (1992). *The ethics of teaching* (2nd ed.). New York: Teachers College Press.

Strike, K., & Ternasky, P. (Eds.). (1993). *Ethics for professionals in education: Perspectives for preparation and practice.* New York: Teachers College Press.

Thiemann, R. (1996). *Religion in public life: A dilemma for democracy.* Washington, DC: Georgetown University Press.

Appendix

The Collegium on Ethics, Policy, and Decision Making

*Background, Methods,
Teaching Case Methods,
Proposals, and General Conclusions*

The purpose of the Collegium on Ethics, Policy, and Decision Making was to develop an effective ethical training program for school-based decision-making committees (SBDMCs) through interpretation of the impact of ethical instruction on the behavior of a group in the analysis of a teaching case and the decision-making process. The Collaborative Research Group on Policy and Ethics (CRGPE), composed of faculty in the departments of special education, child and family studies, and ethics, as well as doctoral students, conducted the Collegium, which consisted of two 1-day sessions and a third day for review and synthesis of lessons learned during the 2 previous days. A total of 19 participants attended the Collegium. They included representatives from elementary schools, middle schools, and secondary schools, as well as parents, a district-level administrator, and a center-based teacher.

Over the course of the 2 days, participants were instructed on ethical issues through the use of the teaching case method. The effectiveness of the use of the teaching case method as a tool for teaching ethical issues was measured and evaluated by several instruments: a Collegium feedback sheet, panel and CRGPE members' feedback sheets, dialogue session reactions, and a suggestions for group observers sheet. The data were then collected and analyzed by members of the CRGPE for the purpose of drawing conclusions and determining implications and applications. Although the analysis of these data has not been included in the material presented in this book, it will be the subject of a forthcoming publication.

Comparisons and contrasts were made between Day 1 and Day 2, through observations, interviews, and audio- and videotape. Differences between Case 1 and Case 2 were also analyzed and noted. Preliminary conclusions were that, overall, a case study seems feasible as an instructional method for ethical deliberation for a variety of SBDMC members. The use of a common reference point engaged participants in facilitative dialogue, permitting them to transfer new information, receive feedback from others, and contribute to the learning process. The Collegium experience enhanced and promoted self-growth for participants and increased their involvement and expanded upon group and individual engagement and thought. Case authenticity, relevancy, and the linkages between cases and ethics instruction were also contributing factors to the efficacy of case method as an implement in the teaching of policy and ethics.

BACKGROUND

Philosophical Context

One of the most challenging features of the school reform movement involves restructuring decision making. The traditional top-down bureaucratic, technocratic approach to policy development and management was targeted as a major dysfunctional feature of the public schools. Consistent with dramatic changes in the philosophy of management in business, school reformers sought to locate more decision-making authority at the bottom of the traditional structure, that is, with teachers and other stakeholders in local schools. The bottom-up focus was institutionalized in the rhetoric of school reform as site-based management.

Several years of experience in attempting to implement a site-based approach to decision making have led to some preliminary conclusions. First, as Michael Fullan pointed out in *Change Force* (1991), the complexities and politics of school management and the myriad policy issues being faced by school leaders, such as diversity and equity interests in the allocation of resources, lead a reasonable person to conclude that decision making needs to be both top-down and bottom-up.

In this context, school leaders, politicians, policy makers, special interest advocates, and others have challenged the technology and art of management to develop a philosophy of management and structure to bear the weight of the goals of school reform. There are many experimental efforts under way, but few conclusions have been reached about a common theoretical framing for practice.

The discourse on advancing knowledge in the management sciences has become increasingly complex since the mid-1980s. There are voices challenging the paradigm of organizations the reform movement is seeking to fix: schools. One of the most articulate voices is that of Senge (1994), who believed that organizations must become learning communities capable of renewing and reinventing themselves. In the learning community, power is shared; knowledge is understood to be constructed; discernible patterns in chaotic systems rather than static rules are sought; and the familiar distinctions such as theory and practice disappear. This paradigm challenge is generating interesting and dramatically different formulations of the management task.

It is in this context of needing to reconsider the basic assumptions and visions guiding the restructuring of management practices that other voices have gained increasing recognition. These are the voices of educational ethicists, such as Kenneth Howe (Howe & Miramontes, 1992), and feminist ethicists, such as Joan Tronto (1995), who are formulating the issues in moral rather than structuralist and functionalist terms. These writers conceptualize the reform of schools more in terms of power and the quality of human relationships and less in terms of rules and procedures. They focus on ways in which gender, ethnicity, social class, and disability are negatively constructed in schools and society. Myriad writers call attention to the values embedded in the interpretation and communication of knowledge and values reflected in the curriculum, teaching methods, assessment philosophies, and placement policies in schools, as well as the approaches to educating teachers.

Local Context

The Department of Special Education and At-Risk Studies at the University of South Florida has a primary commitment to working collaboratively with schools. We have developed four consortia that connect the department with local schools and have developed several collaborative and professional development school partnerships.

The research activities as well as the curriculum for educating teachers in the department are actively guided by the needs in the schools with which we work. One of the key strategies for identifying and attempting to meet those needs is the CRGPE. The CRGPE has been focusing on restructuring and inclusion since 1992. A need that surfaced in that group was the approach to decision making in SBDMCs, one of Florida's principal strategies for implementing site-based management.

Several considerations guided the formulation of our focus on SBDMCs. First, given the confusion and differences of opinion about decision making and the philosophy of management in schools, the nature of the policy authority—if any—of the SBDMCs was not clear.

We anticipated and found considerable variability. Second, since the state's inclusion policy was initially silent on representation of various groups within the SBDMCs, there was reason to question whether the critical interests of children with disabilities would be represented in SBDMCs in each school. Third, the decisions made in each SBDMC would be a function of the values, perspectives, and self-interests of the individual members of each SBDMC. That is, the decisions would be guided by values, with a secondary interest in data. This was an interesting dilemma. How would the needs of children with disabilities be understood and addressed in the policy decisions or advisories generated by these councils? Also, in the absence of any training or assistance in being more self-conscious about the value-laden nature of their work, how could SBDMCs be accountable and perform a responsible policy function? These considerations and the sheer importance of the issues led us to create the CRGPE to address policy and ethics in the context of the work of SBDMCs.

The CRGPE, composed of faculty in special education, child and family studies, and ethics, as well as doctoral students, had been working on this issue for 2 years when a decision was made to try the Collegium approach described herein. Two of the CRGPE members are chairs of SBDMCs, and two others are members in addition to their roles as faculty members or doctoral students. This was an important consideration in keeping our work focused and grounded in the activities of SBDMCs. Our purpose was to have a positive impact on the ethical decision making of SBDMCs, especially with regard to the interests of children with disabilities and their families. A great deal of our focus has been on defining the issues sufficiently well that we would know how to study them. Our commitment is to study the practices of SBDMCs and to examine related literature in policy and ethics to enable us to develop a training program in ethical decision making for SBDMCs.

This background led to a small conference of SBDMC chairs and principals during Fall 1994 to review our work and to obtain guidance about the questions we were raising and our approaches to addressing them. That conference, plus the weekly work of the CRGPE, led to the development of the Ethics Collegium. Consistent with our efforts in the past, we were seeking authenticity in our work and, therefore, needed guidance from SBDMC chairs and principals in different schools. In addition, the Collegium incorporated two research questions that had been formulated in our work to date:

1. Given the abstract nature of ethics, can a valued conversation about ethics occur in a hypothetical SBDMC?

2. What is the impact of ethical instruction on the behavior of a hypothetical SBDMC in the analysis of a case and the decision-making process?

METHODS

Collegium Attendees

Participants were selected to represent the types of constituents who are members of SBDMCs. Panel members were identified during CRGPE meetings as representatives of various disciplines affecting special education who might be interested in participating as active observers in the Collegium's activities. Attendees and observers were people who were involved in varying capacities within the Policy and Ethics Collaborative Research Group and within the Teaching Cases Collaborative Research Group in the Department of Special Education. Some were faculty members in various departments within the College of Education at the University of South Florida; some were doctoral students within the College of Education; and others were involved in activities related to those of the Department of Special Education.

Participant Selection

After numerous lengthy discussions within the CRGPE, several decisions were made regarding the selection of school-based participants. Participants would represent the following categories of school-based stakeholders: principals, special education teachers, general education teachers, exceptional student education (ESE) directors, parents of children who receive special education services, parents of children who receive general education services, SBDMC chairpersons, and representatives of the business community. This representation would reflect the diverse membership on SBDMCs.

Given financial constraints, participants would represent schools from within a 1-hour driving distance of the DaySpring Retreat Center in Ellenton, Florida, the site of the Collegium. This would allow participants to drive to the Collegium and return to their homes comfortably within the same day. Participants would represent a balance of diversity across race and gender, with the recognition that the field of education is overrepresented by women and that administrative positions within education often are dominated by men. Participants would be nominated by school-based people who had been involved in previous activities with CRGPE members. Each participant would be provided with an honorarium of $100 for his or her participation, in addition to receiving mileage and meal expenses. Participants would be recruited by the CRGPE coordinator, who would contact each nominee personally by telephone to describe the Collegium and to secure a commitment to attend. A follow-up letter and description of the Collegium would then be mailed to each participant by the co-ordinator.

As much as possible, each participant would represent a different school. In this way, it could be ensured that Collegium participants, though possibly being small in number overall ($N = 20$), would nonetheless represent the greatest number of schools possible. Over-all, 101 nominations of school-based stakeholders were secured by 18 CRGPE-related personnel. Of the 18, 8 nominators were CRGPE members, and 10 were school-based people known by CRGPE mem-bers. Of the 101 nominations of potential participants, a total of 22 stakeholders committed their participation. Although it is difficult to reconstruct the total number of telephone calls made by the CRGPE coordinator to secure Collegium participation, generally those who were contacted committed their participation during the first tele-phone contact. Therefore, it was not necessary to contact the total number of nominees. Of primary importance in the selection process was the level of diversity of the Collegium participants. Of additional interest, five of the total number of participants ($N = 19$) represented elementary schools, four represented middle schools, three repre-sented secondary schools, five were parents, one was a district-level administrator, and one was a center-based teacher.

It should be noted that occasionally there had been lively discus-sions within CRGPE meetings during decision-making processes re-garding the critical aspect of participant recruitment for the Col-legium. Several CRGPE members believed that it might be difficult for school-based stakeholders to fully appreciate the role that ethics may or may not play within both general and special education. Anchored within the day-to-day realities of parenting and teaching responsibili-ties, ethics may be perceived to be too ethereal to serve any pragmatic purpose, it was feared. Therefore, the process of securing participa-tion would, perhaps, be difficult. In contrast, the experiences of the CRGPE coordinator, upon contacting the nominees, suggested that the opposite seemed more valid—that is, the majority of the people who were contacted engaged the coordinator in 15- to 20-minute con-versations regarding the role that ethics may occupy in some fashion and by varying definitions within education in the 1990s. One of those contacted reported that she was enrolled in a college-level ethics course and found it quite interesting to have been contacted at this time to potentially participate in an ethics collegium. As the parent of a child who receives special education, her opinion was that ethics may have a crucial role to play at this time; and she committed her participation. Another reported that her brother is an ethicist specializing in business ethics and that she was accustomed to participating in lively family discussions regarding ethics. She was pleased to have been invited to attend a forum to which she was invited because a nominator had identified her as a person of strong opinions who might be interested in the ethics underlying education.

TEACHING CASES

In modern times, adults have been tempted to think that they can do without stories—that stories belong to the childhood and adolescence of humanity—before the ages of reason and of science. Having reached the enlightened adulthood of the modern civilization, one must put aside these childish stories. Far from being storyless, however, the contemporary person's actions are still governed by narratives or at least fragments of narratives (Fasching, 1995).

Why Use the Teaching Case Method?

Teaching cases are examples of stories that provide an account of actual occurrences in the lives of the authors of the teaching cases. These real-life events represented in teaching cases are not new in the study of ethics. Since the time of Aristotle, paradigmatic cases of complex ideas and situations have organized the study of ethics (Shulman, 1992). By the presentation of a teaching case to a group of participants and their discussion of the case, knowledge construction and learning occurs. Specifically, the teaching case method used at the Ethics Collegium structured the learning environment by 1) presenting the case; 2) discussing self-constructions and personal beliefs; 3) generating individual and group voice; and 4) identifying change through awareness, understanding, and individual impact. Four attributes of teaching cases influenced the decision to use the teaching case method at the Ethics Collegium. Teaching cases offer 1) a thick description of real events; 2) a situated scenario; 3) a relational, integrated environment; and 4) the opportunity for discussion and social interaction (Richert, 1991).

Description Teaching cases provide the opportunity for school-based stakeholders to record and relate practice. The case materials (e.g., journals, notes, plan books, annotated schedules, even videos) may be transformed into teaching cases. The descriptive aspect of teaching cases allows for addressing the complexities of the school culture. Teachers convey the intensity and understanding of events through the unique characteristics of people, physical environments, time, administrative involvement, and personal dilemmas.

Situational Teaching cases are the representation of life in a specific context. Each case tells of particular actors, particular settings, particular plots, and particular perspectives. Teaching cases are cases of something. They are significant events in the lives of the authors that offer an opportunity for learning because of their anchoring in narrative, time, and place (Shulman, 1992). Teaching cases are stories, but stories for a specific purpose: They are chosen for the purpose of teaching. They are chosen to connect theory with practice in the mind of the learner and offer a piece of experience that is vibrant and engaging. They are unique representations of the complex system of school culture.

Relational Teaching cases demonstrate the interrelatedness and webbing of the multiple components of teaching practice. Activities do not occur in isolation. Teachers and schools operate in a causal environment where ideas, decisions, and actions interact dynamically and multiply in response to numerous perspectives. This dynamic effect is admirably demonstrated by teaching cases.

Social Interaction The foundation of the teaching case method is the discussion and social interaction within the pedagogy of cases. SBDMCs are collaborative groups assembled for the purpose of problem solving, advising, and decision making. The teaching case method and teaching cases parallel the function of these school-based groups. The necessity of understanding and disclosure within the group is facilitated by the use of the teaching case method.

The teaching case method welcomes and acknowledges the participation of people with varying perspectives and backgrounds. It opens a space where diversity is celebrated and freedom of expression is encouraged while an anchor for group interaction is provided. In light of these characteristics, the Ethics Collegium used the teaching case method to engage school stakeholders in developing an ethical awareness of the functioning of school improvement teams and school-based decision-making committees and to stimulate dialogue toward that end.

How Were the Teaching Cases Selected?

For 2 years, a teaching case collaborative research group at the University of South Florida had been involved in assembling a collection of teaching cases. This group had also been interested in the teaching case method and the use of teaching cases at all levels of instruction. The designers of the Ethics Collegium cooperated with the teaching case group to collaboratively identify two cases that represented multi-layered ethical issues. The following were some concerns in the selection of the teaching cases:

- Did the teaching cases present significant issues relevant to SBDMC concerns and/or interests?
- Did the teaching cases present content that reflected ethical considerations?
- Were the teaching cases well written, with enough description, characterization, and detail to engage the participants in the Collegium and allow them to create meaning through group interaction?
- Was anonymity ensured? Was the case presentation risk-free for the characters and authors?
- Could the teaching cases be released for publication?

The teaching case group presented several cases for consideration. Two teaching cases were selected by the Collegium organizers. The ethicists and selected CRGPE members participated in teaching case selection. Each person provided feedback on the selection of teaching cases for the Collegium.

Site Selection   When selecting a site at which to hold the Collegium on Ethics, Policy, and Decision Making, the CRGPE took a number of issues into consideration. First, and most important, the questions the CRGPE was seeking to address required an openness and a substantial measure of trust on the part of the school-based representatives, including parents, teachers, administrators, and SBDMC members. Second, although the University of South Florida provided a central meeting point, the researchers believed that the academic setting might inhibit the open flow of ideas and personal opinions. Finally, the research group felt that a neutral site that was physically removed from the pressures of individual participant workplaces and conducive to introspective thought should be selected. To that end, DaySpring, a rural retreat and conference center in Ellenton, Florida, located an hour south of the university, was selected. The setting proved to be of great value in facilitating the development of the sense of community needed to accomplish the Collegium's work.

Data Collection   A variety of records were kept throughout the Collegium's activities. Audiotaped or videotaped records were maintained for all Collegium activities. Videotaped records were maintained for the presentations by the two ethicists and for the entire day's activities on Day 2. On Day 1, teaching case discussions were not videotaped, to ensure confidentiality of participants and to reduce the obtrusiveness of record-keeping methods. However, the experiences of the day suggested that participants' involvement would not necessarily be reduced because of the presence of videotape equipment. Therefore, more of Day 2's activities were videotaped than of Day 1's.

In addition, individual observers (both panel and CRGPE members) maintained individual records of observation. To complete data collection methods, several CRGPE members are developing an interview format to use with Collegium participants.

Data Collection Methodology A variety of instruments and procedures were used by the CRGPE to gather data relevant to the major questions addressed by the Collegium as well as other questions of interest to individual members of the CRGPE. Overall, there were three data collection techniques based on individual members' areas of expertise, the panel members' academic specializations, individual interests, and professional judgment: 1) questionnaires, 2) participant responses to questions posed by the teaching case facilitator, and 3) observations. This summary concentrates on the instruments that were used by CRGPE members to develop this report and the questions posed by the teaching case facilitator. Reporting on all the data generated by the various questionnaires, participant responses to case facilitator questions, and reporting other CRGPE member data are beyond the scope of this Appendix. It should be noted that the data collected during the Collegium are being used by the CRGPE as part of a data bank that records its ongoing work on ethics, policy, and school advisory structures.

Development of Formal Data Collection Instruments and Procedures Initially, two members of the CRGPE with an interest in the group dynamics variables associated with decision making and deliberations of SBDMCs developed topical outlines for instruments that would be used to observe group development and interactions during the activities scheduled for the first 2 days of the Collegium. These exchanges led to revisions of the instruments to be used for Collegium observations. In the final revision, the scope of the questions was expanded to provide formative evaluative feedback on the group process as well as other aspects of the Collegium's process. In addition, the populations that would use the instruments were expanded far beyond the CRGPE members to included observer and participant feedback. Table 1 provides a listing of the instruments developed, when the instruments were used in the process, who completed the instruments, and a summary of major topics addressed by each instrument.

Participants' Responses to Teaching Case Facilitator's Questions

As part of the two teaching cases used during the Collegium, a variety of questions were used by the facilitator to focus discussion and teach participants. Responses were recorded on wall charts, categorized, and organized for analysis after the Collegium had ended. It is beyond the scope of this report to analyze and discuss all the case study

Table 1. Instruments used to collect data

Instrument	When instrument used	Entity completing instrument	Major topics addressed by instrument[a]
Collegium Feedback Sheet	Case 1 A.M. of both days	Participants	a) Current SBDMC membership status (1) b) Value of teaching case methods to improving one's SBDMC (2) c) Ethical issues arising during case (2) d) Observed group characteristics (3) e) Self-observation of active contributions (2, 3) f) Value of self observation of active contributions (2, 3) g) Value of experience participating in the case (3) h) Recommendations for improving experience to make case more valuable (2)
Panel and CRGPE Members' Feedback Sheets	Case 1 A.M. of both days	CRGPE members and observers	Questions for a, c, d, g, and h are identical to those for Instrument 1 above
Collegium Feedback Sheet	Case 2 P.M. of both days	Participants	a) Same as Instrument 1 above b) Differences between Cases 1 and 2 (3) c) What worked well during case experienced (3) d) Recommended improvements to case experience (3) e) Impact of ethical framework of ethicist on second case analysis (3) f) Three most interesting or useful ideas presented by ethicist (3) g) Disagreeable or objectionable aspects of ethicist's presentation (3) h) Comparison of Collegium group with home school's SBDMC (3) i) Reaction of home school's SBDMC to teaching case methods used to assist in resolving decision-making dilemmas; modifications to enhance utility of case method (3)

(continued)

309

Table 1. (continued)

Instrument	When instrument used	Entity completing instrument	Major topics addressed by instrument[a]
Panel and CRGPE Members' Feedback Sheet	Case 2 P.M. of both days	CRGPE members and observers	a) Questions for a, c, d, g, and h are identical to Instrument 1 above b) Differences between Cases 1 and 2 (3) c) What worked well with Case 2 (3) d) What improvements should be made for Case 2 (3) e) Influence of ethicist's presentation on participation in Case 2 (3) f) Additional comments and observations
Dialogue Session Reactions	Post–Case 2, P.M. of both days	Dyads of CRGPE members and participants	a) Most meaningful experiences of the day (3) b) Could parts of day's activities be omitted without loss (3) c) Value of ethical decision-making processes and SBDMC training (1, 3) d) Other comments (3)

[a]Type of question asked: 1 = Check off, 2 = Open-ended, 3 = Closed-ended.

Teaching Case Questions	Case		Days Used	
	Case 1	Case 2	Day 1	Day 2
What are the problems?	✔	✔	✔	
What else do you want to know?	✔	✔	✔	
Who are the main players?	✔	✔	✔	✔
What do the main players think?	✔		✔	
What are the problems? What are the main players' views?	✔		✔	✔
What else do we want to know?	✔	✔	✔	
What do the main players do?	✔	✔	✔	
What are your initial reactions?		✔	✔	
What could be done to change the decision?		✔		
What are you sad about?		✔		
Who can help?		✔		✔
What do the main players feel?		✔		✔
What's going on here?		✔		✔
Who are the good guys?		✔		✔
Who are the bad guys?		✔		✔
What would you have done?		✔		✔

Figure 1. Teaching case questions and use.

questions posed by the facilitator; however, Figure 1 displays the major questions asked by case and day.

Data Analysis

The following comparisons were made in analyzing the data collected through observations, interviews, videotape, and audiotape. Day 1 was first analyzed as a single entity, comparing Case 1 with Case 2. Day 2 was analyzed in a similar manner. Following that, differences between Day 1 and Day 2 were noted and analyzed.

Day 1: Differences Between Case 1 and Case 2

- Time spent together as a group increased, perhaps resulting in an increased level of comfort for the participants.
- Individual comfort level may have changed due to increased familiarity with surroundings.
- By the afternoon session, leaders had had more time to emerge.
- Fatigue level may have increased by the afternoon.
- The ethicist's presentation may have affected the afternoon session.
- There were additional questions posed to the group by the facilitator in the afternoon session.

All of the differences between the teaching cases listed for Day 1 also apply to Day 2. In addition to the above contrasts, the group identified the following differences between Case 1 and Case 2 on Day 2. Furthermore, a difference existed in Day 2 that did not occur in Day 1: The teaching case facilitator deliberately linked the ethicist's presentation to the second case.

Contrasts Between Day 1 and Day 2

* The school-based participant group changed.
* There was a different ethicist whose presentation differed in content, style, and follow-up.
* Introductory instructions to the participant group were more specific with regard to roles of the observers and panel members.
* The goals of the Collegium were more clearly defined.
* School-based participants were encouraged to speak from their own perspectives.
* The facilitator revisited the ethics presentation during the second case, linking salient points and using key language of the ethics presentation.

The CRGPE had the advantage of a Monday night planning session during which they clarified goals and made suggestions for adjustments in the ethicist's and case facilitator's content and style. Overall, these modifications were aimed at making it more likely that, during Day 2, participants would 1) understand the roles of the different persons in attendance, 2) link the ethicist's paper to the afternoon Case 2, and 3) better articulate the case study questions and discussion to the group's core experience.

PROPOSALS

The CRGPE approached the Collegium as an opportunity to discern basic principles in teaching ethics to a hypothetical SBDMC group. Basic concerns had to do, first, with the abstract nature of discussions of ethics and whether such a discussion would be perceived to be of value to a group that commonly focuses on specific practical issues. Second, there was interest in the impact of the discussion of different approaches to ethics on the group.

An investigation of this kind is extraordinarily complex and does not proceed from a clear set of definitions and assumptions. Furthermore, the complexity of the subject does not lend itself to traditional quasi-experimental research designs. Rather, the general philosophy of the research is more narrative and constructive. The CRGPE reviewed relevant literature and generated some broad propositions that seemed to logically respond to the two fundamental research questions. The Collegium was designed to assist the research group in evaluating the propositions and adding, deleting, or modifying propositions as our experience with the two hypothetical SBDMC groups suggested. Following the Collegium, the CRGPE continued to examine the propositions in group discussions in which each member's perceptions of what occurred and the data collected were used to confirm, contradict, or modify each proposition. This iterative construction-analysis-construction of the propositions resulted in the 20 propositions listed below. They continue to be propositions, subject to ongoing evaluation and development in future experiences designed to help us learn more about ethics instruction for SBDMCs. Some are obviously more basic than others, and it is recognized that the propositions are not mutually exclusive. Neither are they sufficient to ensure successful ethics training. They are, rather, a set of propositions informed by our experience and viewed by the CRGPE to be useful in planning ethics training. They will guide the next stage of our work in developing a curriculum.

Based on our evaluation of the Collegium, the following 20 proposals have guided our work to date and have implications for school-based decision-making committees.

1. Initial instruction in ethics is most effective when there is a common reference point to engage participants. The implication for SBDMCs is that there is a need to have a didactic session on ethics to help the group develop a common language and frame of reference for discussing ethics.

2. Participants enjoyed the experience and appeared invigorated. The implications for SBDMCs are that the study of ethics does not have to be dull. Quite to the contrary: The experience can be an intellectually and emotionally engaging experience. If the discussions are kept relevant with specific teaching case material and the didactic session on ethics is in a language and manner that the group can understand and value, the training can be a satisfying experience for all members of the group. Approaching an SBDMC about ethics instruction should emphasize the positive group energy that can be produced by thoughtful ethics training.

3. An ethical approach to decision making can help participants to feel valued. The implications for SBDMCs are that it appears clear to us that the process of making ethics an explicit concern in a group had the desirable effect of enhancing the perception of each member that she or he is important to the group's work. This implication of ethics training should not be overlooked by those responsible for leading SBDMCs.

4. Participants appeared to feel a sense of self-growth. The implications for SBDMCs are that, in addition to feeling valued and connected to the work of the group, several of the participants talked about their experience at the Collegium as promoting their own growth. This further emphasizes the potential for ethics instruction and teaching case analysis as an approach to group development as well as assistance with decision making.

5. A teaching case approach appears feasible as an instructional method for ethical deliberation for a variety of SBDMC members. The implications for SBDMCs are that the teaching case method helped keep the discussion focused on real examples of policy dilemmas rather than on abstract principles. We believe the teaching case approach should be used with SBDMCs as a practical tool for teaching ethics. It is important to have the cases involve policy dilemmas that are relevant to the work of SBDMCs.

6. A relationship can be drawn among the teaching case, ethics and the teaching case, and ethics and the teaching case and the SBDMC. The implications for SBDMCs are that the fundamental and, perhaps, self-evident issue here is that the approach to ethics should fit the case being used and the context or group, that is, the SBDMC. In planning ethics training for SBDMCs, one must examine the content of the teaching cases to be used and make certain that the didactic session will assist the group with the decisions that must be made.

7. The teaching case method can be an engaging process when properly facilitated. The implications for SBDMCs are that it is essential to have working with the group a skilled facilitator who understands teaching case instruction, group dynamics, and mission of SBDMCs.

8. Teaching cases are enhanced when linkages between cases and ethics instruction are made by the facilitator. The implications for SBDMCs are that the didactic session must be specifically linked to the teaching cases. That is, ethics instruction and teaching cases are not free-standing, independent contents. Groups need help in connecting the two, and this can occur when the ethics instructor makes reference to and uses examples that anticipate the teaching case, and the facilitator draws the ethics content into the teaching case analysis session.

9. Ethical issues can be talked about abstractly, particularly through the use of rhetorical tools, that is, hospitality to the stranger, a metaphor about accepting others used in one of the ethicists' presentations. The implications for SBDMCs are that the frequently reported confusion about abstraction can be significantly reduced by using metaphors, stories, and images that help a person think about an

issue. The use of storied accounts of hospitality to the stranger is an example.

10. Opinions of participants were solicited, contributing to their sense of personal value in the process. The implications for SBDMCs are that it is important to focus on the opinions and perspectives of the participants throughout the process of ethics training. Although there is a specific substantive agenda in the training, that is, an ethical perspective, the group must be assisted in relating this perspective to similar or different perspectives that they have about the subjects being discussed. Again, a skilled facilitator is required, at least initially. The benefit to the group and to individual members of having a facilitator, however, is a positive experience of the process.

11. Informal communications among participants and observers during the day had a determinative effect on the participants' construction of the process and their role in it. The implications for SBDMCs are that it is essential that the planners and leaders of ethics training for SBDMCs account for factors in the environment in which the training is to occur that may be facilitative or distracting. For example, the context of the Collegium included observers whose presence and nonverbal participation had to be considered.

12. Participants received feedback from the facilitator, from each other, and from CRGPE members. The implications for SBDMCs are that ethics training requires each participant to make an investment in learning. Active participation, if it is to benefit the participant and contribute to learning and development, must occur in a dynamic context in which ample feedback on expressed ideas and performance in the group is readily available.

13. The ethicist's use of informal language and delivery style enhance group and individual engagement and thought. The implications for SBDMCs are that SBDMCs should think carefully about what perspective they share. This has implications for the presentation style of the person they should select to speak to the group.

14. Case authenticity and relevancy increased the participants' involvement in the process. The implication for SBDMCs is that it might be desirable for the teaching cases to be developed from local SBDMC experiences. This would increase awareness of issues and generate usable cases. Teaching case writing would become a part of the training. This is a technical process that would be enhanced by participants' understanding the theory of learning on which the teaching case method is based.

15. Information not provided in the teaching case appeared to have an impact on the way a case was handled by the participants. The

implication for SBDMCs is that a lack of information and detail appeared to generate a wider-ranging discussion than would have occurred with more facts provided.

16. The sequencing/nature of the teaching cases appears to affect the outcomes for the participants. The implication for SBDMCs is that it is necessary for planners of SBDMC ethics training to think about the relationship between teaching cases if more than one teaching case is used.

17. The maturity of the group may have an impact on its ability to make decisions. The implication for SBDMCs is that it is important to consider the status of the group when planning ethical training. Some groups are more mature and have had more successful experiences together. Other groups may be less mature in approaching consensus on decisions or may have members who tend to dominate or who are disruptive. These group factors need to be considered in planning for the teaching cases to be used and the sequences in which they are to be presented. It is important, therefore, to know the group.

18. New information, inspiration, and linkages from a common teaching case permit feedback and facilitate the transfer of new information. The implications for SBDMCs are that the teaching case teacher or facilitator needs to have considerable communication with the SBDMC leadership and with the ethics instructor prior to the training. The content and the process of learning should be understood well in advance.

19. There is a responsibility of the ethicist to recognize the theoretical, ethical, and social orientation of the group and to adjust the presentation accordingly. The implication for SBDMCs is that the learning styles of group members must be recognized and the training strategies modified accordingly.

20. The retreat setting is important to the process. The implications for SBDMCs are that SBDMCs need to consider how a retreat-like environment might be achieved for an SBDMC session. SBDMCs might consider a retreat as part of an annual orientation of new members and as a group development exercise.

GENERAL CONCLUSIONS

The Collegium described here was designed to provide descriptive information about how ethics might be taught and applied to complex issues such as those addressed in SBDMCs. More specifically, the purpose of the Collegium was to assist the CRGPE in attempting to understand how case methodology can be used in teaching ethical decision making to members of SBDMCs.

This activity was a part of an ongoing research program investigating ethical decision making in schools, with particular emphasis on issues associated with the education of students with disabilities. The long-range purpose of this research is to generate a curriculum and instructional process that can be used to teach ethical decision making to SBDMCs.

Figure 2 shows the historical background of the work of the CRGPE and is included here to assist the reader with acronyms and references throughout the text to different stages of the process that generated this volume. As indicated in the figure, there have been multiple inputs to and products of the work of the CRGPE that build on 3 years of collaborative research on restructuring and inclusion.

In a project as complex as this, one is limited to modest conclusions that serve primarily to inform the next stages of the study. Our conclusions are therefore limited to observations about the methodology, the relationship between ethics and teaching cases, the source of cases, and the impact of the observational strategies that were used during the Collegium. The following are some observations about the feasibility of teaching case methodology:

- Teaching cases are useful in ethics instruction.
- Teaching cases are helpful in communicating the complexity of issues.
- Teaching cases make people aware of their values, which is necessary in teaching ethical decision making.
- Teaching cases are useful as tools of communication in diverse groups (e.g., gender, ethnicity, ideology).
- Teaching case method evokes openness and participation. Teaching cases provide an opportunity to practice decision making.
- The teaching case facilitator needs to be skilled and flexible, drawing out all voices and analyzing all aspects of the case.

The following are some observations on the linkage of conceptualization or philosophy with teaching cases:

- Teaching cases need to be studied and applied in context.
- The philosophy of case methodology needs to be articulated with the ethical theory being taught.

There is a need to expand the variety of teaching cases that might be used for instructing CRGPE members on ethical decision making in SBDMCs. Important teaching case sources include the following:

- Doctoral students working in community schools
- Collaborative research groups at the university

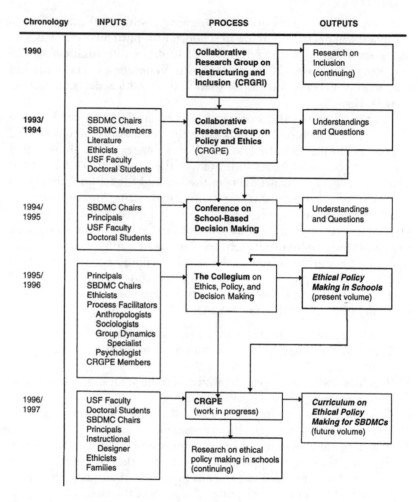

Chronology	INPUTS	PROCESS	OUTPUTS
1990		Collaborative Research Group on Restructuring and Inclusion (CRGRI)	Research on Inclusion (continuing)
1993/ 1994	SBDMC Chairs SBDMC Members Literature Ethicists USF Faculty Doctoral Students	Collaborative Research Group on Policy and Ethics (CRGPE)	Understandings and Questions
1994/ 1995	SBDMC Chairs Principals USF Faculty Doctoral Students	Conference on School-Based Decision Making	Understandings and Questions
1995/ 1996	Principals SBDMC Chairs Ethicists Process Facilitators Anthropologists Sociologists Group Dynamics Specialist Psychologist CRGPE Members	The Collegium on Ethics, Policy, and Decision Making	Ethical Policy Making in Schools (present volume)
1996/ 1997	USF Faculty Doctoral Students SBDMC Chairs Principals Instructional Designer Ethicists Families	CRGPE (work in progress) / Research on ethical policy making in schools (continuing)	Curriculum on Ethical Policy Making for SBDMCs (future volume)

Figure 2. A chronology of the development of a curriculum for school-based decision-making committees. (USF, University of South Florida; SBDMCs, school-based decision-making committees; CRGPE, Collaborative Research Group on Policy and Ethics.)

- Master's-level classes at the university
- Cases written by SBDMC members

The following are some observations about observer presence:

- The large number of observers enabled the collection of a great deal of descriptive information on the process.
- The number and variety of observers provided us with confidence regarding our observations and interpretations of ethically related teaching cases.

- The presence of observers did not appear to inhibit the process.
- The presence of the video equipment seemed to have no negative effect on the participants.

REFERENCES

Fasching, D.J. (1995). *Ethics without choice: Reflections on story, character, and compassion.* Unpublished manuscript.

Fullan, M. (1991). *Change force.* New York: Falmer Press.

Howe, K., & Miramontes, O. (1992). *The ethics of special education.* New York: Teachers College Press.

Richert, A.E. (1991). Case methods and teacher education: Using cases to teach teacher reflection. In B.R. Tabachnick & K.M. Zeichner (Eds.), *Issues and practices in inquiry-oriented teacher education* (pp. 130–150). New York: Falmer Press.

Senge, P.M. (1994). *The fifth discipline field book: Strategies and tools for building a learning organization.* New York: Doubleday.

Shulman, L. (1992). Toward a pedagogy of cases. In J. Shulman (Ed.), *Case methods in teacher education* (pp. 1–32). New York: Teachers College Press.

Tronto, J. (1995). Care for a basis for radical political judgments. *Hypatia, 10*(2), 141–149.

Index

Page numbers followed by "f" or "t" indicate figures or tables, respectively.